Broadcasting Freedom

BROADCASTING FREEDOM

The Cold War Triumph of Radio Free Europe and Radio Liberty

ARCH PUDDINGTON

THE UNIVERSITY PRESS OF KENTUCKY

Publication of this volume was made possible in part by a grant from the National Endowment for the Humanities.

Editorial and Sales Offices: The University Press of Kentucky
663 South Limestone Street, Lexington, Kentucky 40508-4008

04 03 02 01 00   5 4 3 2 1

Library of Congress Cataloging-in-Publication Data

Puddington, Arch.
    Broadcasting freedom : the Cold War triumph of Radio Free Europe
    and Radio Liberty / Arch Puddington.
        p.   cm.
    Includes bibliographical references and index.
    ISBN 0-8131-2158-2 (alk. paper)
    1. Radio Free Europe—History. 2. Radio Liberty (Munich,
    Germany)—History. 3. International broadcasting—Europe,
    Eastern—History. 4. Radio in propaganda—History. 5. Cold War.
    I. Title.
    HE8697.45. E852 P83   2000
    384.54'094—dc21   99-089785

To A.C. Puddington Sr.

Contents

Illustrations follow page 164

Preface

The story of Radio Free Europe and Radio Liberty stands as one of the more intriguing chapters of the Cold War. Radio Free Europe (RFE), which broadcast to the Soviet-dominated countries of Eastern Europe, was arguably the most influential politically oriented international radio station in history. Its audience numbered in the millions, and its listeners ranged from ordinary industrial workers to dissidents such as Lech Walesa and Vaclav Havel to high-ranking Communists, who tuned in because of the unreliability of their own, controlled and censored, media. Radio Liberty (RL), which beamed its message directly to the Soviet Union, also boasted a huge audience, including such dissident luminaries as Andrey Sakharov and Alexander Solzhenitsyn.

These two stations are unique in the annals of international broadcasting. Traditionally, governments have sponsored foreign radio services in order to promote their own geopolitical objectives or to convince a foreign audience of the superiority of their system. Hitler used radio to terrorize neighboring countries; the Soviet Union maintained a vast global broadcast network to promote communism; the American government established the Voice of America to convey the U.S. perspective on world events and familiarize a foreign audience with the American political system and American culture.

The two "freedom radios," however, had a much different purpose. They were, to begin with, pure Cold War institutions. Their goal was not simply to inform their listeners but also to bring about the peaceful demise of the Communist system and the liberation of what were known as satellite nations. The radios pursued these goals not by promoting the American way of life, but by serving as surrogate home radio services, alternatives to the controlled, party-dominated, domestic press. The Polish service of Radio Free Europe, for example, focused most of its attention on developments within Poland; its newscasts featured news about Poland or about the events in the outside world that might have an impact on Poland's future, and its commentaries concentrated on Polish political developments.

There is something daring, even arrogant, in the notion of a country establishing a network of more than twenty radio stations with the ultimate goal of bringing down an entire system of government. Only in America could such an unusual enterprise have been conceived and implemented, perhaps, indeed, only in an America secure in its power and brimming with confidence, as was the case in the immediate postwar era. Radio Free Europe owes its existence to some of the brightest lights of the early Cold War—men, such as Allen Dulles, George F. Kennan, and Gen. Lucius Clay, who epitomized the spirit of the times. They were convinced that the Communist system was susceptible to an aggressive form of psychological warfare and undeterred by the uniqueness of the project, or by the fact that many might regard RFE's broadcasts as a blatant form of interference in the internal affairs of foreign countries.

This book tells the story of Radio Free Europe and Radio Liberty from 1949, when planning for RFE got underway, until the collapse of the Soviet Union and the end of the Cold War in 1991. Concentrating on the evolving role of the two radios (with a greater focus on RFE) in America's Cold War strategy, it explores the relationship between the radios and American intelligence and recounts the extensive efforts of foreign intelligence services to infiltrate and subvert both stations. It also reveals how RFE and RL were affected by the "liberation" doctrine of the early 1950s, which called for the United States to roll back Soviet power in Eastern Europe; the era of "peaceful coexistence"; the rise of the New Left; the collapse of the anti-Communist foreign policy consensus; the onset of détente and Ostpolitik; and the more muscular policies instituted by the Reagan administration.

The source for much of the material on Radio Free Europe is the archive of internal RFE documents stored in RFE-RL's corporate headquarters in Washington, D.C., and scheduled for relocation to the Hoover Institution at Stanford University in 2000. This material includes a great deal of correspondence regarding RFE's relationship with the CIA, State Department, and other government agencies. Much of it is of a highly sensitive nature, never meant for scrutiny by those outside the RFE organization. These documents shed light on various internal RFE controversies; they also tell us something about America's political strategy during various phases of the Cold War.

In addition, I conducted interviews with more than one hundred individuals who have either worked for RFE-RL, were involved in radio affairs as a government official, or were part of the radios' audience during the Cold War. Those interviewed range from well-known public figures, such as Zbigniew Brzezinski, to leading East European dissidents, to some of the most important RFE-RL journalists, men and women whose names and voices were as widely known in the countries to which they broadcast as Tom Brokaw or Sam Donaldson are in the United States. I was also fortunate in gaining interviews with several men who were leading editors and administrators with RFE during its earliest period.

My interest in the history of Radio Free Europe–Radio Liberty derives principally from my experiences as a writer and administrator for the radios. From 1985 to 1993, I served as deputy director of the radios' New York bureau, which was situated in what is now known as the Newsweek Building at Fifty-seventh Street and Broadway.

I was one of the few Americans on the staff, and the only one who had daily dealings with the correspondents for the various language services. My major responsibility was advising journalists on the coverage of American politics and culture. Prior to coming to the radios, I had been involved in various campaigns on behalf of dissidents in the Communist world and was therefore acquainted with Americans who were organizing support efforts for the freedom struggles in Vietnam, Cambodia, Cuba, and Nicaragua, not to mention the countries to which the radios broadcast in Eastern Europe. When a prominent dissident or reeducation camp survivor visited the United States, I would arrange interviews for our staff. Armando Valladares, who survived years in Cuban prisons for advocating democracy, visited us, as did Doan Van Toai, a veteran of the Vietnamese gulag. On one occasion, both Dith Pran, the Cambodian whose experiences were portrayed in the movie *The Killing Fields,* and Dr. Haing Ngor, the actor who portrayed Dith and who was himself a victim of the Khmer Rouge, gave interviews to the staff.

The New York bureau included one or two correspondents from each of Radio Free Europe's eight language services: Bulgarian, Czechoslovak, Hungarian, Polish, Romanian, and the three Baltic services, Estonian, Latvian, and Lithuanian. There were also correspondents from the Ukrainian and Belorussian services, and from time to time from the Armenian service and the smaller Central Asian services, such as the Tatars.

But the Russians were our largest contingent. A sizable proportion of Radio Liberty's Russian-language programs, including some programs that regularly boasted audiences in the millions, originated from New York. The Russian service included four or five full-time editors and correspondents, but since New York was the preferred destination for those among the intellectual elite who were fed up with Soviet restrictions, Soviet censorship, Soviet poverty, and, especially, Soviet hypocrisy, the service was able to recruit literally dozens of talented reporters, writers, poets, musicians, and commentators from among the wave of emigrants who left the USSR during the 1970s.

Most were hired as part-timers or freelancers. Though their pay was hardly extravagant, it could be a life-saver for intellectuals who had left good careers in the Soviet Union for the uncertainties of life in the United States. For some, a more important consideration was the opportunity to work as a journalist or critic in the Russian language. Indeed, after years of censorship (and self-censorship) in the Soviet Union, a job at Radio Liberty for a journalist or critic often provided the first opportunity for honest commentary. It enabled them to earn a decent living and place the spotlight of journalistic truth on the dark corners of Soviet life. Having been unwilling participants in the dishonesty of the Soviet system, the exiled commentators could draw on years of experience to inform their listeners about the corruption of Soviet science, Soviet sport, and Soviet culture and the facts about the natural disasters and man-made catastrophes that were systematically covered up by Soviet authorities.

One of my colleagues, Evgeny Rubin, had been a highly regarded sports writer in the Soviet Union. His passion was hockey; he knew everything about Soviet hockey—the stories that could be told, and those that remained, as Russians put it, "in the drawer." Gene came to the United States in 1979, the last year the Kremlin permitted large-scale Jewish emigration. He was convinced that his years as a sports reporter were over and was therefore delighted when he was hired by RL and given a regular program of sports commentary. Rubin covered the Olympics and other international events, but he also used the Radio Liberty microphone to inform the Russian people about the uglier side of the Soviet sports industry:

Sports journalism in the Soviet Union was dishonest, especially where the professionalism of so-called amateur athletes was concerned. We couldn't write about how athletes were devoting their entire life to sports; we had to write how they were students or soldiers or workers who came to the stadium after working hours to train. All of this was untrue, but we had to write it anyway. And we had to ignore how the officials were sending adult athletes to tournaments supposedly reserved for young people. We had to lie at every level, and we always had the censors looking over our shoulders. Any mistakes, and I could be fired.

Rubin was, in fact, punished for having written that athletes received pensions, a blatant violation of the rule that athletes were to be depicted as amateurs and thus not eligible for material reward. On another occasion, he was nearly fired for quoting a star athlete about the benefits of his profession—a car, nice apartment, and jewelry for his wife. Each month, in fact, the censor would visit his newspaper office, inform the staff of the mistakes they had made the previous month, and explain new rules regulating what could and could not be published. It was even required that photographs be examined by a special photo censor to ensure that no picture of an installation considered off limits—and there were thousands of them—would be published.

There were other prominent Russian intellectuals on our staff: Mark Popovsky, author of a book that revealed the secrets of Soviet science; Solomon Volkov, author of a controversial biography of composer Dmitri Shostakovich; Sergei Dovlatov, a slice-of-life writer whose commentaries were wildly popular back in Russia; Boris Shragin, a philosopher and prominent dissident; Ludmilla Alexeyeva, a leading dissident and author of the most important account of the dissident movement; and Boris Paramonov, commentator on a program called *The Russian Idea*. Paramonov wrestled with the challenge of formulating a modern, nonimperialist form of Russian nationalism, and his radio scripts, which were frequently published as essays in prominent Russian newspapers, were quite influential in the period around the breakup of the Soviet empire.

Among the East European RFE correspondents were men of impressive erudition and linguistic ability. This latter trait was not shared by the Russians, who, like Americans, believed that the rest of the world should learn their language. But several of the East Europeans could converse in a half dozen languages or more. Karel Jezdinský, a Czech, claimed that in addition to Czech, Slovak, and English, he had a passable knowledge of Spanish, Portuguese, Russian, German, Serbo-Croat, French, and Arabic, the last of which he majored in at Charles University in Prague.

Because of the time difference between New York and Central Europe, correspondents operated under intense morning deadlines. They were expected to provide daily reports on breaking political developments in the United States, especially those affecting U.S.-Soviet relations. This required the correspondent to read the most important articles in the English-language press and then write a commentary of several minutes in their native language—all in the space of an hour or two. After their morning report, many correspondents wrote feature commentaries on political or cultural events of up to ten minutes and edited the reports sent in by freelancers.

This was a formidable workload by any journalistic standard. Given that many correspondents had no background as journalists before coming to the radios, and even fewer had experience on radio or television, their performance is more impressive. Some had been political dissidents; others were lawyers, students, academics, teachers. As they soon discovered, writing a two-minute commentary on the SALT negotiations and then reading it in a proper radio voice could pose a much greater challenge than typing a fifty-page essay on the future of Russia after communism.

Several of my colleagues were brilliant analysts of the American political scene. Karl Reyman, who was in effect political director of the New York bureau, had been a Social Democrat in Czechoslovakia and fled after the 1948 Communist coup. Karl was a shrewd observer of world events and was capable of writing trenchant essays on political affairs in three languages: Czech, English, and German. Tom Keri, the chief Hungarian correspondent, knew more about American history and the American system of politics and government than most Washington journalists. Tom was Jewish and had survived some hair-raising experiences during World War II. He was placed in forced labor and barely escaped being shipped to a Nazi death camp. Later, after Hungary was liberated, he was nearly sent into exile in Siberia as a Soviet prisoner-of-war. Tom then became a student of the legendary Marxist philosopher György Lukács, joined and quickly left the Communist Party, and became a devoted follower of Imre Nagy, the Communist reformist who played the leading role in the Hungarian Revolution and was executed after the revolution had been crushed by Soviet tanks. After the revolution, Tom became something of a nonperson and was able to survive by doing translation work. He left Hungary in the early 1970s and eventually found his way to Radio Free Europe.

Tom was a passionate American patriot who admired the United States' democratic institutions, even when they disappointed him. A staunch Reaganite, he would fume and curse when the Great Communicator came under press attack. Yet Tom understood a free press's central role in sustaining democracy, and in his commentaries he treated American press liberties as one of the crown jewels of freedom.

Tom was an early member of Hungary's dissident movement; he wrote one of the first Hungarian samizdat essays in the early sixties, the subject being the split between the USSR and China. By contrast, Jacek Kalabinski, our chief Polish correspondent, had been a well-known journalist for the state radio in Poland before joining RFE. Although never a member of the Communist party, Jacek was among a small group of radio journalists from Eastern Europe who were trained as foreign correspondents during the 1960s; he covered a number of wars and crises in Africa and the Middle East.

Jacek was a strong supporter of Solidarity, the Polish trade union that functioned as the center for anti-Communist initiatives, and thus became a target for arrest when the regime imposed martial law in 1981. Nevertheless, his hiring by RFE was a cause for considerable friction within the Polish service. He was roundly denounced by some staff members because of his prominence as a correspondent for the official Polish media, and his appointment as deputy director of the Polish-language service was eventually vetoed by the American management because of the furor.

Jacek reminded me of American journalists I had encountered through the years. He recognized a good story, he was industrious, he had excellent sources, he was able to explain the story behind the story to his audience. He was, in other words, a born reporter. Unfortunately, much of a journalist's job in Communist Poland consisted of eluding the censor, acquiescing in petty compromises, ignoring facts the authorities might find uncomfortable, and resorting to subterfuge to get a message across.

Had democracy prevailed in their countries, Jacek Kalabinski might have been chief political correspondent for Warsaw Radio, Karel Jezdinský would probably have served as a roving foreign correspondent, Tom Keri would have edited a cultural journal or worked in the film industry, and Karl Reyman would have been chief editor of an important Prague daily newspaper. Instead, what should have been the cream of central European intellectual and journalistic life helped make Radio Free Europe one of the most remarkable experiments in the history of communications.

Our office also had its very own redefector, a young Lithuanian named Bronius. A graduate of Patrice Lumumba University, Bronius had been stationed in Congo Brazzaville during the 1980s as a language instructor, had grown disillusioned, and had asked for asylum at an American embassy in a neighboring African country. Bronius worked in the New York office for about a year until, one day, we received word that he had decided to return to the Soviet Union. Apparently, the KGB had persuaded his mother to make an emotional appeal for his return, and Bronius, who was lonely and isolated in New York, succumbed. On his return to Lithuania he made several obligatory propaganda appearances and gave an interview to a Soviet newspaper in which he criticized RFE in rather mild terms. Among other things, he charged that the staff had regarded the accident at the Chernobyl nuclear power plant first as a huge setback for the Soviet system and only secondarily as a human tragedy for the peoples threatened by the accident.

On this latter point Bronius was not entirely off the mark. Chernobyl occurred shortly after Mikhail Gorbachev had launched his policy of glasnost, or openness, an initiative that won the new Soviet leader considerable acclaim in the West. Most of us at the radios did not know quite what to make of Gorbachev, although the predominant attitude was one of extreme skepticism about the prospects for major internal Soviet reform. Our cynicism seemed vindicated by the Soviet Union's initial denials that anything serious had gone amiss at Chernobyl and that no health hazards existed. Here was the old Soviet Union at its totalitarian worst, flatly denying what the rest of the world knew and jeopardizing the safety of its own citizens, not to mention neighboring countries downwind from the damaged reactor. After having endured article after article in the Western press about Gorbachev the reformer, Gorbachev the democrat, and Gorbachev the peacemaker,

some of us took quiet satisfaction in th
Gorbachev as the true successor to the arc
onid Brezhnev.

Little did we know that Chernobyl w;
the Cold War drama. The process of tearir
Soviet control mechanism actually begar
and accelerated afterward. No longer could
Union be treated as a captive audience, an audience,
Liberty administrator put it, that would "listen hour after hour
broadcaster reading the text of a novel by Berdayev." To be sure, the
Soviet Union was not free. But it was no longer run along classic
totalitarian lines. Journalists were digging into scandals, challenging
official myths, demanding more liberties. Political prisoners were released, emigration policies liberalized, travel restrictions eased. Nothing more vividly testified to the degree of change than the many Soviet
cultural figures and journalists who visited the RL office in New York
and gave frank interviews to our correspondents without fear of reprisal once they returned.

I was particularly impressed by the amount of strategic thinking
the correspondents invested in their broadcasts as the Soviet empire
hurtled toward its crackup. We all shared in the excitement and won-
derment when, starting with Poland, country after country renounced
communism with scarcely a murmur of disapproval from the Soviet
leadership. But even as the liberated people of East Germany danced
atop the Berlin Wall, my colleagues were anticipating the time, not
that far off as things turned out, when disillusionment would replace
euphoria as the people of the post-Communist world realized the
extent of their material impoverishment.

Just as my colleagues rose to the occasion during periods of upheaval and rapid change, they maintained an impressive esprit de corps
during the far more numerous times when it seemed as if nothing of
real significance was occurring behind the Iron Curtain outside of the
arrest of dissidents, the mysterious deaths of labor activists, or yet another purge of liberals from the party leadership ranks. Each day they
would arrive at the office, make their broadcasts, talk to their network
of contacts about political developments back home, study the newspapers and samizdat literature. Although practically all my colleagues
believed that communism would eventually collapse, they saw its demise as occurring well off in the future. Meanwhile, they tried to

their listeners two key ideas: first, that a more prosperous, ing, and honest universe existed beyond the boundaries im- by the Soviet empire; and second, that the United States and its es still considered communism an illegitimate and immoral system.

The radios succeeded in their missions, although it took nearly forty years, much longer than originally envisioned. I consider myself fortunate to have played a small part in that history. And I owe a debt of thanks to the exile colleagues who served with me those years. Certainly I learned much more about the world from them than they learned about the United States from me.

First and foremost, I wish to thank Freedom House, and especially its chairman, Bette Bao Lord, and president, Adrian Karatnycky, for their support and patience during the often difficult period of research and writing.

Many present and former members of the Radio Free Europe-Radio Liberty staff provided invaluable assistance in locating documents, providing clues to research sources, or in deciphering the history of the radios during their early years. Most helpful were Jane Lester of the RFE-RL Washington office and Irene Dutikow and Sara Hassan, who maintained the radios' library in New York. I am grateful to Paul Henze for the many hours he spent explaining the issues and personalities of RFE's first decade. Thanks also go to Thomas Keri, Karl Reyman, Stephen Miller, and Ralph Walter for their many useful comments on the manuscript.

I wish to express my gratitude to several special collections archivists who assisted me in my search through the papers of individuals associated with the radios. These include Betty Austin of the J.W. Fulbright collection at the University of Arkansas; Jaime Rodriguez of the Herbert H. Lehman Library at Columbia University; and Nicholas Scheetz of the special collections division of the Georgetown University library. Thanks also to Dagmara Dominczyk for translating key sections of Jan Nowak's memoirs from Polish to English. Patricia Sowick was instrumental in providing me with important documents from the Board for International Broadcasting. My good friend Alan Kagedan was instrumental in securing critical research material. I also wish to thank Uanda Harris, Sheldon Hendy, Kristen Guida, and Kendra Zaharescu for their assistance.

This book would not have been possible without the financial support of the Lynde and Harry Bradley Foundation. My great thanks to the foundation's board of trustees, and to its president, Michael Joyce, and to Hillel Fradkin, formerly of the foundation staff. I also received crucial financial assistance from Malcolm S. (Steve) Forbes and from the Historical Research Foundation. My thanks to Peter Rodman for his help in securing a grant from the Historical Research Foundation that enabled me to complete the book.

I owe a debt of gratitude to Richard Valcourt, my agent, who believed in the project and devoted his energies to bring it into being.

I could never have completed this book without the love and support of my wife, Margaret, who kept my spirits up during several particularly difficult periods. I cannot thank her enough.

1

"It Will Be Seen Who Is Right"

It was, fittingly, on May Day, the most revered holiday of the international working-class movement, that Radio Free Europe inaugurated its full broadcast service to the peoples of Eastern Europe. Once regarded as an inspirational commemoration of the democratic Socialist vision, May Day had been expropriated by the forces of world communism, which is to say by Stalin and his devoted acolytes in what were then known as the satellite countries. In Eastern Europe, May Day in 1951 was celebrated with the emblems of Soviet militarism and the wooden slogans promoting "peace" and the anti-imperialist cause instead of the traditional symbols of trade unionism and social democracy.

Technically, RFE had been beaming its message to Eastern Europe for the better part of a year; the initial broadcast was made on July 4, 1950, and a regular schedule of daily programs was introduced shortly thereafter. Those early programs, however, were produced by a neophyte staff in New York and then relayed to the audience through a cumbersome process that involved shipping the tapes to Europe and broadcasting the programs over outmoded and weak transmission equipment in Germany. No matter how skillfully crafted the message, the weak signal alone guaranteed that listenership would be limited.

By May 1, 1951, many of the early problems had been resolved. Several transmitters, the most up-to-date and powerful available at the time, had been acquired and strategically located at several sites in West

Germany. A European broadcasting headquarters had been opened in Munich, a city chosen for its proximity to the RFE audience countries as well as its sizable East European exile community. The staff of journalists had been enlarged and strengthened by the addition of a number of highly regarded exiled writers and editors.

The management of the American "freedom radio" treated the May Day broadcast as something of a media event, particularly for the European press. C.D. Jackson, president of the National Committee for a Free Europe, the organization that sponsored RFE, had stirred up a minor furor when he declared at a press conference that RFE broadcasts would encourage defections from Communist-controlled countries. The reaction of the assembled reporters was not to question whether such a policy might endanger the lives and freedom of potential defectors, but to suggest that invitations to defect were unwise, given West European hostility to the rising numbers of East European exiles in their midst.

Aside from the controversy over defections, the inaugural events went smoothly. Although RFE was eventually to form its program around a nucleus of five Communist countries—Bulgaria, Czechoslovakia, Hungary, Poland, and Romania—the May Day broadcast focused on a single country: Czechoslovakia. Considered the satellite nation with the closest links to the West and the most enduring democratic tradition, Czechoslovakia was also the last East European country to succumb to total Communist domination. Indeed, the 1948 Communist coup in Prague reinforced the mounting anti-Soviet mood in Washington and played an important role in convincing policy makers that institutions of ideological persuasion like RFE should be added to America's Cold War arsenal. Although the men responsible for the creation of RFE were experienced veterans of international affairs and realistic about America's ability to influence events in Eastern Europe, they were convinced that communism was especially vulnerable in Western-oriented countries such as Czechoslovakia and Poland. C.D. Jackson had helped implement America's psychological warfare program during World War II, and his experience in the struggle against Nazi Germany persuaded him that hard-hitting propaganda could be a potent weapon against a totalitarian power.

Yet Jackson's opening message to the people of Czechoslovakia reflected the thinking of a liberal internationalist more than an ardent anti-Communist. He reassured his audience that Radio Free Europe had no intention of promoting any particular economic system, a policy RFE would adhere to throughout the Cold War. While he made passing reference to America's historic friendship with Czechoslovakia, he stressed pan-European federation as the solution to the sicknesses that had caused two world wars and now seemed to be threatening to trigger a third. His phrases about the eventual liberation of Czechoslovakia were carefully chosen, emphasizing the thoroughly nonpolemical idea that world peace required self-determination for Eastern Europe. And he demonstrated his awareness of the May Day symbolism by inserting a passage about the "creative spirit and the growing strength and prosperity of the free labor movement" of the Western world.

Jackson was followed at the microphone by Ferdinand Peroutka, chief editor of the Voice of Free Czechoslovakia (VFC), as the language service was to be known in its early, combative days. (All RFE language divisions were identified as the Voice of Free Czechoslovakia, Poland, Bulgaria, and so forth throughout most of the 1950s.) Peroutka was a legendary figure in the intellectual life of Czechoslovakia. He had been a close associate of T.G. Masaryk, the father of democratic Czechoslovakia, and a foremost editor and historian who had been imprisoned by the Nazis and then pushed into exile by the Communists. Peroutka would become famous for his Sunday commentaries on RFE, and for this, the first day of broadcast, he composed a small jewel of an antitotalitarian essay. "Many things can be said in favor of ancient tyrants as compared with present day tyrants," he declared:

> Ancient tyrants were, at least, more sincere. They did not care about their victims after they had crushed them. . . . The present day tyrant does two things at the same time: he tortures the nation and orders it to smile . . . just like a photographer. Meanwhile, a terrible and wretched weapon was invented—the propaganda of the totalitarian states. The present day tyrant always sends out two kinds of emissaries: armed men and forgers of ideas; robust individuals and thin men with glasses and sunken chests; rowdies who beat the nation and other rowdies who give thanks for the beatings in the name of the nation. The policeman is followed—and sometimes also preceded—by the liar.

Peroutka also included a passage on the fate of Czechoslovak journalism—an institution he personally had influenced and shaped over the previous two decades—under Communist rule: "Three years ago they sent after us, into our editors' offices, armed crowds from the street, guarded by police so that nothing could happen to them. Those dark crowds occupied our printers' and editors' offices. . . .When facing us—always a hundred armed individuals facing one unarmed person—they told us: now we have proved to you that you are not right. When this radio station will smash the Communist monopoly on speaking to the Czech nation, it will be seen who is right." And in his ruminations on May Day in People's Czechoslovakia, Peroutka gave evidence of his ability to convey a political message through a personal, almost intimate, vocabulary, a talent that enabled him to remain a presence in Czechoslovak affairs even in exile. "You are walking among pictures of Stalin and Gottwald [Klement Gottwald, Czechoslovakia's first Communist leader] without paying attention to them," he intoned, "while you are carrying Masaryk's picture in your heart."

If Peroutka's hopeful remarks represented one part of the RFE message, another, equally important aspect was reflected by the opening commentary of the next speaker, Pavel Tigrid. Tigrid had worked for the British Broadcasting Corporation (BBC) during the war and was thus a member of the small group of RFE exiled journalists who could boast of actual radio experience. Tigrid would remain at RFE for a few years, after which he became a writer and publisher of exile literature and a guiding force among the Czechoslovak intellectual diaspora; after communism's demise, he would return in triumph to serve for a time as minister of culture under the government of Prime Minister Vaclav Klaus.

Tigrid pulled no punches in spelling out Radio Free Europe's methods for dealing with the Communist enemy. "Our station has, above all, a fighting and political mission," he explained. "Our offensive is directed against Communism and Sovietism, against the representatives of the terrorist regime. . . . It is our task to unmask Communist plans. . . . Today, a terrible enemy rises against all Communist informers, agents provocateurs, and stool pigeons, all inhuman guards of prisons and work camps, all judges and officials of Communist jurisprudence, all propagandists of communist ideology: Radio Free Europe, which will reveal their names, one by one; all of them will be blacklisted by the democratic world and will be dumped on the rubbish heap of contempt by the Czech and Slovak people."Tigrid added that RFE would also speak to Communist Party members and petty functionaries—"to advise them what they should do and how they should behave, so that, when the day comes, their fate will not be that of the Communist big-shots."[1]

Within a few years, the brass-knuckles approach reflected in Tigrid's remarks would be abandoned, as Radio Free Europe evolved into a more normal, if still intensely political, international broadcasting service. Likewise, the semitriumphalist themes struck by Peroutka would be replaced by a more humble approach, as events demonstrated that the overthrow of communism would be a matter of slow, incremental change over decades rather than the quick and total collapse that had been anticipated, by some at least, in 1951.

But if the expectation of early liberation was not to be realized, Radio Free Europe would, in fact, be proved right, as Peroutka predicted. Its strategy, language, and short-term objectives would change during the course of the Cold War, just as American policy toward the Communist world would change. Yet no matter what doctrine predominated in Washington—liberation, gradualism, détente—RFE continued to fulfill its original mission as an instrument of anti-Communist diplomacy. Radio Free Europe, along with its sister organization, Radio Liberty, stood as the most visible institutions of official American anticommunism, and were arguably the most successful Cold War vehicles established by the American government.

Radio Free Europe was not, of course, the only foreign radio station to which the people of Eastern Europe listened. But while the BBC was appreciated for its professionalism and the Voice of America (VOA) valued for its programs on American culture, only RFE was given the status of honorary member of the democratic opposition. This treatment attests to RFE's unusual character. The Radio Free Europe–Radio Liberty model is unique not simply to the Cold War, but to the history of diplomacy. Many countries have established international broadcasting entities, ranging from respected journalistic services such as the BBC to the crudely propagandistic global networks sponsored by Nazi Germany and the Soviet Union. Only with Radio Free Europe and Radio Liberty, however, did a country establish broadcast services whose purpose was to change the form of government in foreign nations by airing news not about the country from which the broadcasts originated but about the countries that were the broadcast targets.

Initiation of this unprecedented project in peacetime propaganda—for RFE was publicly described as a propaganda instrument at its creation—represented a radical departure from U.S. political tradition. Until World War II got underway, the United States had shown no inclination to participate in the global war of the airwaves. Historically, it had been the totalitarian powers that had made the most ambitious use of international radio. The Bolsheviks were the first to recognize radio's political potential; while the Soviet Union did not use its international broadcasts to foment revolution abroad during the period between the Revolution and World War II, it did make carefully targeted broadcasts to countries in which there were border disputes or in which leftist forces seemed on the verge of major gain. During the thirties, the USSR was the only country to beam anti-Nazi broadcasts into Germany; later, after the Hitler-Stalin pact had been signed, Stalin used radio broadcasts to intimidate Finland, threatening the Finns that unless they agreed to certain concessions, they would suffer the fate of Poland.[2]

Hitler also made effective use of radio propaganda. The pattern was set with a slanderous propaganda offensive against the League of Nations occupation regime during the campaign to prepare the way for the reintegration of the Saar region into the Third Reich. Subsequently, Austrian Nazis were put on the air to pave the way for the *Anschluss* by, among other things, advocating the assassination of Austrian chancellor Engelbert Dollfuss. A similar approach was used in the campaign to dismember Czechoslovakia. Konrad Henlein, the leading Nazi among the Sudeten Germans, was placed before a microphone to make patently fraudulent charges of anti-Sudeten atrocities against the Czechoslovak government. Eventually, Hitler established a worldwide propaganda network aimed at expatriate Germans as well as non-Germans. The broadcasts were not as shrill as those directed at Germany's neighbors, and there seems to have been an effort to give a human face to Hitler, the Nazis, and the Third Reich.[3]

The United States, by contrast, chose not to establish a national propaganda or information program until the Japanese attacked American territory at Pearl Harbor and the country entered World War II. To some degree, the lack of interest in propaganda reflected the influence of isolationist sentiments between the wars. Perhaps a more important factor was the absence of state-owned radio in the United States, a condition unique to this country, since in many countries radio was operated exclusively by the government. Furthermore, Americans, while comfortable with business advertising and the propaganda associated with domestic political campaigns, seemed ideologically averse to government-sponsored international propaganda, whose centralized state direction clashed with the American preference for individualistic enterprise.[4]

During the war, the United States created a propaganda agency, the Office of War Information (OWI), and an international radio network, the Voice of America. But while the American public supported international radio during wartime, there was considerable sentiment that, with the end of hostilities, the government should close down its propaganda and information projects; by 1947, the VOA's budget had been slashed and influential members of Congress were advocating the elimination of what remained of American international radio.

The impulse toward a revived isolationism was checked by the onset of the Cold War. Having defeated, at a great cost in life and resources, one great European totalitarian power, the United States found itself confronted by another and in some respects more insidious totalitarian state, the Soviet Union. Communism seemed a more rational, even inspirational, creed than that of the Thousand Year Reich, and it could count as allies the local Communists who existed, in some cases in impressive numbers, throughout Europe. Furthermore, the Soviets approached the challenge of constructing a totalitarian social order with utmost seriousness. Within the satellite countries of Eastern Europe, the Soviets and local Communists moved expeditiously to silence opposition voices, eliminate an independent press, outlaw non-Communist political parties, neutralize religion, and seal off the borders from foreign influence. Countries such as Poland and Czechoslovakia, with centuries of ties to the West, were condemned to a regime of international isolation never contemplated by their old imperial masters in Vienna and prerevolutionary Moscow.[5]

Radio Free Europe was the brainchild of some of the most prominent architects of America's early Cold War strategy, particularly those who believed that the Cold War would eventually be fought by political rather than military means. Here the most important figure was none other than George F. Kennan, author of the famous "X" article and father of the containment doctrine. Unlike some others involved in the creation of America's "freedom radios"—as Radio Free Europe and Radio Liberty came to be known—Kennan was not a proponent of an American policy to liberate Eastern Europe from Soviet domination. But a program of aggressive ideological warfare did not clash with Kennan's preferred strategy of preventing the spread of the Soviet empire beyond its East European boundaries. The logic of containment demanded a policy of creating complications for the Soviets within their own sphere of influence, since the more Moscow was preoccupied with keeping the restive peoples of Eastern Europe in check, the less likely it would be to cast a hungry eye on Western Europe.[6]

Although Kennan was never publicly identified with RFE or with the Free Europe Committee (FEC; originally called the National Committee for a Free Europe), he was clearly one of the key figures in planning this unprecedented propaganda venture. An internal RFE memo from 1949 refers to Kennan as the "father of our project," and Kennan was personally acquainted with most of the men who were officially associated with the FEC and RFE.[7] There was even a university connection tying Kennan to the early RFE leadership: Kennan, Allen W. Dulles, Frank Wisner, and DeWitt C. Poole were all graduates of Princeton who went on to play important roles in shaping policy toward the Soviet Union and establishing RFE as an instrument of American diplomacy.

More important than the Princeton connection was the fact that many of the men who helped get RFE off the ground had firsthand experience with the brutal side of Soviet behavior. Kennan had grown to detest Soviet diplomatic tactics during his wartime service as counsel in the U.S. embassy in Moscow. Wisner had served in the American embassy in Bucharest and was sickened by postwar Soviet brutality toward the local populace, particularly the mass deportations of Romanian citizens to the Soviet Union. For Arthur Bliss Lane, a member of the initial FEC board, the decisive experience was the Sovietization of Poland, where Lane was serving as ambassador. Lane was to leave the FEC in order to carry out a campaign to persuade the American government to disavow the Yalta pact and launch an aggressive policy aimed at the liberation of the satellite countries. General Lucius Clay, the first chairman of the Crusade for Freedom, which raised private funds for RFE, had been U.S. commander in Berlin during the 1948

Soviet blockade of that city. DeWitt Poole had the earliest and most interesting confrontation with Soviet power, having served as an American diplomat both in Moscow and later in Archangel during the first years of the Bolshevik Revolution. As chargé d'affaires, Poole was the last American diplomat in the USSR until President Roosevelt reestablished diplomatic relations during the 1930s. Poole was so appalled by the brutality exhibited by Lenin and other Bolshevik leaders that he took the unusual step of resigning his position to protest what he deemed Woodrow Wilson's overly friendly policies toward the new revolutionary government. Poole wrote that he wanted to distance himself from any policy that "does not include . . . unremitting denunciation of . . . the methods by which the Bolsheviks have come into power." Thirty years later, Poole still identified bolshevism as a deadly threat to civilization, a new form of barbarism that pursued its interests unrestrained by moral or ethical standards.[8]

There is no credible written account relating the precise role that Kennan, Wisner, and other important officials intended for either the FEC or RFE. The explanation provided the public at the time of the FEC's establishment in 1949 emphasized the humanitarian desire to provide useful work for the prominent East European exiles who had sought refuge in the United States after the Communist takeovers of their countries. The first indication that the United States planned to make use of the substantial pool of talented exiles had come in a speech delivered by John Foster Dulles to the Bond Club of New York on May 6, 1948, an address notable for the tone of alarm over the postwar advance of communism. "For the first time since the threat of Islam a thousand years ago," Dulles announced, "Western civilization is on the defensive." Concerned by Communist tactics of internal subversion, Dulles asserted that against Communist methods of political warfare, "armament is as obsolete as the Maginot Line." Prominent among Dulles's recommendations was the extension of political asylum to "those menaced by Communist terrorism" and the creation of an organization or movement composed of exiles that could engage the Communists "at that level where the Communist Party is working and winning its victories."[9]

Frank Wisner had even more ambitious plans for the refugees from East European communism. Wisner was placed in charge of a new, highly secret agency, the Office of Policy Coordination (OPC), to counter Soviet subversion. Until the OPC was folded into the CIA,

Wisner had considerable autonomy in putting together various covert projects. In 1947 Wisner made a tour of the displaced persons camps in Europe and concluded that anti-Communist exiles were an important resource for the struggle to come. Wisner chaired a study group to assess how the exiles might be used to further American objectives; among the conclusions was a recommendation to employ the exiles in the American propaganda machinery.[10]

Historians of a revisionist bent have pointed to the Wisner role in the creation of RFE and RL as evidence that the real nature of the freedom radios was something different—more sinister perhaps and certainly more provocative—than that of a mere propaganda vehicle.[11] Wisner had big plans for his cadre of exiles, but his most ambitious schemes, the liberation of Latvia and Albania by exiles trained in the tactics of insurgent warfare, ended in ignominious failure after the plans were betrayed by Soviet agent Kim Philby.

There is no question that Wisner was a key participant among the small group of men who determined the policies for the FEC and RFE during their first year or so of existence. It also seems likely that Wisner supplied the initial funds for the project from a kitty he controlled at the OPC. He attended many of the planning sessions in 1949 and 1950, initialed budget requests, and was consulted by the public leaders of the FEC on organizational matters as well as such policy questions as whether to include Yugoslavia among the countries to which RFE would broadcast.[12] But there is no evidence that Wisner or others envisioned RFE as having some sort of covert mission to advance the cause of liberation. Radio Free Europe's leadership never concealed the hard-hitting content of the early broadcasts. In fact, RFE bragged about the personal attacks directed at Communist officials and published examples of extraordinarily harsh polemics as part of its public relations campaign. Once RFE got off the ground, there is no evidence of major involvement in its affairs by Wisner or other members of the covert operations team.

In any event, it was not just ardent Cold Warriors like Dulles and Wisner who believed that propaganda would play a crucial role in the struggle with communism. It was, after all, widely acknowledged that the Cold War was in its very essence a war of ideas. The United States, acting through the CIA, funded a long list of projects to counter the Communist appeal among intellectuals in Europe and the developing world. President Truman called attention to the importance of propa-

IAS was openly sponsored by the American government—even—
the station was jointly funded and managed by the United States
West Germany—and staffed almost entirely by Germans, who
ked under the supervision of a small American management team.
station developed many of the broadcast strategies that RFE was
to adopt. It maintained a large research component, which inter-
wed travelers from East Germany and compiled material from the
t German Communist media, and aired programs for special target
ups in the other Germany: youth, women, farmers—there was even
program aimed at border guards. During much of the Cold War,
IAS had a huge listenership in East Germany; it was far and away the
ost popular foreign radio service among its intended audience.
istenership began to fall off only when West German television be-
ame widely available to an Eastern audience.[20]

Although in later years RFE was scrupulous in holding to a
nonpolemical tone, even as the thrust of its programming remained
highly critical of Communist policies, during the early 1950s the station was committed to a muscular brand of political warfare. The men
who represented RFE before the American public made no secret of
the station's combative nature. Frank Altschul once described RFE as
a "citizens' adventure in the field of psychological warfare" that sought
to "sow distrust and dissension among our enemies." To accomplish
these goals, he added,

> we must gain the confidence of our friends—and we must
> constantly remind them that they are not forgotten and that
> while the ultimate date of their liberation is unpredictable,
> its coming is inevitable. At the same time we must under-
> mine the Communist regime by exposing it for the vicious
> fraud that it is. As we are unhampered by the amenities of
> diplomatic intercourse, we enter this fight with bare fists. . . .
> We identify Communist collaborators by name. We give
> their address and give an account of their misdeeds. And
> sometimes, using a formula for which I claim no personal
> credit, "This is the sort of man to whom an accident might
> happen on a dark night."[21]

A sober-minded banker and philanthropist, Altschul was not ordi-

ganda in a major speech that launched "Project Truth," billed as the
American answer to the big-lie technique practiced by the Soviets. In
a speech to the American Society of Newspaper Editors, Truman declared,

> This is a struggle, above all else, for the minds of men.
> Propaganda is one of the most powerful weapons the
> Communists have in this struggle. Deceit, distortion and lies
> are systematically used by them as a matter of deliberate
> policy. . . . Communist propaganda is so false, so crude, so
> blatant that we wonder how men can be swayed by it. We
> forget that most of the people to whom it is directed do not
> have free access to accurate information. . . . In many parts of
> the world . . . where men must choose between freedom and
> Communism, the true story is going untold. We cannot run
> the risk that nations may be lost to the cause of freedom
> because their people do not know the facts. . . . We must use
> every means at our command, private as well as governmen-
> tal, to get the truth to other peoples.[13]

George Kennan mentioned the relevance of propaganda in his famous
"Long Telegram," and justification for RFE was set down in several of
the national security findings issued during the Cold War's early period. Kennan, in fact, drafted NSC 10/2, which authorized the establishment of the Office of Policy Coordination. The finding, issued in
1948, gave the go-ahead for an ambitious covert action and psychological warfare offensive, including "propaganda, economic warfare,
antisabotage, demolition and evacuation measures; [and] subversion
against hostile states, including assistance to underground resistance
groups." These activities were supposed to be planned so that if discovered, the United States government could "plausibly disclaim any responsibility."[14] The most famous Cold War finding, NSC 68, spoke of
the need to "foster a fundamental change in the Soviet system," an
objective that implied a vigorous war of ideas. It also identified the
Kremlin's relationship with the satellite peoples as a principal source
of vulnerability. The document called for "programs designed to build
and maintain confidence among other peoples in our strength and
resolution, and to wage overt psychological warfare calculated to encourage mass defections from Soviet allegiance."[15]

The Free Europe Committee was formed in early 1949. Allen Dulles served as chairman during the committee's first few months, but by June 1, when the FEC's existence was announced to the public, a new chairman, Joseph Grew, had been named. Grew was an old-school diplomat who had spent a half-century in public service. Like several other men associated with the FEC, Grew had been involved in the peace negotiations at Versailles after World War I and was concerned that the West not make the same errors that led to a second world conflagration. He was ambassador to Japan throughout most of the thirties and occupied that post on December 7, 1941, when Japan bombed Pearl Harbor and declared war on the United States. After the war, he was among the first American diplomats to warn that the Soviets posed a danger to American security interests, having written a memorandum in 1945 that Moscow "will constitute in future as grave a danger to us as did the Axis" and having predicted that a future war with the USSR "is as certain as anything in this world can be certain."[16] Joining Grew on the committee was an "A" list of powerful men representing government, the military, business, the press, and organized labor. In addition to Allen Dulles and General Clay, the board included Dwight Eisenhower; Will Clayton, the architect of America's postwar international economic policies; former attorney general Francis Biddle; William Green, president of the American Federation of Labor; A.A. Berle, a prominent New Dealer who had served as assistant secretary of state; Dewitt Wallace, owner of *Reader's Digest;* Henry Luce of Time, Inc.; and Frank Altschul, a prominent New York investment banker. This was an eminent group, especially when the names of interested nonmembers such as Wisner, Kennan, and John Foster Dulles are added. The composition of the committee alone is powerful evidence that those responsible for the formulation of America's Cold War diplomacy regarded the FEC and Radio Free Europe as important undertakings.[17]

Initially, the FEC divided its program into three separate units: exile relations, radio, and American contacts. At the time, exile relations were regarded as the main priority. The exiles were segregated by political loyalties: there were separate organizations for Socialist exiles, Catholic Party exiles, Peasant Party exiles, and so on. It was the committee's hope that the various exile groups, excluding, of course, Communists and Fascists, could be formed into unified national councils, entities that, as Grew put it, "can stand as symbols of democratic

hope for their countrymen in Eastern Europe of exile unity had been achieved, it is not c councils could have advanced the cause of Eas In any event, the relatively limited goal of unitin daunting challenge, due to the divisions and riva political—that separated even the most democr Czechoslovaks, and Hungarians.

The FEC's intellectual projects proved much n publications arm, the Free Europe Press, produced an of reports and analyses on developments in the Comn launched a highly regarded magazine, *East Europe*. The set up the Mid-European Studies Center in New York, was to find transitional jobs for exiled scholars until the positions in Western universities. The center's graduates of the most respected experts in Soviet and East Europe American universities over the past three decades. The FE a Free University at Strasbourg so that East European e continue their studies. There was also an American Contac which introduced prominent exiles to American audiences. the declared objective of this endeavor was to inform the ex American culture and politics, it also appears that the contact was part of a broad program to promote public support for A Cold War objectives. DeWitt Poole, for example, expressed th that anti-Communist exiles could be used to counter Communi paganda in certain East European ethnic communities—he si out the Croats—as well as among Americans in general.[19]

As for radio broadcasting, the United States had already establishe service that stood as a model for the new RFE. It was called Radio the American Sector—RIAS—and it came on the air in 1946 as wired radio service for Germans living in the American sector of Ber lin. The station's importance was magnified during the 1948 Berlin blockade, when it carried the message of Allied determination to resist Soviet intimidation to an audience that embraced West and East Berlin and large parts of East Germany. After the blockade, RIAS evolved into a surrogate home service for East Germans, the first such station of the Cold War. It broadcast news, commentary, and cultural programs that were unavailable in the censored media of the German Democratic Republic.

UNSTABLE
SATELLITES = less SOV cpauty → WE

narily inclined to flights of rhetorical exaggeration. On this occasion, he seems to have been carried away with enthusiasm for the new enterprise, as there is no evidence that RFE broadcasts actually advocated political murder. On the other hand, RFE was clearly regarded as a principal instrument of psychological warfare, a concept much in vogue in the immediate postwar period. C.D. Jackson, who succeeded Poole as FEC president in January 1951, had been involved in America's wartime psywar program, as had several members of RFE's American staff. Jackson said RFE's objective was to "create conditions of chaos in the countries to which our broadcasts reached."[22]

Radio Free Europe was conceived at a time of great concern over the prospect of Moscow's expansion into Western Europe. Three events—the establishment of a Communist dictatorship in Czechoslovakia, the Berlin blockade, and the Italian elections—convinced many Western politicians that Stalin's ambitions stretched well beyond his East European "sphere of influence." The inevitability of Soviet expansionism was, of course, the basic assumption behind George Kennan's proposals to contain Soviet power within its Eastern perimeter. This nervousness over Soviet adventurism seems also to have influenced the early direction of RFE programming. Clearly, some planners believed that fomenting trouble in Moscow's back yard was one means of diverting Stalin from westward expansion.

Thus C.D. Jackson explained, "If we can keep the Russians busy with the people they have already conquered by holding out a genuine hope of freedom, we can, perhaps, prevent the march across Western Europe." Likewise, Gen. Walter Bedell Smith, soon to be appointed CIA director, declared that satellite instability posed "the greatest deterrent to Soviet aggression." He added that RFE was "very effective" in exacerbating this instability.[23] General Eisenhower was perhaps the most eminent public figure to endorse this concept. The United States, he said, "must intensify the will for freedom in the satellite countries. ...These countries are in the Soviet back yard, and only as their people are reminded that the outside world has not forgotten them ... do they remain potential deterrents to Soviet aggression. Therefore the mission of Radio Free Europe merits greater support than before. It serves our national interest and the cause of peace."[24]

Aldous Huxley once asserted that "the propagandist is a man who canalizes an already existing stream. In a land where there is no water he digs in vain." In Eastern Europe, a fast-running river awaited the hydraulic engineers from RFE; the people trapped behind the Iron Curtain were altogether receptive to the RFE message, including the hard-edged polemics of its early years. Nonetheless, men like C.D. Jackson, Grew, and Clay were realistic in their expectations of RFE's ability to move events along the path toward liberation. The FEC leadership was comprised of men who combined a hatred of communism with a powerful belief in democracy, liberal internationalism, and American virtue. Jackson and Grew, for example, were strong advocates of pan-European federation as a means of ensuring that instability in the region did not trigger yet a third global conflict. Nor was Jackson inclined to endorse John Foster Dulles's view that communism represented a dire threat to the future of Western civilization. To Jackson, the real enemy was Soviet imperialism; he once wrote that "a Titoist heresy in one or more of the satellites would be worth fifty divisions." Jackson, in fact, shrewdly understood that communism would quickly collapse without the power of Soviet armaments to prop it up: "If the present Russian regime were to disappear and somehow or other the Russian dynamic of conquest . . . were to cease to exist, would we continue our efforts in order to destroy Communism as a political system in each one of these [satellite] countries? Rather, would we not feel that without the Kremlin dynamic and left to their nationalist selves, the magnetism of the Western system would inevitably encroach and eventually engulf these systems?"[25]

Jackson, it should be noted, expressed his sentiments about the inherent weakness of Communist ideology in a private letter, for in fact such opinions rested outside the mainstream of political debate at the time. Few dissented publicly from the proposition that the United States should aggressively pursue the liberation of the satellites. While Republicans were more likely to press for a liberationist policy, a confrontational approach to the Kremlin's imperial hold over the satellites enjoyed support within both parties. Charles Kersten, a Wisconsin Republican who was generally recognized as the liberation policy's most ardent advocate, proposed that America finance liberation armies comprised of exiles from the satellites. Alexander Wiley, a highly respected GOP senator from Wisconsin, spoke in a similar vein. He condemned containment as overly passive—a "mere 'pantywaist' diplomacy," which he likened to a "wordy Voice of America program." Instead, Wiley proposed a "commando-type program of psychological and revolutionary penetration," and he advocated the distribution of "arms for vengeance" to the peoples of Eastern Europe.[26]

By the ideologically charged standards of the day, RFE represented a voice of Cold War moderation. It steered clear of calls for liberation armies and disavowals of the Yalta accords, a favorite theme of conservative anti-Communists at the time. Nor did RFE impose rigid standards of political correctness on its employees. Often during its history, RFE would be accused of an overzealous and inflammatory broadcast tone. But in its very early years, the station was more responsible than America's political leaders, a major reason for its credibility with its East European audience.

The FEC's initial radio plans were modest. Exiled leaders were placed before a microphone and given free rein to speak to their countrymen. As Grew noted, the goal was to enable those living under communism "to hear the living voices of democratic exiled leaders, to hear from them that neither they nor their countries are (as the Communists would have them believe) forgotten by us in the United States or by the other democratic peoples."[27]

By the fall of 1949 an FEC committee had begun organizing the various components of what would become Radio Free Europe. By mid-April 1950, a skeleton staff of exiles had been hired, including four Romanians and three Hungarians, with "Bulgarians and Poles still struggling to get underway." It was difficult, at first, to recruit a professional journalistic staff. Herbert Gross, the station manager, complained that the exiles were "completely unable to think in radio terms." Although Gross had initiated a crash course in the basics of radio journalism, he remained pessimistic about some of the new recruits. Shortly thereafter, efforts to hire a competent staff were expedited, and by the summer RFE was prepared to begin broadcasting on a limited basis.[28] To help shape the broadcast message, Altschul, who chaired the FEC's radio committee, assembled an advisory committee of respected intellectuals, journalists, and activists; among the early members were Edward R. Murrow, Arthur Schlesinger Jr., and Jay Lovestone, the international affairs director of the American Federation of Labor.[29]

A somewhat clearer sense of RFE's mission had emerged by the time the station went on the air in July 1950. It was to be a "channel of communication by radio with the prisoner states over which things might be said which are in the national interest to have said, but that an official organ of government such as the Voice could not itself say." Those who would speak over the RFE microphone would be "authentic voices of exiled political and intellectual leaders and occasionally the voices of lesser-known or unknown exiles." And whereas VOA programs were "centered in the American scene," RFE broadcasts would concentrate on developments within the target region.[30] A more polemical, but no less accurate, declaration of RFE's objectives was provided by DeWitt Poole. The radio, Poole wrote, sought to "comfort and encourage those now in bondage; to reassure them constantly of the West's steadfast concern for their plight; to keep alive and fortify among them the Western tradition of freedom and democracy; to hold up the prospect of a better future." To further these goals, RFE would, Poole wrote, "work to discredit among the masses the illegitimates who are now over them, namely the native quislings and all Russian personnel, military and civilian." Radio Free Europe would furthermore seek to "sow in their minds and hearts dismay, doubt and defeatism and to foment among them mutual suspicion and distrust."[31]

Another early problem was of a more technical nature. In order to reach the East European audience, RFE would require transmission facilities in Europe. The FEC had failed in its efforts to secure broadcast time over the state networks in Spain, Italy, and Luxembourg. Finally, an interim solution was reached when the Bonn government agreed to allow the installation of a weak, 7.5–kilowatt transmitter near Frankfurt to broadcast via shortwave.[32]

The first broadcast, made on July 4, was little more than an announcement of the impending commencement of regular programming. A daily schedule began ten days later, on July 14, Bastille Day, a European symbol of revolutionary action against state tyranny. The original sign-on announced that RFE would broadcast its message "in the American tradition of free speech, without any interference from government."[33]

The latter part of this statement was clearly deceptive, although the actual government role was less than might have been expected. DeWitt C. Poole, who served as FEC president from its inception until January 1951, once complained of having received "scattered directives" from Wisner that "didn't make too much sense." Poole also complained about the meddling of two of Wisner's colleagues, Tracey Barnes and Carmel Offie, in the exile relations program. There were also occasional rumors that the State Department might assume responsibility for day-to-day broadcast policy, either directly or through an official of the Voice of America. Such plans, if they existed beyond the realm of speculation, never materialized. In fact, top RFE managers were more prone to express discontent over the lack of State Department guidance on the critical question of developing a political line than to fret over an overly intrusive Washington role.[34]

In any event, the CIA's role in RFE operations was to remain hidden from public view for nearly twenty years. Most Americans believed that the station was funded by private contributions raised by a new entity called the Crusade for Freedom. The organization's record at fund raising was, in fact, rather unimpressive. But as we shall see, it proved remarkably successful as a public relations vehicle for Radio Free Europe and the cause of East European resistance to Soviet domination.

2

Crusade for Freedom

For those who were present, the dedication of the Freedom Bell stands as one of the Cold War's more inspirational, if forgotten, moments.[1] Some four hundred thousand Germans lined the streets of West Berlin on October 24, 1950, to cheer Gen. Lucius Clay, the hero of the Berlin Airlift and the figure who symbolized the Free World alliance of the United States and Europe, as he proceeded in a cavalcade from Tempelhof Airport to the Schoeneberger Platz (later renamed John F. Kennedy Platz), the site of West Berlin's city hall. Joining Clay on the dais were a number of West Germany's top leaders, including the chancellor, Konrad Adenauer, and Berlin's mayor, Dr. Ernst Reuter. Representing the United States were such luminaries as Gen. Maxwell Taylor, the commander of American military forces in Germany, and John J. McCloy, U.S. high commissioner for Germany.

And there was the bell itself: eight feet high, weighing more than ten tons, it was essentially a replica of the original Liberty Bell in Philadelphia's Independence Hall. A quotation adapted from Abraham Lincoln—"That this world under God shall have a new birth of freedom"—encircled the base. Above the inscription was a frieze depicting the "five races of man," who stood "with arms outstretched passing from hand to hand the torch of freedom until one day it shall light the whole world." Above the figures, near the shoulder of the bell, was emblazoned a garland of laurel leaves, the symbol of peace.

The bell was designed by Walter Dorwin Teague, a leading industrial engineer from New York, and cast by one of the world's leading bell foundries, an English firm named Gilett and Johnston, Ltd. After the casting was completed, the bell was brought to the United States, where it was given a ticker tape parade down Broadway in New York and then sent on a national tour, including stops in Pittsburgh, Cleveland, Detroit, Chicago, and Kansas City, followed by a Freedom Train tour that took it to another dozen cities, with Philadelphia the final destination.[2]

The Freedom Bell was sponsored and, it was assumed, paid for by a new organization called the Crusade for Freedom. The crusade's ostensible purpose was to raise funds for Radio Free Europe, the new anti-Communist station whose broadcasts to Eastern Europe had begun that summer. General Clay was the organization's chairman; its board consisted of the same prominent men who served on the board of the Free Europe Committee.

Even before the dedication ceremony, the Crusade for Freedom had gotten off to an impressive start. General Eisenhower announced its formation in a nationwide radio address; shortly afterward the Freedom Bell's national tour got underway. Americans were urged to contribute funds to the crusade, which would in turn be used to help finance RFE. They were also encouraged to sign freedom scrolls. Some one hundred thousand scrolls would be delivered to West Berlin as part of the dedication ceremony; in all, the crusade claimed that thirteen million Americans had signed the scrolls.

The dedication ceremonies were held in Berlin because of the city's status as a symbol of East–West division. The event was meant to reassure the German people that America was committed to the ultimate reunification of the country. Predictably, East Germany's Communist Party was incensed by the whole affair, particularly the presence of the hated General Clay. The Communists launched a noisy demonstration several miles from the dedication site, and party propagandists denounced the Freedom Bell as a "war bell," a "hunger bell," a "death bell." A member of the party Politburo, Hans Jendretsky, warned, "The rope of the death bell will become the gallows rope for those who ring it."

The speeches by Clay and the others stressed Free World unity, particularly the emerging alliance between the Federal Republic and the United States. Maxwell Taylor called Berlin the "symbol of democratic resistance," while McCloy spoke of the city's "new courage to resist oppression." As a Social Democrat, Reuter was a member of a party that was ambivalent about West Germany's commitment to the Cold War alliance, but he pledged that Germany "will never rest or relax until freedom . . . will shine over [the countries of Eastern Europe] that are at present forced to live in slavery." General Clay promised that America would engage in a "moral Crusade for Freedom." The Freedom Bell, he added, "will be heard wherever there are human beings who yearn to live, and work, and worship, as free men."

Clay then pressed the button that would ring the bell. Its deep peals could be heard in the Soviet sector of the city, ten miles away. It could also be heard by one of the largest radio audiences to that date, as it was broadcast over stations throughout Europe, as well as the Voice of America, Radio Free Europe, and the Armed Forces Network.

This was an auspicious moment for an organization that would became as familiar to the American people as Ivory soap or Ford automobiles—at least during the early 1950s, when Cold War tensions were at high pitch. The Crusade for Freedom's advertisements were ubiquitous; appeals for support were aired frequently on radio and television, and crusade posters, asking Americans to contribute "truth dollars" to Radio Free Europe, could often be encountered on buses and subways. While the Korean War and American policy toward China were subject to vigorous debate at the time, the organization enjoyed a motherhood-and-apple-pie reputation; its fund campaigns were regarded as no more partisan or controversial than the March of Dimes, the United Way, or Unicef.

Although crusade literature did not claim that its fund-raising drives were the sole or even major source of the RFE budget, it did not mind if people got that impression. The organization, with its prestigious board, its endorsement by Presidents Truman and Eisenhower, and its roster of blue-chip corporate contributors, was ideal as camouflage for the money that was being secretly provided by the American government through the CIA.[3]

It would be inaccurate, however, to look on the Crusade for Freedom as nothing more than a convenient cover for CIA funding. There is evidence that some within the FEC hoped that the crusade would succeed in raising the dominant portion of the RFE budget. Within a year or two, they were disabused of that notion; the crusade, in fact, never raised more than a small fraction of the funds needed to keep RFE on the air. Equally important at the time was the organization's role in mobilizing the support of the American people for the Cold War effort. During World War II, the United States had enlisted the services of thousands of volunteers to sell war bonds and otherwise help support the government's war policies. With the crusade, American policy makers hoped to emulate the wartime volunteer program. As initially organized, the crusade emphasized local participation; there were crusade drives at the national, state, and local levels. The paid staff was small and concentrated in the New York headquarters; the crusade's real strength rested in its network of volunteers around the country. Although corporate contributions accounted for the bulk of its funds, the crusade also raised money through door-to-door solicitations by Boy Scouts and newsboys as well as donations at, among other places, churches, car dealerships, and Broadway theaters.[4]

To stimulate a sense of urgency among its supporters, the Crusade for Freedom adopted annual slogans. In 1950, General Eisenhower supplied the theme in his kick-off message: "Fight the big lie with the big truth." The next year's slogan was "Help truth fight Communism; Join the Crusade for Freedom." The crusade sponsored parades stressing the theme of freedom for the satellite peoples and public forums, complete with speeches by prominent exiles and demonstrations of propaganda balloon launchings, a balloon campaign being the latest and most spectacular RFE undertaking.[5] The crusade also organized trips for large contributors to the Munich headquarters, where corporate executives could tour the broadcast facilities and receive briefings from leading staff members.

By 1954 the crusade had deemphasized its campaigns to raise funds from the general public in favor of corporate sources. After RFE was the target of criticism for its performance during the 1956 Hungarian Revolution, the public campaigns were essentially abandoned, though corporate fund raising continued as before. But the crusade retained its high public visibility through the radio and television announcements placed by the Advertising Council, an organization established to help nonprofit groups reach the public with their message. The council assumed the cost of the crusade's national advertising campaign; the crusade paid only for the production of the commercial spots. It is estimated that the council paid between $12 and $20 million toward crusade advertising campaigns until the ties between RFE and the CIA were severed in 1972 and the station was brought under open public funding.

According to a General Accounting Office study, the crusade raised annually between $2.25 and $3.3 million during the fifties. At the same time, the government was plowing funds into the crusade to enable it to sustain its fund-raising activities, to the tune of more than $2 million in both 1951 and 1952. Eventually, the government contribution stabilized at about 37 percent of total receipts. The crusade's contribution to the RFE budget averaged around 19 percent during the 1950s, a decent figure, but not nearly enough to justify the boast that Radio Free Europé was sustained by truth dollars from ordinary Americans and schoolchildren.[6]

To be fair, RFE did not claim that it was funded by the crusade when journalists would ask about money sources. Spokesmen for the station tended to dodge the issue, or to simply issue a bland "no comment." In those days reporters understood the unwritten rules of the game, and no one probed too deeply into RFE's financial affairs.

We now know that the CIA was the conduit for the bulk of RFE's budget and practically all of RL's budget during the stations' first two decades of existence. A more pertinent question thus is the nature of the relationship between the intelligence agency and the two radios. Did the CIA intrude into the day-to-day administration of the stations? Did the agency set the guidelines for broadcast policy? To what extent were agency employees assigned to work directly for RFE or RL? Did the CIA attempt to use radio broadcasts to send messages to agents behind the Iron Curtain? Were the radios used as intelligence instruments to further Frank Wisner's various projects involving East European exiles?

The most extensive account of the CIA-RFE relationship appears in *Facing Reality,* the memoirs of CIA veteran Cord Meyer. In 1954, Meyer succeeded Thomas Braden as chief of the agency's International Organization Division, the body that had administrative responsibility for much of the CIA's far-flung empire of intellectual committees, magazines and journals, radio stations, and student associations, of which RFE was the most important—and the most expensive. In the early years Radio Liberty operated directly under the supervision of the agency's Soviet division; later, it too would fall under the control of International Organization.

Meyer's most important single responsibility was the radios' budget. Each year RFE and RL would submit budget requests to the agency. The requests would be assessed, and usually reduced, by Meyer and other officials. Meyer then had to defend the radios' proposal against

[handwritten note: 1950's: big START-UP COST fr RFE/RL]

competing claims by other CIA divisions. Since both RFE and RL required heavy spending for transmitters during the fifties, the debates over just where the stations fit in among CIA priorities often became quite heated. As Meyer put it, "There were understandable complaints that the radios were devouring too large a portion of the resources of an organization that was supposed to be primarily concerned with intelligence collection and analysis." He added, "There was an obvious case to be made for breaking the radios out of the agency and providing for open funding by Congress. However, neither the executive branch nor the congressional committees were willing to consider this alternative until events finally forced a decision. The existing arrangements worked tolerably well, and no one at the policy level wanted to face the risk of exposing prior agency involvement that was inevitable in any shift to public financing."[7]

During their formative years the radios had an indispensable asset in the person of CIA director Allen Dulles. Dulles had served as first chairman of the FEC and retained a powerful commitment to the mission of the freedom stations. In the struggle against the Soviet Union, Dulles was often willing to take a calculated risk, especially where the expenditure of money was involved. The radios clearly benefited from Dulles's generosity. For example, Dulles, after some hesitation, gave the go-ahead for a massive and costly transmitter project for Radio Liberty, even though there were serious doubts about the impact of foreign broadcasting to the Soviet Union at the time. Dulles based his decision on the conviction that as Soviet citizens became better educated, they would develop a curiosity about both their own society and the outside world and would be less inclined to accept the official Kremlin explanation of events. Dulles thus based his approval not on the prospect of an immediate payoff, but rather on the hope that at some point in the future the Soviet people would become attached to foreign broadcasts. It turned out to be a farsighted judgment.[8]

Meyer also makes the controversial claim that the agency played the decisive role in formulating broadcast policy—in setting down the political line. This may have been the case during RFE's very first months. Thus an exasperated Frank Altschul wrote in a 1950 memo, "We receive with some regularity a daily selection of what is purported to be significant news items with the condition that they must be used word for word in the form sent, unless changes are cleared by telephone. Only the fewest of these items are of any use at all. . . . [By] way of increasing this appallingly limited flow, our friends have recently been sending translations from foreign newspapers . . . which have no value whatsoever. They are taken from papers anywhere from two to five months old." The radio leadership was, however, hopeful that the CIA might be more helpful in supplying information for broadcast purposes. "We have the impression that a great deal more material useful in character could be supplied by our friends ["friends" was the code word normally used when referring to the CIA in RFE internal correspondence] if liaison with them were better developed," Altschul wrote in 1950. "Needless to say, we recognize the difficulties this presents in view of the sensitive nature of the information and its sources."[9]

In any event, it is clear that officials from the CIA and possibly the State Department were expressing opinions on RFE broadcasts from the very outset. Thus Altschul reports having spoken to a Mr. Kramer from the government within the first week of RFE broadcasts about the Czechoslovak and Romanian scripts. Kramer had found "nothing objectionable" in the scripts, but added that "they had not really hit any of the really vital points." Altschul responded: "We could hardly go further than we had done until we had received the guidance sheets from them—that the desks were working in the dark without any guidance and under this circumstance were doing the best they could."[10] Even before the RFE broadcast schedule was launched, there was some discussion of scripts being written by the CIA itself.[11]

It didn't take long for Radio Free Europe to establish a wide network of information sources, ranging from publications to monitored radio broadcasts to intelligence gleaned from refugees and travelers from the East, that was in many respects superior to anything the American government could provide. As for Meyer's assertion that the CIA took responsibility for the political content of broadcasts, both exiles and Americans who held policy-making positions with RFE during the 1950s insist it just wasn't so. Initially, they assert, broad political guidance emanated from the State Department and was channeled to RFE's policy staff through the CIA. Eventually, a system evolved whereby broadcast policy was determined through a process of negotiation involving RFE, the CIA, and the State Department. Often, political documents were initially drafted by RFE policy advisers after discussion with the exiled editors and then submitted to the various government agencies for approval. This system functioned successfully until the controversy over RFE's broadcasts to Hungary during the 1956 revolution.[12]

Meyer also saw his job as shielding the radios from the designs of the more adventuresome CIA elements:

> Pressure to distort the purpose of the radios also came occasionally from within the agency. Ingenious schemes to use the radios in disinformation campaigns against particular Communist leaders were raised with us from time to time, and my answer to all such proposals was negative. . . . Similarly, we did not attempt to mix apples and oranges by allowing the American and exile staffs to be used for secret agent operations. Contrary to the persistent Soviet allegations that exiles working for the radios were being used by the CIA as espionage agents, this was not the case. It would have been foolishly shortsighted to expose the broadcasts to the kind of regime attack that the apprehension of a single spy behind the Curtain would have made possible.[13]

Meyer's contention that the radios were effectively protected from demands that they cooperate in agency operations is borne out by the testimony of veteran staff members. Jan Nowak, director of the Polish section, recalls an early incident in which he was directed to put on the airwaves special messages similar to those regularly broadcast by the BBC to British agents in Europe during World War II: "I was told that after the news broadcast there would be several special messages which should be broadcast. I complied. But I then went to see Bill Griffith [William E. Griffith, chief policy adviser in Munich] and threatened to quit if the messages continued." According to Nowak, the messages were discontinued.[14] Even at the early stages of RFE development, a policy was established to avoid the use of agents within the satellite countries. "We are to have no agents behind the Iron Curtain under any circumstances," Frank Altschul declared in a note to Robert Lang, the station's director. "And we are to be sure that sources of information that we tap on this side of the Iron Curtain are not based upon the use of agents."[15]

There is, however, some evidence that "elements" within the CIA did involve themselves in RFE projects at least through the mid-1950s. In an October 1954 memo to Whitney M. Shepardson, the president of the FEC, RFE director Bob Lang complained of "intrusion in each and every element of our affairs by characters on the operating side of our friends' organization." Lang's reference to the CIA's "operating side" presumably meant agency officials who were not under the control of Cord Meyer and his staff of prudent Cold War liberals. Significantly, Lang makes no reference to CIA involvement in broadcast policy, although other internal memos referred to complaints by CIA operatives in Turkey about RFE scripts that seemed to be discouraging defections. Lang, however, paints a picture of agency tutelage in a wide range of RFE and FEC activities. According to Lang, "minor level people" within the agency were making budget decisions and trying to exert an influence over relations with exiles, the European University, and other FEC projects, as well as a proposed transmitter project in Turkey (the Turkey project was subsequently abandoned). "By what right do [CIA employees] tell us that we should have two receptionists instead of three?" he asked. "And how did we get in a posture where they could insist upon these small details?"[16]

A careful examination of Lang's complaint suggests that most of the areas in which the agency involved itself related to the RFE budget, and that what seemed to Lang as petty intrusion may have been nothing more sinister than an attempt by the funding source to keep costs under control. In any event, other RFE staff members from the policy and broadcast side reject the notion of heavy CIA involvement in RFE affairs. Jan Nowak recalls the process of formulating broadcast policy as "very democratic," involving the exiled editors, the American policy advisers and, at yet another level, officials from the CIA and State Department. Paul Henze, a member of the policy staff in Munich, recalls an environment of collegial cooperation between RFE and CIA analysts. Agency personnel visited the Munich headquarters regularly; they often attended the morning policy briefings—as did visiting journalists, scholars, and political dignitaries. Henze claims that the notion that there might be anything suspicious or unsavory in the CIA-RFE relationship never occurred to the station's staff. The intelligence agency and radio station were on the same side, pursued similar goals, and were in agreement over RFE's role and policies.[17]

There was also a mutuality of intelligence interests in the early RFE years. Because of the closed nature of Communist societies, RFE employed traditional intelligence gathering techniques to secure the material that would enable the station to air accurate, hard-hitting commentaries on internal political affairs in the audience countries. Journalists from RFE were stationed in bureaus throughout Europe, where they interviewed refugees, defectors, and travelers going to and from the East. The station monitored Communist radio broadcasts and conducted detailed analyses of the Communist press. It collected a massive amount of information on East European communism and then organized the material into a vast archive, which provided a treasure trove of information for scholars, journalists, and, for that matter, intelligence analysts.

Radio Free Europe's listeners assumed that, official disclaimers notwithstanding, the station was supported by the American government. Some former employees, however, claim they were upset when they learned that RFE was funded not by private American sources, as they had been told, but by the CIA, as Communist propagandists contended from the beginning. When Jan Nowak asked about the source of revenues, he was told that corporate contributions would continue to finance the station's operation because companies could write off donations as tax deductions. Nowak's friends called him naïve for accepting this explanation; they said everyone in Washington knew that the CIA provided most of the funding. Nowak then asked Bill Griffith for an explanation; Griffith refused to give a direct response and, as Nowak put it, "this was enough of an answer for me to understand what the reality was." Nowak stayed on, reasoning that RFE was performing an important role without overt interference from the government.

Those in positions of authority—American managers and some exiled editors who held American citizenship—were eventually informed of the CIA's role in RFE affairs and required to sign a statement signifying that they were "witting" to the fact of agency involvement and pledging not to reveal the CIA connection. The statement read, in part, "The undersigned has been informed that Radio Free Europe is a project of the CIA and that the CIA provides funds for the operation of the organization. The undersigned has now been officially informed. If he divulges this information to a third party, he becomes liable for a fine and punishment not to exceed 10,000 dollars and ten years in prison."[18] John Foster Leich, an early staff member of the FEC, reported that he had been informed of the government's funding role early on: "The precise origin, means of transmission, or obligations which this funding imposed upon the Committee were never discussed with any staff member who did not have a direct 'need to know' and had not been 'cleared' for that purpose." As for the exiles, Leich wrote that they "without exception assumed that government funds were involved, and were glad of this evidence of United States interest in their cause."[19]

A few CIA employees were posted directly to the RFE staff in Munich or in corporate headquarters in New York. CIA men were assigned to the security staff (the agency administered the security staff until the station's relationship with the CIA ended), accounting, the policy office, engineering, and personnel.[20] The agency also had a decisive role in chief staff appointments. Thus when Dick Condon, the former director of RFE's Munich headquarters, was named to a high post with Radio Liberty in 1960, the decision was made jointly by Cord Meyer and Howland Sargeant, the president of Amcomlib, the organization that sponsored Radio Liberty.[21]

If given a choice between the CIA and the State Department, RFE clearly preferred the administrative control of the intelligence agency. The natural tension between RFE and the diplomats posted to Eastern Europe was accentuated after Eastern Europe underwent de-Stalinization. As the regimes' isolation gave way to more normal contacts with Western diplomats, regime complaints about RFE broadcast were taken more seriously by American ambassadors and, at times, by the State Department in Washington. At the same time, Washington adopted a policy of differentiation, that is, of treating Communist regimes differently according to their degree of internal freedom and political independence from Moscow. At various times during the Cold War, Poland, Hungary, and Romania were given preferential consideration. Where objections to RFE programs were formerly ignored, now American ambassadors were sometimes inclined to side with the complaining regimes and to view RFE as a nuisance that complicated their diplomatic functions.

By contrast, life with the CIA was free of overt tension. Under Cord Meyer, the agency took the position that as long as RFE and RL had competent managers and editors, the less interference by the government the better. Meyer had been active in the world federalism movement prior to joining the intelligence agency, and he and other agency officials who dealt with the freedom radios were generally liberal men who often preferred liberal and social democratic parties to conservative ones. In choosing candidates for leading staff positions, the CIA preferred men of practical experience to ardent anti-Communists. The CIA seldom interfered in matters of broadcast content. Moreover, the CIA tried to protect RFE when complaints about its broadcasts were voiced by the State Department during the latter half of the 1950s, and Allen Dulles personally intervened when an attempt was made to cut off RFE broadcasts to Poland.[22]

Not that the relationship was entirely free of discord. Retired general Rodney Smith, who served as RFE director during the 1960s, was a determined opponent of CIA intrusiveness. Thus when the agency objected to the appointment of Richard Burks, an East European scholar, as policy director, Smith pushed the appointment through anyway. Smith also had a policy of strictly limiting the number of agency employees serving directly on the RFE staff.[23]

As RFE matured and became more professional, the CIA tended to involve itself less and less in the station's internal affairs. There were, however, exceptions, one of the most notable being the Sino-Soviet split. In a November 1960 memo, Reuben Nathan, a member of the policy staff in New York, complained of "an ever-increasing number of EC suggestions on coverage of the Sino-Soviet conflict" (EC was an abbreviation for Executive Committee, which in turn was code for the CIA in RFE internal memos). Among other things, the CIA was urging that the conflict be handled through master scripts—that is, scripts written by Americans and then translated for the various language desks—rather than simply leaving coverage to the discretion of the desks, as was the usual practice. Nathan also complained that the agency kept changing the political line, making the drafting of policy statements nearly impossible.[24]

Nathan's memo is particularly interesting for what it reveals about agency confusion on the Beijing-Moscow rift. The agency, he noted, "resisted for many months all and any efforts to recommend dealing" with the conflict; when RFE analysts would suggest that something important and worthy of commentary was going on, the proposals were "consistently thrown out as 'speculative.'" Later, when the agency changed course and decided that the rift deserved coverage, it demanded "extremely emphatic treatment" by RFE. "They went so far as to ask that we 'envenom' the conflict," Nathan wrote. At the same time, the CIA complained when RFE desks attempted their own analyses, and demanded that the station rely on secondary sources from the world press.[25] The CIA also sent their own intelligence reports to the

structions that they be given to Americans in the policy
ould rework the material for the exile staff to translate.

)60, memo, presumably from a CIA source, RFE was
....u to "not emphasize split.... Allow this to develop along current
lines since fear that if any US comment it would only serve to unite
the two camps."[26]

For some within RFE, the CIA connection was a source of singular
embarrassment. Among other things, they believed that CIA funding
and oversight made the station vulnerable to Communist accusations
of involvement in espionage operations. Those of a more liberal persuasion grew increasingly uncomfortable as the CIA became identified in the public's mind with American foreign policy failures and
covert operation excesses. They welcomed the day when the CIA link
was broken and RFE and RL were brought under direct congressional funding, as was achieved through legislation enacted in the early
1970s.

Some later came to regret their enthusiasm for severing the relationship with the intelligence agency. Despite legislative efforts to in-
sulate RFE and RL from political pressure, the radios actually suffered
a much higher degree of governmental intrusion than during the bad
old days of CIA administration. Congressmen and their staff began to
nose around in internal radio affairs. Allegedly insensitive scripts became the subject of congressional hearings. The Office of Management and Budget, whose role had been minimal when the stations'
budget was enfolded into the general CIA budget, began to ask pointed
questions about the radios' operations and repeatedly attempted to
reduce their allocations. Projects that had once been completed with a
minimum of bureaucratic complication became ensnarled in the congressional budgeting process and dragged on for years. The political
ideology of top radio management, a nonissue under the CIA, emerged
as a source of internal contentiousness. For some radio veterans, the
lesson of all this was that reform does not always signify improvement.

3

"The Mills of God Grind Slowly"

[handwritten: SWIATLO defects ...]

On a December day in 1953, Lt. Col. Josef Swiatlo, one of Poland's highest ranking secret police officials, slipped away from a traveling companion during a shopping expedition in West Berlin, made his way to a Western embassy, and asked the astonished officials there for asylum. Swiatlo was not the first Communist functionary to have defected to the West. But Swiatlo was no ordinary member of the party apparatus. He had served as chief of Department Ten of the UB, as Poland's secret police were popularly known. Department Ten was responsible for the political and ideological purity of Communist Party officials, a counterintelligence force against deviation. Swiatlo was uniquely positioned to know the most intimate details about the private lives of the men who had reached the pinnacles of power—details about their financial affairs, their mistresses, their acts of betrayal, and their relations with high Soviet officials.[1]

The Swiatlo affair would eventually reverberate throughout the Soviet satellite system. Swiatlo's revelations would lead to a major shakeup of the Polish Communist Party and contribute to a softening of Soviet control over its East European empire. They would accelerate the pace of de-Stalinization.

Swiatlo's defection would, furthermore, have widespread implications for the future of Radio Free Europe. For it was over RFE's Voice of Free Poland (VFP) that Swiatlo told the inside story of Polish communism. He began his broadcasts on September 28, 1954, nearly ten months after his defection, and his scripts were aired almost nightly for the next three months. Eventually Swiatlo took part in more than one hundred programs, in which he recounted the details of secret police torture, rigged elections, and, especially, the mechanisms through which Soviet officials controlled Polish life.[2]

The broadcasts' impact derived from the secret policeman's remarkable memory for details. He recounted minute specifics of the methods of repression and reported who had committed crimes, and where and when they had occurred. In a series of powerful broadcasts, Swiatlo described the elaborately plotted campaign to subvert the Catholic Church, an institution the Communists saw as an unreconstructed source of nationalism and anti-Sovietism. He emphasized that the plan to control the church originated with Ivan Serov, a high KGB official, thus reinforcing the image of Polish Communists as Moscow's lackeys. Swiatlo named the four prominent Polish party officials who were selected to implement the antichurch campaign, giving particular attention to Boleslaw Piasecki, chairman of the Communist Party's "Catholic" organization, Pax. Swiatlo revealed that Piasecki had collaborated with the Nazis during World War II and had avoided execution after the war by agreeing to cooperate with the Communists, with the specific assignment of weakening the church's influence.

Swiatlo told what he had seen during a visit to the monastery where Cardinal Stefan Wyszynski, the Polish primate, was interned on orders from Moscow. There Swiatlo witnessed battalions of secret police officials, electricians, plumbers, and masons preparing the cardinal's new residence. Two rooms were reserved for police agents: a "priest" and a "nun." Other rooms were set aside for guards and other police officials. There was a master control for the recording devices located throughout the residence and the various electronic signaling devices placed strategically to enable police agents to monitor the prelate's every move. Microphones were installed in each room, and the door to the garden was rigged so that an alarm would sound when Wyszynski stepped outside. The garden was surrounded by a wall, protected by a wire netting that prevented the cardinal from reaching the wall, and there were guards placed on the wall and around the perimeter. As a final touch, Swiatlo reported that measures had been taken to limit the cardinal's access to the chapel: a glass door had been installed in the passageway from the living quarters to the chapel, and Wyszynski was denied entrance unless he received permission from the commander of the guards.[3]

Swiatlo's sensational accounts represented much more than a tabloid version of political journalism. Swiatlo was an intensely political man; he had personally arrested Wladyslaw Gomulka when Gomulka was purged from the party ranks for nationalist tendencies. His message was that in People's Poland, a hierarchy existed in which the party was ruled by the police and the police were ruled by the Soviet Union. That Poland lacked genuine sovereignty was hardly news. But by piling on one episode after another, by naming names, by providing places, times, and dates, the Swiatlo broadcasts aroused the nation and rattled the Communist Party. Jakub Karpinski, a historian of Polish postwar politics, believes that the Swiatlo commentaries rank with Khrushchev's secret speech and the Poznan worker riots as events that changed the course of communism in Poland. As to the practical consequences, the revelations led to the removal of Stanislaw Radkiewicz as minister of Public Security, provoked a shakeup of the security service, expedited the release of Gomulka from house arrest, and triggered a spate of Communist self-criticisms clearly influenced by the Swiatlo broadcasts.[4]

The Voice of Free Poland, meanwhile, had become the most influential source of news in Poland, a remarkable achievement for a foreign radio station whose signal was frequently rendered unlistenable by jamming. During the Swiatlo broadcasts, residents of Warsaw, where reception was often dreadful, tuned in during the late-night hours when jamming was least effective and spent their days in conversation over the incredible things they had heard through the static. The Voice of Free Poland had attained what RFE had originally set out to do: win acceptance as surrogate home service, with all that implied for the totalitarian project. Polish communism could no longer claim a media monopoly or even media domination. The party retained political power, of course. But if it raised prices by decree, or jailed a dissident writer, or ordered its police to shoot striking workers, it would do so with the knowledge that the action would be covered by a free, uncensored, and widely credible radio station—one that, despite its American sponsorship and German headquarters, was regarded as more genuinely Polish than the official party press would ever be regarded.

Few who were familiar with its operations in 1950 would have predicted that Radio Free Europe was destined to alter the course of

Communist history within a few years. With no studios of its own, RFE made its recordings in facilities owned by WMCA, a popular New York radio station, during its first months. The tapes were shipped by air to West Germany, and then beamed to the target countries via a weak 7.5–kw. transmitter located at Holzkirchen, a village not far from Frankfurt. The early broadcasts were often crudely argued and amateurishly produced. Nevertheless, RFE's existence was duly noted, and objected to, by Communist authorities, and information percolating through the Iron Curtain indicated that the intended audience was aware of the new radio service as well.

Soon after broadcasts to the East were inaugurated, it was decided to abandon the original conception of RFE as a forum for exile political leaders. The Korean War had broken out, and the government responded by beefing up projects designed to stir matters up in Moscow's backyard. It was felt that a broadcasting service dominated by exile politicians was no longer sufficient for RFE's mission. The role envisioned for RFE was spelled out in a memorandum for the FEC board: "The aim of Radio Free Europe is primarily to supplement the Voice of America in the field of propaganda, using the voices of exiled leaders incidentally as this seems consistent with its fundamental purpose." The non-governmental status of RFE, the memo added, "permits us . . . to shape our programs sympathetically in the familiar terms of the audience to which they are addressed. Above all, it allows us a far wider latitude than is allowed the Voice in the selection of news and the slanting of commentary."[5]

The decision also was motivated by exasperation with the exiles. The exiles had been figures of importance in their native countries; in the West they were shunted off to the margins of political life. Where the affairs of entire nations had once been their domain, they now functioned in the constricted environment of exile committees with little influence over Western policy. In their homelands, politics had been a rough and risky occupation, in which the spirit of compromise and bipartisanship was rarely invoked. Predictably, they often treated exile affairs as a small-scale version of politics back home and dealt with adversaries with a mixture of polemics, vituperation, and deception. At RFE, the American managers were constantly faced with accusations that this or that faction was preventing members of other groupings from gaining access to the airwaves, as well as charges that an exile leader had attacked another exile leader over an RFE microphone.[6]

Beginning in late 1950, RFE began to assemble the staff that would transform the radio station from a mouthpiece for exiles to a full-scale foreign broadcast service. Most of those hired as editors and commentators came from the postwar emigration of East European non-Communist journalists and intellectuals. Very few had a background in radio news; most had worked on newspapers or journals or had served as teachers, academics, or in the diplomatic corps.

Among the criteria that influenced hiring decisions was political balance. It was RFE's goal to hire a team of journalists for each language service that reflected the audience country's range of political parties, from Social Democrats on the left to the Peasant Party on the right. For obvious reasons, RFE hired no Communists or party sympathizers; it was, however, thought worthwhile to have one or two former party members on staff to help in formulating RFE's message to party members in the audience countries. There was also a policy against the employment of Fascists or extreme nationalists. The Czechoslovak service, for example, refused to consider applicants who were supporters of Slovak separatism. The RFE management allowed exiled leaders to play a prominent role in staff hiring for the Hungarian and Czechoslovak services, the first two to be assembled. This policy came to be regretted, and when a staff for the Polish desk was hired, the chief editor, Jan Nowak, was given near total power over employment decisions.[7]

Finding Hungarians, Czechoslovaks, and Poles with potential as radio journalists proved not as difficult as might be imagined. There were thousands of bright young exiles, many with writing experience, and a few with established journalistic reputations, adrift in Western Europe. They were often poor, subsisting on the small change they earned writing for exile journals or scraping by as university students. One can hardly imagine a more appealing prospect for these political exiles than to earn a decent living as a journalist while simultaneously striking a blow against their Communist persecutors. The RFE management began to talk seriously about establishing a full-scale Voice of Free Hungary (VFH) in the summer of 1951; within a half year, a staff of over one hundred had been hired, complete with German technicians, a few American managers, and over seventy Hungarian exiles. But while a competent staff for the Hungarian, Czechoslovak, and Polish services was assembled rather quickly, problems were encountered in finding Bulgarians and Romanians. This was due principally to the relatively small number of Bulgarians and Romanians living as exiles in the West. A further difficulty for the Romanian service stemmed from the fact that the political biographies of many exiles were tainted by involvement with Fascist or ultranationalist causes. Even more difficult was finding a staff for an Albanian-language service, which was launched in 1951 at the behest of the American government. The Albanian service was discontinued after two years. The government finally abandoned its hopes of an overthrow of the Communist regime there, and it was determined that, given the few number of Albanians who owned shortwave receivers, RFE's impact was minimal.[8]

Once the basic broadcast staff was in place, the next priority was securing information about the target countries. To prove that it was superior to the Communist media, RFE required thorough files on the individuals and institutions it targeted, and it needed reliable material about events inside the Iron Curtain. The development of a system of intelligence and file gathering was an even more critical requirement for RFE than for other media because it operated entirely outside audience countries, which were run along classic totalitarian lines, their leaders maintaining an expansive interpretation of what constitutes state secrets.

Thus even before it inaugurated its full broadcast schedule, RFE had begun to construct a news and intelligence gathering operation that would become the envy of scholars and journalists all over the world. In addition to the major Western newspapers, wire services, and magazines, RFE acquired a long list of Communist bloc publications, right down to small provincial weeklies. The next step was to set up a series of monitoring stations in which broadcasts from the official Communist radio stations were recorded, transcribed, and sent to the desk editors as background information. Although it was eventually centralized in the Munich headquarters, monitoring was at first organized on a catch-as-catch-can basis. For example, one man, supplied with a room and typewriter, took care of the monitoring for the entire Czechoslovak regime radio output. To monitor Romanian and Bulgarian radio broadcasts, a staff was hired in Istanbul; it took nearly a week for the staff's transcripts to reach RFE headquarters in New York.

In addition to its monitoring program, RFE opened a network of news and information bureaus throughout Western Europe. The chief of each bureau was an English-speaking journalist; the rest of the staff were usually exiles. The bureaus eventually came to function like normal news operations, supplying reports relevant to the audience countries from London, Bonn, Rome, and Paris. At first, however, the bureaus' main purpose was intelligence gathering. The original plan called for a division of intelligence gathering between the CIA and RFE, with the CIA providing general information about conditions behind the Iron Curtain and RFE providing material elicited in interviews with defectors. Thus the decision on where to locate the bureaus depended less on the news potential of the city than on how often it was frequented by travelers or refugees from the East. Bureaus were opened in Hamburg and Stockholm because these cities were often visited by ships from Poland. A bureau was opened in Istanbul because it was the destination of travelers and refugees from Bulgaria and Romania. Bureaus were opened in various cities in Austria because of their proximity to the Hungarian border. The bureau staff conducted in-depth interviews with travelers and often employed standard defector interrogation techniques. Some of the information was sent to Munich as news reports, but sometimes the format resembled interrogation or intelligence reports. Because civic life was heavily politicized under communism, the inquiries were quite broad. Radio Free Europe journalists asked about life on the "factory farm," the income of collective farmers, whether peasants were withholding grain (as RFE was urging them to do), what music people listened to, what books they read, whether there were strikes or industrial sabotage, the role of Soviet advisers, prices on the black market, the status of sports clubs and paramilitary organizations, and much more. The information allowed RFE to broadcast information that the Communist media would not send over the airwaves and that rival foreign broadcast services such as the VOA could not broadcast because they lacked the research capability.

Radio Free Europe did not maintain paid agents inside the Iron Curtain. It did, however, retain a network of well-connected émigrés in Paris, Vienna, Rome, and other European cities who kept abreast of political developments through contacts within the East European countries. These agents would pass along information gathered from their various sources, and the material would then be analyzed and occasionally used in special broadcasts about internal conditions in the audience countries. RFE also received information on developments within the Communist world from letters sent to its special Box 52–20 in Munich. Listeners were invited to write to this address, and the information was sometimes used in RFE's *Messages* programs, in which announcers would reveal the names of Communist spies or informers.[9]

Critics have occasionally cited the role of the information bureaus as evidence that intelligence gathering occupied a more important part of RFE's mission that has ever been acknowledged. Radio Free Europe certainly shared its vast trove of information with agencies of the American government, including the CIA, without ever suspecting that routine cooperation with a government organization dedicated to the same broad objectives would ever be regarded as sinister or unethical. Indeed, as the CIA's networks within the Iron Curtain countries fell apart, the agency came to rely more and more on the information RFE acquired from its bureaus. In any event, most of the material compiled by the bureaus could be categorized as national secrets only by the unusual standards of Communist regimes. In other countries, including many dictatorships, the information about industrial production and farm life that RFE so eagerly sought could be routinely read in newspapers or publicly available government reports.

Over the years, as Cold War tensions relaxed somewhat and RFE shifted away from an emphasis on psychological warfare, the station relied less on information from travelers and defectors. It was, nevertheless, the repository of a remarkable collection of material about the Communist world, most of which was categorized, filed away, and analyzed by a team of researchers. Radio Free Europe's archives contained the biographies of literally thousands of party officials, the details of industrial and agricultural policy from the time Communists seized power, the ups and downs of satellite relations with Yugoslavia, the shifts and detours of regime policies toward religion, the arts, the schools. Scholars, journalists, government officials, and intelligence analysts came to regard RFE as the ultimate source of information about communism in Eastern Europe.

The material produced by the monitoring and research units was also invaluable to the language service editors. The editors of the Polish service, for example, would receive a thirty-to-fifty-page report each morning containing transcripts of the previous day's Warsaw Radio news broadcasts. They would also be given reports filed by the bureaus and any other information sent in by sources throughout Europe or within Poland. Jan Nowak, the chief editor of the Voice of Free Poland, says the monitoring and information operations were critical to RFE's success in breaking the information blockade that the regime had worked assiduously to perfect. The Polish service could respond to breaking developments within hours, with analyses and commentaries that conveyed a grasp of local realities that rivaled that of any domestic media.

To further bolster its local coverage, the Polish service would hire the more insightful of the recent Polish refugees to advise the service on its programming. The refugees were asked to listen to broadcasts, read scripts, offer an honest critique, and provide briefings on internal conditions, the popular mood, and the response to RFE and other international radio services. Nowak subscribed to the theory that one conversation with a recent escapee was worth dozens of written reports.[10]

Radio Free Europe was unique among international broadcasting stations in the autonomy enjoyed by its editors. Whereas other services employed scripts that were centrally written and then translated for use by the language services, RFE practically never used centrally written scripts. Nor were the various language services compelled to broadcast specific commentaries. It was assumed, of course, that the editors shared RFE's objectives. There were also guidelines relating to broadcast tone, admittedly loosely enforced in the early years. Otherwise, editors had considerable latitude in the selection of the daily broadcast schedule.

The American management did play a crucial role in the determination of broadcast policy. In the original conception, political direction was to be decided initially in the State Department after consultation with key officials at RFE and the FEC. In practice, the directives, or, as they were generally known, guidances, on political coverage were written by RFE political advisers and then given routine approval by government officials at the State Department or CIA.[11]

The guidances could take various forms. There were daily guidances with suggestions on coverage for breaking news stories. There were broad guidances that provided the framework for covering a specific subject—agricultural policy in Hungary, for example—or setting forth the broadcast strategy for a particular country. On the one hand, guidances might entail a few paragraphs suggesting useful points to buttress an argument or urging that certain issues be avoided. On the other hand, they might consist of lengthy, and sometimes erudite, essays, including extensive background analysis, a report on the current state of affairs, and recommendations on broadcast treatment

Before the Munich headquarters opened in May 1951, most guidances were written by Frank Altschul in his capacity as chairman of the FEC's radio committee. But during most of the 1950s, the development of political strategy was entrusted to two men: Lewis Galantiere and William E. Griffith, with Galantiere composing most of the important policy directives. Galantiere was a man of wide-ranging intellect who had earned something of a reputation as a literary critic and translator from French and German. He had worked at the Federal Reserve Bank and, during the war, was director of French operations for the Office of War Information. Griffith was a young scholar who had worked in the de-Nazification program for the Allied Occupation Forces in Bavaria. That neither Galantiere nor Griffith—nor the staff of policy assistants who worked under Griffith in Munich—could boast of a special knowledge of East European history or languages was not regarded as a handicap. At that time, there were few competent scholars in Russian history in American universities, and an even smaller number of specialists in Eastern Europe, a situation that would change only with the deepening of the Cold War.

For its first director, RFE chose a man from the world of advertising. Robert E. Lang was working in the product advertising department of the Post Cereal Company in Battle Creek, Michigan, when he was asked to come to New York to help get the new enterprise underway. Like many of the men associated with RFE, Lang had served with the Office of Strategic Services (OSS) during the war. Lang had limited experience in network radio. As manager of the far-flung business empire of big band leader Fred Waring, he had gotten a taste of broadcast radio work and had been involved in placing advertising on radio networks for Post Cereals, but otherwise, Lang's main qualifications for the job were enthusiasm, energy, administrative skill, and a can-do attitude—the latter an essential quality, given the daunting nature of the assignment.[12]

From the beginning, scripts were written by the exiles themselves, "incorporating their own ideas and sense of humor," as Lang put it. He believed it was essential that RFE project an idiomatic voice, and this meant avoiding the use of centrally written scripts.[13]

This left RFE with the problem of ensuring that scripts were competently written, were not overly polemical, adhered to broadcast standards, and did not deviate from the political line. There was some early talk of adopting a policy of censoring scripts before they were put on the air. It was feared that "if the exiles were left to themselves, they would be carried by their feelings and/or wishful thinking" and might be "inclined to support the idea of preventive war."[14] Initially, all scripts were reviewed prior to broadcast by analysts from the FEC. This practice was quickly scuttled as too cumbersome and as an impediment to the authenticity of the exile voice. Instead, scripts were reviewed only after they had been aired. To facilitate script control, detailed discussions were held between the policy advisers and the exile editors each morning over which stories would be given priority and the policy line to be adopted. An American policy adviser was assigned to each language service; the adviser in turn was assigned an assistant who spoke the particular language. The assistant read or listened to the scripts and would report to the adviser on the content of sensitive broadcasts, but only after the broadcasts had been aired. "It was fundamental to RFE's success that there be no pre-broadcast censorship," observed Ralph Walter, who served as policy adviser to the Polish desk, and was later appointed RFE director. "We felt it was essential that broadcasters have not only responsibility, but authority. And they understood that in comparison to other broadcast services to Eastern Europe, RFE gave them wide authority and independence."[15]

The exile editors were also consulted when policy was being set. Jan Nowak described the process as one of free-wheeling give-and-take. Once policy guidelines were established, however, the language services were obligated to adhere to the political line. There were, in addition, certain subjects on which commentary was ordinarily proscribed, most notably issues of particular sensitivity to the West German government and minority questions in the target countries.

The first attempt at an overall policy directive came in November 1951, with the RFE Policy Manual. A true product of its time, the manual gets right down to the point in its opening passages. Radio Free Europe's purpose, it observes, is to "contribute to the liberation of the nations imprisoned behind the Iron Curtain by sustaining their morale and stimulating in them a spirit of non-cooperation with the Soviet-dominated regimes by which they are, for the time being, ruled." Radio Free Europe would achieve this objective, the manual goes on, by reminding our listeners constantly that they are governed by agents of a foreign power whose purpose is not to further the national interest but to carry out the imperialistic aims of the rulers of the Soviet Union;

by displaying the moral and spiritual emptiness of Communism as an ideology and the material incapacity of Communism as an economic system to provide an acceptable standard-of-living for the working class;

by inculcating hope of eventual liberation through a convincing display of the superiority of the skill, resources, and military strength of the West, and through reiteration of the promise that the West intends that our listeners shall be free;

by sowing dissension in each regime through exposing the ineptitude of its officials, and sowing fear among the officials by denouncing confirmed acts of oppression and cruelty, and threatening retribution.[16]

In addition to a statement of principles, the policy manual provided advice on a number of questions that were being debated by the best minds among Western Cold War policy makers. There was, for example, the matter of what constituted the main enemy: communism as theory, indigenous Communist parties, or Soviet-Russian imperialism. The answer, RFE suggested, was that while all three were thoroughly objectionable, the source of the most serious trouble was Soviet imperialism. Thus from the outset RFE took a relatively positive view of Titoism. While RFE disapproved of any regime, including Tito's, that called itself Communist, its broadcasters were encouraged to "make judicious use of the independence of the Kremlin" that the Yugoslav dictator had won. Furthermore, RFE's sponsors in the government decided, after some initial debate, against establishing broadcasts to Yugoslavia as acknowledgment of the positive role Tito was playing in East European politics.[17]

Radio Free Europe's approach to anti-Semitism, an eternal East European malady, was nuanced. The guidance identified two strands of anti-Semitism then prevalent in the broadcast region. The first was a carry-over from traditional anti-Jewish suspiciousness, which, the guidance asserted, was a particular problem in Hungary and Romania. But while broadcasters were urged to warn the Hungarian populace against making Jews the scapegoats for the country's troubles, the Romanian service was told to soft-pedal the issue because Romanian Jews were being allowed to emigrate to Israel due to an agreement between Bucharest and Tel Aviv. The second variety of anti-Semitism might be described as Communist anti-Semitism, deriving from the Soviet conviction that as a cosmopolitan element the Jew is destined to become a citizen of the world and is incapable of accepting the true Communist faith. Communist anti-Semitism was reflected in the practice, widespread at the time, of naming Jewish Communists to highly unpopular positions, especially within the security apparatus, and then exploiting native anti-Semitism by blaming the Jews for repression and policy failures. Broadcasters were encouraged to make special appeals to Jewish party members by stressing the insecurity of their position given the Communist view that Jews could not be loyal citizens.[18]

This was not the only occasion in which anti-Semitism was made the focus of RFE broadcast strategy. In November 1952, a guidance on the Slansky trials in Czechoslovakia, in which most of the defendants were Jewish officials of the Communist regime, urged broadcasters to draw attention to the anti-Semitic nature of the purges. The guidance suggested that Jews were singled out by the regime in order to win favor with what were described as the "many ex-Nazis in high positions in East Germany and with the neo- and crypto-Nazis in Western Germany." In other words, RFE was suggesting that the persecution of Jews in the Soviet orbit was evidence of renewed alliance between communism and Nazism, toward the ultimate goal of destroying democratic forces in Germany. In broadcasts to Communist Party members, editors were urged to stress "that all party officials live a brief life of power, and that Jewish party officials live a shorter life of power than the rest. Stress . . . that the Kremlin is prepared to sacrifice any Jewish party leader, however brilliant, however great his past services to the party, on the altar of the Kremlin's plan for a Soviet-Nazi partnership against civilization."[19]

There were practically no exiles with radio experience among the staff assembled in New York and Munich in 1951. Indeed, many had no real experience as newspapermen, either, having worked as critics, teachers, or government functionaries back home. Managers with radio backgrounds undertook to train the exiles, but the task was complicated by the fact that many didn't understand English.

The problem was summed up in a 1952 memo from William Rafael, an RFE manager, to the staff of the Voice of Free Hungary. The Hungarian editors, he complained, were still "writing as [print] journalists and not as radio men." "You have got to remember that the cardinal principle of good radio writing is not oratory but conversation," he instructed. "When you speak over the radio, you are talking to just one man," and not, he added, pontificating to the entire Hungarian nation.[20]

Similar problems were detected in an analysis of a series of 1951 Czechoslovak broadcasts. While the staff's enthusiasm was noted, the scripts were criticized as too preachy, too long, and too prone to include irrelevant material. A farmers' program was dismissed as a "long, tedious lecture" on the shortcomings of Soviet agricultural policy. Another script, directed to Communist Party members, "takes a long time to say that Communism cannot exist without despotism."[21] A 1952 evaluation found the Voice of Free Poland programs exhibiting "an attitude to the Polish audience that was largely emotional and negative." The memo criticized a tone of "sympathy and moral indignation from which small propaganda gains can be expected" and urged a more positive mindset, suggesting that "every writer and announcer should be inspired with the conviction that those powerful forces working against the regime really exist," here referring to the Catholic Church, the peasantry, and the industrial working class.[22] There were also problems with scripts that minimized the significance of Western institutions, such as free trade unions. Thus in the course of a Czechoslovak script dealing with the antiworker aspects of Soviet labor policy, the broadcaster noted that "capitalism too had such a type of people, the so-called greedy workers," which he implicitly compared to the Stakhanovite worker of Soviet notoriety. The script went on to characterize the notion of workers laboring for themselves as "fairy tales," whether propounded by Communists or Capitalists. Galantiere issued a memorandum describing the script as "counter-propagandistic," noting that speedups had been abolished due to the opposition of Western trade unions and adding that millions of Americans did in fact "work for themselves" by virtue of stock ownership in their enterprises.[23]

Despite the long-winded speeches and overheated vocabulary, RFE soon found itself with a growing and loyal audience. Reports from inside the Iron Curtain indicated that RFE was most appreciated for its harsh brand of anticommunism; at the top of the list of favorite programs were the *Messages* broadcasts, in which RFE announcers denounced by name Communist spies and informers. In contrast, a Romanian listener asserted that programs on science or literature were "of small interest." Radio Free Europe was also gaining listeners by simply broadcasting reports about important news items that the Communist media either ignored or presented hours or even days later than the Western broadcasting stations. According to an internal survey conducted in 1953, the Voice of Free Hungary aired items about the free world an average forty-four hours earlier than Communist media, and thirteen hours earlier on items about Communist countries. In some cases, the differences were astonishing. Thus RFE aired reports about the East Berlin uprising a full twenty-seven hours earlier than Hungarian radio in 1953; RFE even beat the party press in reporting the selection of Imre Nagy as prime minister.[24]

Radio Free Europe gauged its effectiveness as much by the vehemence of regime attacks as by the testimonials of listeners. The first serious response by a Communist government was an official Czechoslovak protest in 1951 over the Voice of Free Czechoslovakia's broadcasts, which were denounced as interference in the country's internal affairs. Otherwise, Communist counterpropaganda was crude, bombastic, and ineffective. A typical example, published in *Scinteia,* the major party newspaper in Romania, was notable for its boilerplate venom, referring to General Eisenhower as a "warmonger," calling labor chieftain William Green a "vile traitor of the working class," and denouncing General Clay as a "bloody executioner." The article carried the byline of one S. Brucan; nearly four decades later, RFE would broadcast a letter critical of the Romanian dictator Nicolae Ceausescu's policies signed by a number of well-known Romanians, including, most prominently, a dissident Communist named Silviu Brucan.[25]

Radio Free Europe was unusual in that while its message was intensely political, its principal appeal was to a popular audience, rather than to the elites who ordinarily make up the core supporters of political journalism. Workers and peasants—the very classes exalted in Communist scripture—were the prime targets of RFE's message, not intellectuals. In later years, as dissident intellectuals and disillusioned party members began to press for democratic reforms, RFE's broadcast focus would change as well.

The program schedule was divided into two broad categories. The first consisted of programs aimed at specific audiences. Each language service broadcast programs for workers, peasants, young people, women, religious believers, and those interested in the arts. The second category consisted of programs with generalized anti-Communist themes. For example, one program, called *The Other Side of the Coin,* offered refutations of party propaganda.

All programs except the newscasts featured some political content. For example, a musical program on the Voice of Free Hungary might include a composition by Béla Bartók, whose works were effectively banned by the regime. A literary program on the Voice of Free Poland might consist of readings from a nineteenth-century patriotic poem in which the tyranny of Russia was decried. A youth program might contrast the freedom that young people enjoyed in the West to the regimentation and constricted opportunity under communism.[26]

When asked about their favorite programs in RFE's repertoire, listeners in the early 1950s almost always mentioned the *Messages* broadcasts. The reason for the program's popularity is not hard to grasp. Although RFE would occasionally single out a cabinet minister or other prominent official for attack, the target was more likely to be a Communist of local notoriety—a factory chief, trade union official, petty bureaucrat, or police chief. Or simply an ordinary citizen whom RFE believed to be functioning as an informer or stooge. While the language may seem florid and excessively moralistic, the style was compatible with the vocabulary of traditional East European journalistic polemics.

In a 1951 broadcast of the Voice of Free Hungary, Vilmos Vizi, factory official and sexual predator, was singled out:

> The mills of God grind slowly, but thoroughly. Each day
> new voices are added to our Black Book. No traitor, no
> helper of the Russians should believe that his acts will
> remain unknown. Disgusting, treacherous eyes are persecut-
> ing the pretty girls working at the textile factory of
> Ujszeged. They are sly, these eyes, and the unfortunate young
> girls do not know which of them will be the next victim of

the Almighty Activist of the factory organization. For by
now you will have discovered, Comrade Vilmos Vizi, that I
am talking about you. Aren't you ashamed, Vilmos Vizi, of
using the advantage originating in your party position not
only to exploit physically the working women and to
torture their minds, but to lay claim to their bodies in order
to satisfy your filthy urges? How many young women have
you denounced, Vilmos Vizi, as reactionaries and enemies of
popular democracy and of the party merely because they
had sufficient courage to refuse your immoral and dishonor-
able suggestions? . . . You are worse than a beast, Vilmos Vizi. . . .
The mills of God grind slowly but thoroughly. We know
everything. We are watchful. . . . Some day everything will
have to be paid for. Tomorrow it may be too late, but you
can still find in yourself the human being, the Hungarian.
The free Hungarians are looking at you with open eyes and
will not forget.[27]

The case of Vilmos Vizi was prized by RFE because the broadcast
elicited a thankful response from the factory women who had been
subjected to what appears to be an extreme form of sexual harassment.
One of the women expressed her "deep gratitude" for the broadcast,
which apparently put a temporary end to Comrade Vizi's assaults. "You
can hardly imagine what we have had to endure until you have warned
that filthy Communist," she wrote. "But we have had peace ever since
and it is a pleasure to see how scared he is."

Vilmos Vizi was by no means the only Communist industrial boss
to merit a stern RFE warning. In 1954, the Voice of Free Hungary
zeroed in on mine official Joseph Goda: "We are calling Joseph Goda
at Tatabánya. Listen carefully, Goda. We know how you abuse and exploit your miners, and the inhuman conditions under which you force
them to live. Your name is in our black book. Unless you change your
habits at once, you will never escape trial and punishment when liberation comes. This is your last chance, Goda."

Likewise, the Voice of Free Czechoslovakia made an example of
Comrade Absolanova, an official with the reconstruction bureau in
Bratislava: "We warn you against her as emphatically as possible. She is
a dangerous spy for the Communist police. Her task is to recruit for
the state security police new agents and informers from among young

people. Absolanova is about 170 cm. tall and blond. She concentrates her attention on young men whom she seduces and then blackmails into collaborating with the police. We warn you against this fanatical Communist informer."[28]

Veterans of RFE's early days react with defensiveness when the subject of *Messages* is raised. To the sophisticated ear of today, these polemical broadsides, with their spooky references to black books, the mills of God, and watchful eyes, sound almost ludicrous. Yet neither RFE nor the Crusade for Freedom regarded them as embarrassing; indeed, excerpts from *Messages* scripts were featured in Crusade press releases. The *New York Times* quoted from the script regarding Comrade Absolanova in an article that described the personal attacks as a psychological warfare technique heretofore never employed by American international radio, and quoted an RFE spokesman as asserting that the broadcasts were based on information from sources "known to be reliable." Nor were the women who worked in Vilmos Vizi's factory the only listeners to pass along testimonials. Thus a Hungarian worker wrote that his factory manager, Joszef Varga, had become more conciliatory toward the workers after serving as the object of a *Messages* broadcast, only to revert to his former autocratic ways after a few weeks had elapsed. The writer suggested that RFE periodically repeat the names of Communist malefactors in order to achieve "permanent results."[29]

Radio Free Europe also devoted exhaustive coverage to the periodic escapes, some quite spectacular, which reinforced the perception of the early Cold War as a time of heroism. Defections were a staple of RFE news coverage throughout the Cold War. In later years, however, defection was often made possible by the liberalized travel policies adopted by Communist regimes and involved nothing more risky than filling out an application for asylum at a Western embassy in Paris, Munich, or Vienna. But during the early fifties, before the regimes had perfected their system of border controls, and when few East Europeans were permitted to travel outside the bloc, escaping communism often involved treks over mountains and through forests, payoffs to guards, dashes to freedom under a hail of bullets.

One of the most spectacular mass escapes occurred in September 1951, when a Czechoslovak train engineer tied down the throttle and barreled through a border checkpoint into West Germany. Of the one hundred or so passengers, thirty-two decided to stay in the West; twenty-two of these said they were regular RFE listeners, an impressive figure given that RFE had inaugurated a full broadcast schedule to Czechoslovakia a mere five months earlier. The others returned home, where they were apparently forced to sign documents asserting that they had been the victims of an American kidnap plot and had been treated with brutality. That evening, on the 7:00 P.M. news, Radio Prague jeered that the passengers had refused "to the last man" to remain in Germany. Just before the broadcast, RFE urged its listeners to first tune in to Radio Prague, and then, at 7:30, to listen to RFE to learn "what really happened." Sure enough, at 7:30, the train engineer came on the air, telling the audience, "The Communists are lying when they tell you that every passenger had gone back. . . . Thirty-two of us have chosen freedom."[30]

The Voice of Free Poland reinforced its stature with its Polish audience when, on the heels of the Swiatlo broadcasts, it succeeded in winning the release of Polish soldiers who had been held as prisoners of war in the Soviet Union. The issue arose in 1955, when Moscow allowed thousands of German POWs to return to their homes. On their return, the Germans reported that many Polish POWs still languished in Soviet camps; the Kremlin was apparently unwilling to admit that it was holding the citizens of a "fraternal" Socialist country. The Polish Communist regime was also reluctant to raise the issue publicly. In response, RFE interviewed former German prisoners, compiled lists of Polish prisoners, including names and camp locations, and pounded away at the Polish regime day after day. Warsaw was finally shamed into making a formal request for the return of the POWs, and the Soviets, after initially issuing denials, finally acknowledged the truth and released several thousand Polish military officers.[31]

Radio Free Europe scored another coup when it covered the story of eight Czechs who smashed through the border in a homemade tank. The tank consisted of a World War II British scout car, which had been fitted with steel plates and treads, and had been built over several years by a man who worked in secret in an old shed. He then gathered his wife, two small children, and four friends and headed for the border, where the astonished guards made no attempt to stop the strange vehicle. Eventually the tank and its occupants went on tour in the United States to raise money for RFE.[32]

In addition to reporting about successful defections, RFE from time to time encouraged them. A 1953 broadcast by the Voice of Free

Czechoslovakia urged air force pilots to emulate the example of a pilot who had landed his craft in Austria some months earlier:

> It is no oversimplification to tell you that you are standing at a crossroad that offers you two possibilities: the first one leads to your doom and means that you may be able to go on flying for a bit, but then—if you survive—other people will come and ask you unpleasant questions. . . . The second possibility means that when Communism is only an unpleasant memory you will still fly. . . . Or let us put it differently: everyone has the choice today of either serving Moscow to the bitter end by flying an airplane whose wings bear the Czechoslovak cockade, under Moscow's orders; or serving the Czechoslovak people by learning and preparing to restore to the sovereign insignia of the aircraft their original significance, emblematic of a state which never stood on the side of slavery and lawlessness when there was fighting going on.[33]

Sometimes RFE promoted change through less dramatic broadcasts. In 1952 the Polish section began broadcasting Christmas carols after discovering that the regime radio would not allow carols on the air. A year later, the regime capitulated and began to offer regular broadcasts of carols at Christmas time. Around the same time, the Polish section began broadcasting Wyspianski's play *Wesele,* a work that had not appeared in Poland since 1948. After RFE broadcast the play several times, *Wesele* was suddenly produced by the Polish National Theater.[34]

Devising a broadcast strategy for the working class posed something of a challenge, since communism portrayed itself as champion of the proletariat. But by the time RFE introduced its full broadcasting schedule, few workers harbored illusions about the Communist system.

Radio Free Europe sought to exploit growing worker restiveness with a two-pronged strategy. First, broadcasts aimed at industrial workers stressed the oppressive features of Communist labor policy, including work quotas and work books, as well as peculiarly Soviet innovations, such as the Stakhanovite phenomenon. Second, RFE aired numerous programs that focused on the rights enjoyed by workers in the West, especially the right to free trade unions uncontrolled by party or state. These broadcasts often included interviews with Western labor leaders such as William Green, a member of the FEC board, or David Dubinsky, the legendary leader of the garment workers and a staunch anti-Communist. To further bolster its labor coverage, RFE established close relations with Jay Lovestone, a one-time leader of the American Communist Party who had, after becoming a virulent critic of communism, assumed the post of chief adviser on international affairs to the American Federation of Labor. Lovestone attended many of the early RFE strategy meetings, gave advice on personnel matters, and introduced RFE editors to European contacts who were knowledgeable about labor developments in Eastern Europe.[35]

If there was such a thing as a natural audience for RFE, it was, in the early years, the East European peasantry. Communism appeared to the farm sector as a threat to everything the independent peasant cherished. Communism seized the peasant's land, herded him into a Russian-inspired system of collectivization, and took his sons from the land and put them in the army. Communists seized his crops and, it was widely believed, shipped them off to the Soviet Union where hunger was rampant because of the failure of the Soviet collectivization system. As added insult, communism persecuted the church, a cherished institution of the countryside. Radio Free Europe thus regarded the peasantry as the "natural enemy of Communism as a creed and as a practice" and instructed that editors should "never assume that a peasant audience has been converted to Communism."[36]

Although RFE was careful to avoid promises of Western military assistance to set the satellite states free, broadcasts repeatedly emphasized the commitment of the United States and other Western nations to the defeat of world communism, citing as Exhibit A the military intervention in Korea. Whether the Korea example reassured the RFE audience is open to some doubt, as East Europeans were inclined to regard events in the more exotic parts of the world as irrelevant to their own plight. They cared about Europe and Europe alone and were adept at discerning the hidden meanings of diplomatic statements that suggested an acceptance of the status quo. Radio Free Europe's American policy makers were sensitive to the impact of Western political developments, lest they suggest to the audience or, for that matter, to their own exile staff, that the East Europeans were being abandoned to their fate. One notable setback to staff morale was the 1955 Four-Power Summit Conference in Geneva, with its talk of peaceful coexistence and images of a grinning President Eisenhower shaking hands with a beaming Premier Khrushchev. To the more cold-blooded among the exile staff, Geneva provided powerful evidence that liberation was not on the agenda of the American government.

Among the RFE exile groups, the Poles were the least inclined to place their bets on Western intervention. Poland's experiences with Western diplomacy had repeatedly led to bitter consequences, and the Polish exile leadership was wary of glib pledges from American politicians. Even before the Voice of Free Poland got on the air, eminent exile leaders such as Stefan Korbonski were advising RFE that it would be folly to tell a Polish audience that liberation must come from an internal uprising rather than from external force; the Polish people, he reminded the American radio policy makers, had vivid memories of the Warsaw uprising and would not regard calls for yet another insurgency as helpful. Korbonski also cautioned RFE against emphasizing the military assistance America was sending to Europe, since the five divisions the United States was assigning to the continent paled in comparison with the twenty-five divisions Poland alone could muster.[37]

Although the Polish staff was as resolutely anti-Communist as the Hungarians or Czechoslovaks, they were considerably more cautious in their broadcast strategy. During World War II Jan Nowak had served as liaison between the Polish resistance and the British government. His real name was Zdzislaw Jezioranski; he adopted Jan Nowak, a common Polish name, during the war. Nowak underwent some hair-raising experiences in his trips in and out of Poland. He also acquired firsthand experience with Western diplomacy at its most cynical. He and his staff were convinced that the Yalta treaty represented a Western betrayal of Polish interests and counseled against programming about the agreement. Nowak had strong beliefs about the Voice of Free Poland's responsibilities to the Polish people; he was also endowed with a legendary stubborn streak. He often resisted program guidances that the other services adopted, and he was prone to skepticism about the special psychological warfare projects that RFE periodically took on. Thus an August 1953 memo from the policy staff complained that Polish service programs were "still designed not only to prevent any popular outburst, but any thought of it." Another memo, by Paul Henze, observed that "the Poles still feel a heavy sense of responsibility not to go too far and provoke premature disturbances." Three years later, when events did threaten to spin out of control in Poland, Jan Nowak's cautious approach would be vindicated.[38]

István Deák, who worked in the Munich headquarters in the early 1950s, speaks for many RFE exile journalists when he asserts that he "never imagined that this would be a job to retire on." Deák, in fact, spent only a few years with RFE, after which he earned his scholarly credentials and established a reputation as a leading authority on central European history. But others remained in Munich for forty years or more, not the one or two years that, they felt, would be all that was needed to help push communism toward a swift and inglorious demise.[39]

How the collapse of communism was to be achieved—whether through internal resistance, the intervention of the West, or an implosion triggered by the system's internal contradictions—was never made clear. But there could be little doubt that the East European regimes were on shaky ground. Radio Free Europe hardly needed to exaggerate the difficulties facing East European communism. Reports of food shortages, plan failures, police state terror, and internal party division, as reflected in wave after wave of purge trials, represented powerful testimony to the inherent instability of East European communism.

By 1953, some within the American government, and within RFE as well, were convinced that the hour of decision was at hand. Indeed, the pace of events did seem to be accelerating. First, Stalin died, triggering a Kremlin power struggle that was to stretch over many months and lead to the execution of one of the leading contenders for the succession. Rather quickly, many satellites adopted a political New Course, entailing a shift away from crash industrialization, forced collectivization, and the hunt for deviationists from the party line. Within the RFE audience countries, the most notable development was a series of disturbances in the Czech city of Plzen provoked by a currency reform and general dissatisfaction with the regime's policies.

The most important event, however, was the uprising in East Germany, in which workers rebelled against Communist industrial policies and order was restored only with the intervention of armored units of the Soviet army. On one level, the June 17 uprising was powerful evidence of the vulnerability of East European communism, and of the abject failure of the Stalinist regimen to which each satellite country had been subjected. The East German security forces had refused to fire on their countrymen, more proof of the yawning gap that divided the rulers from the ruled. But while June 17 had revealed communism's weakness, it ultimately had to be judged a failure. The Red Army crushed the resistance rather quickly, the uprising's ringleaders were executed, and order was restored. An outpost of the empire had challenged Moscow's hegemony, and Moscow had responded with the necessary measures to reassert its authority. Meanwhile, the West, and especially the United States, had little to offer beyond sympathetic phrases, clear evidence, for all who cared to notice, of the hollowness of the new Republican administration's liberationist rhetoric.

The period from Stalin's death to the East German uprising was a crucial juncture in RFE's history. Some within the radio station advocated the adoption of an ultraliberationist approach in which every trick in the psychological warrior's bag would be utilized to press developments behind the Iron Curtain toward their ultimate denouement. Although the evidence is not entirely clear on this point, it would appear that the liberationist stance was favored by certain CIA elements. Almost coincidental with the Berlin rising, a directive was prepared, apparently by CIA officials, trumpeting the arrival of an entirely new political situation in the Soviet bloc, a situation that demanded a much more aggressive response from RFE. Although the document's analysis applied throughout the Soviet bloc, it singled out Czechoslovakia as a test case for the new and more robust propaganda line.

Radio Free Europe, the guidance declared, was to announce that it "has knowledge, not all of which can be revealed, to the effect that the present regime in Czechoslovakia is in a much more precarious position than meets the eye":

> As the process of its disintegration assumes increasing
> momentum, events of the greatest significance are bound to
> develop. . . . It is essential that our listeners be made to
> realize the extent of the crisis in which the Czechoslovak
> regime finds itself. . . . Once the peoples of Czechoslovakia
> disabuse themselves of the notion that they are hopelessly at
> the mercy of a powerful regime, they will begin to under-
> stand the truth—namely, that they are again in the process of

becoming masters of their own destiny. . . . It is essential in these circumstances that all freedom-loving Czechs and Slovaks be prepared to play their roles. . . . The time has come to call Moscow's bluff. The hands of the stooges who claim to be the government of Czechoslovakia, by increasing passive resistance and by taking all positive steps by which fighters for freedom are capable without jeopardizing the even more active role they may have to play in the future. . . . Chances are that passive resistance and beginning of sabotage will meet with weaker reaction on the side of the regime than previously—not only because the position of the Kremlin has deteriorated, but also because Kremlin does not desire repressive action at this time.[40]

The radical course implied by this guidance was never, in fact, implemented. As A.A. Berle, an FEC board member, summed up the situation in his memoirs, "Now a split in the organization: One-half wants a violent campaign strictly in American interest. The other and more intelligent half wants a more cautious, better thought-out campaign: that we are presently pursuing."[41]

Lang, Galantiere, Griffith, and most of the exiled editors regarded the notion that the revolution was at hand as irresponsible folly, particularly in light of the fate of the East German workers who had tried to practice what the guidance was advocating and had paid a heavy price. While urging that RFE concentrate its attention on the working class in the wake of events in Berlin and Plzen, Ferdinand Peroutka declared that the people behind the Iron Curtain were "suspicious of revolutionary appeals transmitted by exiles who are at a safe distance from the events."[42] Indeed, RFE adopted a tone of restraint in the immediate aftermath of the East German events. "June 1953 is not the moment when we can say positively to the Iron Curtain peoples that they are in fact stronger than their governors and that they should prepare to rise up and liberate themselves," one guidance declared, adding that editors should use caution in proclaiming that a new phase in the struggle for freedom had arrived. "The peoples we address simply cannot be expected to count upon their own strength alone; they still count in the largest measure upon the USA; and as long as the USA makes no material gesture towards their liberation, we cannot seem to be limiting ourselves to supplying the words while they supply the deeds."[43]

Eventually, the ultraliberationist stance was rejected, but not before a struggle over the future direction of RFE programming took place over the better part of a year, creating a measure of confusion over the station's political direction. Griffith advocated what came to be known as gradualism, the notion that liberation would be achieved in incremental stages, and not with one cataclysmic burst.[44] The compromise strategy that was temporarily adopted was, in any event, hardly one that conceded the inevitability of Soviet control of the satellites. Radio Free Europe stressed the division within the Kremlin, the chaos within the satellite parties, and the new-found power of the people. It urged East Europeans to demonstrate their rejection of communism through acts of personal resistance, ranging from party members refusing to inform on their neighbors to industrial workers carrying out work slowdowns. Even Peroutka, a normally cautious man, urged a strategy that encouraged "economic sabotage, absenteeism, slow work" and other measures designed to undermine the East European economies.[45] A July 1953 guidance on conditions in Hungary declared, "The regime is growing weaker, the people are growing stronger. . . . The Communists in Moscow and Budapest are rent by ever-increasing dissension. To the peasants we say: The regime is in your power. It must have the harvest and it can only get it from you. Therefore sabotage the state delivery system, sabotage the state threshing machines, keep the harvest yourself and use it as you know best."[46]

Broadcasts to party members were regarded as especially important in the post-Stalin period. The goal was much the same as before: to unnerve Communists by reminding them of just how dangerous a career in the party could be. The difference was that now RFE had powerful evidence to fortify its arguments. Purges and counterpurges had occurred throughout the bloc, and some of those who had been persecuted a few years previously were now regaining their freedom and undergoing rehabilitation, a process that raised questions about the fate of those implicated in their persecution. Furthermore, the ghost of Lavrenti Beria, Stalin's secret police chief, hovered over the Communist parties, and especially over the security forces. Beria had been arrested and liquidated during the summer of 1953, a chilling development for the many "Beria men"—Josef Swiatlo was a prominent example—in the satellite parties. Beria's fate carried a message for all Communists: if the most powerful party officials can be brought down, the same fate could just as easily befall the humble party official serving as a trade union steward or collective farm manager.

Radio Free Europe reminded Communists of the untrustworthiness of party bosses and of the impossibility of honest initiative in an environment of suspicion. Commentators continued to denounce cases of abuse by party officials. And they drove home the concept of party members crossing the "Golden Bridge," a form of psychological defection in which party members defend their neighbors against the depredations of the system.[47]

Most broadcasts were addressed to lower-level party officials, who were reminded of the many times they had been made the scapegoats for policy failures. In Hungary, for example, petty agricultural officials had been blamed for the failures of the collective farm system. "We tell you that your oppressive attitude to the people has now placed you between the anger of the nation and the vengeful spirit of the party," a broadcast on the Voice of Free Hungary declared.

Clearly, a broadcast strategy that contributed to divisions within party ranks would have been judged a success. But RFE commentators sometimes encountered difficulties in achieving the proper tone for broadcasts to party members. An evaluation of scripts from the *Calling Communists* program of the Voice of Free Hungary decried an inability of the broadcasters to speak sympathetically or to demonstrate a grasp of the party member's concerns. The reviewer noted, "The effectiveness of certain scripts is frequently impaired by a failure to recall that we are speaking to human beings and not to abstractions called 'dirty Reds.'" Broadcasters were reminded that the goal was "not to insult and injure, it is to persuade, to convince, to convert."[48]

The party was not, however, the most important audience for RFE during this period of communist ferment. Once again, RFE strategists pinpointed the peasantry as the weak link in the Communist scheme of things. Even Communist officials, in a rare burst of candor, acknowledged that their agricultural policies had failed, with peasants abandoning the collective farms and food shortages nearing crisis proportions. Radio Free Europe's strategy was simple: encourage the peasants to employ their increasing leverage to extract concessions from the state, the sum total of which would amount to a renunciation of socialized agriculture. In the context of the times, these were not un-realistic goals: collectivization was never achieved in Poland and was in ruins in Hungary until, in the aftermath of the 1956 revolution, János Kádár imposed agricultural socialization on a defeated populace.

The Voice of Free Hungary broadcast two agricultural programs each day: *Farmer Balint,* in which the announcer, depicting a typical Hungarian farmer, talked to his countrymen back home about farm problems, and *Farmer's Program,* in which another typical farmer carried on a dialogue with his brother-in-law. In both cases the tone was conversational: ordinary Hungarians talking to ordinary Hungarians about farm affairs. But each program had an unmistakable political message. Thus one script reminded Hungarian farmers how Ukrainian peasants had foiled collectivization by ruining machinery and explicitly urged Hungarians to emulate this example. The audience was also encouraged to take measures to prevent the state from achieving its grain quotas.[49]

Even under the new gradualist course, RFE had not lost its polemical edge, as the suggestions that Hungarian peasants sabotage machines and undermine the harvest make clear. In later years, RFE broadcasters were strictly forbidden to urge their audience to undertake acts of defiance. But in the period of post-Stalin ferment, few doubted that Radio Free Europe's principal mission was to stir matters up in an increasingly unstable Eastern Europe. The leadership of the FEC was convinced that the station had achieved a remarkable influence over the course of East European developments. "There is no question that RFE is now the recognized head of the non-Communist opposition in great parts of Central Europe and that it can force changes in the governments and the policies both in Czechoslovakia and Hungary," wrote A.A. Berle in 1954. "The question now is how best to use the power."[50] Furthermore, RFE was soon to add another weapon to its arsenal, the balloon operation, a psychological warfare campaign par excellence, which was to reinforce the message that an increasingly powerful citizenry could win change, and eventually freedom, through acts of resistance.

4

"We Tore a Big Hole in the Iron Curtain"

One of the most spectacular projects undertaken by Radio Free Europe was the balloon operation. From the night in August 1951 when the first balloons were sent aloft until the project's end in November 1956, millions upon millions of leaflets, newspapers, stickers, and political souvenirs were dropped into Communist Eastern Europe bearing messages that reinforced the themes featured in RFE broadcasts. Balloon leaflets urged Hungarian peasants to abandon the collective farms, encouraged Czechs and Slovaks to boycott national elections, and provided Poles with written versions of the Swiatlo revelations. The balloons also provoked a degree of official Communist fury never elicited by RFE broadcasts; regime leaders were reduced to profanity when the subject of the balloons came up, and the balloon campaign ultimately wound up as an issue before the United Nations.

Propaganda leaflets had been used with some effectiveness in both world wars as well as the Korean conflict, and given the substantial representation of OWI and psychological warfare veterans among the RFE leadership, a curiosity about the usefulness of airborne messages as a cold war tactic was inevitable. In the past, however, airplanes had usually been used to transport the leaflets to their destination; there was widespread doubt about the effectiveness of balloons as vehicles for leaflet drops because their flight pattern could not be controlled.

Nevertheless, the image of millions of Free World balloons penetrating the Iron Curtain appealed to Frank Wisner's sense of audacity.

Wisner, as head of the OPC, had inherited a stockpile of surplus weather balloons, some of which found their way into Eastern Europe under various sponsorships during the Cold War.[1] Dr. Robert Millikan, a prominent participant in World War II balloon work, was also an enthusiastic proponent of propaganda balloons as a complement to RFE broadcasts. After discussions with Dr. Millikan, the FEC turned to General Mills, which had been involved in World War II balloon efforts, to develop long-distance balloons capable of reaching targets in Eastern Europe.[2]

Initially, the balloon operation's most notable achievement was the publicity it gained for RFE and the Crusade for Freedom. The crusade was the official sponsor of the 1951 inaugural launch, which took place on a field near Regensberg in West Germany. Drew Pearson, the fabled Washington columnist and an RFE booster, was on hand for the ceremony, as was Harold Stassen, at the time a rising star within the Republican Party and chairman of the Crusade for Freedom.[3] According to Abbott Washburn, who organized the launch, the event started inauspiciously when the balloons began drifting westward, away from the intended target of Czechoslovakia. As the assembled eminences watched nervously, the balloons hovered for a time until finally setting off in the proper direction, triggering a celebration that was punctuated by a keg of German beer.

Thousands of balloons filled the sky, carrying messages of freedom to captive peoples while at the same time delivering an insult to Czechoslovakia's Communist leaders by breaching the sanctity of the country's otherwise tightly sealed borders. Unfortunately, the first balloon campaign, dubbed the Winds of Freedom, had little impact on the target country. The leaflet messages amounted to rudimentary propaganda, featuring a picture story of the train that had crashed through the West German border, and a message from the engineer: "There were no terrorists, no secret foreign plot. The only terrorists are the Communists; the only foreigners are the Russians." The leaflets also provided the times and wavelengths of Voice of Free Czechoslovakia broadcasts.

When asked about the impact of Winds of Freedom, Harold Stassen commented, "We tore a big hole in the Iron Curtain."[4] Unfortunately, the hole was discernible only to Americans. Although the initial balloon campaign bolstered the Crusade for Freedom's reputation for aggressive anticommunism, it did little to strengthen RFE's credibility in Eastern Europe. Refugees often spoke highly of RFE broadcasts, but they seldom mentioned the balloons. Even the regime in Prague chose to ignore what it surely regarded as a blatant violation of its airspace. Within a few years, however, RFE launched a much more ambitious balloon operation amounting to a psychological warfare action program that sought to coordinate and inspire popular opposition to communism, and instill fear in the party leadership.

The first project combining RFE broadcasts with leaflets dropped by balloon came on the heels of the June 1953 riots in Plzen and other Czechoslovak industrial centers. The project was named Operation Prospero and was run jointly by RFE and the Free Europe Press (FEP), the publications arm of the Free Europe Committee. The FEP had already issued a series of impressive reports on internal conditions within the satellites and published journals and newsletters in the languages of the RFE target countries. For this campaign, the FEP put its pool of exiled writers to work drafting the texts for leaflets and newspapers that would be conveyed by balloon and then dropped behind the Iron Curtain.[5]

Operation Prospero was designed to reach workers in Czechoslovakia's principal industrial cities, including Prague. The balloons carried three different messages. One was a copy of Czechoslovakia's crown note, which had been devalued due to the regime's much-hated currency reform. On one side of the note the message "Men call this the Hunger Crown, gift of the Soviet Union" was written; the reverse side carried the message "Czechs and Slovaks, know this: The regime is weaker than you think. Power lies with the people, and the people stand opposed. With unity and courage, organize your strength. Down with the collective. Insist on workers' rights today. Demand concessions—tomorrow, Freedom." A second message consisted of a one-page leaflet recounting the story of the East German uprising, along with news about developments behind the Iron Curtain. The third item was a facsimile of a twenty-five-heller coin, stamped with the Crusade for Freedom's freedom bell.

Over sixty thousand balloons filled the skies in the four days of the campaign, during which the Voice of Free Czechoslovakia broadcast program after program promoting Prospero and its themes. Radio Free Europe sought to increase uncertainty among party officials while encouraging a mood of popular resistance. "The Soviet Union is growing weaker," one script announced. "Only those will survive who detach themselves from the Communist boat in time. . . . Everywhere in the Free World your friends are with you. . . . All power to the people." On Prospero's final night, lighted lanterns were attached to the balloons for dramatic effect.

Although the authorities had ignored previous balloon drops, they responded to Prospero with fury. MiG fighters were ordered to shoot down the balloons; when they proved too fast to get an accurate bead on the targets, slower, propeller-driven Messerschmitts were dispatched, and antiaircraft guns fired at the invaders as they crossed the border. After an emergency session of the Politburo, police cars were told to patrol the streets with sound systems, demanding that citizens turn in any Prospero leaflets they encountered. Ultimately, the Foreign Ministry sent a sharp protest note to the U.S. State Department; the text of the American rejection included a lecture on freedom of expression.[6]

The balloon operation was not the only project that sought to penetrate the Iron Curtain with the printed word. There was, for example, a series of mailings to East European Communist officials, their names and addresses provided by the voluminous files the RFE research department had compiled. The pamphlets were mailed in unmarked envelopes and sent from different European cities in order to elude the censors. The texts stressed the Golden Bridge theme of Communists committing a form of psychological defection and serving the people instead of the party.

But RFE was convinced by the success of Operation Prospero that a combination balloon-broadcast campaign represented a new model for political warfare action programs. Thus Prospero was followed by a much more ambitious undertaking, again aimed at Czechoslovakia, called Operation Veto. The new campaign was tied to a series of elections scheduled for 1954, ranging from the national parliament to local government councils and trade union committees in the factories. Radio Free Europe projected itself as the Voice of the Opposition; through radio broadcasts and the balloon leaflets, RFE encouraged Czechs and Slovaks to make use of the meetings and consultations built into the preelection process to demand changes in government policy. There was, of course, no serious organized opposition in Czechoslovakia, and RFE actually discouraged its listeners from forming resistance organizations. But even under Czechoslovakia's repressive system there were mechanisms through which dissident views could be raised, and RFE urged that these instruments be exploited to the fullest extent.[7]

Operation Veto was organized around a series of ten demands that RFE suggested Czechs and Slovaks address to candidates for office. Most of the demands centered on workers' rights (independent unions, better pay, the right to change jobs voluntarily) and agriculture (an end to forced collectivization, abolition of compulsory deliveries). Taken individually, the demands did not imply a radical transformation of the Communist system, and they could by no means be interpreted as reflecting a conservative or free market philosophy. For example, a demand for the denationalization of consumer trade called for cooperative rather than private ownership, and a housing demand advocated state allocation based on family need instead of political influence, and not for private enterprise in real estate. Nevertheless, adoption of the demands as a package would have moved Czechoslovakia well along the road to social democracy. But while Operation Veto implied rather dramatic change, it nevertheless reflected the new RFE focus on gradualistic measures—"liberation through liberalization," as the radio station's motto of the time declared. The RFE audience was urged to treat liberation from communism as a process of incremental change rather than to wait for a Western intervention that was not in the offing.

The role of the balloon operation was not merely to provide Czechs and Slovaks with printed versions of what they heard on RFE. At the beginning of Veto, the FEP showered the country with stickers, on which were inscribed simply the number ten, the campaign's official symbol. A few days later, RFE began an around-the-clock broadcast offensive on the ten demands and the idea of a people's opposition.

Then, just prior to local elections, the FEP launched a massive balloon drop featuring a "Ballot of the People's Opposition." The ten demands were printed on the ballots, and Czechs and Slovaks were asked to circulate the leaflets by placing them in mailboxes and under doors. Another series of drops featured the Masaryk letter; it resembled an ordinary air-mail letter with the Masaryk stamp, a regular issue. The cancellation, however, read "The Truth Prevails," and where the return address would normally be found was printed the inscription "In Unity, Strength."

The next phase of Operation Veto was launched in late summer; the target group was the peasantry, and the campaign was called the

Harvest of Self-Defense. The demands included a retreat from socialized agriculture and compensation for agricultural losses incurred during heavy summer rains. Independent farmers were urged to withhold delivery quotas; peasants were encouraged to resign from the kolkhozes; and party members, government officials, and the police were asked to demonstrate their solidarity by refusing to implement sanctions against the peasants. In the fall, when trade union elections were conducted, Veto focused on the working class. Through broadcasts and balloon leaflets, RFE encouraged workers to insist that proper election procedures be observed with secret ballots and workers as tellers, and to insist that candidates come from the ranks of genuine workers rather than the party *aktiv*. Because younger workers had never experienced anything except Communist unions, RFE broadcast programs on the principles of democratic trade unionism, citing the experience of Western unions as well as the labor movement in prewar Czechoslovakia.

There were signs that Operation Veto had made an impression on developments in Czechoslovakia. Although RFE had urged Czechs and Slovaks to participate in the local government elections and in the balloting for trade union councils, it took a much different stance toward the balloting for parliament, which it regarded as a party-controlled ritual. It thus advised its audience to display disapproval by boycotting the election or crossing off the names of the official candidates. In fact, the regime acknowledged that five percent had voted against the party, an unusual admission given the normal Communist policy of claiming 99 percent support. Furthermore, the regime once again responded angrily to the balloon barrage, sending fighter jets to shoot the balloons and directing the police to collect the leaflets. The regime press made four times the normal number of attacks on RFE, and even began to make sarcastic references to the ten demands and the "so-called People's Opposition."

To those who have come of age with the Internet, satellite dishes, and CNN, the very idea of promoting political liberty via propaganda balloons must seem odd, amusing, or even absurd, but it must be remembered that in 1954 the revolution in communications technology was decades away. At that time, East Europeans lived in societies in which controls over information were almost total, save for the broadcasts of foreign radio services. Outside the controlled and discredited regime press, the only printed matter available was publications of foreign Communist parties and the modest supply of proscribed literature published by exile organizations and smuggled into the country.

Thus a major goal of the balloon campaign was to provide the RFE audience with something approximating a free press. In addition to gimmicks like the "Hunger Crown" and the Masaryk letter, the FEP produced small newspapers in editions of two million, which were dropped more or less regularly to Poland, Hungary, and Czechoslovakia between 1954 and 1956. The newspapers were given names—the Czechoslovak version was called *Svoboda Evropa* (Free Europe). Sometimes they were devoted to the themes of special action campaigns, such as Operation Veto; at other times they carried news items about the latest developments in the Soviet bloc or the Cold War, or special material, such as extended coverage of the Swiatlo revelations. They also offered lengthy essays about the current state of affairs in the particular country and the prospects for change. Occasionally they included important works of banned literature; the balloon operation was responsible, for example, for introducing many East Europeans to George Orwell's antitotalitarian classic, *Animal Farm*.[8]

There was nothing haphazard about the balloon operation. It was meticulously organized by the Free Europe Press, and it was no doubt expensive; the annual cost of maintaining one launch site was nearly $500,000. The FEP eventually built at least three launch sites in Bavaria and near the West German–Austrian border. The launch sites were located so as to allow the balloons to reach practically all parts of Czechoslovakia and large sectors of Hungary and Poland. The village of Tirschenreuth, a few miles from the Czechoslovak border, was the principal launch site. It included barracks, a mess hall, and a research and meteorological center. A staff of professional meteorologists gathered information about wind direction and speed, and then determined the most propitious time for launching.[9]

During the balloon campaign's initial phases, the FEP used small rubber balloons that were inflated so as to burst when they reached a certain altitude. These were useful only for short distances; another drawback was that they dropped the leaflets in one place, often in one package. Soon the operation graduated to large plastic balloons that were inflated to float at a certain altitude for a predetermined time. Timing devices that allowed the balloons to discharge the leaflets in various locations during the journey were developed. The FEP also used direction finders to plot the balloon path with a high degree of accuracy. By employing a pilot balloon, the FEP was eventually able to plot the time and wind path the balloons were likely to follow, and to adjust the timing mechanism on later balloons to drop leaflets at specific locations along the path.

In an attempt to reach the more distant parts of Eastern Europe, the FEP made use of massive balloons capable of carrying four hundred pounds of leaflets and of soaring up to seventy-five thousand feet. The leaflets were attached to a device resembling a horizontally attached bicycle wheel, and a device with a razor blade clipped the packets at prescribed times, sending them earthward. The leaflets were reported as far away as central Turkey. But while the long-range balloons were never accused of having been responsible for an incident with commercial aircraft, the FEP eventually discontinued their use, presumably to avoid blame for an air tragedy.[10]

The final coordinated balloon-broadcast project, Operation Focus, basically represented a Hungarian version of Operation Veto. It encouraged Hungarians to exploit local elections to raise demands for change in Communist domestic policy. Because of the greater distances involved in ballooning into Hungary, a new launch site was found, near Berchtesgaden, Hitler's notorious hideaway in southern Bavaria. And a new type of balloon was developed, one capable of traveling relatively long distances before dropping its payload of leaflets. The leaflets were carried in a box suspended underneath the balloon; the ingenious twist was using slow-dissolving dry ice as ballast. When the dry ice finally melted, the container tipped over and the leaflets were dispatched to their target. The FEP took special pride in the accuracy of the Hungarian drops. It claimed that by calculating the amount of hydrogen, the weight of the leaflets, and the direction of the wind, it could achieve pinpoint drops hundreds of miles away.

Like Veto, Operation Focus presented the regime with a series of demands—twelve, in this case, adding freedom of religion and cultural independence to the earlier list. Focus urged Hungarians to participate in what it called a National Opposition Movement. The Hungarian acronym—NEM—also spelled "no," and the FEP thought this would serve as a vivid emblem for the campaign.[11]

Once Focus got underway, the Voice of Free Hungary broadcast a series of programs that reinforced the leaflet messages. Thus a *Calling*

Communists script had this warning for party members: "In all probability, local party agent, you are feeling slightly chilled, since in the past few days millions and millions of leaflets have been added to my [the announcer's] occasional discreet admonitions. . . . I remind you that I myself have warned you at least fifty times—do not be a blind tool in the hands of the usurpers of power. Now you have received this warning from the Hungarian people in writing so you cannot claim that no one has warned you." Operation Focus was phased out in 1955 after party hard-liners removed Nagy from his leadership position and reinstalled Mátyás Rákosi in the number one position. But the balloon drops continued until the end of 1956 in the form of the mini-newspapers that the FEP had published during the various action campaigns. The FEP also added Poland to the list of countries targeted for balloon drops. Although Jan Nowak was unenthusiastic about political warfare projects of the Operation Veto type, he did agree to a balloon project that provided written summaries of the Swiatlo revelations.

By the mid-fifties, the countries of Communist Eastern Europe were inundated with balloon leaflets sponsored by a variety of sources. The CIA had its own balloon project. So did the shadowy anti-Soviet organization, Narodno Trudovoi Soyuz, the National Labor Union, usually known by its acronym, NTS. The NTS boasted a global network of agents and a core of devoted supporters within the Soviet Union who championed an ideology of anticommunism and Russian nationalism. The NTS tried to reach the Soviet Union by launching their balloons from West Berlin.

It was, however, the RFE balloons that caused Communist officialdom the greatest distress. A Czechoslovak border guard who defected to the West reported that all frontier units had been mobilized to collect leaflets and balloons from the very beginning of Operation Veto, and refugee reports indicated that units of the army, border guards, and the secret police were mobilized to track down leaflets in both Czechoslovakia and Hungary. A report from Gdansk indicated that military units there were assigned to scour the barracks for balloon leaflets, with orders to give special attention to public toilets, where leaflets were often found. The balloon campaigns also compelled the regimes to make adjustments in their propaganda and indoctrination programs. In Poland, the political officers of military units gave special lectures on the leaflet contents, while in Czechoslovakia the basic propaganda manual, *Handbook for Agitators,* included a refutations of Veto's ten demands. The Prague regime went so far as to dispatch an agent to West Germany with orders to destroy a launch site; he was arrested by West German police as he was reconnoitering the target area.[12]

Not surprisingly, the balloons sometimes created incidents when they fell to earth in populated areas or were blamed for air travel complications. In January 1956, the Czechoslovak regime suspended all night flights into Prague, claiming that the balloons were creating air traffic hazards. Subsequently, KLM airlines cited the balloons in its decision to halt flights into Czechoslovakia. In February the regime charged that a DC-4 aircraft had collided with an RFE balloon and crashed. The case was taken to the United Nations, where the Prague regime demanded compensation from the American government. Washington requested that a team of American investigators be allowed to inspect the crash site; after the request was turned down, the United States rejected the Czechoslovak complaint, noting that the airliner was flying in poor weather and had faulty equipment, and claiming that the balloon allegedly involved was not a type used by RFE. The United States also carried out test collisions, and concluded that the damage claimed by Prague could not have been inflicted by an RFE balloon.[13]

Ultimately, it was a shift in the international political environment rather than fears about airliner catastrophes that brought the balloon operation to a conclusion. Balloon campaigns represented a pugnacious kind of political warfare that was inconsistent with the "Spirit of Geneva" and the Eisenhower administration's abandonment of the vocabulary of liberation. Whether West Germany would continue to permit balloon launches from its territory in the face of angry East bloc protests was unclear; at one point, the FEP considered shifting the launch sites to ships on the Adriatic and Baltic Seas. There was, finally, the tragic defeat of the Hungarian Revolution. Radio Free Europe's performance during the revolution was the target of a number of serious charges, some highly exaggerated, some justified. In the revolution's aftermath, RFE took steps to ensure that it would never again be accused of irresponsible or incendiary broadcasts. The shutdown of the balloon operation was one part of a process that would transform RFE from an agency of open political combat to a radio station that pressed its agenda through more nuanced methods.

Some within RFE were never comfortable with psychological

warfare projects like Operation Veto and were not unhappy to see the end of the balloon campaigns. Gen. Lucius Clay is said to have temporarily disengaged himself from the Crusade for Freedom because of his skepticism about the balloon operation.[14] And a controversy over extending the balloon campaign to Poland—a step strongly resisted by several well-known exiles—triggered the resignation of Robert Lang as RFE director.[15] Not surprisingly, the balloon campaign was highly unpopular with American diplomats posted to embassies in Eastern Europe. They complained that the leaflets were dull and difficult to acquire; they also worried, somewhat contradictorily, that the creation of a People's Opposition might provoke a hardening of repression by the authorities. Since the embassies were often unenthusiastic about RFE broadcasts, their coolness toward the balloon operation can be seen as a reflection of irritation at any project that complicated the conduct of diplomacy through normal channels. On the other hand, the argument that it is bad strategy for psychological warfare efforts to outdistance political and military capabilities had to be taken seriously, since the Communist regimes regarded the balloons as not just another Cold War propaganda instrument, but as a violation of their sovereignty and air space, and thus as a hostile act.

Yet it would be wrong to write off the balloon operation as little more than a publicity stunt. Leaflets were found in almost all parts of Hungary and Czechoslovakia, and surveys of refugees indicated that familiarity with the balloon campaign was nearly universal among Czechoslovaks and Hungarians. It is, however, quite possible that many people became acquainted with the balloon campaigns through the near-hysterical polemics of the Communist authorities and never actually saw a leaflet. East Europeans believed that one was much more likely to invite punishment if caught with an FEP leaflet than if discovered listening to RFE broadcasts. People were under strict orders to turn in leaflets to the police, and there were reports of Hungarians collecting three or four leaflets and retaining one while handing the others to the authorities. There were also accounts of leaflets being treated like espionage documents as they were passed from one person to another. As one Czechoslovak described his first encounter with an Operation Veto leaflet,

> I was sitting with three friends in a restaurant. All of a
> sudden one of them, a railroad employee, handed me some-

thing under the table. I felt some paper in my hand, which I slipped into my pocket. After a while I went to the restroom and locked myself in. I took the paper out of my pocket. . . . One after the other, friends disappeared into the restroom to read the leaflets. The place was certainly not adequate, but nowhere else could one read the leaflet undisturbed. . . . None of us discussed it or asked our friend . . . from where he had gotten it; we were satisfied with the fact that he was there—and the expression on the faces of our group showed the deep impression it had left on our minds. Just as I, they were enthusiastic and confident that the free world has not forgotten us.[16]

But if the people of Eastern Europe welcomed the leaflets as a symbol of Western solidarity and an insult to the Communist authorities, they often regarded the leaflet texts with indifference or disdain. Some dismissed the leaflets as boring. According to a Czech engineer, "The most interesting thing is that [the leaflets] traveled such a distance through the air, and nothing else. The contents are not interesting. People don't pay attention to the Ten Demands. The only important thing is that it is against the Communists."[17] Others claimed to detect a foreign mindset or even a leftish bias in the texts. Neither Hungarians nor Czechoslovaks took the list of demands or the idea of a people's opposition as seriously as their rulers did.

While the balloon operation generated considerable publicity for RFE, its ultimate effect was to divert attention from the station's main mission of broadcasting news and commentary across the Iron Curtain. In the future, RFE would avoid references to non-existent oppositions and lists of demands that the people were to address to their rulers. Radio Free Europe grew in influence and stature as it jettisoned the balloon campaign and the special psychological warfare projects like Operation Veto. Unfortunately, the radio's transition to journalistic professionalism would be accelerated by one of the great tragedies of the Cold War, the Hungarian Revolution.

5

Right-Wingers
and Revanchists

Throughout the Cold War, Radio Free Europe's principal broadcasting facilities were located in Munich. Munich was not the preferred site for RFE's European operations; feelers had been extended to France, Italy, Luxembourg, and Spain by the Free Europe Committee during its search for a broadcast headquarters, and in each case, the response had been negative, for either political or technical reasons. Germany, on the other hand, was still under military occupation, and John J. McCloy and other American officials in the office of high commissioner for Germany were actively promoting the integration of West Germany into the Atlantic Alliance. Locating the broadcast studios of an American-sponsored anti-Communist radio service in Munich was another means of tying the new Federal Republic of Germany to the Atlantic Alliance.[1]

In some respects, Munich had much to offer RFE. Its proximity to the Czechoslovak border made the city a magnet for East European and Soviet exiles, and its appeal to exiles intensified after both RFE and Radio Liberty set up headquarters there. Munich was also within easy reach of the major camps for East European refugees in West Germany and Austria. Another advantage was that Munich was not a traditional center of exile politics, as were Paris and London; the staff was thus insulated from the factional bickering that proved such a distraction in New York, where the FEC's exile relations division had its offices. Furthermore, the political climate in West Germany was decidedly more pro-American and anti-Communist than in Italy or France.

But the German location presented drawbacks as well. There was an understandable popular resentment at RFE's having been imposed on the country by an occupying force. Later, RFE's German presence was legitimized through licensing agreements between the radio station and a sovereign FRG government. To the more nationalist-minded, however, RFE's continued broadcasts from German soil contained the rankling message that their country lacked total sovereignty, a theme later picked up by the German New Left. While RFE kept a relatively low profile out of consideration for German sensitivities, its presence in headquarters on the outskirts of the Englishcher Garten, Munich's splendid municipal park, was a constant reminder, in ways more vivid than the NATO military installations that ringed the city, of Munich's role as a forward base in the Cold War strategy of the United States.

Munich posed an additional problem because of what it symbolized to the people of Eastern Europe. World War II had been over but six years when RFE inaugurated its broadcasts over the Voice of Free Czechoslovakia; to Czechs and Slovaks, Munich was the most hated city in the world, the place where Hitler, with the West's complicity, had implemented the destruction of their little country. Munich was also home to Hitler during the formative years of his movement, thus further reinforcing the city's identification with Nazism. Communist propagandists in Czechoslovakia and Poland, audience countries that had suffered harsh fates at German hands, pounded home the argument that RFE was an instrument of unregenerate German Nazis as well as greedy American capitalists—a tool, so to speak, of the Rockefellers and the Krupps. To emphasize the German connection, the Communist press routinely referred to the radio station as "Munich Free Europe."[2] Radio Prague broadcasts routinely denounced Ferdinand Peroutka as a Nazi supporter (a hardly credible approach, given that Peroutka spent much of the war in a concentration camp) and described the European federation that RFE promoted in its broadcasts as a "Europe of Krupp, Schacht, and Adenauer." A fairly typical reflection of the regime's strategy to link RFE with German militarism was included in a Radio Prague broadcast of October 28, 1953: "The Munich station of lies and swindles is one and the same thing as the Bonn crew of monopolists, Hitlerite generals, and war criminals. . . . After the occupation of our country Ferdinand

Peroutka immediately found his way and held on to the SS man. . . .
Today he rules Radio Free Europe and therefore quickly found a way
to join Hitler's successors."[3]

In RFE's early years, however, the phrase "German problem" usually referred to the radio station's difficulties with the population of
Germans who had been expelled from various East European countries after the war. The total number of expellees amounted to some
nine million, with the largest group, four million, having been pushed
out of the parts of Silesia that had been ceded to Poland under the
Yalta accords in compensation for the parts of Ukraine and Belorussia
that had been handed to the Soviet Union. Another two million had
been forcibly driven from the Sudetenland, that part of Czechoslovakia that historically had been populated by ethnic Germans.

The Sudeten issue was marked by moral complexity. Many
Sudeteners had welcomed Hitler's arrival and the dismantling of the
Czechoslovak state, and some were complicit in the atrocities committed against the Czech population. On the other hand, they had
been the victims at war's end of a brutal form of ethnic cleansing in
which little distinction was made between the guilty and the innocent. Ultimately, only a few hundred thousand Sudeteners remained
in postwar Czechoslovakia, the rest having been pushed into Germany, sometimes under horrible conditions.

The expellees constituted a potent electoral bloc in West Germany, and an even more powerful force in Bavarian politics, many of
the expellees having settled in that state. The Sudetendeutsche were
well organized politically: they exerted an influence on all the major
parties, and they pressed their case with skill and aggressiveness. The
Silesian expellees demanded that the lost territories be returned to
German control, an impossible goal, as most German politicians realized, but one that had resonance among Germans. Feelings on the
Polish border question were intense enough so that no German official could endorse a recognition of the Oder-Neisse line, the boundary set at Yalta, and remain in public life. As for the Sudetendeutsche,
their minimum demand was compensation for their lost property, although most insisted on accepting nothing less than the right to return to their homes in Czechoslovakia. Some went further, proposing
a new state relationship in central Europe. They refused to recognize
the legitimacy of the Czechoslovak state, on the grounds that their
position from 1919 to 1938 was intolerable because of anti-German

discrimination by the government. They demanded that, when Eastern Europe was liberated, what was then Czechoslovakia be incorporated within a confederation that would include all the peoples who lived in the Danubian basin.[4]

Although the expellees were quite loud in their professions of anticommunism, they were cool toward the United States due to its role at Yalta and its tacit approval of the Sudeteners' expulsion. The Sudeteners also considered themselves authorities on Eastern Europe and had a real influence on the debate over the "Eastern question," that is, Germany's relations with the Soviet Union and its satellites in Eastern Europe. On matters of Eastern policy, the Sudeteners regarded Americans as bumbling interlopers and tended to look at Radio Free Europe as a product of American naïveté.

At the heart of the conflict between the expellees and RFE was the question of Czechoslovakia. Or to be more precise, Edvard Benes. Benes had been the last democratic president of Czechoslovakia; his replacement by Klement Gottwald marked the consummation of the Communist takeover of the country. Benes had been the leader of the National Socialists, a left-of-center party with a moderately nationalist orientation and a commitment to liberal democracy. Benes was also the architect of a controversial policy of accommodation with the Soviet Union and Czechoslovakia's Communist Party after World War II, and for this was looked on as a dupe or worse by many anti-Communists after the Communist seizure of power.

It was Benes, acting with the concurrence of the Allied powers, who ordered the expulsions of the Sudetendeutsche, an act that earned him the undying hatred of the expellees. The Sudeteners maintained a similar antipathy toward Benes's associates, a number of whom were prominent members of the Council of Free Czechoslovakia, a group affiliated with the Free Europe Committee, or served on the staff of the Voice of Free Czechoslovakia. The list included Hubert Ripka, minister of foreign trade under Benes; Peter Zenkl, a deputy premier in the Benes government; and Ferdinand Peroutka and Julius Firt, both pro-Benes journalists. Ripka and Zenkl were among the leaders of the Council of Free Czechoslovakia, Peroutka was director of the Voice of Free Czechoslovakia, and Firt was a leading editor of the VFC.[5]

If the Sudeteners regarded Benes as the devil incarnate, they treated the FEC-RFE Czechoslovaks as Satan's willing minions. They hated Ripka and Zenkl because, it was claimed, they were the government officials responsible for implementing the Sudeten expulsions. The Sudeteners tried to compromise the pair by accusing them of preparing the way for the Communist takeover of Czechoslovakia through collaboration with the Soviets and by hinting that they were Soviet agents assigned to torpedo a reconciliation between Czech exiles and the Sudeten Germans.

The Sudeteners carefully monitored VFC broadcasts, searching for phrases that could be interpreted as justifying the expulsions or glorifying Benes. They vilified Peroutka and the other hate objects in the Sudetener press, and worked tirelessly to insinuate their views in the general media. They pressed their concerns about RFE on the government and the political parties. They formed coalitions with Slovak separatists, who shared their animus toward RFE because the station, in line with official U.S. policy, opposed the breakup of the country into separate Czech and Slovak states and refused to establish separate divisions in the Czech and Slovak languages. And they cultivated American public opinion, with a particular focus on the conservative wing of the Republican Party. They rode the wave of anticommunism by tarring Americans whom they considered unfriendly to their cause as crypto-Communists, condemning the "Roosevelt-Morgenthau clique" for its support for the Benes government and "pinks" in the State Department for the success that Ripka and Zenkl enjoyed in the United States. They even supplied damaging material on the Czechoslovak desk to right-wing critics of RFE in the United States.

Radio Free Europe's first line of defense was to forbid on-air commentary on sensitive German subjects, a form of censorship unusual for the station. At the suggestion of William E. Griffith, who was dispatched to Munich in June 1951 to ascertain the extent of the German problem, C.D. Jackson directed that RFE coverage of the Sudeten and Oder-Neisse questions be limited to straight news reporting; under no circumstances were RFE journalists to broadcast opinion pieces on the troublesome topics. The RFE management also gave thought to prohibiting commentaries on Benes, but eventually decided against this measure given the strong feelings of Peroutka, who was writing a biography of the Czech statesman.[6]

The directive restricting broadcasts on the Sudeten question posed no special problems for the Czechoslovak desk. Even those Czechs and Slovaks who felt the expulsions justified given the Sudeteners behavior during wartime felt little pride in the tactics used to drive the Germans from the country. If anything, the Voice of Free Czechoslovakia went overboard in celebrating West Germany as a democratic member of European civilization and ally in the struggle against Soviet imperialism.[7] Broadcasts emphasized Bonn's commitment to democracy and its willingness to compensate Jewish victims of the Holocaust. Another theme was the substantial number of former Nazis in positions of authority in East Germany. Broadcasts emphasized that measures had been taken to ensure that the new European defense force would not be dominated by Germany; RFE also attacked the Soviet proposal, which was advanced in the early fifties, for a unified Germany as posing a serious threat to the future security of Europe.[8]

For the Polish desk, however, the restrictions on coverage of the Oder-Neisse boundary presented a real dilemma. Jan Nowak believed that the Oder-Neisse dispute went straight to the heart of RFE's credibility in Poland. The Polish people felt betrayed at Yalta not only because Poland subsequently came under Soviet control but also because Poland was compelled to surrender its eastern territories to Moscow's rule. Under these circumstances, Western support for a return of the German lands awarded Poland would be interpreted as proof of the West's perfidy. While the Bonn government was not pressing for a border adjustment, West German politicians gave lip service to the Silesian expellees' demands. Meanwhile, the United States carefully refrained from pressing the Adenauer government to accept the Oder-Neisse. In Nowak's opinion, RFE risked its support in Poland if it could not take an unequivocal position in favor of the Oder-Neisse, and he fought the guideline, to the point of threatened resignation, until the policy was softened in the late sixties. Needless to say, Communist propagandists took note of RFE's reticence on the subject, which they gleefully interpreted as further evidence of German control over the Voice of Free Poland.[9]

To the American management, the German question was a source of apprehension and occasional disagreement. Lewis Galantiere once proposed that RFE broadcasts advocate compensation for the Sudetendeutsche; William E. Griffith countered that if RFE were to follow this course it would simply prove that the radio station was what its Communist critics said it was: a "German station." Griffith prevailed, as he generally did where matters of German policy were concerned.[10] The station's American advisers were, nevertheless, kept off guard by unexplained shifts in the attitude of the Bonn government. At times, German officials let it be known that they regarded the Sudeteners as a garrulous special interest, not to be taken too seriously. On other occasions, unsettling hints were dropped about the difficulties and complications associated with the expellees' plight. Thus RFE officials were disturbed when a Foreign Ministry official demanded, in the course of a letter reminding them of Bonn's cooperative attitude on licensing and personnel matters, that RFE avoid comment on the Oder-Neisse controversy some time after the guideline on coverage had been issued.[11] On such occasions, RFE officials would invariably respond with patience and reason; they might invite the official for lunch and a tour, explain policy on controversial matters, and request evidence of policy violations (such evidence was almost never forthcoming). On one sensitive matter, however, RFE remained adamant: requests for a German role in broadcast policy were invariably rebuffed, on the grounds that even a minimal German participation in the formulation of the RFE message would pose a threat to the station's credibility.[12]

Despite the self-censorship and attentiveness to German feelings, relations continued to deteriorate. Of particular concern was an article that appeared in an October 1952 issue of *Rheinischer Merkur,* a newspaper that often reflected the views of the Adenauer government. The article said that RFE's policy of silence on expellee issues was no longer sufficient; the only satisfactory course was open support for the Sudetener cause. The article further observed that the end of the occupation regime was approaching, and added ominously that from then on RFE's future would be determined in negotiations between two equally sovereign governments. The author declined to speculate on the fate of such negotiations but did say that it was a "contradiction" for Germany to allow a radio station to broadcast material inimical to German national interests from its territory.[13]

The appearance of this disconcerting item coincided with signs of an emboldened anti-RFE campaign by the most powerful expellee organization, the Sudetendeutsche Landsmannschaft. Among the demands were a radical change in the leadership of the Council of Free Czechoslovakia, a shift away from the council's commitment to a unitary Czechoslovakia, support for a separate Slovak state, a change in RFE policy from silence to open advocacy of the expellees' positions, and participation by the Sudeteners in the affairs of both the council and RFE.[14]

The worsening political environment finally prompted Lewis Galantiere to propose that the Free Europe Committee consider formulating a plan to relocate RFE broadcast facilities outside Germany. To Galantiere, the failure of responsible German politicians to defend RFE from its critics was a more serious problem than the expellee attacks. Galantiere's mood was affected by a difficult encounter with a Foreign Ministry official. Although clearly unacquainted with Peroutka's writings, the official had criticized the Czechoslovak editor, explaining that he "knew the type," by which he meant a Czech patriot. The official added that many Germans, and, by implication, the official himself, believed that the United States should avoid matters about which it was ignorant, such as Eastern Europe. Galantiere detected more than a whiff of traditional German imperialism from this unfortunate meeting.[15]

While RFE did not follow up on Galantiere's relocation proposal, its American advisers did consider various strategies to deflect the mounting tide of German criticism. One plan called for RFE to establish a semiofficial relationship with NATO on the theory that the sanction of the Atlantic Alliance would prod the West German government to be more forthcoming in its public defense of RFE. Bob Lang argued that a compromise might be necessary on the question of a German role in the management of RFE. He also suggested that scripts on sensitive German themes be shown to Germans with favorable attitudes toward RFE, an idea that was, in fact, implemented.[16]

Eventually, the station's strategy of patience, the cultivation of relations with influential Germans, and a broadcast policy that remained sensitive to German feelings succeeded in bringing the situation under control. By September 1954, Ernst Langendorf, a German American hired by RFE as a combination public relations man–troubleshooter on German matters, reported that government officials in Bonn maintained a positive attitude toward RFE and regarded the radio station's presence in the FRG as a nonissue.[17] Although a Cold War between RFE and the Sudeteners simmered for a number of years, the station managed to win over some of the more moderate leaders of the expellee community, and as the years passed and the expellees became enmeshed in the political life of West Germany, their self-identity as Sudeteners or Silesians underwent a natural decline.

Although the expellee controversy would die down, the German problem would reemerge, albeit in different form, some years later. At a 1955 meeting of the RFE American leadership, Bill Griffith predicted that Bonn's reestablishment of diplomatic relations with the Soviet Union would be the source of more long-term problems than the rumblings of the expellees. This was a shrewd prediction, as later events would demonstrate.[18]

Radio Free Europe also faced problems with critics in the United States. The radio station's adversaries came almost exclusively from the ranks of ultraconservatives, who were convinced that its message was insufficiently anti-Communist. Given the wrenching divisions that erupted over America's Cold War policies in later years, the fact that ardent right-wingers were RFE's chief detractors might strike many as unusual. In the 1950s, however, the real debate over American foreign policy did not involve a division between Right and Left, but pitted mainstream anti-Communists against ultra-anti-Communists. To some of the ultras, RFE's brand of anticommunism did not measure up.

To be sure, RFE did not suffer the fate of the Voice of America, which was the target of a series of investigations led by Senator Joseph McCarthy. That Radio Free Europe was not subjected to the full-scale McCarthy treatment must be largely ascribed to its nongovernmental status. Whereas the VOA was run by government bureaucrats with little political clout, RFE was protected by the FEC board of directors, composed of some of the most influential men in public life. An added layer of protection was provided by the CIA and its director, Allen Dulles, the most powerful intelligence chief in postwar America and a founding member of the Free Europe Committee.

But Radio Free Europe was vulnerable because of its intensely political nature. The station's most gifted personalities enjoyed putting their thoughts on paper, often in provocative form. Each week the station issued hundreds of policy documents, guidances, memos, background papers, and scripts, most marked "Confidential" and not meant for circulation in the outside world. The desks were divided along several different lines: Left and Right, religion, exile party affiliation. The exiles quickly learned that if their position did not prevail through normal channels, they could at least embarrass their adversaries by taking their case outside the station, leaking information or passing guidances or controversial scripts to exile politicians or friendly journalists. From its inception, RFE leaked like a sieve; in a report prepared in 1958, the RFE security staff listed no less than thirty-seven station staff members as suspected of passing information to outsiders, including officials of exile groups hostile to RFE. All were Czechs or Slovaks, and a number were members of exile groups critical of the Voice of Free Czechoslovakia's policy orientation.[19]

Sometimes the station's American managers found it necessary to defend staff members from accusations of Communist sympathies. Thus in 1951 William E. Griffith assured C.D. Jackson that a group of Hungarian exiles were untainted by Communist association. Among those accused (by a member of the American embassy at Lisbon) were István Deák, later a distinguished scholar, and Zoltán Szabó, a brilliant writer and the most talented commentator on the Hungarian desk during the 1950s.[20] Occasionally the charges of Communist influence were voiced by more formidable personalities. Senator Bourke Hickenlooper, an Iowa Republican, complained in a letter to David Sarnoff that the VOA and RFE "are still dominated, in some departments at least, by left-wingers of a very pinkish hue." C.D. Jackson assured Sarnoff that nothing was amiss: "Every single exile working for us—in fact, everybody working for us in a sensitive position—has been subjected to the most careful checking, and while I will not pretend that we have not been infiltrated from time to time, these are isolated cases; they almost always reveal themselves after not too long a time and they are always dealt with firmly and immediately." Jackson added that in exile politics, "character assassination is the rule rather than the exception."[21]

By itself, the American ultra-Right represented a minor nuisance to RFE. The station's domestic critics, however, discovered unexpected allies from within the exile world, especially among the Sudeten-deutsche. The Sudeteners developed a network of sympathizers within the McCarthyite wing of the Republican Party, a group that included congressmen, congressional investigative staff, and columnists. They provided the Americans with damaging information about the political biographies of RFE staff, along with internal memos and scripts. If the Americans found it politically imprudent to advocate the Sudeteners revanchist demands, they were often willing to join in the campaign against the Sudeteners' enemies in RFE.

The first indication of possible trouble came in 1954, when a Senate internal security subcommittee chaired by Senator William Jenner, Republican of Indiana, announced plans to question three of the FEC-RFE's leading Czechs: Hubert Ripka, Ferdinand Peroutka, and Julius Firt. Ripka was given a rough going-over during his session with the

old-Fashioned imbeciles

committee; Senator Herman Welker, an Idaho Republican, reportedly called Ripka a Communist and accused the Council of Free Czechoslovakia of subversion.

Fortunately, the unedifying spectacle took place behind closed doors. Ripka had been an eminent statesman in his native country and in exile had devoted himself to the overthrow of his country's Communist oppressors. As reward, he was bullied by one of the Senate's more primitive members and stood accused by a battery of fringe element witnesses that included a Slovak separatist, a Czech Fascist, and a publicist for the Sudeten cause. The regime press in Prague had a field day recounting the sad fate of exiles who come to America to fight communism.[22]

Lewis Galantiere subsequently met with Richard Arens, counsel to the Jenner committee and a prominent antisubversive investigator. Arens had no complaints about RFE, save for its Czechs, whom he attacked along lines already set down by Sudeteners, Slovak separatists, and other exiles. Arens called Ripka the leader of a "secret ring" of crypto-Communists who had "sold out Czechoslovakia to the Communists."[23]

The main worry for RFE was Peroutka, who was under relentless attack by exiles and the American right. Peroutka was vulnerable. Although never formally aligned with a particular party during his years in Czechoslovakia, Peroutka was drawn to democratic socialism. His postwar writings repeatedly struck the theme of capitalism's demise, something Peroutka seemed to welcome. He was also for a short time favorably disposed toward the Soviet Union, partly for reasons of Czechoslovak realpolitik and partly out of a sense of obligation toward the country that had liberated Czechoslovakia from the Nazi grip. He attacked anti-Communists, criticized Catholic political parties, denounced the Marshall Plan, and took a conciliatory stance toward the Czechoslovak Communist Party right up into 1948, when the Communists assumed total control of the state. There were, to be sure, mitigating circumstances. Peroutka believed that given Czechoslovakia's geographical realities, opposition to communism and the USSR would prove fatal to the country's democratic system. He also feared that the collapse of Soviet power in the region would lead to a reoccupation of his country by the Sudeteners, and he came down unequivocally for a socialism that was democratic and nonbureaucratic.[24]

Peroutka's critics were an unsavory bunch, not above taking his opinions wildly out of context in their efforts to depict him as pro-Soviet. To counter the campaign of vilification, RFE launched a project to translate the entire opus of Peroutka's postwar speeches and newspaper columns. This was no small undertaking. The Prague newspapers in which Peroutka's work had appeared were housed in libraries in various European cities; they had to be located and then translated. Eventually, teams of researchers and translators were put to work in Vienna and London (many of the newspapers were filed in the British Museum) until the project was completed.[25]

Unfortunately, RFE was limited in its ability to defend Peroutka because many of his writings did reflect a tolerance toward communism. Meanwhile, the anti-Peroutka campaign was drawing blood. In July 1952, Peroutka was scheduled to receive permanent residence status in the United States; at the last moment, the Immigration and Naturalization Service declined to approve Peroutka's status, and launched an investigation based on evidence supplied by his critics. Peroutka's chances were further damaged by his involvement in a personal scandal—he apparently left his ailing wife for a younger woman. In any event, despite the earnest entreaties of the Free Europe Committee, the CIA declined to intervene on Peroutka's behalf, and it took several years before the issue was resolved.[26]

Peroutka and the Voice of Free Czechoslovakia were thought to be major targets of another 1954 congressional investigation, chaired by Rep. Charles Kersten, Republican of Wisconsin. Kersten was a vocal critic of containment and an ardent liberationist, best known for the Kersten amendment to the 1951 Mutual Security Act, which called for the allocation of $100 million to train military units of East European exiles. The goal, Kersten said, was to "make some trouble for Joe Stalin in his own back yard."

Like other Republican ultra-anti-Communists, Kersten was influenced by fringe exile groups. Kurt Glaser, an energetic champion of the Sudeten cause and confirmed enemy of RFE, served on the staff of Kersten's Committee on Communist Aggression. When the committee announced plans to conduct hearings in Munich, RFE officials anticipated at minimum another attack on the Voice of Free Czechoslovakia. A further source of concern was the presence on the committee of two Polish American congressmen, Thaddeus Machrowitz, Democrat of Michigan, and Edward J. Bonin, Democrat of Pennsylvania, who had made clear their lack of confidence in RFE's work.[27]

The most unsettling aspect of the hearings was their Munich location. Americans were not likely to take seriously charges advanced by exiled politicians. On the other hand, for American congressmen to repeat the arguments made by the Sudeteners would represent a powerful vindication of the expellee cause in the eyes of many Germans, and, it was feared, might deal a crippling blow to RFE's status in the FRG. And if it was not Kersten's intention to destroy RFE, that was clearly the objective of Glaser and others who were providing the congressman with anti-RFE ammunition.

Radio Free Europe mobilized whatever support it could muster in Congress, the State Department, the CIA, and the administration to contain the potential damage. The damage control may have worked. Galantiere met with Kersten shortly before the hearings and found him, somewhat surprisingly, "thoughtful, rational, coherent, speaking words and not meaningless phrases, and altogether sympathetic."[28] A more important factor, however, may have been the behind-the-scenes activities of Jan Nowak and other prominent Poles, who, according to RFE veterans, dropped unsubtle hints that Kersten might encounter problems with his sizable Polish American constituency if he used his hearings to launch an attack on RFE.[29]

In the end, the hearings actually bolstered RFE's standing. Kersten focused exclusively on the tactics used by the Communists in taking control of the satellites. The RFE staff helped organize the hearings, secured witnesses, provided translators and background material. Station officials also used the opportunity to give the visiting congressmen a tour of the Munich facilities, with the result that Machrowitz and Bonin adopted a much friendlier attitude toward RFE and promised to persuade skeptical Polish American newspapers of the station's merits. The committee's final report praised RFE's contribution to the anti-Communist cause and urged support for it.[30]

Radio Free Europe's most determined American critic during the 1950s was Fulton Lewis Jr., a radio commentator of McCarthyite sympathies. He had been a fierce critic of the New Deal and, according to information uncovered by British intelligence from German foreign ministry cables, was favorably disposed toward the Third Reich quite late in the game, having offered German diplomats advice on how to deal with the United States as late as 1940.[31] His programs nevertheless appeared almost nightly over the Mutual Broadcasting System, and he wrote a syndicated column that boasted a wide circulation.

During 1957–58, Lewis carried out an obsessive campaign against the station, devoting over one hundred broadcasts to RFE's alleged shortcomings. Lewis made good use of his many contacts among the network of countersubversives, Sudeteners, disgruntled exiles, and dissident RFE staffers. Like RFE's other rightist adversaries, Lewis made the Czechoslovak desk a special target. He described Peroutka as a "long-time open collaborator with the Stalinists,"[32] and labeled Hubert Ripka as "one of the greatest mass murderers of modern times." Sometimes he would broaden his assault, asserting that RFE had been "systematically manned by many confirmed Marxists." If he wasn't questioning the staff's political reliability, he was expressing contempt for their journalistic talents. He called RFE "pretty much of an amateur operation, ridiculously overstaffed by people who, for the most part, would never be tolerated in a successful commercial operation." He derided the American advisers as "Ivy League trench coat and dark glasses playboys" and labeled the emigre staff "hack politicians in exile."

The name calling caused few problems for the station. Lewis, however, shrewdly began criticizing the corporations that gave large contributions to the Crusade for Freedom and encouraged employees and shareholders to raise questions about the donations. Soon, RFE officials were compelled to answer the questions that arrived from various corporate headquarters about the charges contained in the Lewis broadcasts. And Lewis showed considerable skill in interweaving half-truths, innuendoes, and outright falsehoods with a few serious points, and then giving the whole mixture a veneer of authenticity by quoting from the guidances and scripts that had fallen into his hands. On one occasion, Lewis actually got hold of a coded cryptogram, sent by a CIA official to Whitney Shepardson, then president of the FEC, in which the intelligence agency inquired whether RFE had implemented a policy of promoting the Titoist version of national communism as a model for the satellites. Lewis baited RFE further by admitting that an RFE official had translated the coded message for him.

On those occasions when Lewis was able to shake free of his Reds-under-the-bed obsessions, he sometimes stumbled on questions of significance to the debate over America's Cold War policies. Lewis's RFE series took place after the Hungarian Revolution, by which time

American policies—and RFE policies—had moved in a decidedly moderate direction. It was not true, as Lewis often charged, that RFE was following a line that was anti-Russian but not anti-Communist. Nor was it the case that RFE presented Tito's Yugoslavia as a model for the satellites. It was true that RFE broadcasts spoke favorably of Titoism as a way station between Soviet-style communism and Western-style democracy. Indeed, RFE's Polish desk had supported Wladyslaw Gomulka, who was then regarded by some as a national Communist, in his effort to supplant the old Stalinist leadership in 1956. A serious debate over the most effective strategies to liberate the satellites from communism and Soviet imperialism in the post-Hungary period might have served a useful purpose. But Lewis yearned for the days of anti-subversive investigations and the Kersten amendment. Charles Kersten, in fact, was a guest on Lewis's program; he alleged that the RFE staff included "collaborators" and asserted that the station should be renamed "Radio Co-existence" because of the capitulationist line it was following.

While Lewis's influence should not be exaggerated, there is no denying that his broadsides drew blood. Influential Americans began asking questions about his charges, as did the press. During an appearance in Richmond, Konrad Kellen, an RFE official, was inundated with questions from reporters clearly inspired by the Lewis broadcasts. The journalists were particularly keen to find out if RFE would welcome a congressional investigation, a frequent Lewis demand. Other conservative organs, including *National Review* and *Human Events,* began asking similar questions, although in less strident tones. The *National Review,* then just emerging as a leading journal of conservative thought, devoted a four-page editorial to the RFE-Lewis controversy. The editorial demurred from some of Lewis's wilder generalities (such as his repeated assertion that RFE was a "discredited" institution) but came down much harder on RFE and concluded by calling for an investigation of the station's internal workings by a commission of anti-Communist notables.[33]

Fulton Lewis Jr. eventually lost interest in RFE and moved on to other targets. Although his charges were usually off the mark and often irresponsible, Lewis can probably be credited as the first journalist to directly address the relationship between RFE and the CIA. He announced straight out that RFE got the bulk of its funds from the intelligence agency, placing the amount at $20 million, a reasonably close estimate. Lewis did not uncover this information through investigative digging, but rather relied on his sources within RFE or the CIA. Other journalists had the same information but chose not to break with the reigning consensus on coverage of American foreign policy. Although an extreme conservative, Lewis was not a fringe figure; his program had a regular listenership in the millions, and his columns appeared in some of America's leading newspapers. His revelations, however, were ignored; it would be another decade until the mainstream press, goaded by the "engaged" reporters of New Left publications such as *Ramparts,* would deal openly with RFE's reliance on government money channeled secretly through the CIA.

6

Revolution in Hungary and Crisis at Radio Free Europe

During the entire Cold War in Eastern Europe, no single event produced as much death and destruction as the Hungarian Revolution. The immense human toll included between ten and twenty thousand dead, and thousands more wounded, imprisoned, deported to the Soviet Union, or forced into exile. The revolution also destroyed many of the assumptions on which American policy toward the satellite regimes was based, or seemed to be based. Having stood aside, impotently, as the Red Army ruthlessly smashed the first real attempt to overthrow the yoke of Communist oppression, the United States was to abandon all pretense that its policy was driven by the rollback of Soviet imperial authority or the liberation of the satellites. After Hungary, America was to essentially concede Soviet domination of the region, more or less for the remainder of the Cold War, so that when America challenged Soviet expansionism, the venue would be in Third World outposts such as Vietnam, Angola, or Nicaragua. Washington never again gave serious consideration to disputing Moscow's hegemony in its own back yard, even when Poles or Czechoslovaks rose up to demand freedom and national independence.

The Hungarian tragedy was also to have serious consequences for the projects that America set in motion to wage war against commu-

e of the émigré fighting units that Frank
us European bases. (The units were dis-
ftermath.) But the deepest wounds were
Europe.[1] Before the revolution, RFE was
tion of American Cold War strategy; after
ould be forever tarnished, as historians,
used the station of having made a bad
st extreme cases, of actually having trig-
shrill and irresponsible broadcasts. The
latter charge is unfair. Communist oppression caused the revolution,
not American propaganda; and Americans typically exaggerate their
own power and the power of their institutions. Nevertheless, the charge
of incitement became embedded in Cold War mythology; one latter-
day commentator even coined the phrase "Radio Free Europe syn-
drome" to describe situations in which the United States eggs on a
tyrannized people to rebellion without providing the means for victory.[2]

While in the past the question of RFE's performance during the
revolution has been a source of bitter controversy, it is now possible to
reach a reasonably definitive conclusion about the station's broadcasts.
If the ultimate charge of incitement is unjustified, there is little question today that the station's broadcasts to Hungary during the
revolution's first eleven days violated—repeatedly and sometimes flagrantly—many of the accepted canons of professional journalism. There
were, to be sure, mitigating circumstances: the intense emotions of
exiles driven from their countries by communism, the absence of reliable information from inside Hungary, the incapacitating illness of the
Voice of Free Hungary's chief editor. One is tempted to add that RFE's
confused response to the Hungarians' attempt at liberation reflected
the confused state of mind that prevailed in Washington. As Ralph
Walter, an RFE assistant policy adviser at the time, pointed out, "Nobody was prepared for the Hungarian Revolution, and nobody knew
how to respond when it broke out, including the American government, the Soviet Union, or Radio Free Europe."[3] Ultimately, however,
the responsibility for RFE's flawed coverage of the revolution belongs
squarely with the Hungarian staff, the American management, and, to
a certain extent, RFE's sponsors in the government. Radio Free Europe had been established to encourage a spirit of anti-Communist
resistance among the people of Eastern Europe, and when nonviolent

resistance escalated into open rebellion, RFE found itself unprepared to deal with the consequences.

To properly assess RFE's performance during the revolution, it is first necessary to examine the events preceding the Hungarian crisis, events that were to make 1956 a watershed year in Cold War history and fundamentally alter both the relations between the Soviets and their satellites and American policy toward the Soviet bloc.

The year opened with the Twentieth Congress of the Communist Party of the Soviet Union, the gathering at which Nikita Khrushchev stunned the Communist world by delivering a speech that revealed the crimes of Stalin against the Soviet people—the famous "Secret Speech." The secret speech was appropriately named, for while the congress took place in February, Khrushchev's address did not filter through to the West until May, when the CIA, after a frantic search, managed to obtain two copies of the speech through various sources. The text was turned over to the intelligence agency's top Soviet analysts, who soon concluded that they had obtained the genuine article.

At this point, a controversy broke out within the CIA over the release of the speech. One official, Ray S. Cline, proposed that the full text be made public almost immediately, arguing that it would provide invaluable insights to scholars and students of the Soviet Union and would vindicate everything the West had been saying about the Soviet system over the years. To Cline's surprise, both Frank Wisner and James J. Angleton, the legendary head of counterintelligence, opposed this plan. Instead, they urged that the secret speech remain secret, and proposed that select portions of the document be released to carefully targeted audiences in the Soviet bloc; they wanted to "exploit" the speech rather than simply let people read it.

The adoption of the Wisner-Angleton plan would have enhanced RFE's role in the gradual dissemination of the speech, since, everyone agreed, the most critical audience comprised party members in the satellites, for whom the infallibility of Stalin was an article of faith. Furthermore, Wisner hoped to link release of the speech to a covert action plan called Red Sox/Red Cap. This project involved refugees from the RFE audience countries who were being trained for eventual paramilitary operations inside Eastern Europe. The commando trainees were judged not yet ready for action, and Wisner and Angleton reasoned that, once the exile units were combat-ready, strategic use of the speech might trigger unrest and create opportunities for the exile armies to initiate paramilitary operations. On June 2, Cline finally took his case to Allen Dulles, who decided on the spot to give the speech to the *New York Times,* which published the text almost immediately.[4]

Though not given exclusive rights to the secret speech, RFE nevertheless played an important role in acquainting its listeners with Khrushchev's anti-Stalin message. The text was read over the air night and day, accompanied by commentaries that speculated on its implications for communism's future.[5] Not that the speech required much analysis; the words themselves had a powerful impact on Communist Party members in both East and West and were absolutely devastating for those party members who took seriously communism's more inspirational ideals. The speech was also circulated throughout Eastern Europe in pamphlet form via the Free Europe Press balloon operation.

No one could predict with precision whether the speech would trigger upheaval in the Soviet bloc. But RFE analysts were sensitive to the potential for some sort of violent reaction to years of Communist repression and sent frequent warnings to Washington about the deteriorating situation in the satellites during the summer of 1956—warnings that were ignored by the State Department, according to Cord Meyer, the CIA official whose portfolio included oversight of RFE.[6] Even before the secret speech was made public, challenges to the party's authority over artistic and cultural affairs were mounted by intellectuals in two key satellites, Poland and Hungary. In both countries, the leaders of the burgeoning protest movement were writers who were either party members or had party approval. While party leaders resisted demands for cultural freedom, they proved unwilling to take the repressive steps necessary for a reassertion of total control. As a result, important intellectual publications fell under the control of the liberalizers and functioned as forums for pointed criticisms of the political system, the party's control over culture, and the lack of democracy. Naturally enough, liberal forces interpreted the secret speech as a vindication of their views and a sanction for change from the highest possible authority.

It was not the intelligentsia but the working class that mounted the first direct challenge to communism in the postspeech period. In late

June a protest over increased norms at the ZISPO works in Poznan, an important Polish industrial center, rapidly escalated into violent disorder. Workers shouted down party officials, invaded office buildings, and, in an act of anti-Communist rage, destroyed the equipment used to jam RFE broadcasts. Local police refused to fire on the workers and order was restored only after troops were dispatched by the regime in Warsaw.

By the summer of 1956, Radio Free Europe was arguably the most influential source of information for the Polish people. Thus RFE's coverage of the Poznan riots was crucial to how Poles might react to what was clearly a regime-threatening crisis. The policy of gradualism, of promoting liberalization rather than liberation, was the overarching theme of RFE broadcasts. When the news of the Poznan events reached Munich, the response of both the American advisers and Jan Nowak was to pursue a course of extreme caution. One of the first guidances on Poznan coverage contained this instruction for writers: "We understand and appreciate the motivations which have driven the workers of Poznan to desperate measures. However, riots and revolts are not likely to improve matters in Poland, for the police may be given an opportunity for reprisals which only make things worse. No government which bases itself exclusively on the tanks and bayonets of armed forces will endure. But the Polish people must husband their strength and hold on for the time of freedom." The broadcasts over the Voice of Free Poland adhered strictly to this admonition, not surprising since Nowak played a major role in the policy's formulation. Thus one of the first broadcasts to Poland included an unambiguous call for restraint: "Let us have no illusions. Incidents like [Poznan] play into the hands of [Communist Party leader Edward Ochab] and his Stalinist clique, who want the return of terror and oppression. The struggle for freedom must end in victory, for no regime based on repression can last. But in that struggle prudence is necessary. And therefore in the name of the ardent desire, common to us all, Poland's freedom, we must call on the people to preserve calm and refrain from acts of despair."[8] The Voice of Free Poland did not, of course, restrict its coverage to entreaties for calm. The Poznan upheaval had conveniently taken place during an international trade fair to which many Western visitors had been attracted. Their eyewitness testimonies were broadcast back into Poland by RFE, as were the declarations of support by Western trade union leaders, such as George Meany, president of the American Federation of Labor, and Mike Quill, the president of the Transport Workers Union who had once been notorious in labor circles for his pro-Communist sympathies. The Voice of Free Poland also defended those Poznan workers who had been arrested in the aftermath of the riots and were being charged with serious crimes against the Socialist state. Eventually, the workers got off with light sentences or had their cases dropped.[9]

In light of subsequent developments, the coverage of events during and after Poznan by RFE's Hungarian service is worth noting, for there is no question that the Polish upheaval served as an inspiration to those most responsible for propelling the Hungarian Revolution forward. Poznan was, not surprisingly, item number one on the Voice of Free Hungary's program schedule; in addition, Polish developments supplied the backdrop for programs on conditions in Hungary and the growing ferment in the world Communist movement. Hungarian broadcasts talked about the desperate plight of the Hungarian working class, the counterparts to the workers who had taken to the streets in Poznan. Other programs reported the outpouring of world support for the Polish workers, on the demands for cultural freedom put forward by Polish intellectuals, and on the apparent chaos within Communist parties throughout the world in the wake of the secret speech and Poznan. There was nothing necessarily inflammatory or irresponsible in these commentaries. Collectively, however, the coverage of the secret speech, Poznan, and the rebellion of the intellectuals might well have projected a deceptive picture of world communism as a movement wracked by internal division, weakened by upheaval, and quite possibly on the brink of collapse. That communism was on the defensive during this period is beyond dispute. Equally as significant, however, was the cautious response of the Eisenhower administration to the Polish events, a response that provided further evidence that the "spirit of Geneva" meant an acceptance of the East European status quo by the governments of the Free World.[10]

For Jan Nowak, there was no contradiction between the long-term goal of liberation and the policy of gradualist caution that the Voice of Free Poland had embraced. Nowak was convinced that the Kremlin was not prepared to allow a strategically situated satellite like Poland to detach itself from the Socialist camp. And his experience with Western diplomats had left him skeptical, to put it mildly, about the readiness of the United States to intervene on Poland's behalf in

the event of a Soviet invasion. As No
lieved that there was in 1956 an oppo
gin of freedom. The international situa
events in Russia. But we could not c
thing would be lost. My staff was in
should remain the voice of the peop
anti-Communist masses whose one
made in Poznan. At the same time,
self-defeating for RFE to enthusiast
liberal opposition within the Con
identification with a "Capitalist" radio station might —
vulnerable to charges of collusion with the forces of foreign imperialism.[11]

The Voice of Free Hungary was an enormously popular radio station
in 1956. Surveys taken after the revolution placed RFE's Hungarian
listenership at well over 50 percent; RFE commanded a particularly
wide audience among workers and peasants, the educated classes expressing a preference for the BBC.[12] The VFH's first editor was Gyula
Dessewffy, a man nicknamed the "Red Count" for his aristocratic pedi-
gree and vaguely leftish politics. Dessewffy had recently resigned as
chief editor to take a less demanding position with RFE in New York;
his replacement, Andor Gellert, was respected by the American managers for his administrative skills and, it was believed, superior political
judgment.[13]

Gellert inherited a staff of uneven abilities, ranging from brilliant
commentators such as Zoltán Szabó to less talented writers who preferred polemics to analysis. The VFH's political configuration was also
a problem. The Budapest regime accused the VFH of having fallen
under the domination of Fascists and Horthyites, that is, supporters of
the authoritarian interwar leader Nicholas Horthy. While this charge
was clearly exaggerated, there is no question that the service included
a number of journalists of distinctly rightist sentiments.

There had been concern about RFE's broadcasts to Hungary for
some time, both among RFE managers and the U.S. diplomatic corps
in Budapest. In June 1955, the American embassy wrote a sharply
worded critique of the VFH's programming that laid particular emphasis on the overly propagandistic tone of the broadcasts. The evaluation did contain some good news for RFE. "RFE's popularity among

s substantial," the note said, adding dryly that its cred-
to increase as one descends the educational ladder." The
ted that RFE "symbolizes for the Hungarian people the
erest of the American government in Hungarians and Hun-
he report lauded the VFH for demonstrating that it was famil-
with developments inside Hungary, and observed that the station
ad a knack for "talking the true language" of the Hungarian people.

It was the very popularity of RFE that seemed to worry the diplomats more than anything else. In fact, the report claimed that the
lack of "flexible subtlety"—the VFH's propagandistic hard edge—
seemed to account for its acceptance by the masses. The problem, the
memo declared, was that the Hungarian people were beginning to
think seriously about ridding themselves of Communist rule. The Soviet Union had entered into a rapprochement with its former sworn
enemy, Yugoslavia; more important, Hungary's neighbor, Austria, had
recently won a status of neutral sovereignty through a treaty that had
been negotiated by the Americans and Soviets. Embassy officials worried about the propensity of Hungarians for "wishful and speculative
thinking," especially regarding the prospects of joining Austria in non-
Communist neutrality. Radio Free Europe, the memo charged, was
encouraging what was regarded as a dangerous mindset; RFE and other
foreign broadcast services were guilty of "arousing what may be false
hopes" and must therefore evolve from "a symbol of future Western
liberation into a symbol of Western concern that Hungarians force
concessions from their regime."[14]

Not surprisingly, RFE officials judged the embassy report as patently unfair. Paul Henze wrote at the time that the embassy recommendations were already embedded in RFE's policy emphasizing
incremental, gradual change and passive resistance by the people in
the face of regime oppression. Henze also noted that RFE was careful
in its coverage of the Austrian treaty to avoid giving the impression
that, under prevailing international conditions, neutrality was a realistic option for Hungary. It may also be that RFE's response to the
embassy report was colored by the station's history of difficult relations with the diplomatic corps. Indeed, there were reasons for RFE
to regard criticisms from American embassies in Eastern Europe as, in
some cases, a reflection of an ambassador's irritation at the radio for
complicating his diplomatic functions rather than as an evenhanded
assessment of broadcast quality.[15]

There were, however, other signs of government apprehension over the quality of RFE programs—all its programs, not simply those beamed to Hungary. A survey, apparently commissioned by the State Department or, less likely, the CIA, and conducted in September 1956, suggested that RFE broadcasts were overly propagandistic and strident. While the survey was hardly conducted along accepted social science lines, it included comments by a reasonably wide range of foreign service officers, government officials from foreign countries, American news correspondents with experience in Eastern Europe, and East Europeans who listened to RFE broadcasts. Here again there was a division between the responses of the Westerners—largely critical—and those of the East Europeans—often quite favorable. The East Europeans, in fact, seemed to like the very items that diplomats and foreign correspondents most intensely disliked, such as balloon leaflets and personal attacks on individual party officials. Once again, the group with the most negative views was the diplomats; the journalists, while also skeptical of RFE's tone, acknowledged its wide audience among the common people.[16]

But as the fall of 1956 approached, the concerns about the quality of RFE's broadcasts such as were expressed in the report seemed overdrawn. In a memo written September 26, less than one month before the Hungarian Revolution exploded, Bill Griffith expressed satisfaction with the coverage of the momentous developments in Poland and Hungary. He predicted that while the cultural thaw would continue to gain momentum in both countries, the possibility of a revolutionary outburst was remote. As for RFE's mission at this delicate moment, it was to "assist in prolonging and extending the thaw" and not to foment revolution. On an optimistic note, Griffith declared that hostility toward the emphasis on gradual change rather than liberation had dissipated within the staff; all agreed that real change had taken place and that further liberalization was possible, even under conditions of continued Communist rule. There was, he noted, a danger in overpraising reform leaders lest RFE provide ammunition to hardliners preparing for counterattack. One further problem stemmed from the fact that the East European people were better informed about world events, which presented RFE with the challenge of maintaining an authentic voice—"of our sounding like a completely informed home service." But in general Griffith regarded events at this juncture as "encouraging."[17]

Griffith could not have foreseen that within a few weeks, RFE would have not one, but two crises on its hands. The first occurred in Poland. For months, tension had been building within the Polish United Workers Party, the Communist Party's official name, for a change in leadership. Although it would be inaccurate to describe the forces pressing for change as reformers, they wanted Poland to be less subservient to Moscow's dictates in its march toward socialism and were thus more national in orientation than the old Stalinists then in charge. The one man who had credentials both as an anti-Stalinist and as a devoted Communist was Wladyslaw Gomulka. Gomulka actually owed a debt to Radio Free Europe, for it was during the broadcast of the Swiatlo revelations that the fraudulent nature of the regime's case against him was first made public. He had been released from house arrest during the spring; on October 16, he was elected to the party's central committee, and three days later the central committee took the daring step of dismissing the Polish-born but Soviet-trained—and Soviet-imposed—defense minister, Gen. Konstantin Rokossovsky. Rokossovsky was a Soviet citizen and former Soviet vice minister of defense when he was named defense minister in Poland, an act that symbolically marked the beginning of Stalinism in Poland. His dismissal set off alarm bells in the Kremlin, and Moscow's displeasure grew more intense when Gomulka was elected party first secretary and the remaining Stalinists were eliminated from the Politburo.

Soviet troops were already stationed in Poland; the Red Army initiated a series of menacing maneuvers that brought troops closer and closer to Warsaw. For a few days, it appeared that a Soviet assault was imminent. Suddenly a plane carrying Nikita Khrushchev and a delegation of Soviet potentates landed near the Polish capital. Summoned to a meeting with the Soviet delegation, the Poles were subjected to the Khrushchev treatment of threats, bullying, and bluster. Gomulka, however, retained his composure during this hair-raising encounter and in the end succeeded in convincing the Kremlin leadership that the new Polish team would remain loyal to the Socialist camp and continue to acknowledge Moscow's leading role.

In its coverage of the Polish crisis, RFE followed the policy line set down during the Poznan riots. The Voice of Free Poland reported the facts and urged calm and restraint while denouncing the Soviet visit as interference in Poland's internal affairs. More to the point, the VFP urged that Poles support Gomulka during the hour of danger.

While conceding that Gomulka remained a convinced Communist, RFE declared that his retention of power represented Poland's only opportunity to carve out a measure of independence from the Soviet Union and to maintain the process of internal change.[18]

The policy of critical support for Gomulka was maintained for some time after the informal agreement with Khrushchev had been reached. The radio broadcast numerous expressions of support from Western leaders, and admonished Poles to avoid violence at all cost. That the new Polish leadership recognized the role RFE was playing was made clear when the regime stopped jamming RFE broadcasts, the first time jamming had been ended by any satellite leadership.

Once again, RFE had encountered a crisis and had, by all accounts, acquitted itself with honor. There was no reason to expect that it could not cope with the next challenge looming on the horizon.

The Hungarian Revolution began on October 23, with demonstrations, a huge rally at the Parliament building, and a dramatic speech by Imre Nagy. Later that night shots were fired on a crowd assembled at offices of the national radio. Events quickly gathered force; there were massive demonstrations in Budapest and other cities calling for a new government under Nagy and the withdrawal of Soviet troops. Nagy, the one party leader to command widespread popular respect, was named prime minister; almost simultaneously, Soviet tanks opened fire on unarmed demonstrators. It was this action that transformed what had been a relatively peaceful protest into a national revolution, as regular Hungarian army units fought with students, workers, and peasants against Soviet troops and units of the secret police. Within a few days, Soviet forces had withdrawn, apparently beaten, and Nagy announced a new program of democratic reform and neutrality. After Nagy and János Kádár, who had joined the government as party secretary, negotiated with the Soviets, the occupation forces withdrew. But on November 1, Kádár was kidnapped and taken to the Soviet Union, where he was persuaded, under threat of death, to go over to the Soviet side. Soviet forces then returned in strength and, in a second intervention, crushed the revolution despite desperate resistance from the freedom fighters.

Although Hungary had been in ferment since 1953, the revolution caught RFE by surprise. While the guidances issued by the American advisers were in the main prudent and cautious, the political line was more ambiguous and less confident than in the Polish crisis, which contributed to the mistakes committed in the coverage of Nagy. To be sure, Hungary presented RFE with a more formidable challenge than did Poland. RFE did not have the option of urging the people to remain in their homes and avoid bloodshed. Hungary was at war; thus the challenge for RFE was to support the goals of the revolution through honest, nonpolemical reporting, to provide a realistic evaluation of the international response to Hungary's plight, and to avoid becoming a participant in the upheaval. Unfortunately, RFE fell short on all three goals.

In retrospect, Bill Griffith, RFE's chief policy adviser in Munich, acknowledged that his office should have imposed stricter script controls once violence broke out in Budapest. In fact, the adoption of control measures seems not to have been seriously considered.[19] For the American policy staff to implement what amounted to precensorship of scripts would have been an unprecedented step. Indeed, RFE took great pride in its refusal to employ script preclearance; the freedom the staff enjoyed was what differentiated RFE from other international broadcast services. Additional control mechanisms had not been imposed during the Polish crisis, and everyone agreed that RFE's coverage had been factual and responsible. Moreover, to have had every Hungarian script analyzed in advance would have been a logistical nightmare, given the few staff members with a knowledge of Hungarian.

One problem was the condition of Andor Gellert, the Hungarian service director. Gellert had been sick prior to the revolution but dragged himself to the office during the first few days of the upheaval. He then collapsed and was replaced by a relatively weak lieutenant, a man with limited English and a hearing problem who did not enjoy widespread respect from the staff.[20]

The first sign of trouble came on November 2, when the director of RFE, W.J. Convery Egan, sent a sharply worded memo from New York reminding the staff to adhere to a policy of strict neutrality in discussing personalities or parties in Hungary. A day later, Egan sent another, almost panicky, memo: "The serious if not flagrant violations of . . . Radio Free Europe policy, particularly on the Hungarian desk[,] . . . have caused sharp and distraught reaction in highest circles." The reactions were not so distraught as to prevent the government from encouraging RFE to maintain a polemical stance toward those Hungarians who collaborated with Moscow. Thus on November 5, Egan sent a memo, obviously drafted after consultation with officials in the CIA or the State Department, demanding an all-out propaganda offensive against János Kádár and other Communists who served in a new, collaborationist, cabinet: "All restraints have gone off," Egan wrote, "and we assail Kádár and other quislings with no holds barred. Repeat: no holds barred."

This latter memo gives evidence of the confusion that gripped RFE and, presumably, the American government as the revolution collapsed under volley after volley of Soviet tank fire. A spate of newspaper articles, appearing on both sides of the Atlantic, were accusing RFE of tendentious and bombastic commentary, of giving the freedom fighters tactical military advice, and, most seriously of all, of telling its Hungarian audience that Western military assistance was on the way. Yet the government was encouraging RFE to escalate the polemics, albeit against a target whose traitorous conduct certainly merited universal contempt.

What exactly had RFE been saying? On this score, no one seemed quite certain, although the accounts filtering through from Budapest suggested that a serious scandal was brewing. Among the thousands of refugees who were pouring across the border into Austria, there were reports of having heard RFE broadcasts that tutored the listeners in guerrilla war methods and dealt rather harshly with Imre Nagy. Western reporters who had heard RFE broadcasts or, since few understood Hungarian, had had the broadcasts translated, were if anything more embittered than the Hungarians. Perhaps the most extreme critic was Leslie Bain, a correspondent for the North America Newspaper Alliance. Bain was an American of Hungarian origin who understood the language and who, as a devoted follower of Cardinal Mindszenty, was personally involved in the revolution. He proved something of a fanatic on the question of RFE broadcasts, writing that the Voice of Free Hungary was controlled by right-wingers of Fascist tendencies and included on its staff "discredited fascists and war criminals." Bain wrote widely for influential magazines of the day, and his book *The Reluctant Satellites* included a lengthy section on RFE that set the pattern for subsequent assessments by scholars and journalists.[21]

The first serious control measures taken by RFE occurred on November 4, at which time the VFH was placed on a restricted schedule, with political commentaries, which, it was believed, were the source of the most serious policy violations, reduced to a bare minimum.[22] But RFE's public response to the mounting criticism was to simply deny that anything irresponsible had gone out over the air and to cite official guidances that forbade inflammatory language or the promise of Western assistance. While some observers were in fact accusing RFE of having triggered the revolution, à la Leslie Bain, the real question was whether RFE's broadcasts reflected responsible journalism or, if you prefer, responsible propaganda.

Radio Free Europe also pointed out that many foreign broadcasts were beamed into Hungary during the revolution, and that in some cases the broadcast sponsors were of dubious character. The broadcasts of Radio Madrid were thought to have crossed the line dividing responsible from irresponsible commentary. The NTS, a shadowy organization of Russian émigrés (which, however, received support from the CIA), also initiated special broadcasts to Hungary during the revolution from its station in Frankfurt. According to reports from the period, the NTS claimed that its broadcasts were sponsored by a fictitious Association of Former Hungarian Servicemen, led by one General Zako. These broadcasts promised that an army of exile warriors was heading toward the border, and urged the freedom fighters to rendezvous with the general and his forces.[23]

Another source of possible confusion was the dozen or so "freedom stations" that broadcast information about the progress of the revolution from various locations inside Hungary. The Voice of Free Hungary relied on these stations, most of which were regular provincial stations, for firsthand information. In addition, since their signals were weak, RFE either summarized the freedom stations' broadcasts or, in some cases, beamed their programs throughout Hungary over frequencies normally used by RFE. The freedom stations were staffed by revolutionary partisans, not journalists, and their appeals were often highly emotional, even poignant, as they begged Radio Free Europe to tell the world about the Red Army's atrocities. They beseeched the West for assistance, and they urged their countrymen to continue the struggle, no matter what the odds. Their accounts of fighting were gripping, but not necessarily accurate. In retrospect, Griffith admitted it may have been a mistake for RFE to have put its facilities at the service of the freedom stations.[24]

It was RFE's contention that Hungarians may have confused Radio Madrid, NTS, or freedom station broadcasts for RFE programs.

There was, clearly, a cacophony of voices giving comfort and advice to the beleaguered freedom fighters, and it is conceivable that some of the blame heaped on RFE was misplaced, but RFE was the most popular foreign station in Hungary, and listenership was reported to have been much larger than normal during the crisis. Radio Madrid and the NTS were by contrast marginal enterprises.

In any event, despite the public denials, RFE managers knew that something had gone seriously amiss. Even before a thorough script analysis had been concluded, Richard Condon, the director of the Munich operations, was raising serious questions about the competence of the Hungarian staff. He described the VFH as containing many rightists who "tended over the years to become more and more shrill, emotional, and over–general in tone, to an extent where we have for some time felt that rather drastic measures are needed to deemotionalize their scripts, make them more specific, and prevent them from antagonizing our listeners." Condon concluded this astonishing report by urging that a search for new blood be undertaken among the new group of refugees then lingering in camps in West Germany and Austria.[25]

Eventually, investigations into RFE's role during the revolution were conducted by four outside organizations: the United Nations, the West German government, a congressional subcommittee, and the Council of Europe. Neither Germany nor the Council of Europe probed very deeply, and both reports cleared RFE of serious wrongdoing. The Bonn government, however, was aware that RFE's performance left much to be desired. The foreign ministry assigned a woman who understood Hungarian to listen to a selection of broadcast tapes; while her conclusions were never issued in official form, they were privately passed along to RFE. Although absolving RFE of the most serious charge of having incited the revolution, the report in other respects was quite harsh, with, as an RFE memo put it, "pointed criticism on tone, irresponsible statements, gratuitous tactical advice, errors in political judgment."[26] Radio Free Europe officials feared that release of the report might seriously damage the Western position at the United Nations, where debate over Hungary was underway, and there is evidence that American diplomatic influence was exerted to encourage the Adenauer government to employ discretion in releasing the report's conclusions. The government, for its part, was not inclined to press the issue. But it did worry that RFE's presence on

German soil could become an election issue. The German press had given widespread publicity to the charges made against RFE, and at least one major party, the Free Democrats, issued scathing statements against the American station. The party's newspaper, *Freies Wort,* went so far as to assert that RFE's "aggressive propaganda is responsible to a large extent for the bloodbath."[27] Some trade unions were also weighing in on the issue. "What we want is a real European radio station . . . subject to democratic control exercised by the free European countries," declared Erwin Esal, a prominent Bavarian labor official.[28] Yet despite concerns that the opposition might demand the station's removal from Germany or a German role in the station's management, Adenauer announced in the course of a January 25, 1957, press conference that RFE was innocent of the charges brought against it and would remain in Munich.[29]

Radio Free Europe was less fortunate in the findings issued by a congressional subcommittee that made a study of American policy toward the satellites. Chaired by New York Democrat Edna Kelly, the subcommittee was not directly critical of RFE's performance in Hungary. But its comments about American propaganda were obviously meant as a rebuke to the station, as well as a dig at the Eisenhower administration. "We must not talk more strongly than we are prepared to act," the report said, adding that "publicity and propaganda must be geared to a policy." The report also compared, unfavorably, the VOA and RFE to the BBC on issues of factual news coverage.[30] The United Nations report was basically a blistering attack on Soviet actions, but it contained a brief section on RFE, based primarily on refugee interviews. Like most other studies, the UN cleared the radio of provoking the uprising but indicated that RFE broadcasts may have given the impression that Western aid was forthcoming.[31]

The most thorough, and blunt, evaluations of RFE's performance came from within the radio station. One report, conducted rather quickly and issued internally in early December, declared that the Voice of Free Hungary's broadcasts were "inexpert due to poor content, emotional tone, and inadequate programming techniques." Sam Walker, the director of the Free Europe Press and the report's author, was scathing in his comments about the Hungarian subeditors, describing them as "out of touch with the situation in their country, inadequately trained in professional radio techniques, and politically out of tune with the patriots." By contrast, the Polish service's programs were judged as "consistently excellent, showing restraint, strict adherence to policy, and masterful programming techniques."[32]

The most extensive, and most damning, report was prepared by Bill Griffith and his policy staff deputy, Paul Henze. About 70 percent of the scripts between October 24 and November 3—the critical period during which most of the controversial broadcasts took place—were analyzed by reading translations of the scripts.[33] The basic conclusion was that "although there were few genuine violations of policy . . . the application of policy lines was more often than not crude and unimaginative. Many of the rules of effective broadcasting technique were violated. The tone of the broadcasts was overexcited. There was too much rhetoric, too much emotionalism, too much generalization. The great majority of programs were lacking in humility and subtlety. VFH output for the first two-week period in particular had a distinct 'émigré' tone; too little specific reference was made to the desires and demands of the people in the country." The report identified four scripts as containing outright violations of broadcast policy, three of which were featured on a military affairs program entitled *Colonel Bell*. One of the worst scripts was written by the program's editor, Julius Borsanyi, and was aired October 27, during the first round of fighting. The Griffith report summarized the script: "The program gives detailed instructions as to how partisan and Hungarian armed forces should fight. It advises local authorities to secure stores of arms for Freedom Fighters and tell the population to hide Freedom Fighters who become separated from their units. . . . The writer tells Hungarians to sabotage ("disconnect") railroad and telephone lines. It fairly clearly implies that foreign aid will be forthcoming if the resistance forces succeed in establishing a 'central military command.' The program is cast entirely in the form of advice from the outside; there is no reference to information coming from within the country." A second Borsanyi script was again cited for gratuitously handing out warfighting advice. "Hungarians must continue to fight vigorously because this will have a great effect on the handling of the Hungarian question by the Security Council of the U.N.," the script declared. A third military script was criticized for both encouraging Hungarians to fight on and for instructing them in military tactics—in this case, the techniques of antitank warfare.

The most serious policy violation occurred in a program that reviewed world press commentary on the revolution. The program was broadcast on November 4, by which time the freedom fighters were being pummeled by Soviet artillery. The broadcaster, Zoltán Thury, quoted extensively from a *London Observer* dispatch: "If the Soviet troops really attack Hungary, if our expectations should hold true and Hungarians hold out for three or four days, then the pressure upon the government of the United States to send military help to the freedom fighters will become irresistible." At this point, Thury summarizes the article's conclusion thusly: "This is what the *Observer* writes in today's number. The paper observes that the American Congress cannot vote for war as long as the presidential elections have not been held. The article then continues: 'If the Hungarians can continue to fight until next Wednesday [the day following the American presidential election] we shall be closer to a world war than at any time since 1939.'" Thury then added his own final observation: "The reports from London, Paris, the U.S. and other Western reports shows that the world's reaction to Hungarian events surpasses every imagination. In the Western capitals a practical manifestation of Western sympathy is expected at any hour." The Griffith report theorized that it was this script Hungarians had in mind when they claimed that a broadcast pledging Western assistance had come over the air on the weekend of November 4. It should be noted that Thury quoted the *Observer* accurately; in later years, RFE journalists might have been forbidden to quote from the more speculative passages in the *Observer* article during a period of crisis. Comprehensive controls on the use of news source materials were not, however, put in place until after Hungary.

In addition to the four scripts cited for policy violations, a number of other broadcasts were criticized for inaccuracies, irresponsible tone, or excessive partisanship. Among the charges: supporting one party or faction against other parties in the opposition, describing members of the government as "political prostitutes" and "vile traitors," exhorting Hungarian workers to fight on when the struggle was doomed, and finally and most unfortunately, attacking Imre Nagy, often in the most bitter terms.

The Nagy case was complicated by RFE's having adopted a stance of cautious neutrality toward the prime minister at the beginning of the crisis. Bill Griffith himself was skeptical of Nagy's abilities. In an interview years later he lumped Nagy together with Alexander Dubček as Communist liberals who, though sincere in their reformist impulses, were naïve about Soviet intentions and too weak and indecisive to provide leadership during a revolutionary situation.[34] As for the staff of the VFH, it included a number of commentators who hated Nagy simply because he was a Communist, only marginally preferable, if preferable at all, to the discredited Stalinist leaders Mátyás Rákosi and Ernő Gerő.

The policy guidances issued from New York headquarters at the beginning of the revolution urged neutrality toward Nagy and other Communists in his government. An October 24 document declared, "Actions of the new Communist leaders in Budapest . . . are better not prejudged at this time. That Nagy called upon foreign troops to restore 'order' is a fact he will have to live down. He can live it down only by keeping his promises and helping to establish the climate of freedom and material satisfaction . . . which the people . . . will achieve with or without the cooperation of the present Communist leaders." Similarly ambivalent was the official policy toward Nagy as prime minister. A guidance urged that support be withheld until Nagy removed from his cabinet those Communists identified with the old, Stalinist policies. At the same time, RFE journalists were enjoined to avoid dogmatically anti-Nagy positions until an alternate figure capable of assuming leadership of the revolution emerged.

Thus the ironic situation in which RFE gave cautious, but firm, support to Gomulka, a devout Communist, while treating Nagy, whose Communist faith had eroded rather considerably, as an adversary. And, of course, commentators for the VFH went well beyond the carefully worded strictures contained in the policy guidances. They called Nagy an "inveterate liar," a man who hid behind Soviet tanks, a puppet of Moscow, a traitor, and, in a commentary by VFH chief editor Andor Gellert, a man who had "Cain's stamp on his forehead" and was "one of the biggest traitors of Hungarian history who will be talked of for centuries to come."[35]

In fact, Nagy never requested foreign intervention; the Soviets entered Budapest uninvited, not the first or last time they would take such extreme liberties with their neighbors. Nevertheless, RFE can be excused for believing that Nagy shared in the responsibility; there is evidence that a Hungarian government radio broadcast announced that Nagy had called for Soviet assistance. The murkiness of conditions inside Hungary is, however, a powerful argument for an RFE policy of extreme caution. Instead, some RFE commentators seized upon vague reports of Nagy's complicity in the Soviet intervention as justification for an envenomed tirade against the man who would prove to be one of the revolution's heroes.

More to the point, RFE can be faulted for its generally hostile attitude toward Nagy. Nagy enjoyed widespread support among Hungarians, including nonparty members. During the Stalinist years, he had been excluded from the inner circle of party leaders because of his revisionist tendencies. Among the first acts upon being named prime minister in 1953 was to close the prison camps for political offenders and allow those who had been deported from the cities to the provinces to return to their homes. He also made agricultural collectivization voluntary, and permitted peasants who had been forced into collectives to become independent farmers. There was nothing murky about this record, nor about the antipathy toward Nagy of Rákosi and other hard-liners. Nagy was, in other words, precisely the sort of reform Communist RFE would support in subsequent years. That RFE did not treat him as such is perhaps the most scandalous aspect of the Hungarian affair, and both the Voice of Free Hungary and the American management share in the blame.

Gyula Borbandi, a member of the VFH staff in 1956 who later wrote a history of the Hungarian service, acknowledges that some broadcasters were hostile to Nagy: "The revolution was anti-Communist; Nagy was a Communist. Some wondered how a Communist could lead an anti-Communist revolution." Although admitting that some of the criticisms directed at the Hungarian staff was justified, Borbandi believes that the RFE management contributed to the problem by failing to exercise firm political leadership. He said that while Griffith's observations about the Hungarian situation were consistently moderate, some guidances issued from New York only deepened the environment of confusion. Borbandi asserts that one policy advisory urged that Cardinal Mindszenty receive favorable coverage in the hopes of his succeeding Nagy as the leader of the revolution. He also completely rejects comparisons between the Polish and Hungarian situations: "What were we to say to the Hungarians: 'Be moderate; go back to your homes, be restrained'? We had from the very beginning of RFE been urging Hungarians to resist Communism. Should we now have told the workers to return to the factories? Or the soldiers to return to their barracks? We couldn't say to the Hungarians: 'Please be moderate.' The Soviet army was in Budapest."[36]

For a brief time at the revolution's high point, Hungary effectively abandoned its system of controls at the border with Austria. Freedom fighters went back and forth at will; some even drove to Vienna to secure medical supplies and then returned to Hungary, unmolested by border guards or Soviet troops. Although RFE had occasionally paid foreign correspondents or travelers to gather information during trips to the Soviet bloc, it had never sent staff journalists across the Iron Curtain. That is, until the revolution. On October 28, a team of RFE reporters crossed into Hungary at the border town of Szentgotthard. Subsequently other teams of RFE journalists and interpreters penetrated as far as the regional center of Győr and the mining town of Tatabánya. Radio Free Europe was thus the only international broadcast service to provide coverage from inside Hungary, and one of the few news outlets to cover events from the provinces.[37]

On November 3, however, the Soviets reasserted their authority and closed the roads between Győr and the border, leaving a team of three RFE staff members trapped. The three—Fritz Hier, an American, Gabor Tormay, a Hungarian, and Jerzy Ponikiewski, a Pole—had acquired a treasure trove of secret police documents from the Győr police station. But instead of returning in triumph, they were compelled to sit tight in Győr, since an attempt to return to Austria might provoke an international incident if the Soviets chose to arrest representatives of the "criminal" Radio Free Europe. They were finally allowed to leave on November 11, but only after the American government had initiated a diplomatic complaint in Moscow.[38]

The RFE presence in Austria was substantially augmented after the revolution broke out, a development the government in Vienna regarded with a distinct lack of enthusiasm. It had been a little over one year since the treaty ending the country's foreign occupation had been signed, and Austrian officials wanted to avoid giving the impression that they were allowing the country's neutrality to be compromised. Radio Free Europe maintained several bureaus in the country in order to keep close contact with travelers from the East and refugees from Hungary. The staff presence mushroomed with the revolution, as additional reporters, interpreters, and technicians flooded into the border area. Radio Free Europe also shifted much of its monitoring of foreign broadcasts to the Austria-Hungary border in order to pick up the broadcasts of the revolutionary freedom stations.

The government finally took action by banning RFE staff from the border. The government cited as justification a report, inaccurate as it turned out, that RFE had "kidnapped" the wife of Pal Maleter, the military leader of the freedom fighters who had been arrested by the Soviets. The kidnapping story was probably a pretext; Austria seems to have been motivated by an anti-RFE mood that pervaded governing circles. The chief of state police made sweeping, and illogical, charges against the radio during a meeting with Allan Michie, the deputy director of the Munich headquarters. Higher-ups in the government threatened to expel RFE entirely from the country, retreating only after American Ambassador Llewellyn Thompson told the foreign minister than so drastic a step would damage Austria's reputation in America. The issue was resolved when RFE agreed to limit its presence in the country.[39]

Throughout its early years, RFE periodically considered a program of broadcasts in the Russian language. During the revolution, RFE actually launched a special series of broadcasts aimed at troops in the Red Army invasion force. The project enjoyed American government approval and was actually intensified after the second Soviet intervention on November 4. According to a memo from RFE director W.J. Convery Egan, the programs were to be crafted along the following lines:

> Why have you been ordered to kill your Hungarian brothers—workers and peasants like yourselves? The men in the Kremlin have ordered you to carry out their own mad ambitions. You and your family suffered under Joseph Stalin for twenty years. Then the men in the Kremlin said they would wipe out the crimes and oppressions of Stalin. But they have lied. They are new and worse Stalins. What are they doing to your wives and children and families while you are fighting for the Kremlin in Hungary? Worse still, they are risking the safety of the Russian fatherland and your families by defying the world. Every moment you go on fighting endangers your fatherland and your loved ones. Lay down your arms. Refuse to obey your officers. Refuse to bring your own country to its doom.[40]

The Russian scripts were translated into Hungarian and broadcast repeatedly over RFE's normal frequency. In the memo, Egan cautioned that commentators should deal with the theme of Russia's endangered fatherland "with utmost care" in order to avoid any suggestion to the Hungarian audience "that broadened military action is contemplated."

The balloon operation was an indirect casualty of the revolution. Although RFE had judged the balloon campaign a modest success, the project had never been popular within the American government. Diplomats hated the balloon drops because they provoked noisy complaints from Communist regime officials. According to an oft-repeated story, the U.S. ambassador to Czechoslovakia was mortified when a load of balloons fell on a sports stadium during an event he was attending. Furthermore, non-Communist governments were unhappy with the balloons. The Austrians protested because the balloons passed over their air space en route to Hungary, raising questions about their neutrality. On this point, Vienna had the firm support of Ambassador Thompson, a man of some influence within foreign policy-making circles. Though it tolerated the balloon launchings, the Adenauer government was coming under increasing criticism from Moscow for permitting the balloons to be sent aloft from German soil. After the revolution, a quiet agreement was reached between the United States and Moscow, and the balloon campaign was stopped.[41]

The Hungarian debacle has haunted Radio Free Europe ever since. During the Cold War, the myth of RFE as the nerve center of the uprising was carefully cultivated by Communist authorities in Budapest and elsewhere. In 1981, on the twenty-fifth anniversary of the revolution, the *Chicago Tribune* noted, "The party's position on what happened . . . remains basically unchanged: that naive workers and students, urged on by Radio Free Europe and the late Josef Cardinal Mindszenty, took to the streets without knowing what they were doing."[42] The question of RFE's role was a point of bitter contention even after the collapse of communism; a 1996 Budapest symposium on the fortieth anniversary of the revolution featured a loud debate over the Radio's guilt or innocence. If they deal with RFE at all, Cold War histories usually mention two, and only two, facts: RFE was funded by the CIA and RFE was widely blamed for inciting the Hungarian people to a doomed revolution.

The charge that RFE was responsible for the revolution is absurd.

Bill Griffith is almost certainly right in asserting that "propaganda cannot control or decisively influence events within a country in a state of revolution."[43] A more relevant question might be whether the very existence of Radio Free Europe contributed to popular discontent and therefore laid the foundation for the revolution. This, basically, was the argument of Senator J. William Fulbright when, in the early 1970s, he attempted to eliminate American support for both RFE and Radio Liberty. There is, of course, a risk in broadcasting even straight news reports to societies under totalitarian control, whose only recourse to misrule is resistance, violent or otherwise. Under totalitarian conditions, people are prone to hear what they want to hear. Where a Western audience will understand a politician's ritual denunciation of tyranny for what it is, a person living in a state of oppression may interpret boilerplate rhetoric as a promise of help. In any event, important changes were afoot in Eastern Europe in the period leading to the revolution, and those changes were reflected in RFE broadcasts. As a memorandum prepared by the CIA observed, "During this period RFE . . . played the Khrushchev 'secret speech' heavily; reported Western reaction and the reaction of various Communist party leaders in the West to the secret speech; gave full play to the Belgrade Declaration of 'differing roads to socialism'; gave appropriate treatment to the rehabilitation of various 'titoists' and national Communists throughout the satellite area; reported all evidences of the liberalization process wherever taking place; and gave full play to the attempts of Gomulka to establish greater freedom from Soviet control in Poland."[44] In addition, RFE gave extensive coverage to the declarations of President Eisenhower, Secretary of State Dulles, Democratic presidential nominee Adlai Stevenson, and other political leaders pledging that the cause of East European freedom would remain a fundamental goal of American policy, and informed its listeners of congressional resolutions and party platforms calling for freedom of the captive peoples.

Ultimately, the Fulbright argument asks that the United States cooperate in the legitimation of totalitarian rule, and it is to America's great credit that even during the era of détente it continued to sponsor Radio Free Europe and Radio Liberty, thereby sending a message, however muted, that the United States did not acquiesce in the Sovietization of Eastern Europe. There is, however, merit in Griffith's observation that there was in 1956 a gap between American rhetoric and realpolitik where Eastern Europe was concerned. After the Geneva conference, it was understood throughout the government that the United States would not seriously challenge the East European status quo. On the other hand, no American political figure was willing to assert anything that might be interpreted as an abandonment of the satellites. While no American president ever indicated that the United States would go to war to change East European boundaries or to change the political system in a particular country, America's most important leaders, including Eisenhower and Dulles, made statements that could easily have been judged by even skeptical Hungarians or Poles as a signal of an American willingness to provide some, unspecified, form of assistance. In a 1955 Christmas message, Eisenhower declared that "if any East European shows a visible opposition to the Soviet oppression, it can count on our help."[45] Radio Free Europe's mission included broadcasting the foreign policy declarations of America's top officials; at the same time, RFE was not likely to have cautioned its listeners that what they heard was not what the President really meant. As Ralph Walter noted, "We broadcast the foreign policy statements of responsible American officials. But we did not interpret them or explain their real significance."[46]

Some critics fault RFE for failing to present an accurate picture of communism's strength. In the years leading up to the revolution, RFE pounded home the notion that the regimes were weak and the people were strong. As the events of 1956 demonstrated, this was a reasonably accurate assessment of East European reality in 1956. Indeed, Griffith and other RFE analysts were anticipating a crackdown in Hungary and Poland during the summer; instead, the forces of change continued to gather strength while the Communist parties in both countries seemed on the verge of collapse. A more appropriate question was whether RFE was sensitive to Soviet determination to retain control over the satellites. Yet even here, events could lead to different interpretations. The Soviets were not engaging in the sabre-rattling that preceded the 1968 intervention in Czechoslovakia. And without Soviet intervention, or the threat of Soviet intervention, communism would have been overthrown in both Hungary and Poland; ultimately, the people were much stronger than the party. Nor is it fair to describe the Hungarian Revolution as predestined to fail. That the Soviets would use force to keep Hungary in the Socialist camp was by no means certain; the power struggle that divided the party after Stalin's death was unresolved, and recently released evidence from the Kremlin archives indicates that Khrushchev went through a period of profound uncertainty before opting for military intervention.

The flawed coverage of the revolution was to be RFE's first—and last—major public scandal. This is an enviable record by any reasonable standard, all the more so given the sensitive issues that RFE dealt with on a daily basis, the microscopic scrutiny devoted to its broadcasts by Communist officials, and the intense emotions of the exile staff. Yet it took some years before the radio enjoyed the degree of trust and esteem that it had enjoyed before the Hungarian debacle. Ironically, it would be RFE's performance in future periods of crisis—during the 1968 invasion of Czechoslovakia, the successive upheavals in Poland, and the collapse of communism in 1989—that would solidify the station's reputation for calm, responsible broadcasting under conditions of intense pressure.

7

Peaceful Coexistence

Shortly after the Hungarian Revolution had been crushed, Ferdinand Peroutka was summoned to a meeting to discuss the future of broadcasting to Czechoslovakia. As the chief editor of the Voice of Free Czechoslovakia and the service's most respected political commentator, Peroutka would ordinarily be expected to take a principal role in formulating the political line, particularly when the request for new propaganda strategies originated in the American government, in this case the CIA. Peroutka, however, was less than enthusiastic. As he saw things, Czechoslovaks were unlikely to respond to appeals for resistance given a recent history that included the dismantling of their country by the Nazis, a Communist takeover, and the failure of the 1953 upheavals to elicit Western assistance. Considering the repeated instances of Western betrayal, Peroutka suggested that his audience was unlikely to support anything beyond the policy of cautious gradualism that guided programming at the time. Nevertheless, he declared himself willing to give the matter serious thought if a crucial question could be answered: "Does the U.S. government want a revolution in Czechoslovakia, or does it fear one?"[1]

Although no responsible American official would say so publicly, the answer to the uncomfortable question posed by Peroutka was that if the United States did not exactly fear another satellite rebellion, it certainly did not favor one. The Hungarian tragedy was a setback for Moscow's international prestige, especially in Western Europe, where leftist intellectual sentiment strongly backed the freedom fighters. America, however, did not emerge from the revolution unscathed, having been revealed as a country that talked a great deal about freedom for those oppressed by communism but then stood by passively when the people of a satellite nation took its words to heart.

The changes introduced into American post-Hungary policy related less to its actions—under Eisenhower, the United States had moved toward an acceptance of the division of Europe in the aftermath of the Geneva conference—than to its words. Henceforth, the gap between realpolitik and rhetoric would be closed. And Radio Free Europe, which had borne the burden of blame for the West's mistakes in Hungary, was placed under an unprecedented degree of government oversight.

The most important immediate change was in the leadership of the Munich headquarters. Dick Condon was dismissed as director; his replacement, Erik Hazelhoff, was a former Dutch airman with a reputation as something of an adventurer but with little knowledge of Eastern Europe. Bill Griffith remained as policy director until the beginning of 1959, when he left to take up a career as a specialist on Communist affairs at the Massachusetts Institute of Technology and as a roving editor for *Reader's Digest*. Most of his deputies also departed: Paul Henze returned to Washington, where he held a series of posts in the intelligence world, the National Security Council, and the RAND Corporation; Bill Raedemakers moved to *Time* magazine; and Ralph Walter took a post with the Free Europe Committee in New York for a few years before returning to Munich as RFE policy director.[2]

The departure of Griffith's team would have serious repercussions for both RFE and the Free Europe Committee. Prior to the Hungarian Revolution, the FEC played an important role in setting East European policy. The policy of promoting evolutionary change, initially elaborated in an FEC paper, formed the basis for a 1954 NSC policy document. Griffith was personally credited with having persuaded the State Department that Poland, not Hungary, was the most important, and most vulnerable, of the satellite states. Griffith was also credited with having established the Munich headquarters as a center of intellectual inquiry into the Communist world, a place where eminent scholars such as Hugh Seton-Watson and Franz Borkenau gave regular lectures, and where scholars, journalists, and government officials from Western Europe looked for analysis about the Soviet bloc.[3]

Among the language services, only the Hungarians experienced significant changes. Not surprisingly, morale in the Voice of Free Hungary was at a low point. Nor was the inevitable overhaul accomplished with ease. A memo written by Paul Henze described the Hungarian staff as riven by personal and political differences, with editors refusing to work with other editors in an atmosphere of finger pointing. Eventually, Andor Gellert was eased out as chief editor and replaced by István Bede, whose previous experience in the diplomatic service proved valuable in rebuilding staff esprit de corps. His task was made easier by a purge of a dozen or so VFH broadcasters and editors, with those considered politically extreme, journalistically weak, or inclined to office intrigue made special targets for dismissal. Ironically, Julius Borsanyi, the infamous Colonel Bell, was retained; as the service's representative on the union-management works council, Borsanyi was effectively immune from dismissal. Bede, the new chief editor, was a Social Democrat who had served in Hungary's diplomatic corps. A 1957 memo indicated that the Hungarian service's postrevolution political composition included a "preponderance of liberal progressive elements" and a cross-section of the non-Communist Left. Furthermore, the service found a wealth of new blood among the revolution's exiles.[4]

In addition to staff changes, proposals were advanced for a more rigorous system of script control to ensure that broadcasts avoided the excesses that had marked the coverage of the Hungarian Revolution. Some were far-reaching, calling for a review of all scripts prior to broadcast or the use of master scripts, composed by Americans and then translated into the various audience languages. In his memoirs, Jan Nowak says he mobilized a petition campaign within the Polish section, complete with the threat of en masse resignations, to protest what the exiles regarded as impending censorship.[5] The plan that was finally adopted was moderate, and ensured that RFE journalists would retain a large degree of autonomy in their day-to-day broadcasting. The key element was the creation of the Broadcast Analysis Division, a unit that analyzed scripts after they were broadcast and then issued cautions or warnings when broadcasts departed from the political line of the day or failed to meet accepted standards of journalistic professionalism or accuracy.[6]

The most sweeping changes affected RFE's role in formulating a political line. Previously, the FEC had drafted the policy documents and then sent them to the State Department. The State Department could veto the policy guidances and send them back to the FEC for revision. In practice, this system worked rather well; few guidances were vetoed, the FEC's judgment on East European matters was respected, and RFE enjoyed considerable autonomy in setting its political priorities.

After Hungary, the State Department assumed responsibility for the major policy guidances. In 1957 the State Department, in conjunction with the interagency Committee on Radio Broadcasting, an entity that included representatives from the State Department, CIA, and United States Information Agency, issued a series of policy documents that were to provide a framework for American broadcasting to Eastern Europe, both for the VOA and RFE. But instead of drafting five distinct country guidances that took into account the often striking differences between one country and another, one basic document was issued for all five RFE countries, with minor variations to take account of individual country conditions. The purpose of the guidances, then, was less to provide political direction than to drive home the point that American radio propaganda was to proceed along a much more cautious path in the post-Hungary environment.[7]

Thus in spelling out American policy objectives, the guidance for Czechoslovakia observed that while the ultimate goal was freedom from communism, the short-term, realistic objective was "to foster an evolutionary development resulting in the weakening of Soviet controls and the progressive attainment of national independence." To accelerate the slow march toward liberty, the guidance declared that American policy favored the "establishment of a 'National Communist' regime which, though it may be in close military and political alliance with the USSR, will be able to exercise to a much greater degree than in the past independent authority and control in the direction of its own affairs." And in a passage that provided an answer to Ferdinand Peroutka's question, the guidance said it was "neither feasible nor desirable that the U.S. run the risk of instigating either local or general hostilities" by encouraging popular resistance.

The guidance reaffirmed RFE's unique role by referring to it as an instrument of "grey" propaganda as distinct from the VOA's position as the official broadcast service of the American government. As such, the guidance declared, RFE might sometimes be used for the dissemination of "unannounced" government policies: "As an instrument for furthering unannounced policy, RFE will be governed strictly by the policy guidance furnished to it through appropriate channels. The guidance will relate to specific events and conditions, and may in some instances appear to be in conflict with announced policy. (In most instances, guidances on unannounced policy will relate to objectives which can be undertaken by RFE as an unattributable radio, but which would be inadvisable or inappropriate positions to be taken by an official organ or spokesman of the U.S. government.)" This passage can be interpreted as assigning RFE some sort of covert policy assignment, similar to its role in promoting the campaigns to destroy harvests. Or it can be read as acknowledgment that RFE could continue to criticize certain government officials or internal policies of regimes to which the American government gave general approval. Whatever the case, during the next few years the State Department seemed much more intent on telling RFE what not to say than in giving the radio special policy tasks.[8]

Of more practical significance was a statement that henceforth RFE was to regard itself as a European rather than as an American or exile station. In covering world news, RFE broadcasts "should generally be in the European context as seen through European eyes." Radio Free Europe was encouraged to provide more coverage of European news, broadcast more interviews with European leaders, and emphasize the success of the movement toward European integration as an example of voluntary cooperation in contradistinction to the imposed unity of the Warsaw Pact.

Considerable attention was devoted to broadcast tone. Radio Free Europe was instructed to "avoid a tendentiously negative approach" and urged to "inject constructive criticism into its commentaries." In discussing internal conditions, RFE was to "avoid alienating ... listeners by dwelling on those internal conditions and shortcomings of which the Czechoslovaks are well aware." Broadcasts were to avoid inflammatory material, "excessive polemics," "vituperation," and a "patronizing or condescending tone." Also to be avoided were calls to action that might invite official reprisal, "direct incitement to armed uprising," or tactical advice during an uprising.

The strategic goal was modest compared with the ambitious agendas of previous years. Radio Free Europe's broadcasts were to encourage common people, intellectuals, and party members to think and act independently of Moscow, to the degree that prudence permitted. The guidance recommended that RFE "seek to keep the people in touch with Western life and thought" and acquaint the listeners with alternatives to Communist methods of organizing and administering society.[9]

The significance of the new guidances related less to the content of RFE programs—the radio had been evolving in the direction of a normal, politically oriented broadcast service—than to the State Department's intention to play a more intrusive role in shaping the station's political approach. The first important manifestation of the new regime was a decision, dictated by the government, to abandon the identification of the language services as the Voice of Free (Bulgaria, Czechoslovakia, Hungary, Poland, Romania); henceforth, each language division was to be identified as the Hungarian (or Polish or Romanian) service of Radio Free Europe. Jan Nowak vehemently protested this decision; he worried that the change would be interpreted by Poles as a concession to Gomulka, but to no avail. The State Department was determined to ensure that RFE would never again be looked on as a representative of a political opposition or an outlet for émigré opinion.[10]

If it was not clear before October 1956, it was certainly clear afterward that Poland was the most vulnerable chain in the Soviet bloc, and the most responsive to the RFE message. The radio's already considerable prestige was reinforced by its intelligent coverage of the "Polish October" and the rise of Gomulka; in a sense, RFE had achieved recognition as the voice of the responsible opposition to communism and Soviet imperialism.

Radio Free Europe's decision to provide critical support to Gomulka was not lost on the new Polish leadership. In mid-December 1956, Oskar Lange, a Polish economist who functioned as a kind of liaison between the "responsible" elements of the Communist Party and the West, approached an RFE Polish editor with a request that the radio become even more supportive of Gomulka. During a meeting in Rome, Lange told the editor that disturbances had nearly broken out in the Polish provinces after the Hungarian Revolution had been crushed. He asked that RFE take the precarious internal situation into account when planning its broadcast strategy and urged that the radio adopt a tone that would have a "tranquilizing influence" on Poland. Furthermore, Lange insisted that important internal reforms were in the offing, adding that RFE could make an important contribution to the country's revival by teaching Poland about Western institutions and ideas instead of attacking the shortcomings in the regime's program. Criticism of Gomulka, he added, would only drive the regime toward closer alliance with the Soviets.[11]

The argument that Western criticism would set back the Polish reform process was repeatedly advanced by emissaries like Lange over the years. Although it found a ready audience among many American officials, it was never accepted by RFE. Jan Nowak was from the very first a skeptic about Gomulka's claims to the reform mantle; he was convinced that the Polish leader was cynically manipulating Western diplomatic opinion by sending go-betweens like Lange to argue for a policy of ignoring the mounting evidence of the regime's retreat from the liberal ideas of the Polish October.

Nevertheless, RFE did recognize that Poland could easily explode in the months following the historic meeting with the Soviet leadership. Election to the Polish parliament, the Sejm, were scheduled for January 20, 1957, and there were many who feared that the election campaign might trigger a popular insurrection that would in turn trigger a Soviet invasion. As after the Poznan riots and the October crisis, RFE's Polish service stressed the dangers of violent upheaval and discouraged public demonstrations on the grounds that they might be used to justify Moscow's intervention or a renewed drive for power by the Communist Party's Stalinist wing. A guidance asserted that in the event of a popular eruption, RFE's policy was to "suspend judgment on such actions" and "keep listeners informed of the political and military realities."[12]

The critical election issue was not which party to vote for—it was assumed that Gomulka's coalition would win overwhelmingly—but whether to boycott the election as an act of protest. On this question at least, RFE did accept the argument, advanced by the regime but supported by the Polish Catholic Church, that a boycott would play into Soviet hands. To be sure, RFE attacked Gomulka's insistence that voters support only candidates running under the banner of the Communists or one of their satellite parties. It also ran a series of "black list" programs in which voters were urged to oppose candidates with known Stalinist sympathies. Nevertheless, RFE believed that under the tenuous state of affairs in Poland, the prudent—and, ultimately, patriotic—option was a backhanded endorsement of the Gomulka position. As Nowak observed in an election eve commentary, "In the present electoral campaign, the [Communist] party has only one argument, but this argument is weighty and—alas—convincing. If you refuse us your support, they say, if you bring about our downfall, the alternative is a return to Stalinism. This argument is cruel, but entirely correct."[13]

Over the next several years, RFE found itself in a constant struggle with the State Department over coverage of its audience countries. The radio found an ally in the CIA, whose director, Allen Dulles, remained a committed RFE champion. In a 1958 memo, Stuart Hannon, an RFE official, noted that he frequently passed along material to CIA liaison officials to enable the agency "to work more effectively against the opposition," meaning the professional diplomats who constituted the radio's severest American critics.[14] In another memo, John Dunning, an RFE executive, noted with satisfaction that a series of Polish scripts had received high marks in separate analyses by the CIA and the State Department. The State Department team, however, raised objections to a series of programs on an American military buildup, complaining that the scripts might make it appear that the United States was insufficiently committed to peace.[15]

The major difference between RFE and the State Department involved coverage of Poland. To the State Department, Poland had emerged as the most open of Communist societies, with the possible exception of Tito's Yugoslavia. Poland had opened its borders to Western visitors, businessmen, and even private foundations (the Ford and Rockefeller Foundations had both established projects there). American diplomats in Warsaw enjoyed friendly relations with Polish officials whom they regarded as Poles first and Communists second. To embassy officials in Warsaw, the overriding objective was to forge even closer ties with the regime in the hope of stimulating further liberalization; under these conditions, an RFE broadcast attacking an official or government policy was an impediment to better ties; when a regime official expressed outrage over a script, the embassy often sided with the regime rather than defend RFE.

There was also the issue of Jan Nowak. To some American diplomats in Warsaw, Nowak seemed a loose cannon, too quick to criticize the regime's shortcomings and too unsympathetic to the pressures on Gomulka from sources inside and outside the country.[16] Given Nowak's steady, cautious guidance of Polish broadcasting during 1956, his reputation as an enfant terrible might seem strange. But Nowak had never been a Gomulka partisan, and he believed that Gomulka was justifying policies of Communist orthodoxy by exaggerating the Soviet threat. To Nowak, American diplomats were naïve and the comparison of Poland with Yugoslavia an absurdity.[17]

The gap between the RFE view of Polish reality and the version accepted by the diplomatic corps was vividly revealed in the course of a 1958 meeting involving Thomas Donovan, the political officer in the Warsaw embassy, and Bill Griffith. Donovan objected to RFE's use of secret party documents on the grounds that official party declarations were often meaningless. He objected to accounts of prison conditions broadcast by recent refugees. He objected, vehemently, to a series of broadcasts, based on interviews with a defecting wife of a Polish dignitary, which detailed the life styles of high party officials; even if accurate, such programs were "over-sensational," he declared. He declared that RFE coverage of church-state controversies should be more evenhanded. And he insisted that Polish retrogression from the program of October 1956 was exaggerated by RFE, and added that whatever regression had occurred was due to Soviet pressure and did not reflect the objectives of Gomulka.

Not surprisingly, Donovan failed to convince RFE that change in its broadcasting policy was in order. Communists, RFE believed, often did mean what they said, and even if their internal documents were never implemented as policy, the fact that they entertained certain ideas was news. Reports on the private lives of party leaders, their wives, children, and relatives were popular with the Polish audience; moreover, there was an important political message in the evidence of corruption, privilege, and favoritism among the nomenklatura, a point that had been brilliantly elaborated by Milovan Djilas in his account of Communist bureaucracy, *The New Class*. Where Djilas had provided a theoretical discussion of the rise of a privileged class of officials, RFE was now detailing how the nomenklatura acquired and held on to its privileges in real life. And RFE was contemptuous of suggestions for an "on the one hand . . . on the other hand" type of coverage of church-state problems, given that the Polish people were overwhelming supportive of the Catholic Church and strongly hostile to the Communist Party.[18]

By the summer of 1959, the friction between the State Department and RFE reached the point where intervention by President Eisenhower and other high officials was necessary. Jacob Beam, U.S.

ambassador to Poland, shared many of Thomas Donovan's misgivings about RFE. On July 7, CBS reported that Beam had demanded the elimination of the Polish broadcasts, claiming they were too critical of Gomulka. Beam subsequently told the *New York Times* that RFE was airing blatant propaganda and included too many broadcasts in which conditions in Poland were placed in the worst possible light.[19] Nor was Beam alone in feeling that RFE did more harm than good. Milton Eisenhower, the president's brother and confidant, was skeptical about the usefulness of RFE Polish programs, as was George V. Allen, director of the United States Information Agency. In a memo to the president, Allen declared, "Even our best friends in Poland . . . think these broadcasts are carried on primarily in the interests of Polish refugees in New York." He added, "The present Communist officials, who are Communists but loyal to Poland, regard the quarrel carried on by RFE as a fight between two groups of Poles—the outs attacking the ins. Since the outs in RFE are known to have U.S. government support, the ins (Gomulka and Co.) consider the broadcasts to be directed against them personally and the regime is thereby thrown closer into the arms of the Soviets for protection."[20] While Milton Eisenhower proposed to change the nature of RFE programs and to limit on-air staff to American citizens—an unworkable solution, to say the least—Allen advocated outright elimination of the Polish service, arguing that even major changes in the broadcast schedule would fail to convince officials in Warsaw that the station was not simply a "refugee outfit." Allen claimed that Gomulka feared an attempt by the United States to destroy his regime and install a government composed of exiles from New York and London. Allen claimed that unnamed East Europeans regarded the "refugees" as wanting to "turn the clock back to days that are past and gone."[21]

Allen's observations betray surprising ignorance of RFE programs given his wide experience in international broadcasting. That an official of such importance could gain a presidential hearing for such views was all the more disturbing, since it suggested that other officials might entertain similar misconceptions about the nature of RFE's work. In his memo, for example, Allen claimed that Llewellyn Thompson, then ambassador to the Soviet Union, favored a discontinuance of Radio Liberty broadcasts. Furthermore, Allen's memo, combined with anti-RFE statements from other officials, indicated that the Gomulka regime's strategy of blaming RFE for Gomulka's drift toward orthodoxy was paying dividends.

The Allen memo prompted a hasty response from C.D. Jackson. Though he was out of government, Jackson retained an interest in America's psychological warfare potential, and remained a firm supporter of RFE. Jackson wrote the President to propose a high-level meeting to discuss RFE, Poland, and political warfare in general.[22] The meeting took place over dinner on September 10. In addition to the president, those on hand included Vice President Richard Nixon; Douglas Dillon, Robert Murphy, and Neil McElroy from the State Department; Gordon Gray; Gen. Andrew Goodpaster; Press Secretary James Hagerty; Allen Dulles; George V. Allen; and Jackson.

Jackson made a straightforward case for maintaining a political warfare program targeted on Eastern Europe. As Jackson saw things, the satellite nations represented the Soviet Union's principal point of vulnerability; for the United States to refuse to exploit the weakest link in the Soviet empire raised fundamental questions about the entire thrust of American Cold War policy. Jackson conceded that certain American ambassadors were unenthusiastic about RFE and RL broadcasts. But he asserted that it was entirely proper for the goals of political warfare to differ from those of formal diplomacy, and added that "for ambassadors to be getting high blood pressure because an instrument of political warfare is 'making trouble' for them is ridiculous."[23]

Jackson's direct approach seems to have deflected a concerted drive against RFE. The State Department representatives, particularly Dillon and Murphy, protested that their concern was not with the idea of political warfare, but only certain details of RFE programming. Vice President Nixon seconded Jackson's perspective, while Allen, who held the strongest anti-RFE position, remained silent throughout the evening. The radio's position may have been strengthened by a lobbying campaign by Polish Americans, a project instigated by Jan Nowak.

Radio Free Europe's cause was given a further boost by its role in making a visit to Warsaw by Vice President Nixon a success. Prior to his arrival, RFE aired numerous broadcasts on Nixon's life and encouraged its listeners to give the American a warm welcome. Then, RFE learned that the regime had directed Nixon's plane to land at a different airport than the one originally announced. This information was relayed to the Polish audience. Nixon, in fact, was not expecting a large turnout, assuming that the Polish regime would not want the American to receive a more favorable reception than Nikita Khrushchev had received during a visit to Warsaw a few weeks earlier. To Nixon's surprise, the streets were thronged with cheering Poles, some holding banners that read "Long Live America." "As we drove through the suburbs . . . the crowds grew larger and larger. . . . As we reached the downtown area, the situation got completely out of hand. The crowds overflowed the sidewalks and pressed into the street, stopping the motorcade altogether. . . . We moved at a snail's pace, stopping time and time again because of the throng of people who surged around us. . . . Whenever our car was stopped, I had a chance to look closely into the faces around me. Some were shouting, others were singing, and many were crying—with tears running down their cheeks. It was the most moving experience of all my trips abroad." Nixon added, "The official blackout of all news concerning my visit and the time of my arrival . . . was considered a failure because the Polish government had not taken Radio Free Europe into consideration."[24]

During the visit, Ambassador Beam attempted to convince Nixon that RFE was serving as an obstacle to closer Polish-American ties. Nixon, would have none of it. He reportedly told Beam that in addition to the need for good relations with the Polish government, it was an American diplomat's responsibility to maintain a close relationship with the people. In Nixon's opinion, the reception accorded him was proof of the importance of an American radio station that spoke directly to the people.[25]

Yet despite the White House meeting and Nixon's support, the tensions between RFE and the diplomatic community continued to fester. On October 21, a delegation of FEC–RFE officials, accompanied by Allen Dulles and Cord Meyer, met with Ambassador Beam, Foy Kohler, and several other State Department officials. Kohler, generally a hard-liner who later rose to serve as ambassador to the Soviet Union, declared that it would be difficult for RFE to implement the new broadcast guidelines with "the same old exiles" behind the microphone. He further suggested that RFE might have been responsible for the poor performance of Polish agriculture through the years because of its broadcasts urging resistance to collectivization. Nor was Beam reassured about RFE's Polish programs. While conceding that RFE was empowered to make critical commentaries about internal Polish affairs, he urged that it switch its focus to news about the West, a proposal, in other words, to transform RFE into a version of the VOA.[26] (Beam would later have a complete change of heart; during the 1970s he served as chairman of the RFE board of directors.)

Relations between the professional diplomats and RFE eventually improved, to the point where the State Department pulled back from its strict control over broadcast strategy. While a measure of tension between diplomacy and political warfare (or, as it would later come to be called, public diplomacy) would be a constant throughout RFE's history, the Beam controversy would be the only occasion in which a clash with the State Department posed a threat to the RFE mission.

Meanwhile, RFE confronted other problems as its first decade drew to a close. One of the most vexing was the challenge of replenishing its staff. Most exiled journalists had fled their countries between 1945 and 1948, when Communist regimes were consolidating their control over the societies of Eastern Europe. Some had died; some were nearing retirement age. A serious problem was created by the shifting character of the station. Many staff members had been hired when RFE encouraged a polemical approach of the kind used in the "black book" broadcasts of the early 1950s. Now, broadcasters who were hired because of their skills at denunciation were finding the transition to journalistic professionalism difficult. As Jan Nowak observed, "The Polish editorial team was selected almost eight years ago to suit best the fighting nature of the station which at that time had been conceived as a sharp, hard-hitting instrument of propaganda warfare. It consists of people who throughout the eight years have become trained and top experts in domestic problems and polemics with Communist propaganda. Under normal circumstances the only logical thing in the present situation would be to replace some editors by hiring people who are better equipped and qualified to prepare programs of the 'Projection of the West' type."[27] Unfortunately, the normal process of staff replacement was impossible. There was, to begin with, a general reluctance to fire exile staffers, which sprang from humanitarian motives. There was, in addition, West German labor law, already in place by the late fifties. German regulations gave extraordinary protection to employees; they could be dismissed if the employer could provide an economic justification, not always an easy undertaking. Otherwise, employees hired in Germany could more or less rely on lifetime employment. For this reason, RFE employees in the United States were more vulnerable to layoff or dismissal than those situated in West Germany, with its elaborate, social democratic, worker protection regulations.

Nor was it a simple matter to fill staff vacancies. Through the years, the Communists had become more sophisticated in their prevention of "defections" to the West. There was no longer a large pool of exile talent from which RFE could pick and choose. The dearth of new talent was acute among the Romanians and Bulgarians. A Bulgarian with a journalistic background would prove a prize catch for RFE in 1960. The obvious exception was the Hungarians, who could recruit from the large number of exiles who had fled after the revolution was crushed.

The Czechoslovak service posed a special dilemma for RFE. Although Czechs and Slovaks had a much more successful history of coexistence than Hungarians and Romanians or Croats and Serbs, the relationship was not without its tensions. Czechs believed in their cultural superiority and were mindful that the Slovaks had established, with German encouragement, a separate, Fascist state during World War II. Slovaks believed that they were the victims of discrimination in the allocation of jobs and resources in the unified state, and there lingered some support for Slovak separatism, especially in the diaspora.

Since American policy supported a unified state, RFE ruled out separate Czech and Slovak services. But RFE recognized that special measures would be required to maintain credibility with the Slovak audience. In practice, this meant that if a Czech was appointed service director (as was almost always the case), a Slovak would be named as associate director. It also meant keeping something of a staff balance between Czechs and Slovaks and implementing a balance between Czech and Slovak programs. The program schedule included frequent reports on successful examples of interethnic amity in the West, such as existed in the United Kingdom, Canada, and Belgium, as well as scripts on the positive aspects of European integration. At the same time, RFE retained its strict policy of refusing to hire advocates of Slovak separatism.

In 1960, this delicate balance threatened to unravel. Julius Firt, the Munich service director, announced his retirement. Firt was a popular and effective editor; his successor, Oswald Kostrba, was disliked by the staff for his militarylike management style. Kostrba then further alienated the staff by naming as associate director a Slovak whom the staff regarded as an incompetent. Kostrba's first weeks on the job were marked by constant arguments with subordinate editors, some of whom he exiled to the fringes of the service, where they were put to work on such menial tasks as correcting grammar in program scripts. The staff, in turn, took to writing memorandums, which were passed along to the American management, and office intrigue, for which the RFE émigré staff displayed genuine talent.

By December the situation had deteriorated to the point where decisive action had to be taken. Erik Hazelhoff, the Munich director, summarily fired eighteen editors whom he regarded as ringleaders of the rebellion; in response, most of the remaining Czechoslovak staff walked out in sympathy, leaving the service in the hands of a skeleton staff of Kostrba loyalists. Top officials of RFE and the FEC, both located in New York, were unable to resolve the dispute.

At this point, the CIA stepped in out of fear that the entire radio was in jeopardy. Hazelhoff and his chief deputies were dismissed; as a replacement, Allen Dulles supported retired general G. Rodney Smith, who had been working for the FEC in New York.[28] The appointment of Smith was accompanied by a series of organizational and personnel changes. The most important of these was a decision, demanded by Smith before he accepted appointment as director, that the radio's headquarters be shifted from New York to Munich. Henceforth, the RFE director, his chief aides, and the language service editors were assigned to Munich, and New York functioned as a large bureau.[29]

Smith proved a decisive but fair-minded manager who actually gave the service editors more authority in the day-to-day operation of their units. In a more controversial move, Smith gave the news division much more authority over the content of news broadcasts. He named Gene Mater, a professional journalist who later moved on to a high position with CBS news, director of the news division. Although Mater could not control the content of commentaries and analyses, he had power over news broadcasts, and he used that power to kill items that smacked of rumor, speculation, or conjecture. Mater established a requirement that a story have two sources before it could appear on the news broadcast, a standard that was more restrictive than the policy followed by major newspapers and broadcast services. The émigré editors complained bitterly; Nowak in particular argued that Mater's policies would rule out sensational stories like the Swiatlo revelations. But Smith backed Mater up.

In another change, RFE no longer supported "information bureaus" in cities such as Salzburg, Linz, and Graz, whose principal function was the interview of refugees. Instead, bureaus were limited to cities in which important news was made: Berlin, Bonn, London, Rome, Paris, Vienna, Brussels. They were staffed by professional newsmen, whose sole role was to report on the stories of relevance to the RFE audience.[30]

Another change occurred at the Free Europe Committee. Since the departure of C.D. Jackson in 1952, the FEC had had four chairmen, none of whom provided the steady leadership with which Jackson had been credited. The absence of strong leadership was particularly notable during the 1956 crises; the chairman, retired general Willis D. Crittenberger, a golfing buddy of President Eisenhower, was ineffective in pleading the radio's case, and failed to provide leadership in rebuilding staff morale in the wake of the Hungarian controversy.[31]

In 1961, Allen Dulles chose John Richardson Jr., a New York investment banker who had been involved in humanitarian projects in Eastern Europe, to succeed Archibald Alexander as FEC chairman. The choice was a good one, because Richardson, who was to serve seven years in the FEC post, enjoyed the respect of both the staff and the government officials with whom the FEC had regular dealings. During the latter years of Richardson's tenure, pointed questions were raised about America's Cold War institutions. That RFE emerged from this period relatively intact must in part be attributed to the maturity and professionalism the radio displayed during Richardson's tenure, as well as to the continued support it enjoyed from its audience.[32]

In July 1961, *Foreign Affairs* magazine published an essay that urged a new direction in American policy toward Eastern Europe. The article was of more than passing interest to RFE, since the authors were Zbigniew Brzezinski, then just emerging as a leading expert on the Communist world, and William E. Griffith, the former policy adviser in Munich. Brzezinski and Griffith advocated a policy of "peaceful engagement" toward the satellite countries, with the aim of stimulating greater diversity within the bloc, encouraging independence from Moscow, and, ultimately, creating a neutral belt of countries, not hostile to the Soviet Union, but enjoying freedom of choice in domestic affairs.[33]

The authors argued that America should adopt a dual approach to Eastern Europe, seeking improved relations with the Communist leadership where feasible, while expanding the range of contacts with the East European people. They explicitly warned against a policy that seemed to recognize the permanence of Communist rule and Soviet domination, and they described Western radio broadcasting as the most effective instrument for maintaining indirect contact with the East European people: "Given the Soviet violations of the Yalta and Potsdam agreements, the West has a right and obligation to maintain direct contact with the peoples involved. . . . In broadcasting to the captive peoples, the West is performing one of the roles of a free democratic opposition which the Soviet Union and the East European Communist parties deny to their peoples. We should not consider stopping these broadcasts in return for some Soviet concession." As prescription for American policy, the *Foreign Affairs* article made eminent sense, as the authors balanced realpolitik and moral values and never lost sight of the eventual goal of freedom for Eastern Europe. But despite its endorsement of foreign broadcasting, the article pointed to looming dangers for Cold War radio broadcasts, and for RFE most of all. For anti-Communists like Griffith and Brzezinski, the value of a home service radio for Eastern Europe was self-evident. But there was no guarantee that officials with their sophisticated understanding of the Communist world would be setting the tone for American policy. What would be RFE's fate if America sought détente with the Soviet Union and stability in Europe? Would RFE be seen as an obstacle to peace, a relic of the past, something to be bargained away in return for the suspension of Soviet broadcasts, which had a tiny Western audience and even less influence?

Such apprehensions, which were shared by some within the radio management, seemed vastly overdrawn in 1961; the new Democratic president, John F. Kennedy, had vowed to escalate the struggle against communism. His brother and chief adviser, Robert, was an enthusiastic supporter of RFE, and his administration announced its intention to engage the Soviet Union in an aggressive war of ideas all over the globe.

And despite the lessening of Cold War tensions and a growing East European cynicism over Western intentions, RFE clearly stood as the most popular foreign broadcast service in the Eastern bloc. A survey conducted in 1959–60 by several European research institutes for RFE found the station with far more regular listeners than either the BBC or the VOA. While the BBC was regarded as the most objective station, RFE was deemed the most influential. The VOA had suffered a notable decline in listenership since the Hungarian Revolution. The

Voice's management had instituted major restrictions on broadcasts to the Communist world; critical commentaries on internal affairs had been prohibited, and programming emphasized world news, American culture, and jazz music.[34]

Nevertheless, RFE was concerned about retaining its audience. East Europeans were suffering from political exhaustion. They had accepted the unwillingness of the West to support a liberation policy. While the Communists were less internally brutal, they were if anything more efficient in imposing order. The authorities also benefited from a gradual improvement in material conditions. In each Soviet bloc country, moreover, a nomenklatura class had emerged that, although by no means committed to Communist ideals, identified its well-being with the maintenance of party rule.

The Communist press also posed a stronger challenge. Stories that had once been ignored were now covered, albeit with a particular slant. Newspapers and radio covered the news more extensively and professionally; now it was RFE that was at times late in covering stories that had already appeared in Communist newspapers or radio. And there was the challenge of television, which had just been introduced in Eastern Europe. Some in RFE were sufficiently concerned by the new threat to propose that RFE explore the possibilities of international television broadcasts. Jan Nowak was among those most worried about television's impact; he suggested that if international broadcasts prove unfeasible, the United States government consider giving financial support to Free World countries that bordered the Soviet bloc so that they might strengthen their television signals and give the East European audience a greater access to non-Communist programs.[35]

The period between August 1961, when the Berlin Wall was erected, and 1968, with its upheavals in Poland and Czechoslovakia, was a time of relative calm in Eastern Europe. Political developments in the people's republics moved at a glacial and often obscure pace. There were no leadership purges, popular upheavals, or reform initiatives; organized dissent hardly existed. Nevertheless, the esprit de corps at RFE remained high, a tribute to the steady leadership of John Richardson and General Smith, but also a reflection of the strong sense of mission the exile journalists retained. Their commitment may have derived from the belief that in what some were calling a post–Cold War environment RFE remained the one institution committed to East European freedom. "Resolute, strong, and dangerous," is how Mieczyslaw Rakowski, an official Polish journalist, described the station in 1964.

One of the most important stories of the 1960s was the rise of Mieczyslaw Moczar and his group of "Partisans" in Poland. A leading party member, Moczar could count on a core of support from the security forces and from a group of army veterans, thus the name, Partisans. Moczar harbored ambitions to replace Gomulka as party chief and sought support by portraying himself as a populist nationalist who was prepared to purge the country of alien elements, namely Jews. In 1962, Jan Nowak was summoned to Rome for an urgent meeting with a high-ranking Polish Communist, who demanded anonymity and thus was dubbed Mr. X by Nowak. Mr. X told Nowak that the Moczar group posed a serious danger to Poland, given its ties to the police, the support it enjoyed from certain elements in the Soviet party, its anti-Semitism, and its access to security files. Mr. X claimed that the Partisans were readying a power grab, and begged Nowak to mount an anti-Moczar campaign in RFE broadcasts.

The RFE Polish section was divided over involvement in Communist Party factionalism; some reasoned that it was no concern of RFE whether one group of scoundrels prevailed over another group of scoundrels. Nowak, however, believed that it was important that Poland not fall under the control of the Moczar group, and in 1963 RFE began what was to be an eight-year campaign against the Partisans. Radio Free Europe here benefited from inside information provided by party and security sources. The campaign eventually found its way into the European press, and Nowak claims that he was at one point asked by the State Department to keep out of internal Polish politics. But the Polish section persevered, and many believe that RFE's campaign played an important role in thwarting Moczar's ambitions.[36]

Radio Free Europe also played an important role in its coverage of the 1967 Israeli-Arab War. With the exception of Romania, the Communist press gave the conflict thoroughly distorted coverage, placing blame for the conflict on Israel and the United States. Radio Free Europe provided factual coverage, emphasizing Arab battlefield defeats and the loss of Soviet prestige both in military action and in maneuvers at the United Nations. A professor who was visiting Warsaw during the conflict reported that every social gathering was interrupted as Poles listened to RFE war coverage; even party members acknowledged reliance on RFE for accurate news of the war.

Finally, RFE devoted hours upon hours of coverage to the Cuban Missile Crisis in 1962. It broadcast the complete text of President Kennedy's October 22 speech revealing the crisis, and stressed the themes of American determination, the risk of nuclear war, and the subservience of East European governments, most of which were giving various forms of aid to Cuba, to the dangerous policies of the Soviet Union. When the crisis finally ended and Khrushchev agreed to withdraw the missiles, RFE received, for perhaps the only time in its history, instructions that veteran staffers claim emanated directly from the White House. The guidance consisted of just two words: "Don't gloat."[37]

8

"The Iron Curtain Was Not Soundproof"

That American youth culture has never been given due credit for its contribution to communism's demise is not altogether surprising, given that many of those who wrote the Cold War's history were convinced that rock music exercises a pernicious influence on all societies, especially the Capitalist democracies of the West. Yet while historians may consider it regrettable, there is no doubt that for Eastern Europe's younger generation, rock music's anarchistic rhythms and message of individualism and personal freedom signaled a rejection of the entire fabric of state socialism, with its stodginess, its censorship and prohibitions, its limits on travel, its bogus proletarian culture, its elevation of political reliability over merit and imagination.[1]

It may come as something of a surprise that Radio Free Europe played a critical role in spreading American youth culture to Eastern Europe. The station's strength, after all, resided in the political shrewdness of its exiled editors, and not in their imaginativeness. The men who devised RFE's broadcast strategy were the antithesis of cultural radicals. They were firmly grounded in the history of the audience countries, the dialectics of Marxism-Leninism, the economics of peasant agriculture, the intricacies of the Sino-Soviet rivalry. Not that they dismissed culture as irrelevant to the RFE mission. Each broadcast service, in fact, offered several programs devoted to cultural themes. But these programs appealed to adults, particularly to those with an attachment to the music, art, and literature that had been repressed by the new Communist rulers, and their content was often highly political, in a very direct sense, with readings from patriotic (and often anti-Russian) poems or books from the proscribed list or performances of musical compositions by banned composers or as played by exiled musicians. One of the Czechoslovak desk's proudest moments occurred on March 15, 1956, when it broadcast a concert of the Vienna Philharmonic Orchestra conducted by the renowned Czech exile Rafael Kubelik. The program featured compositions by the two great Czech composers, Dvorák and Smetana, and the date was the seventeenth anniversary of the Nazi takeover of Czechoslovakia. As a final touch, the concert was held in the Berlin Sportpalast, the site of many of Hitler's harangues.[2]

The appeal of the Kubelik broadcast to all patriotic Czechs and Slovaks is obvious; just as obvious are the reasons why Prague radio, with its relentless hostility to West Germany, could not have broadcast this moving and historically important event. Similarly, Hungarians appreciated programs featuring recordings or live recitals of compositions by Béla Bartók, whose music was officially out of favor under the Stalinist regime of Mátyás Rákosi. Indeed, it required little strategic ingenuity to compete with communism for the audience with an appreciation of music. Thus in Hungary, the Stalin-Rákosi period saw an attempt to manufacture a proletarian culture in which favored composers and hack musicians wrote oratorios and songs in praise of the Red Army, Stalin, Rákosi, and the Five Year Plan. This was a time when Radio Budapest could promote a song with the memorable title "Produce More than the Machines."[3]

Radio Free Europe did not ignore popular music. Jazz was effectively banned in the Soviet Union and the satellites—it was variously described as "the music of putrescent capitalism" and "sexual perversion in sound." But young people wanted to hear jazz; by the late 1950s, Willis Conover, the jazz disc jockey for the Voice of America, had acquired a huge audience behind the Iron Curtain, and RFE jazz programs were popular as well. But a thaw set in after Stalin's death, and jazz was once again tolerated by the officials who set the Soviet Union's cultural standards. Faced with more demanding competition, RFE bolstered its jazz programming by hiring respected Western experts as commentators on the music or by rebroadcasting programs that originally appeared on radio stations in New York City. While the music was first-rate and the commentary knowledgeable, these programs had one drawback: their featured experts were Americans whose remarks had to be translated, thus depriving the broadcasts of the intimacy that only native speakers could convey.[4]

The pragmatism that communism displayed in its acceptance of jazz did not, however, extend to the newest American fashion: rock and roll. Rock music was forbidden on state radio throughout the bloc, rock recordings could be obtained only by those few who were allowed the rare trip to Austria or some other Western country, and rock musicians were vilified in the regime press of some satellites (less so in Hungary and Poland), much as jazz had been during Stalin's time.

How did he ever get in in Munich?

Radio Free Europe got into the disc jockey business almost by accident. Charles Andras, a hard working, nonsmoking, nondrinking, and culturally conservative Hungarian service editor, had been transferred from New York to Munich and named assistant editor of the service in the aftermath of the Hungarian Revolution debacle. Andras was given the formidable challenge of reviving staff morale and rebuilding RFE's credibility in Hungary.

One day Andras complained to a young colleague, Géza Ekecs, that his teenage daughter was driving him to distraction by neglecting her studies while constantly listening to rock music on the American Armed Forces Network. The two Hungarians were impressed by rock music's power over Western youth and soon talked over the possibility of launching a program to introduce rock to the young people of Hungary.[5]

Andras encountered resistance from some older Hungarian editors when the idea for a popular music program was broached. A few of the more hidebound veterans complained to the American managers, Ekecs recalls, insisting that a Hungarian radio station "should not play 'nigger' and Jewish music." But the American management approved the idea, perhaps out of desperation for new programs that could revive RFE's fortunes in Hungary. In 1958, then, Radio Free Europe inaugurated its first disc jockey program. It was called *Teenager Party* and aired once a week (with two repeats) for thirty-five minutes a program. Géza Ekecs was the disk jockey, a job he was to hold for the next three decades.

Ekecs was not an aficionado of rock music when his program was introduced; his success was due to a youthful, open mind and a unique ability to communicate his enthusiasms to the young people of Hungary. His early biography was not atypical for an RFE journalist: a few years spent as a newspaper reporter on a journal of social democratic leanings in Budapest, dismissal after the arrival of Communist dictatorship, prohibition from newspaper work because of "bourgeois origins," escape to the West, occasional work on an émigré publication in Paris, and finally, employment by RFE, beginning in December 1951, three months after the Hungarian service began broadcasts from Munich.

Ekecs was initially assigned to cultural affairs, with a particular focus on cinema. Ekecs was an ideal cultural reporter, for he combined an aesthetic astuteness with a genuine passion for the new trends in music and movie making. He was not as intensely political as some of his colleagues; he believed that it was less productive to natter at the Communists about the ruin they had brought to Hungarian culture than to talk about the remarkable new films produced in France and Italy, and gently contrast the exciting developments in free societies with the wasteland that communism had created in a country with a rich central European cultural tradition.

Ekecs likewise kept *Teenager Party* free of overt politics. It was enough, he decided, to play the music young people loved; his audience would be alienated by lectures contrasting Western freedom with Communist repression. Hungarian youngsters instinctively understood the superiority of democracy and told him so in the thousands of letters they addressed to him at RFE.

Ekecs borrowed the top-forty format popularized by American rock stations. He would occasionally play a Sinatra recording, or something by Doris Day or Dean Martin, but his core audience wanted rock, and that is what he gave it. He kept his listeners informed about the shifts in the *Billboard* magazine ratings, explaining which songs were moving up and which were heading down. He scanned American newspapers and magazines for features about the latest rock sensations, so that he could tell his listeners something about Little Richard's biography, explain why Jimi Hendrix used a particular guitar, or delve into the relationship between African American history and rhythm and blues.

For a few years *Teenager Party* enjoyed something of a corner on the Hungarian youth market. The regime refused to poison the minds of its youth with this most execrable example of capitalist degeneracy.

Other foreign stations did broadcast rock; indeed, popular music was the staple of Radio Luxembourg, which boasted an impressive listenership in Western Europe. But only Ekecs spoke to Hungarians in their language. As the program's popularity grew, its air time was increased, until a new music program, also featuring Ekecs, was added to the schedule; it was broadcast daily at about the time when Hungarian youngsters returned home from school. And as *Teenager Party* gained in listenership, the other RFE language sections added disc jockey programs, some of which became important fixtures in the station's program mixture.

Ekecs worked diligently to translate the often absurd titles into Hungarian and interpreted the American slang. He also copied the American practice of listener requests. Because writing to RFE from Hungary could be a perilous exercise, Ekecs instructed his listeners to substitute code names for their real names; he would then announce the code names on air when he played the songs they had requested. He also invited listeners to send in a series of requests, which he would then play uninterrupted to enable young Hungarians to tape record their favorite numbers. He even interviewed many of the most popular performers, including the Beatles and Louis Armstrong.

The popularity of *Teenager Party* infuriated Hungary's cultural bureaucrats. They especially resented the brazenness of the program's listeners. Members of the older generation had, of course, listened to RFE. But they did so discreetly, in the privacy of their homes, and remained circumspect in discussing their listening habits with outsiders. Now their children flaunted their Western radio preferences. They listened to RFE's subversive, criminal, broadcasts in trains, on the street, at the beach, in school. The authorities were also disturbed by what they dubbed RFE's "sandwich strategy," that is, placing the nonpolitical *Teenager Party* between two openly political broadcasts as a means of spreading anti-Communist ideas to a generation that, having no memory of life before state socialism, was expected to accept the system much more readily than their parents. One publication suggested that *Teenager Party* had been introduced at the personal behest of President Lyndon Johnson as part of a sinister strategy "to gain the confidence of politically immature strata."[6]

Radio Budapest capitulated in 1965 by introducing its own version of *Teenager Party*. The state radio borrowed heavily from Ekecs's example, even to the point of using his translated titles. The regime could not, however, resist the lure of ideology; it translated "Penny Lane," the Beatles' hit, as "Penny Lane: Street of the Poor." The station had to apologize after receiving a deluge of letters from listeners who, due to Ekecs's broadcasts, knew that Penny Lane was a street in the Liverpool business district.

Like most RFE journalists, Ekecs used a radio name to protect relatives back in Budapest. As Laszlo Cseke, he became a household name, a beloved personality whose voice was known throughout the country. Letters addressed to "Uncle Laci" poured in from all over Europe, from Hungarians living in Yugoslavia, Slovakia, and Romania, from Hungarians working in Moscow and East Germany, as well as from Hungary proper. Many letters were postmarked from Vienna, Belgrade, or West Germany; they had been given to travelers for mailing because some Hungarians still feared official reprisals for sending any sort of communication to the criminal radio in Munich. (Although the BBC would send Western records on request to the Soviet bloc, RFE did not, for fear of provoking official sanctions against listeners.) And some simply didn't trust the Hungarian postal service; correspondents complained of having mailed over thirty letters before Ekecs received just one.

Some wrote simply to express regard for their beloved Cseke; they called him their "best friend," a "vitalizing force," the person "who keeps us from falling into despair." Others reassured Ekecs that the Budapest rock program was but a pale imitation of *Teenager Party*. But many letters conveyed a political undertone. One inquired about prospects for political asylum; his class origins had disqualified him from dental studies, and he had been compelled to join the Communist youth organization to secure any kind of education. Another sent this plaintive message: "Uncle Laci, tell me please how I could get over to your country? There, perhaps, I could further develop my painting talent. I get no admission to school here, because I did not join the Red youth organization, because I did not want to become a Communist. Even if they killed me." Another lamented, "The Communists always plan in such a way which must lead to failure." But while Ekecs took understandable pride in the many listener tributes, he was less than pleased by a backhanded compliment from none other than János Kádár. When asked to comment on RFE broadcasts, the Communist leader replied laconically that the station "played good music," leaving Ekecs to fret over whether the American public would appreciate its tax dollars subsidizing an ostensibly political station known best for its popular music.[7]

Ekecs continued his music programs into the mid-eighties, despite his dislike of some of the rawer musical fads—heavy metal and rap, for example. As the rhythms grew darker and the lyrics degenerated into obscenity, Ekecs provided fewer commentaries and translations. He would, however, occasionally do battle over censorship by production supervisors. He once persuaded RFE to make an exception in its antiobscenity policy for a song by Country Joe and the Fish that included the word "fucking" in the refrain.

When communism collapsed, Ekecs returned a hero to the country he had left forty years earlier. The response overwhelmed him: "In cabs, people recognized my voice; in shops they recognized my voice." Such was his popularity that Ekecs was invited to revive *Teenager Party* on a private radio station in Budapest after RFE eliminated the Hungarian broadcasting service in 1993. Now Ekecs travels to Budapest every two weeks to tape his programs, which run on Sunday afternoons.

He remains a passionate defender of popular culture's liberating qualities and argues that American rock music undermined the Communist system as surely as did the intellectual arguments of anti-Communists. Naturally enough, he has a far more benign view of rock's social impact than do many of his RFE colleagues, even those who may have welcomed rock's subversion of state socialism: "The message of rock is, 'Please don't accept everything the older people say.' Remember, it was the younger Hungarians who changed the system; the older people were the Bolsheviks. In the end, the Iron Curtain was not soundproof."

9

August 21, 1968

pos. in reform commun / = more "nuanced" view of / RFE in gen'l ...

By 1968 the changes that were introduced in the wake of the Hungarian Revolution had transformed Radio Free Europe's coverage of the Communist world. This was particularly true of the station's positive attitude toward the controversial phenomenon of reform communism. Whatever the predisposition of the individual broadcaster, some of whom found the very notion of reform communism difficult to swallow, the station's official policy was to give a degree of credit to regimes that instituted policies of incremental change or that seemed to inch away from lockstep endorsement of Moscow's international stance.

Radio Free Europe remained, of course, a powerful anti-Soviet voice. Every policy, every statistic, every claim of a successful harvest or overfulfillment of the plan, was placed under microscopic scrutiny. Furthermore, Radio Free Europe gave extensive coverage to the first stirrings of intellectual dissent in the bloc; if disaffected party members issued an appeal for democracy in Poland, Radio Free Europe ensured that, among others, disaffected party members in Czechoslovakia and Hungary were immediately informed of the most recent developments. And while a measure of control over broadcast content had been instituted, prebroadcast censorship was still rejected, and RFE remained by far the most freewheeling of the major international broadcast services.

In accepting the potential utility of reform communism, RFE reflected the official policy of the American government. Reform communism, however, came in many varieties, and each presented a special problem for RFE editors. By the late sixties, it was clear that János Kádár was leading Hungary in a cautiously reformist direction; nevertheless, many Hungarians still despised Kádár for his betrayal of the revolution and his role in Imre Nagy's execution. In Romania, a new party leader, Nicolae Ceausescu, gained immediate popularity with Western diplomats for his country's shift toward a foreign policy stance that appeared to be independent of Moscow. To RFE's Romanian audience, however, Ceausescu's international maneuvering was less important than his authoritarian internal policies and the ominous early signs of a developing personality cult. And in Poland, the time had long passed since Gomulka was seen as a reformer; the only argument supporting his continued rule was the spectre of Moczar as the likely alternative.

To those responsible for the formulation of RFE's broadcast strategy, the argument for reformism was sustainable only if initial modest change was seen to be leading to the ultimate goals of freedom and independence. No one quite knew how the process of change would transform state socialism into something approaching social democracy, although it was assumed that the reform impulse would originate within the party, not from forces outside the system. The superiority of Western democracy was, however, self-evident, given the growing prosperity in Western Europe, especially in Germany. After the Hungarian Revolution, the credibility of Communist leaders depended increasingly on their ability to satisfy consumer needs, but it was abundantly clear that communism could not compete with the regulated market systems of Capitalist Europe without a significant economic reorientation. Thus RFE devoted program after program to the ruminations of economic planners whose ideas challenged the orthodoxies of the Soviet model. In practice, "market socialism" proved only marginally more effective than the Stalinist system of economic organization. But reformism's economic consequences were a secondary consideration to RFE, which was predominantly concerned with the impact of economic change on the ability of the Communist state to maintain strict political control.

As events developed, Czechoslovakia was to be the proving grounds for the most serious attempt at reform communism ever undertaken. Although widely considered as the most Westernized country in the Soviet bloc, Czechoslovakia had suffered under the rule of a series of dogmatic hard-liners, the latest of whom, Antonín Novotný, had retained power since the fifties through a strategy that combined the neutralization of potential domestic rivals with the reliable support of the Kremlin leadership. By 1968, however, opposition to Novotný's uninspiring leadership had gathered force, and at a party Congress in early January, Novotný was removed as Communist chief and replaced by a little-known figure, Alexander Dubček.

The changes in party leadership were to trigger one of the most astonishing chapters in the annals of communism. Ultimately, the Prague Spring was to reveal not the potential of reform, but communism's utter inability to withstand real change. When the Prague experiment was finally crushed by a Warsaw Pact invasion, it was not simply the Czechoslovak reforms that were destroyed, but the then prevalent idea that communism was moving inexorably in a liberal direction. In January 1968, however, no one was predicting that the Dubček leadership was inclined toward radical change. To much of the world, it seemed as if one thoroughly mediocre leader was being replaced by a colorless party bureaucrat who was not likely to preside over major liberalization and would certainly not pose a challenge to Moscow's hegemonic authority.

This, in any event, was RFE's cautious response to the results of the party congress. Still, early commentaries were calculated not to emphasize the possible negatives. They stressed Dubček's roots in Slovakia and interpreted his election as largely due to the demands of Slovak Communists (Dubček was the first Slovak elected party leader) for an equal share in political power. An RFE policy document described him as an undynamic career party man. "We are probably going to witness a period of collective and cautious leadership in which it could turn out that Dubček is a transitional figure," the memo observed. "The new regime will very likely go to some lengths . . . to avoid startling policy changes of any kind. It will be important not to offend important sensitivities either inside or outside the country. Hence, in spite of the shakeup, we do not foresee a dramatic reorientation of major policies."[1]

Given the modest expectations for the new leadership, it is hardly surprising that RFE broadcasts did not greet Dubček's elevation with unalloyed enthusiasm. Early commentaries stressed the Slovak factor, the fact that Dubček represented a generation untainted by direct participation in Stalinist excesses, and the new leadership's apparent lack of the older generation's anti-German attitudes. The station's analysts also believed that Dubček's having been elected by the entire central committee, instead of simply installed by a tiny clique, was an encouraging sign. Finally, RFE was convinced that after the stagnant years of Novotný, the new leadership deserved to be treated with cautious optimism until it proved itself unworthy of respect.

Within two months, it became clear that the Dubček group was not only prepared to advance bold plans for change but also willing to tolerate radical ideas from outside the party. Extensive democratic reforms were instituted, including near freedom of speech and press, the rehabilitation of the victims of political persecution, the restoration of the rule of law and the independence of the judiciary, a fair sharing of power among Czechs and Slovaks in a new federal state, and the acceleration of previously promised and far-reaching economic reforms. Political debate was freewheeling; there was practically no subject that was regarded as taboo, including the country's loyalty to the Socialist camp. To be sure, in public Dubček and the rest of the leadership continued to swear total loyalty to its East bloc allies. At the same time, they held to a reform course and refused to crack down on those who were impertinent enough to raise uncomfortable questions about Czechoslovakia's international commitments.

This was an exhilarating time for Czechs and Slovaks. The prevailing mood is vividly and, in light of subsequent events, tragically, captured in a letter written by a Czech intellectual and sent to Jiří Horák, a Czech exile academic who worked as a free-lance commentator for RFE: "I don't know what to do first: to read newspapers, watch tv, or listen to the radio. Panel discussions, interviews, and reports are so interesting we can't get enough of them. You probably can't imagine what this means to us. We are now living in a new world. To hear, after so many years, an open criticism and candid words. . . . We breathe better nowadays, people are shedding their passivity and indifference. . . . I envy our little Helene [their thirteen-year-old daughter]; her future looks better than ours did twenty years ago."[2] The media that so thoroughly fascinated the author of this letter, and millions of his countrymen, was Czechoslovak media, not, by and large, Radio Free Europe. For the first time since it initiated broadcasts in 1950, RFE was confronted by competition from a truly free press, a press committed to asking all the many forbidden questions that had accumulated during two decades of reactionary Communist rule. Radio Free Europe had been asking the right questions for years, but RFE was located in Munich and New York, not Prague. To even suggest assigning journalists to cover Czechoslovak developments directly from Prague would have been regarded by Moscow as an act of brazen provocation. Thus RFE continued to cover the fast-moving events secondhand, leaving the station at a real competitive disadvantage.[3]

Compounding RFE's dilemma was a growing fear that the Prague reformers were inviting catastrophe by their aggressive challenges to the Kremlin's authority. Ralph Walter, who had recently been appointed the station's director, had served on the policy staff during the Hungarian Revolution and was determined that RFE would not repeat the mistakes of 1956. During the spring, RFE went on a crisis footing over the prospect of two potentially explosive challenges to the East European status quo. Whereas in Czechoslovakia, the party had opened the door to a challenge to Communist authority, in Poland student demonstrators posed a threat to the already shaky Gomulka regime. No dreamy reformer, Gomulka resorted to force in dealing with his adversaries, and order was restored, for the time being.[4]

To some degree, the Prague Spring stood as a vindication of RFE's endorsement of reform communism adopted after the Hungarian Revolution. The 1965 Czechoslovakia country paper—a document that set forth the station's broadcast strategy—emphasized that while the eventual objective was a total transformation to democracy, the growth of reform sentiment within the party represented the most effective available means of moving in that direction. The document stressed the importance of broadcasts directed to party functionaries, and suggested a policy of encouraging revisionist tendencies within party ranks and the stimulation of national consciousness among party members as well as the general population. Moreover, the document encouraged a policy of advocating socioeconomic models different from American-style capitalism, laying particular emphasis on European social democracy as an alternative to the Communist brand of state socialism. While endorsing a continuation of RFE's traditional support of a unitary Czechoslovak state, the guideline proposed an emphasis on a new system that guaranteed a fair division of power for Czechs and Slovaks in a federal state. The document also cautioned against any suggestion that the West might intervene militarily in the event of invasion by the Soviet Union.[5]

Three years after its adoption as official broadcast policy, this document seemed remarkably prescient. But while RFE was enthusiastic in its embrace of the Prague Spring, the enthusiasm was tinged with caution. Once it was clear that the Prague reformers were intent on instituting serious changes, including guarantees of freedom of expression, Radio Free Europe refrained from exhortations to push matters even further. Instead, RFE took on a role that was, in certain respects, quite modest. A guidance issued in late February, entitled "The Winds of Change in Czechoslovakia," indicated that RFE intended to function as a national communications center for the reform forces by amplifying what was being said in a particular region or by a particular interest group or by forces outside Czechoslovakia.

This was relatively tame stuff, given the direct challenges to both the Communist system and the country's participation in the Warsaw Pact, which were being publicly aired in Prague itself. "Prague Radio said things which Radio Free Europe didn't dare broadcast," recalled Karel Jezdinský, a reporter for Czechoslovak radio who later left Czechoslovakia and joined the RFE staff after the invasion. Jezdinský himself produced a program for Prague Radio on the jamming of foreign stations that included an interview with the official who administered the jamming operation.[6] In-depth reporting of this sort was beyond the capacity of RFE; it was, on the other hand, normal fare for the Czechoslovak media in the months before the invasion.

Not surprisingly, RFE's listenership declined, giving rise to rumors, apparently unwarranted, that plans were being made to shut down broadcasts to Czechoslovakia. But while RFE strategists were constantly debating how best to reach the Czechoslovak audience during this period of political upheaval, the policy of broadcast caution was maintained throughout the period. "We heeded the lessons of the Hungarian Revolution," said Walter. "We were cautious, because we were conscious of the possibility of an invasion. We were more cautious than Czechoslovak journalists were, because we did not want to be out in front of people who, we feared, were out in front of what the situation would allow. We felt that we had to be more responsible than the people who were enjoying this period of liberation."[7]

Walter's apprehension at the possibility of an invasion was, in fact, a minority view among the chief editors and policy advisers. Walter recalls that following a sharply worded note from the Warsaw Pact leaders to Dubček in July, he was almost alone in predicting that an intervention was in the offing unless the government backed off from some of the more confrontational policies. Only István Bede, the chief editor of the Hungarian desk, was in agreement. As Karl Reyman, a key member of the policy staff, remembers the period, "We really didn't believe that the Soviets would invade, and this affected our judgment. President Johnson had just met with Kosygin, and the 'spirit of Glassboro' (their meeting was held in Glassboro, New Jersey) had been declared, signaling progress toward détente between the United States and the Soviet Union. We did not believe that Brezhnev would risk the new relationship with such a blatant act of aggression. We were convinced there would be no invasion, right up to the last minute."[8]

Nevertheless, Ralph Walter began to prepare for the worst, determined that RFE should not be caught by surprise if an invasion should materialize. He also was intent on ensuring that coverage of an invasion would not be subject to the emotional levels that had negatively affected broadcasting during the Hungarian Revolution. In mid-July he established contingency plans for centralized control of programming in the event of military intervention. Walter wrote in a memo that broadcast tone would be monitored "as part of an effort to keep down excitability in any form."[9]

Walter was also concerned about the attitude of the American government toward the disturbing rumblings from Moscow. In the past, RFE could usually depend on reliable sources from within the government to provide an accurate assessment of Washington's thinking on the controversial issue of the day. As momentum toward an invasion gathered force, however, Walter was given conflicting signals: either Washington had quietly warned Moscow that an invasion would damage the developing détente relationship, or the Johnson administration had decided to take a hands-off stance in the event of intervention, with little more than a pro forma condemnation. A few weeks before the invasion, he received a message indicating that "as regards U.S.-Soviet relations and progress towards disarmament and other things, the State Department feels that the Czechoslovak crisis should not cancel out things that have been in the works for years." The prediction that the United States was preparing a relatively mild response to Soviet military action was beginning to creep into the reports of the savvier diplomatic correspondents as well, leaving RFE with the dilemma of covering American policy both accurately and responsibly. While RFE was certainly not about to report that America was preparing to impose economic or diplomatic sanctions, much less a military response, it also did not want to bolster Soviet confidence by reporting that the United States had decided to eschew a strong response in the name of détente. In the end Walter issued guidelines forbidding the broadcast of analyses that speculated that the administration had reached a decision to allow the Soviets freedom of action within their sphere of interest.[10]

With the arrival of August came an intensification of invasion rumors. Radio Free Europe's coverage stressed international solidarity with beleaguered Czechoslovakia, with a special focus on sympathetic quotes from Communists in Italy, China, and elsewhere, along with strong declarations of support from the non-Communist European Left. The broadcasts cast both Yugoslavia and Romania in a favorable light for their statements on behalf of the right of sovereign states to chart their own course of Socialist development. The coverage of America emphasized the debatable point (to put it mildly) that the administration's soft words were enabling the Kremlin to follow a moderate, non-interventionist path.

By mid-August, RFE was expressing outright concern over the confrontational steps that the Dubček government had taken or was tolerating. In a policy guidance issued on August 16, less than one week before the invasion, RFE was counseling the government to make concessions to the critics of their internal reform among more orthodox minded Warsaw Pact members to ensure breathing space for the reform process. The guidance, however, reflected RFE's internal agony, for while urging prudence on the Czechoslovaks, it also noted that "any attempt to restrain the hard won liberties or define the limits of democratization . . . raises the question of how much internal discipline is consistent with liberal reform." The Dubček government was thus advised to weigh "what particular gestures toward [Warsaw] Pact allies are justified and which threaten the national unity which was a response to pressure from those allies."

Within a few days, RFE actually concluded that intervention pressure had eased. A policy evaluation asserted that the Czechoslovaks had "won a victory in maintaining the integrity of key sections of their reforms," while the Soviets were thought to have abandoned a policy of immediate pressure in favor of tactics to contain the Prague disease over the long term. In the future, the evaluation went on, it would be increasingly difficult for the Kremlin to impose its will on foreign Communist parties. There was a prediction that an informal coalition of Communist mavericks—Tito, Ceausescu, Dubček—might undermine Soviet hegemony in Eastern Europe, and, finally, a suggestion that Moscow might actually reap benefits from its toleration of the Prague experiments "if it accepts the limitations which modern political conditions place on superpowers."

This guidance was issued during the day of August 20. A few hours later, just before midnight, Red Army units, joined by troops from Poland, Hungary, and East Germany, crossed the Czechoslovak border. Once again, a challenge to Soviet authority was to be crushed by a massive show of military force.

On this occasion, however, there would be no question of RFE complicity in the tragedy. Immediately upon receiving news of the invasion, Walter imposed sweeping and, for RFE, unprecedented controls over the broadcast content of the Czechoslovak service. He or another member of his staff scrutinized every Czechoslovak script relating to the events in Prague, right down to the news items adapted from the wire services. This policy was accepted with good grace by the exile broadcasters and carried forward without serious dispute. But if the process of script analysis meant that news coverage would be delayed, and thus somewhat less timely, that was a price Walter was willing to pay in order to ensure accurate and responsible coverage. Karl Reyman, a chief policy aide during the invasion period, recalls a labored debate over how to characterize a declaration by President Johnson cautioning the Soviets not to "unleash the dogs of war." The wire service dispatch described Johnson's statement as a "warning"; Walter, however, thought the term too strong and, furthermore, believed that to report to an East European audience that the American president had issued a "warning" to the Kremlin might be construed as a threat of military response. Walter, of course, was proved right by the course of events; Johnson's words were meant as more of an admonition and certainly did not amount to any kind of threat. And while Walter did permit some information from clandestine, freedom radio stations in occupied Czechoslovakia to be broadcast over RFE, he absolutely forbade RFE's repeating the calls for Czechoslovak neutrality, which the underground stations and various groups were issuing in the wake of the invasion. "I more and more fear that Czechoslovakia is headed for disaster," Walter wrote in an August 23 memo in which he theorized that the Soviets were cynically allowing the underground stations to remain on the air "in the near certainty that their demands will become more and more extreme" and thus provide the Kremlin with an excuse "to put finish to the whole business with as much violence as may be necessary."[11]

Although forced to rely on the Western press for most of its invasion coverage material, RFE was uniquely equipped to interpret one of the most critical aspects of the crisis—the invasion's international ramifications, especially within what remained of the world Communist movement. As it turned out, the invasion's international implications were a major part of the story. Few Communist parties outside the Warsaw Pact supported the Soviets, and some parties were sharp in their denunciation of the action. The invasion also provoked a mood of anti-Sovietism among non-Communist leftists in Europe and the nonaligned bloc. That "progressive" world opinion had, however briefly, interrupted its perpetual crusade against American imperialism to express its anger at the Soviets may have been of little solace to the beleaguered Czechoslovaks. Likewise, Czechoslovaks may not have been overly moved by another RFE theme—that the Dubcek leadership had throughout the Prague Spring affirmed its loyalty to the Soviet camp and repeatedly denied any desire to subvert the Communist system. While technically accurate, this line of argument fudged the essential truth of the reforms, which is that they were leading Czechoslovakia almost inevitably, and rather quickly, to social democracy, something that most Czechoslovaks strongly supported.

On balance, however, RFE's performance during the crisis was an impressive combination of comprehensive news reporting, wise if cautious commentary, and expert analysis. In addition, many listeners appreciated the station's appeals for moderation and calm, such as was contained in a broadcast that urged Czechoslovak youth "not to risk too much, not to provoke the occupiers, and not to demonstrate heroism." A particularly important highlight was the intense coverage devoted to Foreign Minister Jiri Hajek's moving protest against Soviet aggression to the United Nations.[12]

With an independent press muffled, Radio Free Europe's listenership rose dramatically after the invasion; a poll taken by the Czechoslovak Academy of Science in the spring of 1969, and apparently suppressed by the normalization regime of Gustáv Husák, gave RFE a rating only slightly below that of Radio Prague and Radio Bratislava, an impressive figure given the difficulty of reception under jamming conditions. At least part of RFE's enhanced appeal can be traced to the addition of several of Radio Prague's most respected political commentators, such as Sláva Volný and Karel Jezdinský. No less a figure than Gustáv Husák gave testimony to RFE's influence, referring on two occasions to the station's baleful role in the course of his inaugural speech as party first secretary. Attacking "anti-socialist" forces inside the country, he said, "If one monitors Radio Free Europe one hears the same sort of talk and the same phraseology used by some of our editors."[13]

And again, referring to fears that Czechoslovakia might return to a Novotný-type regime, Husák declared, "We know how cunningly Radio Free Europe plays this tune, with Sláva Volný and similar heroes . . . spreading rumors about the horrible things which might happen. . . . The people who are doing most of this shouting are those who a few years ago were talking in an entirely different way. Now they are such torchbearers of freedom as the world has never seen before. Some of them went abroad, and now then want to enlighten fourteen million people about democracy and independence."[14]

Despite their superficial defiance, Husák's words betrayed the leadership's insecurity. Clearly, RFE was regarded as a powerful adversary, made even more formidable by the addition of journalists who represented the "generation of '68" and were still regarded back home as heroes of the failed experiment in liberal reform. Radio Free Europe's commitment to a broadcast strategy that stressed nonviolence and caution did not change. On the first anniversary of the invasion, a commentator urged his listeners to eschew violence. "In August last year our people refused to accept the standards of those who invaded our country," he observed. "They have no reason to sink to their level today. . . . Violence is not the Czechoslovak method."

10

From Liberation to Liberty

On March 1, 1953, a new international broadcasting station, Radio Liberation from Bolshevism (RL), inaugurated programming to the peoples of the Soviet Union. According to the recollections of RL veterans, Boris Shub, a Russian American intellectual who was a guiding spirit in the station's early years, had proposed that broadcasts include, over the ticking sound of a metronome, the announcement "The era of Stalin is coming to the end, the era of Stalin is coming to the end." The idea was rejected on the grounds that Stalin, then seventy-three years old, might rule for many years to come.[1] In fact, Stalin was to rule for just five more days, his reign of terror coming to a close with his death on March 5.

Conceived as a weapon of psychological warfare during the darkest days of the anti-Stalin struggle, Radio Liberation—the original name for Radio Liberty—confronted a new political situation almost immediately. Nor was the challenge of crafting a message for the post-Stalin era the station's most immediate problem. Even before RL began its broadcasting schedule, internal strife had caused serious divisions within the organization that sponsored the station, the American Committee for Liberation from Bolshevism, generally known as Amcomlib. Amcomlib had set itself the goal of forging unity among the more important of the Soviet exile organizations, Russian and non-Russian alike. What emerged from this undertaking was a series of acrimonious faction fights, pitting Russian exiles against other Russian exiles,

Russian exiles against non-Russian exiles, and Russians and non-Russians alike against Amcomlib's American management.

To these problems were added several of a more technical nature. There was the question of the number of shortwave radio receivers in the Soviet Union. The Free Europe Committee had conducted surveys of East European countries that indicated that there were a sufficient number of shortwave receivers to guarantee a substantial audience for Radio Free Europe broadcasts. No such survey was possible in the Soviet Union. Moreover, the distances involved in transmitting programs from Munich, where RL was located, to the major Soviet cities was much more substantial than transmitting programs from Germany to Prague, Warsaw, or Budapest. To reach a mass audience in Moscow, Leningrad, or Kiev would require much more powerful transmitting facilities than the antiquated equipment with which RL began operations.

There was also the problem of finding competent broadcasters. Soviet emigration offered nothing to match the core of exiled East European writers and editors that made up the nucleus of the RFE staff in the early years. Indeed, the very phrase "Soviet journalist" was something of an oxymoron, since all vestiges of an independent press had been eliminated with the coming to power of the Communists in 1917.

Finally, Radio Liberation needed an overarching broadcast theme, or message. For Radio Free Europe, the political theme was obvious: freedom from communism and liberation from Soviet (or, as some preferred, Russian) imperialism. Radio Liberation's audience, however, was primarily Russian. Communism had not been imposed on Russia by outsiders; it was a home-grown affair. Unlike Eastern Europe, where evidence of unrest was manifest, there was little sign that the Soviet Union faced significant popular opposition to the system; by 1953 the postwar unrest that had flared periodically in the Baltic republics and Ukraine had been suppressed. Russians may have detested certain aspects of the Communist system, but they also identified Stalin with victory over Hitler and with a modest improvement in living standards. Russians were isolated from the outside world and had no experience of free institutions or Capitalist economics. They were not likely to respond favorably to an appeal based on the evil nature of their leaders, the superiority of the American economy, or to lectures about the immorality of imperial aggression against smaller neighbors.

Within a few months after the opening broadcast, the name Radio Liberation from Bolshevism was shortened to Radio Liberation. In 1959 it would be changed again, to Radio Liberty, a name symbolizing the softening of the station's message and tone. Not only did the political line undergo a process of refinement but the other problems that plagued the station in its first months were resolved as well. By the 1970s, Radio Liberty ranked as one of the most influential international broadcast stations in the world. It boasted an impressive staff of exile writers and intellectuals, the most powerful transmitting facilities available, and a large audience of Soviet listeners.

Radio Liberty emerged from the same Cold War environment that produced Radio Free Europe. Especially after the Soviet Union gave proof of its atomic weapons capacity, American officials thought it essential to develop strategies to counter Soviet aggression through nonmilitary methods. George Kennan, C.D. Jackson, Allen Dulles, Frank Wisner—the same men who had been responsible for Radio Free Europe—favored a similar instrument of political warfare targeted at the Soviet Union itself.[2]

The American Committee for Liberation from Bolshevism began operations in 1950 and was officially incorporated in January 1951.[3] Amcomlib did not begin operations with the fanfare and high visibility that had marked the launching of the Free Europe Committee. There were no public campaigns or crusades on Amcomlib's behalf. It did not send leading exiles on public speaking tours, nor did its board of directors consist of a blue-ribbon roster of eminent leaders from business, labor, the military, the press, and the entertainment world. Amcomlib's funds were provided exclusively by the American government through the budget of the Central Intelligence Agency. To questions about its source of revenue, Amcomlib officials would say that the money was donated by wealthy individuals who were interested in the organization's mission. No names were mentioned, and reporters did not press the matter further.[4]

The man responsible for assembling Amcomlib's board of directors was Franklin A. Lindsay, an aide to Frank Wisner at the Office of Policy Coordination. Whereas board members for the Free Europe Committee were selected for their wealth, public visibility, and influence in Washington, the principal criterion for membership on Amcomlib's board was a familiarity with conditions in the Soviet Union.

The first chairman was Eugene Lyons, a *Reader's Digest* editor and former correspondent in Moscow who, having become disillusioned with the Soviet system, had written *The Red Decade,* a classic study of Communist influence in American culture. Another journalist with Moscow experience, William H. Chamberlin, also served on the board, as did William Y. Elliott of the Harvard faculty; William L. White, publisher of the *Emporia Gazette* in Kansas and son of William Allen White; and Allen Grover, a vice president at Time, Inc. and assistant to Henry Luce.[5]

The decision to maintain a low public profile was driven by several factors. First, the exiles Amcomlib was recruiting were of a different caliber from those hired by Radio Free Europe. They had not held high positions in government, culture, or the press. Most did not speak English. They had no history of leadership in democratic political parties or opposition movements. Some had questionable political histories, having collaborated with Nazi Germany while engaged in anti-Soviet activities during wartime. Furthermore, Amcomlib's leaders were convinced that a radio station sponsored by émigrés would carry more credibility with a Soviet audience than one operated by a committee of Americans, and therefore made it a matter of policy to minimize the relationship between the parent organization and Radio Liberty. Finally, there is evidence that the CIA was unhappy with the independent-mindedness of the Free Europe Committee board and intended to exercise a stronger degree of control over Amcomlib.[6]

In announcing its formation, Amcomlib was blunt about its purpose: to provide assistance to anti-Communist exiles who were working for the overthrow of the Soviet regime. How this was to be accomplished was not clear, although Amcomlib from the outset planned to establish a radio station to broadcast propaganda to the Soviet Union. Beyond radio broadcasts and the publication of anti-Soviet literature, the committee's principal objective was to forge a unified political center out of the politically, linguistically, and ethnically divided Soviet exile community.[7]

At the time of Amcomlib's founding, several hundred thousand exiles still languished in displaced persons (DP) camps throughout Europe. The number of Soviets who had fled their country in the wake of the retreating German army had been much larger. But Stalin had demanded the return of Soviet exiles, and in a shameful episode, the Allies had complied, sending thousands of exiles to a term in the

Gulag or death by firing squad. By the late forties the forced repatriations had ended. But the remaining exiles, some 260,000 in 1947, existed in dreadful conditions in the DP camps. They were unable to work, build homes, or establish any semblance of a community life.[8]

A common feature among the postwar exiles was their hatred of communism or, in the case of the non-Russian nationalities, Russian domination. Some were essentially nonpolitical but nevertheless fled because of the persecution of religion, mistreatment of the peasantry, cultural repression, or simply because of the everyday brutality of the Stalinist system. Others left because they had been active in anti-Soviet causes. Some were Balts, Ukrainians, Belorussians, or Azeris who had participated in movements for national independence. Others had been part of the army organized by Gen. Andrei Vlasov, a Red Army officer who, after having been taken captive by the Germans, organized a unit of Soviet prisoners of war who fought the Red Army during the latter stages of the conflict. Vlasov was captured by the Soviets and executed, but many of his followers managed to escape repatriation and remained in Germany.

Amcomlib had ambitious plans for the émigrés. In its founding declaration, the committee expressed its intention to "encourage the establishment . . . by the refugees from every part of the Soviet Union of a central organization embracing all democratic elements which will give them effective and coordinated leadership and will be a worldwide symbol of the resistance of the peoples of Russia to the tyrannical Soviet regime."[9]

As experienced observers of Soviet politics, the leaders of Amcomlib understood that factionalism was rife among the exiles. The Russians alone were divided over political ideology, personal rivalries, and differences between the generation that left Russia after the revolution and the generation that left after the war. Compounding the problem was the shrewd work of Soviet intelligence, which had penetrated every important exile group and was promoting, with some effectiveness, a campaign to encourage the exiles to return to the motherland. The Americans, however, were undaunted by the formidable obstacles against exile unity. And, of course, the Americans had considerable leverage in negotiations with exile organizations. There was the planned radio station, which according to the initial conception was to be run by a coordinating center of the unified exile groups. In addition, Amcomlib was handing out regular stipends to those exile organizations that were cooperating with the unity effort, not unimportant given the impoverished condition of the émigré community.[10]

In the fall of 1950, Amcomlib dispatched Spencer Williams to serve as its European representative with the assignment of beginning the exile unification process. Williams was soon replaced by Isaac Don Levine, a Russian-born intellectual who had written a number of books about the Soviet Union and was known as an ardent anti-Communist.

Amcomlib did record some early achievements. The radio station was operational in 1953. The committee was also able to project its activities into the Middle East by sending two exiles from the Soviet Union's Muslim republics to the annual *haj,* or pilgrimage, in Mecca. According to a committee report, the two—a Tatar and a Turkestani— "were singularly successful in countering the propaganda efforts of pilgrims who had been sent by the Soviet government to Mecca." The committee also dispatched exile representatives—Muslims and Kalmyks—to the 1955 conference of the nonaligned nations in Bandung, Indonesia, where the Kalmyks told the delegates of Stalin's liquidation of the only Buddhist group in the Soviet Union. To explore the prospects for establishing a permanent presence in the Middle East, an Amcomlib official visited Turkey, where he discussed the feasibility of various anti-Communist projects.[11]

But the major project of creating a unified center of émigré activism proved a drawn-out, frustrating failure. To begin with, Russians and non-Russians were deeply divided over the future of a post-Communist Soviet Union. Russians favored the overthrow of communism but opposed the breakup of the union. The non-Russians wanted to both destroy Communism and win freedom from Russian domination for their people. The differences between Russians and the other nationalities was serious enough to cause Amcomlib to undergo two name changes in its early years, from the American Committee for Freedom for the Peoples of the USSR to the American Committee for the Liberation of the Peoples of Russia to, finally, the American Committee for Liberation from Bolshevism. In the first instance, Russians objected to the phrase "Peoples of the USSR"; in the second, the non-Russians regarded "Peoples of Russia" as an insult. The result was the use of the somewhat archaic-sounding "Liberation from Bolshevism" as a compromise.[12]

Then there were divisions among various Russian factions over ideology, tactics, and personalities. Of the four principal Russian émigré groups, the best organized—and most controversial—was the National Labor Union, or NTS. Founded during the 1930s, the NTS advocated an ideology called solidarism, which called for the establishment in Russia of a corporate state modeled after Mussolini's Italy or Portugal under Salazar. The NTS had branches throughout Europe at the beginning of World War II; after the Germans declared war on the USSR, the NTS was permitted to set up headquarters in Berlin and preach its doctrine to prisoners of war, conscript laborers, and the civilian population in parts of the Soviet Union under German control. After the war, the NTS made a serious effort to spread its ideas among the new wave of émigrés by circulating propaganda publications and by building schools and churches.

A second major organization, comprised of followers of General Vlasov, was the Union of Struggle for the Liberation of the Peoples of Russia (SBONR). Two other organizations had their headquarters outside Europe: the League of Struggle for the People's Freedom and a group led by Alexander Kerensky, the exiled former prime minister and Menshevik leader.[13]

The involvement of Kerensky proved a mixed blessing. He was the only émigré with an international reputation. He was also self-important, stubborn, and publicity hungry. Whereas Amcomlib preferred a low-key approach while unification was under negotiation, Kerensky sought out the press. The result was a series of embarrassing headlines in European newspapers. "Kerensky's Strange Secret Conference—What is the Liquidator of Russia Doing in Germany," proclaimed the headline of a Frankfurt newspaper, while the London *Economist* accused Amcomlib of having lifted the old Menshevik "from the dustbin of history."[14]

And while Kerensky was not as zealously nationalistic as the followers of the NTS, he was totally opposed to cooperation with non-Russians who favored separation from the Soviet Union. In January 1953, Kerensky met with Walter Bedell Smith, then director of the CIA, and Allen Dulles, who would soon take over direction of the intelligence agency, to express his concerns about the participation of certain Ukrainian and other nationality organizations that were committed to independent nationhood. Smith and Dulles assured him that Amcomlib would exclude the groups to which he objected.[15]

Initially, Amcomlib had offered the émigrés a major role in policy making for Radio Liberation. At a 1952 conference in the German city of Starnberg, Isaac Don Levine told the assembled exiles that the new radio station "must be built on the basis of one principle: a radio from the emigration, for the people behind the Iron Curtain. . . . We will give you an excellent and powerful radio station . . . if the emigration will meet us half-way." Subsequently, the exiles established a radio commission, consisting of Russians, non-Russian nationalities, and Americans, to set policy for the station and appoint the chief editors of the language services.[16] Unfortunately, the exile organizations did not name their most talented people to the radio commission, and with the exception of several national representatives who had worked for German shortwave propaganda during the war, none of the commission members had experience in broadcasting.

To compound Radio Liberation's problems, factional divisions insinuated themselves in the broadcasting operations. In their attempts at unity, the émigrés had operated on the principle of strict, one-to-one parity between Russians and non-Russians in the appointment of leaders and committees. Now they demanded that the parity concept prevail in radio operations, with a strict division of program time between Russian and non-Russians and the appointment of a two-person directorate—one Russian, the other a nationality representative—to oversee station operations, a proposal the Americans rejected outright.

Eventually, Amcomlib abandoned the attempt to create a unified émigré center and made formal that its representatives, and not the émigrés, would make the crucial decisions about the future of Radio Liberation. This led to a Russian withdrawal from both Amcomlib and RL, which in turn provoked the Americans to eliminate the subsidies that had been allocated to the exile organizations. The exiles demanded that the subsidies be revived, but Amcomlib was adamant, having decided that the viable exile groups would survive without American assistance. This assessment proved accurate, as the principal casualties were organizations Amcomlib had built up despite their lack of support within the emigration. Meanwhile, leading figures in a number of the émigré organizations found their way to positions with RL, some as chief editors. But there was no more discussion of RL as a project of an émigré coordinating center; the key decisions would be made by Amcomlib and the radio's American managers.[17]

Within a few weeks of the inaugural broadcast, RL launched programs in Armenian, Azeri, Georgian, Turkestani, and the languages of the peoples of the North Caucasus. Finding staff for some of the smaller services was a chronic problem, given the tiny exile communities. There were, by contrast, a substantial number of qualified Russians among the two waves of emigration—that which left after the revolution, and that which departed after World War II. Many lived in the United States, and some of the brightest were hired to work in RL's New York office.

These were the days before satellite communications, which enabled broadcasts from New York to be relayed immediately to the target audience in the Soviet Union. In these relatively primitive times, tapes produced in New York were transported by air to Munich, where they were edited and then sent along to RL's transmitting facilities. The process of transporting the tapes from the Munich headquarters to the transmitters was something of an adventure. The transmitters were situated in Lampertheim, two hundred miles from Munich. To get the broadcasts on the air required that the tapes be physically carried by a combination of train and motorcycle courier from Munich to the transmitters, a six-hour trip.[18]

A more serious problem was that practically no one in the Soviet Union could hear RL's broadcasts because of the weakness of the station's small, outmoded transmitters. Only after CIA director Allen Dulles decided to spend the necessary funds to build a network of high-powered transmitters in Spain—a project that was not completed until 1960—was RL able to reach a mass audience.[19]

Meanwhile, RL began to hire a staff of journalists and managers. Boris Shub, a brilliant writer with a deep feeling for Russian history and culture and a moderate political sensibility, was hired away from RIAS. Edmund Stevens, a foreign correspondent with experience in Moscow, was named chief of the news division.[20] Stevens would later return to the Soviet Union as an American correspondent; years after his death evidence would emerge that led some to believe that he had been a Soviet agent. As chief political adviser, Amcomlib, presumably at the behest of the American government, appointed Robert A. Kelley. Kelley had had a distinguished career at the State Department; during the 1930s, he established the department's East European Division and was responsible for having trained the first generation of Soviet experts in the foreign service.[21]

The most important personnel move was the appointment in 1954 of Howland H. Sargeant as president of Amcomlib. Sargeant was the fourth Amcomlib chief. Eugene Lyons was succeeded in 1952 by Adm. Alan G. Kirk, and Kirk, after serving less than a year, was succeeded by another military man, Adm. Leslie C. Stevens. Both had Moscow experience, Kirk as ambassador to the Soviet Union and Stevens as naval attaché to the U.S. embassy. Sargeant had been assistant secretary of state for information during the Truman administration, a job that included administrative responsibility for the VOA. (In addition to his government credentials, Sargeant brought a bit of glamour to RL as the husband of actress Myrna Loy.) When asked by Thomas Braden and Cord Meyer, the CIA officials responsible for the freedom radios, whether he would consider accepting the Amcomlib position, Sargeant is said to have retorted that he was not interested in "the care and feeding of exiles." On the other hand, Sargeant was intrigued by the idea of developing a type of communications different from an official government radio like the VOA.[22]

Before accepting the offer, Sargeant set down several conditions. First, he demanded minimal interference from the CIA. Second, he insisted that Amcomlib focus its energies on turning RL into a first-rate international radio station. Finally, he was adamant that exile groups have no say in the affairs of Amcomlib or RL. This last condition the CIA was especially willing to grant, having had more than enough of the byzantine world of émigré politics. Sargeant also took a hard line on the NTS. He decreed that no one who adhered to NTS organizational discipline could work for Amcomlib or Radio Liberation. Sargeant objected to the NTS both because of its antidemocratic philosophy and because it functioned in cadre fashion, infiltrating legitimate organizations for the purpose of dominating them.[23]

Sargeant remained as chief of Amcomlib until 1975, when RFE and RL were brought under a consolidated management. During his long tenure, Sargeant protected RL from outside interference, oversaw the modernization of the station's technical facilities, and pressed for enhanced professionalism among its broadcasters. He is probably more responsible than any single individual for the evolution of RL into one of the most influential international radio stations of the Cold War era.

According to a declaration drafted by the short-lived émigré coordinating center, the purpose of Radio Liberation was to wage "implacable struggle against the Communist dictatorship until its complete destruction." The statement went on to say that RL's theme was "Liberation—liberation from the tyranny of Bolshevism and one-party rule, from poverty and suffering forced on the people by the Bolshevist regime and from the threat of war imposed by Bolshevist foreign policy and ideology."[24]

Although the death of Stalin suggested that a rethinking of the "implacable struggle" approach might be in order, early broadcasts betrayed a certain confusion over the new station's role. For example, in a broadcast in June 1953, in the midst of the uprising by the workers of East Germany, an RL Russian announcer declared, "Soldiers and officers of the Soviet Army, the German workers struggle against Kremlin oppression is unfolding before your eyes. . . . [On] order to fire on the defenseless, remember that they are not enemies of our country but are defenders of freedom. They seek liberation from the same yoke which oppresses our fathers, mothers, brothers and sisters. . . . The workers of East Berlin are fighting for the cause of all mankind and for the delivery of the whole world, including our motherland, from Communism. Help them!"[25] This was not to be the last time that RL appealed to the spirit of proletarian solidarity. Three years later, special Russian language broadcasts were beamed to Hungary during the Hungarian Revolution. A critic who studied RL broadcasts during its early years said that appeals were addressed to Red Army troops "not to shoot the Hungarians because they also were building socialism; regrets were expressed because 'our' brave soldiers murdered Hungarian women and children; appeals were made to members of the Communist Party and to the 'politrabotniki' [political officers] of the army to stop the mass slaughter of the population."[26]

Radio Liberty was not alone in its confusion over how to regard the Soviet Union in the post-Stalin period. The American government was similarly afflicted, oscillating between hopes for a more peaceful relationship and continued calls for the rollback of Soviet power in Eastern Europe. The station was, nevertheless, moving in fits and starts toward a more moderate vocabulary. In a September 1, 1954, memorandum, Admiral Stevens, then president of Amcomlib, indicated that broadcasters should adopt a less contentious voice in their political commentaries: "Encourage reliance on traditional indigenous spiritual concepts; stimulate independent thinking and a spirit of free inquiry; present specific democratic political, economic, and social processes as an attainable and attractive alternative to the Communist dictatorship; develop basic concepts of justice and humanity for the protection of the individual against the power of the state; present realistic and practical alternatives to passive submission to the Soviet system."[27] The RL staff shared RFE's confidence that the Soviet system would collapse rather quickly. Francis Ronalds, an American who worked at RL on and off from 1952 to 1977, recalls: "We did not think in terms of the Soviet Union collapsing in forty years. We believed that the system was bad, that the people hated the system, and that if we provided them with reliable information which proved how bad the system was, the people would work to gradually bring about its demise."[28]

This belief in the imminence of communism's collapse may help explain why RL featured polemics and exhortation along with news and commentary. In any event, by 1958, with Hungary crushed, Poland no longer threatening rebellion, and Nikita Khrushchev seemingly in charge, it was clear to all that those who had signed up for the anti–Communist struggle were in for the long haul. A memorandum from Howland Sargeant reflected the sober new environment. It cautioned against assuming that a mood of radical alienation prevailed among the Soviet people. While the country's youth might feel "disillusioned," this did not suggest the existence of a political or spiritual crisis. Sargeant noted that the most discontented group, the peasantry, was difficult to win over through radio broadcasts and was reluctant to take action against the system. Furthermore, Sargeant advanced the once-heretical notion that the Soviet people took pride in their country's technological achievements (he no doubt had the Sputnik launching in mind) and might even give the political leadership credit for the country's accomplishments. Under conditions of gradual social improvement, he concluded, RL should not assume that the people hated the system or detested their leaders.[29]

While RL moved to professionalize its broadcasting operations, it engaged in a never-ending debate over the proper tone for its Russian listeners. According to a 1960 internal program review, the tone suffered from an "impersonal nature, not intended for Russians." Commentaries, the reviewer said, did not seem to be written by Russians for Russians, but rather "by some foreign outsider, flinging accusations at the outsider, Mr. Khrushchev." Robert Kelley concurred with this assessment. "It seems to me that the highest priority should be given to the correction of this shortcoming with a view to the establishment of that intimate rapport between Radio Liberty and its listeners." Broad-

Howland Sargeant (left), president of
Amcomlib from 1954 to 1975.

General C. Rodney Smith (right)
won respect from staff during
his stint as RFE president.

W.J. Convery Egan (left), president of
RFE during the dark hours of the
Hungarian Revolution.

(All photographs courtesy
of RFE-RL archives.)

Broadcasts featuring stories from escapees were often featured during the early
Cold War years. RFE journalist (above right) tapes interview with escapee from
Czechoslovakia during the early 1950s. (Below) Children interviewed for RFE
after their family escaped from behind the Iron Curtain.

(Above) Man on the street interview in London, early 1960s. (Left) An early drawing of an RFE microphone.

Averell Harriman addresses the Radio Liberty audience.

(Above) Radio Liberty editor Francis Ronalds interviewing Dr. Martin Luther King Jr. (Below) Archbishop Alexander, head of the Independent Russian Orthodox Church in West Germany, in a 1961 RL interview.

(Above) Interviewing actress
Juliette Greco for RFE in 1968.
(Right) RFE monitors listen to
Communist bloc radio broadcasts; the more important
programs were transcribed for
the use of the RFE broadcast
staff.

(Above) An RFE Hungarian broadcaster interviews British pop star Tom Jones during the 1960s. (Right) A Bulgarian announcer during the 1960s.

(Above) James F. Brown (far right) leads one of RFE's daily policy meetings during the 1970s. (Below) Radio Liberty held the world's largest collection of Soviet samizdat literature. Here an RL researcher compares an original document with the newly typed version.

casters should, Kelley declared, "sit alongside their listeners and engage in friendly talks with them," instead of "talking down to their listeners from a platform."[30]

To improve broadcast staff quality, RL sent Boris Shub on scouting missions throughout North America and Europe. Shub's father, a Socialist, had come to the United States before the Revolution. As a result, Shub inherited a Socialist tradition, a Russian tradition, and a solid grounding in American democracy, an ideal combination for a man responsible for RL staff recruitment. One of Shub's prime catches was Victor Frank, the chief of the BBC's Russian-language broadcasts. While the BBC could boast an impressive tradition as the world's premier international broadcasting entity, RL paid more handsomely, and was thus able to grab of a number of talented BBC employees. Frank himself was installed a head of RL's Russian service.[31]

Ironically, RL's American managers developed a preference for Russian émigrés of the older generation as opposed to those who had come West after the war. The older exiles were better educated, spoke a purer and more literary form of Russian, were more likely to speak English, were more democratic in their personal dealings with colleagues and more moderate in political outlook.

Many of the older Russians were knowledgeable about Russian history and culture. This was an important asset, since a major theme of RL's broadcasts was communism's suppression of Russian culture and its systematic rewriting of Russian history. Boris Shub's father, David Shub, wrote a series of scripts on the country's democratic heritage. He also acquainted his listeners with the writings of democrats like Alexander Herzen. Another important contributor was Father Alexander Schmemann, a Russian Orthodox priest whose son, Serge, went on to a distinguished career as a foreign correspondent for the New York Times. Father Schmemann made regular broadcasts on religious themes, and he had a wide and devoted following in the Soviet Union. None were more devoted than Alexander Solzhenitsyn; in an interview after his expulsion from the USSR, Solzhenitsyn referred to Father Schmemann as "my priest."[32]

Although both were located in Munich, Radio Liberty and Radio Free Europe had little contact with one another. Only in the late 1960s, when serious threats to the existence of both organizations rose to the surface and talk of consolidating the radios began, did RFE and

RL begin close collaboration. Many RFE officials regarded Radio Liberty with an air of superiority. They considered the Russians and other Soviet nationalities as culturally inferior to East Europeans. They suspected that RL's programs lacked the level of professionalism that RFE had achieved. They believed that many RL staff were political extremists who knew little about radio work. They also suspected that RL was much more tightly controlled by the CIA than was Radio Free Europe. James Critchlow entitled the entertaining memoir of his years at RL *Radio Hole-in-the-Head,* a name he claims was attached to Radio Liberty by an RFE staff member during the 1950s. Critchlow's account contains an undertone of bitterness over RFE's condescending attitude; he notes with special glee that RL never experienced a scandal to rival the controversy over RFE's coverage of the Hungarian Revolution.

Veteran Radio Liberty staff also deny significant interference by the CIA. Indeed, their accounts of relations with the radio's sponsoring organization resemble those of RFE administrators. Americans such as Ronalds and Critchlow testify that while they knew of the CIA link from the beginning, they never considered the relationship especially important since the intelligence agency seldom tried to exert influence over broadcast policy. In the first few years, Ronalds says, the CIA did ask RL to encourage defections by Soviet citizens, a policy that bothered some staff members because of the shabby treatment Soviet defectors had received from American officials. The CIA and RL did, of course, share information, although, according to Critchlow, the radio would independently verify inside tips it received from the intelligence agency before putting a report on the air.[33]

Radio Liberty faced a more formidable challenge in building an audience than did Radio Free Europe. From the moment it went on the air, RFE had a guaranteed audience consisting of the millions of Hungarians, Poles, Czechs, Slovaks, Bulgarians, and Romanians who hated both communism and Soviet imperialism. In Russia, by contrast, generations were coming of age having experienced no other system than Soviet-style communism, complicating the task of convincing an audience that a better and more humane alternative was possible.

Radio Liberty was thus constantly seeking special opportunities to reach its audience. The station devoted extensive coverage to Khrushchev's eventful 1959 visit to the United States. McKinney

Russell, an American journalist who had been hired by RL, followed Khrushchev in his travels around the country and gave regular reports that were translated into the various RL languages and beamed back to the Soviet Union. The Soviets actually suspended jamming during the RL broadcast of the Soviet premier's speech to the National Press Club, only to resume jamming when the American secretary of state, Christian Herter, addressed the assembled journalists. The next year, RL gave complete coverage to Khrushchev's infamous United Nations address, during which he pounded the table with his shoe to make a polemical point. The shoe pounding was removed by the censor in the version broadcast by Soviet radio, which apparently did not want the leader of the first country of socialism to appear a buffoon.[34]

On two occasions, RL directed special programs to Soviet troops abroad. The first was during the Hungarian Revolution; the second during the Cuban missile crisis. In the latter instance, RL contracted for two fifteen-minute broadcasts per week with a Charlotte, North Carolina, station with a powerful medium-wave transmitter. In 1955, the radio contracted with the government of what was then known as the Republic of China, on Taiwan, to establish a powerful transmitter that could enable broadcasts to reach the Soviet maritime provinces and Siberia. Radio Liberty even hired a special program staff for the Taipei operation, along with a correspondent in Hong Kong to keep up with the twists and turns of Soviet-China relations. The Taipei operation lasted until 1973, when it was closed for budgetary reasons.[35]

Radio Liberty also established what would develop into one of the world's most respected Soviet research entities. The research unit was begun during the 1950s by Victor Zorza. Zorza was a Pole who had been evacuated to the Soviet Union during the war and had eventually found his way to England, where he served in the air force and flew several missions as a wartime pilot. Despite his imperfect English, Zorza went on to serve as a foreign correspondent for several Western newspapers. During a brief stint at RL, Zorza organized what were called the Red Archives. The archives contained massive files on everything from agricultural production, biographies of party officials, industrial output, foreign policy—just about everything a researcher might want to know the personalities and policies of the Soviet Union.[36] Later, under the direction of Albert Boiter and Keith Bush, Radio Liberty research developed a global reputation for both the thoroughness of its file keeping and the astuteness of its analysis.

Another research organization connected to RL was the Institute for the Study of the USSR. Established in Munich during the early 1950s, the institute was planned as a research and conference center for émigré scholars. For a time it issued publications in several of the Soviet languages and published long studies about developments in the USSR, but it never developed into a major vehicle for Soviet studies. Many of the researchers were elderly and unfamiliar with Western languages, a serious weakness given that most important scholarly material on Soviet affairs was produced by American, British, or French researchers. The institute was closed in the early seventies for budgetary reasons.

Another special undertaking was audience research. For both RFE and RL, determining the size of the audience and the likes and dislikes of listeners posed a serious challenge, given the closed nature of the countries to which they broadcast. Opinion surveys could not be conducted in the Soviet Union itself, leaving as the only alternative the solicitation of opinions from visitors to Western countries. Unfortunately, Soviet citizens did not make frequent trips to Western Europe, and those who did usually traveled in carefully chaperoned groups and were wary of contacts with strangers.

The man chosen to build an audience research unit was Max Ralis, a Russian-born, German-educated social scientist who had served in both the French and American armies and then studied under Paul Felix Lazersfeld, an early expert on mass communications. Ralis hired Soviet émigrés, trained them in interview techniques, and directed them to approach Soviet travelers and ask pertinent questions about their listening habits and attitude toward specific RL programs. Initially, the information was used to help RL in gauging the effectiveness of its programs. Later, Ralis worked with Ithiel de Sola Pool, an authority on mass communications, to develop a method of using the RL data to assess the audience share for RL and other Western international broadcasting services. The audience research unit eventually moved to Paris because of the greater volume of Soviet visitors in that city.

The Soviets viewed the audience research operation with an attitude that at times bordered on the hysterical. Because the audience research interviewers found ways to make contact with Soviet citizens out of earshot of their tour guides or delegation leaders, officials assumed that Ralis's people were spies seeking intelligence secrets or, even worse, attempting to convince gullible Soviets to desert the motherland and defect to the West.[37]

Radio Liberty's audience rose dramatically after the new transmitter facilities were made operational in 1960. Some listened for news broadcasts, some for cultural programs, some for political commentary or meditations on Russian history, some out of attachment to a particular broadcaster.

Broadcast tone remained a perennial problem. Jon Lodeesen, an American who was hired in the 1960s to monitor adherence to the policy guidelines, had frequent occasion to complain of a strident or propagandistic vocabulary. In a 1969 memorandum, Lodeesen chastised a commentator for using the phrase "liberation struggle" in the wake of an assassination attempt on Leonid Brezhnev.[38] He objected to a series of 1970 scripts along similar lines: "There was such a tone of hostility to the system expressed from a superior position it would be particularly easy for our listeners to conclude that the hostility was directed at them."[39] Lodeesen also criticized a Russian commentator who had excoriated a study of prerevolutionary Russia written by the eminent historian Richard Pipes. The commentator had dismissed the book as "coming from the school which draws a straight line from Ivan the Terrible to Joseph Stalin." The same commentator wrote that "because Poland rejected the police state, it died." Lodeesen called this analysis "junky history" and admonished that a police state "cannot be referred to in a positive or neutral light."[40]

On another occasion, Edward van der Rhoer, a policy official at the station, cautioned against vituperation against individual Soviet personalities. His warning was motivated by scripts that were critical of the internationally famous poet Yevgeni Yevtushenko. Yevtushenko's poems raised themes that cautiously challenged certain precepts of official ideology, and as a result he was lionized by Western critics. At the same time, the poet never directly attacked the Soviet system, leading some to suggest that he had maneuvered his way to acceptability by both liberal Western opinion and Soviet cultural officialdom. Van der Rhoer, however, declared that Yevtushenko should be given credit for trying to encourage "Soviet citizens to think for themselves and to consider without reference to the opinion of the party such issues as guilt, duty, personal concern...." "When we comment on the author of a published work," he added, "we should never assume that what he has written and published under the Soviet system is what he would have if he had been free to express himself without fear of retribution. When we disagree with his work and with what has been published we can and must do this without feeling obliged to engage in personal assault on the author."[41]

As RL entered the 1970s, its most serious problem was not its message but the aging of its staff and the need for new programming that could draw the interest of a younger and increasingly independent-minded Soviet audience.

The staff issue was approaching crisis proportions. The most valuable broadcasters hired during the 1950s had come from the first wave of emigration. Many joined RL in their fifties or even sixties, and by 1970 had either died, retired, or were nearing retirement. The situation of some of the smaller nationality services was especially dire. Some had to reduce broadcast hours and attempt to train the westernized children of staff members in their ancestral language in a desperate attempt at staff replenishment.[42] While the Soviet Union was a less oppressive society than under Stalin, emigration or even foreign travel were not recognized as among the rights of the citizen. A reasonably well educated Russian who managed to escape to the West stood an excellent chance of being hired by any of the western broadcast services.

Ironically, it was the Soviet Union that came to Radio Liberty's rescue—in two ways. First, the repression of Soviet dissent and official refusal to permit the publication of nonconformist writing gave rise to the samizdat phenomenon. Samizdat were essays or reports typed and retyped in editions ranging from several dozens to a few hundred. Some reflected the opinions of dissidents who favored democratic reforms for the Soviet Union. Others were written by those seeking autonomy, cultural freedom, or independence for the non-Russian peoples.

In typed editions, a samizdat document might reach an audience of a few hundred or several thousand at best. If the document were broadcast on a Western radio station, however, it could reach millions. Because it broadcast many more hours each day than its Western competitors, Radio Liberty was able to devote hours of air time to the broadcasting of samizdat documents. Soon enough, a major goal of samizdat authors was to arrange for the document to be smuggled to the West and given to Radio Liberty.

One of the earliest samizdat documents to reach the West was a transcript of the trial of Andrei Sinyavsky and Yuri Daniel, the first dissidents tried and sentenced to the Gulag for antistate activities. The document was duly delivered to RL's bureau in Paris. Francis Ronalds, bureau chief at the time, verified the document's genuineness and turned it over to the *New York Times,* on the theory that the news would have a greater impact if carried first by the *Times* rather than on the avowedly anti-Communist RL. Radio Liberty then broadcast details of the trial after they had appeared in the *Times.*[43]

Radio Liberty next established a special program at which samizdat was read. Soon enough, the station was inundated with documents from the Soviet Union. The station established a samizdat archive and hired an archival staff to sift through, catalogue, verify, and circulate the thousands of documents that reached the station. Mario Corti, a Russian-speaking Italian who became chief of the samizdat unit, says that the RL staff subjected each document to a meticulous fact-checking procedure. If, for example, a document mentioned a party official or KGB operative, the staff combed through the Soviet press to ensure that the name and position in the document corresponded to information published in the press.

As a matter of strict policy, Radio Liberty never solicited samizdat; to have done so would have placed the author in jeopardy of a sentence in the gulag. The samizdat unit was also careful to verify that each document was legitimate, in part out of fear that the KGB might concoct a report that, if taken at face value by RL and put on the air, might serve to discredit the dissident movement.[44]

More important than samizdat to RL's future was the wave of emigration the Brezhnev regime permitted as a concession to the United States during the early years of détente. Quite unexpectedly, tens of thousands of Soviet citizens were allowed to leave for the West. Many of the émigrés were educated, and a few had a journalism background. The emigration included well-known cultural figures—writers, singers, musicologists, artists—as well as authorities of Soviet science, economists, and others of the technological intelligentsia.

It was almost too good to be true. Indeed, some station veterans believe that RL officials, perhaps nervous over the possibility of a renewed curb on exit visas, were insufficiently discriminating in their initial hiring decisions, grabbing off any new emigrant who might conceivably be taught the rudiments of radio broadcasting.[45] Eventually, hiring decisions became more selective, and the new staff formed the cornerstone for what was to become the golden period in the station's Cold War history.

One issue RL had to face with the new emigration was a shift in the ethnic balance of the Russian service. The Brezhnev emigration was overwhelmingly Jewish, in line with American demands that Jews be allowed to leave the Soviet Union as victims of systematic bias. Some non-Jews were given exit visas, as were the non-Jewish spouses of Jewish emigrants. But Jews were the main beneficiaries of the emigration relaxation, and thousands came to settle either in the United States or Israel.

There had always been Jews on the RL staff; there had, as well always been Russian nationalists who could never accept Jews as genuinely Russian. Both groups had worked in peaceful if uneasy coexistence. With the influx of new Jewish staff members, some Russian nationalists became concerned about the shifting ethnic balance within the staff. Several staff members from the second generation made their concerns a public issue by circulating reports to émigré publications that the staff was becoming "too Jewish."

The rancor between nationalists and Jews was to plague the Russian service for the next decade. Nevertheless, the 1970s were a time of growth and improvement for RL. It boasted a staff of educated professionals, some of whom were familiar personalities to the Russian audience. It offered the most complete coverage of samizdat and the human rights movement. Its coverage of Soviet affairs was clearly superior to that of the VOA, whose Russian broadcasts, critics contend, were made to conform to the dictates of U.S.-Soviet détente. Since RL paid well, it was able to woo the best and brightest of the new emigration away from the BBC, where compensation was comparatively low.

Radio Liberty's message had, of course, changed dramatically from the days when emphasis on the "implacable struggle" against the Bolsheviks had set the tone for broadcasting. By the 1970s, many authorities were describing the USSR as a status quo power that had attained political stability and satisfied the basic material needs of its people. Today, of course, we know from the testimony of Soviet officials that it was during this period that the era of stagnation—political and cultural, as well as economic—set in. To the outside world, however, and to RL the Soviet Union seemed a military and diplomatic power whose long-term existence as a Socialist state and multinational empire was not in doubt.

Thus the guidances issued by management as a road map to the coverage of the most important issues of the day seem altogether moderate, and in some cases even timid, given what has been learned since the collapse of the Soviet Union. Rather than fostering the overthrow of communism, the overarching objective of RL coverage was to "give expression to and encourage those trends . . . which can lead to democratization, social justice, and national self-determination." Radio Liberty saw its prime audience as the Soviet Union's political elites—"real or potential decision making elements," "thinking members of the Communist Party and Komsomol," "the scientific, technological, and creative intelligentsia," "skilled workers and their supervisors."[46]

A guidance on Soviet agriculture, a notorious failure of the system, eschewed calls for the dismantling of the collective farms in favor of proposals to democratize and transform them into something akin to a cooperative. Likewise, a guidance on relations between the Soviet Union and Eastern Europe did not ask commentators to condemn Moscow's imperialist domination of its neighbors. Rather, it urged that commentators discuss the reforms that had been adopted by countries such as Hungary and Yugoslavia and condemn the Brezhnev doctrine, under which the Soviets claimed the right to intervene anywhere to rescue a Socialist system, as a threat to peace. In a similar vein, commentators were encouraged to give credit to the achievements of the Soviet economy, such as full employment. They were warned against "negative comparisons of Soviet reality with Western models": "The portrayal of the virtues and achievements of the market economies should be tempered with a frank discussion of their shortcomings—the unemployment and pockets of poverty in the U.S., as well as the vulgarity of American commercial life."[47]

In broadcasts dealing with Lenin, a guidance urged broadcasters to keep in mind that the father of the October Revolution was a popular figure in the Soviet Union: "Among all elements of the population there persists in general a strong positive attitude toward Lenin and the democratic ideals with which he is identified." In covering Lenin, the guidance declared, the goal should be to "show our audience that the officially propagated Lenin legend has little relation to the man and his work." The guidance urged broadcasters to differentiate between the prerevolutionary Lenin, "insisting on democratic principles and human rights," the revolutionary Lenin—"the heroic and cruel utopian"—and the postrevolutionary Lenin, "who had to abandon or revise some of his theoretical principles in order to keep and strengthen the grip of power."[48]

Drafted during the era of détente, Radio Liberty's policy guidance would have found few critics within the American government. To what degree the moderate position laid down in the guidances were reflected in RL broadcasts is, however, not clear. It is not likely that many of the émigré journalists would have sympathized with the notion of Lenin as an advocate of "democratic principles and human rights" at any point in his career as a revolutionary. Despite their many differences, RL's journalists, whether monarchist or democrat, Orthodox Christian or Jew, admirer of Solzhenitsyn or follower of Andrey Sakharov, Ukrainian, Georgian, or Russian, were near unanimous in their conviction that communism was the ruination of their native land. More telling than the content of the policy guidances was the statement by Solzhenitsyn that "if we ever hear anything about events in our country, it's through them (Radio Liberty broadcasts)."[49]

Within a few years, détente would be replaced by a heightening of U.S.-Soviet tensions. In the United States a new political leadership, one which believed that the country's foreign broadcasting stations had become overly influenced by détente, would assume power. Committed to a more robust American presence in the ideological contest against the Soviets, it was convinced that Radio Liberty's role in the war of ideas should be enhanced and its message sharpened. As the 1980s approached, RL was about to enter its period of greatest influence. Just as the eighties would bring RL's greatest triumphs, however, the decade would be notable for a degree of strife and controversy unprecedented in the station's history.

11

The Perils
of Ostpolitik

By the late 1960s, the anti-Communist consensus that had enabled the United States and Europe to maintain a more or less unified policy of containment had clearly broken down. A shift toward a vague kind of neutralism was particularly noticeable among the parties of the liberal Left. In varying degrees, the Democrats in America, the British Labor Party, and the social democratic parties of the Nordic countries were beginning to distance themselves from a foreign policy ideology grounded in anticommunism. While no important party was prepared to advocate the jettisoning of the Atlantic Alliance, significant elements were beginning to call for a thoroughgoing détente in which the Soviet Union and the satellite countries would be recognized as normal states, with legitimate governments and reasonable security concerns. And where "outmoded relics" of the early Cold War, like Radio Free Europe and Radio Liberty, would be sacrificed in the interest of international harmony and global peace.

Unfortunately for the radios, no country took the question of relations with the Communist world as seriously as did the Federal Republic of Germany. And in no country save the United States did the outcome of the détente debate have as critical an impact on the future of the Cold War. West Germany was the most economically powerful country in Europe, and its geographic situation on the front line of the East-West divide made it strategically more important than other European countries. Under the leadership of Chancellor

Adenauer, West Germany had earned a reputation as a trustworthy NATO partner, certainly more reliable than the French under De Gaulle and perhaps more dependable than the British, whose Labor Party was burdened by an influential faction of hard leftists. Meanwhile, the German Social Democrats (SPD) were moving steadily toward the center. The party had abandoned doctrinaire socialism and accepted the Federal Republic's partnership with the United States.

In 1969 the SPD came to power as the dominant party in a coalition with the Free Democrats. The new chancellor, Willy Brandt, moved quickly to set the country on a different foreign policy course centered on détente, or Ostpolitik, with the Communist world. Even today, controversy rages over Ostpolitik's ultimate goal, as envisioned by Brandt and other party leaders. Some critics are convinced that Brandt's objective was a form of neutralism in which West Germany would pursue international objectives independent of the alliance. Others contend that Brandt and his successor, Helmut Schmidt, had more modest ambitions—a détente with the East bloc that was grounded in Germany's continued adherence to the West's strategic and political aims. Whatever his private thoughts may have been regarding Germany's geopolitical future, Brandt was usually cautious in advancing Ostpolitik during his tenure as chancellor and carefully avoided actions that might alienate the American government.

There were many anti-Communist organizations active in West Germany at the time; the country was a magnet for East bloc exiles, research institutes that studied the Soviet system, and organizations devoted to the cause of freedom for East Germany, including several radio stations.

But the most visible stars in the anti-Communist constellation were the two American freedom radios, Radio Free Europe and Radio Liberty. The radios were vulnerable on several counts. They were Cold War symbols at a time when the liberal Left was inclined to regard such symbols as relics of a discredited policy, and they were American-operated, and thus a reminder that the FRG lacked total sovereignty in the formulation of its foreign policy. Most important, they were hated by Germany's neighbors and soon-to-be-partners in Ostpolitik. Whereas exile organizations were treated as a minor irritant and NATO accepted as an emblem of a tolerable European status quo, the freedom radios were regarded with much the same kind of fear an autocrat might reserve for an opposition political party, trade union, or newspaper.

Ostpolitik involved a series of bilateral negotiations with the Soviet Union and the East European countries. These talks could be protracted and delicate affairs, involving issues that stretched back to Germany's conduct during World War II. For some countries, the presence of the radios in West Germany was a subsidiary issue and was disposed of after Communist officials made pro forma requests for the radios ouster. Others, especially the Poles, made the removal of the radios from Germany a major diplomatic priority.

Yet while the Poles complained, threatened, and issued demands, they were not prepared to see the talks fail because Bonn refused to expel Radio Free Europe. Much more important questions were involved, in particular trade expansion and the West German government's explicit recognition of the Oder-Neisse boundary. Had the German government been firm and unequivocal in defending the radio station, the issue of RFE would have dropped off the table rather quickly. In 1967 Bonn had responded sharply when Hungary called RFE, Deutsche Welle, and various exile groups an impediment to normal ties, and the issue was dropped without serious discussion.[1]

By 1970, however, the political climate had undergone a decided shift. Like other Europeans, Germans took the revelations that the freedom radios had been secretly funded by the CIA with calm indifference. Most German politicians understood that RFE—and it was RFE, not RL, that posed the most serious problem—had changed considerably since the days of propaganda balloons and the encouragement of defections. And they knew, via reports from diplomats posted in Eastern Europe, that RFE had a wide and devoted audience—larger than the Communist domestic media, in some cases.

Nevertheless, there was sentiment within Brandt's inner circle to accede to East bloc demands by revoking the radios' operating licenses. They considered Poland as a major test of Ostpolitik, and the Poles were not inclined to accept vague assurances that the question of RFE's presence would be given further thought. An aggressive anti-RFE propaganda offensive had been launched during the period leading to Bonn-Warsaw talks, involving some of the country's highest officials. In the course of an October 1969 interview on German television, Polish foreign minister Stefan Jedrychowski pointedly attacked "various centers of ideological diversion" as obstacles to normal relations. "I am thinking here of the aggressive radio station calling itself Free Europe," he added, "for whose activities West Germany is also responsible because this subversive station is located on German territory. In our opinion, neither the existence of two opposite social systems nor ideological differences need to be obstacles if [the two parties] are resolved to resist tensions and psychological warfare."[2]

In fact, the Polish Communists' emotional insistence on RFE's elimination was a sign of the leadership's instability, as well as a tribute to RFE's influence. Through its coverage of Poland's recurring crises—the Swiatlo revelations, the Poznan riots, the confrontation with Khrushchev, the rise of Gomulka, the Moczar movement, and student protests and anti-Semitic purges of 1968—RFE had established itself as the most influential source of information in Poland. And it had been some time since RFE had looked on Gomulka as a potential reformer; his dogmatism, mismanagement of the economy, and capitulation to extreme nationalism were constant targets of RFE broadcasts. For its part, the regime treated RFE as its most dangerous adversary. Thus after the authorities banned the play *Forefather's Eve* in 1968, Jerzy Putrament, head of the party cell in the Polish Writers Union, convened a special meeting to denounce RFE, which had broadcast a number of programs on the student protests that followed the prohibition of the play. Even Jakub Karpinski, an opposition leader at the time, was taken aback by the regime's obsession with the radio. It seemed to him that "activists listen to nothing else and consider its opinions the way other governments would public opinion."[3]

A clue to the regime's mindset was provided by Henryk Birecki, a former official in the Foreign Ministry:

> Communist leaders who have become prisoners of their own monopoly need [RFE] for their own private enlightenment, but at the same time fear its impact on others. It is this deep concern over the impact of Radio Free Europe, not only on the population, but above all on the Communist Party itself, that has finally prevailed. . . . Decisions were taken at the top level in Warsaw to use all available diplomatic as well as secret channels to bring about the closure of Radio Free Europe. Considerable resources were earmarked for this purpose and plans for this operation were already

made three years ago with Washington and Bonn the main targets of diplomatic pressure.[4]

Polish communism had been sustained throughout its history by depicting itself as the victim of forces that were not only the enemies of communism but also the enemies of Poland. During the 1960s, the principal enemies were Jews, students, and West Germany. But the Jews had been driven out, the students marginalized, and West Germany was to become a partner in détente. To now portray RFE as the major source of the regime's troubles was an admission of Communist weakness, and certainly not an argument likely to persuade the Polish people. On the other hand, a successful détente required an internally stable East bloc, and the contention that RFE was an impediment to mutual understanding and cooperation was taken seriously by advocates of an accelerated Ostpolitik.

Furthermore, a growing number of SPD officials were coming to the view that RFE, RL, and similar institutions were, as the Communists claimed, "relics" of the past and deserved to be shunted aside to clear the way for the new era of European harmony. Brandt himself may have believed this. Although the chancellor was careful to shield his innermost thoughts on the radio question, he occasionally hinted that he favored the departure of the two stations, albeit through a formula that did not make it appear that his government had capitulated to East bloc pressure. During a 1970 appearance in Saarbrücken, Brandt blurted out that "both sides should stop defaming each other and using silly propaganda by throwing it where it belongs, on the garbage pile of history."[5] Further evidence can be found in the notes Brandt took during December 1970 negotiations with the Polish regime in Warsaw. The notes quote Gomulka as asking, "What would a German court say if we sued Radio Free Europe?" Brandt summarized his own response thusly: "Reference to overall developments, relations with USA, possible changes through passing of time."[6]

Brandt's response was not exactly a ringing endorsement of RFE. In fact, RFE officials were receiving clear, although indirect, signals that the station's presence in Germany was in jeopardy. Journalists from RFE's news division who had developed solid contacts with Bonn's political establishment through the years suddenly found that formerly friendly officials would no longer return their calls.[7] More disturbing were the reports filtering in from acquaintances in the European press and sources within the Foreign Ministry. Ralph Walter received an ominous message from Rudiger von Wechmar, a Foreign Ministry official, that the highest circles within the Brandt government had an unfavorable opinion of RFE.[8] Another Foreign Ministry official who as recently as 1968 had described RFE's mission as "very important" because of the Warsaw Pact invasion of Czechoslovakia, was in 1970 expressing irritation at the American government for treating the question of RFE's future location as a major issue instead of "helping" Bonn by taking the initiative and offering to move the station to another country.[9]

By the summer of 1970, articles in the press began to appear quoting anonymous government sources as saying that Brandt had decided to deny RFE and RL their broadcasting licenses, and remove them from German soil before the summer Olympics in 1972. When an article in the *Financial Times* asserted that the fate of the American radio stations had been discussed during West German negotiations with the Soviet Union, the government, concerned about the appearance of bending to Communist pressure, issued an official denial of any intention to expel the radios.[10] Typically, the government statement was considerably less than definitive, so that while the question of the two radios' immediate future was clarified, their ultimate disposition was left open, thus encouraging the radios' adversaries to maintain pressure for their removal.

The Soviet bloc was further emboldened by evidence that the SPD government was attempting to bring the message of the German international broadcasting service, Deutsche Welle, into line with détente. A 1975 article in *Die Zeit* claimed that the government was planning to appoint two deputies to the chief editor to oversee broadcast content. The article indicated that the government might squeeze the service through budget restrictions, or by shifting some of its East Europe language services to another, less aggressive German broadcasting service, Deutschland Funk. According to *Die Zeit,* the government was carrying out its plan to take editorial control of Deutsche Welle quietly, in the hope of averting public discussions during election time.[11]

The seriousness of the German threat to the radios' existence was driven home during a meeting involving RFE officials and a group of midlevel functionaries from the Foreign Ministry in May 1970. The most senior German official got right to the point: RFE had emerged as a "problem" in the course of Bonn's negotiations with the East bloc and was very much "on the table." He made clear his generally favorable attitude toward RFE and declared it his goal to resolve the issue so that Bonn's interests were served and RFE's position was not undermined.

The main problem derived from repeated Polish complaints that RFE broadcasts slandered high officials and interfered in the country's internal affairs. He added that a study undertaken by the Foreign Ministry concluded that there was some merit in the Polish complaints; furthermore, he said that the counter argument that Poland's media was grossly unfair in its treatment of West Germany could no longer be advanced, since a study of regime propaganda indicated a positive change in the coverage of German themes. Although the Soviet Union had not raised the issue of Radio Liberty in talks with Bonn, the official warned that there were important German officials who would be happy to be rid of the American radio stations and were looking for justifications for a license revocation. Some had proposed shutting the radios down during the Olympic Games, although the official added that this idea had not been taken seriously. At the same time, German officials were aware that influential Americans supported RFE, and that a move against the radios would complicate overall relations with Washington.

To the Germans, the crux of the matter lay in the commentaries on internal political affairs, which were featured items on each RFE language service. The official thus proposed that RFE shift to a broadcast formula similar to the BBC's, emphasizing straight news reporting, with little or no commentary. Here the Germans were requesting a fundamental change in the nature of the station, since RFE's popularity derived in large measure from the political analysis and opinions of its commentators. Indeed, RFE distinguished itself from the Voice of America and other foreign broadcasting services through its commentaries on internal politics in Eastern Europe. Ralph Walter, who represented RFE at the meeting, politely declined to undertake the proposed changes. He explained in detail the procedures to ensure a responsible broadcast tone and stressed that the station's management made sure that the guidelines were enforced. He then reminded the German officials that RFE broadcasts had presented West Germany in a consistently favorable light and quoted a Polish émigré who contended that the reason Poles did not regard the FRG as an enemy nation was due to RFE broadcasts, whose treatment of Germany stood in sharp contrast to the relentlessly anti-German propaganda that had dominated the Polish media. Radio Free Europe's presentation of Germany as a humane and democratic society, Walter added, had come at a risk to the station's credibility, since it reinforced regime attempts to depict the station as Bonn's puppet. A dramatic change in the station's tone along the lines suggested by the ministry officials would provide Communist propagandists with further evidence that the station was under German control, while encouraging yet further demands from the East bloc on the theory that the appetite grows with the eating.[12]

The inconclusive result of this meeting was in keeping with the broad pattern of RFE-German relations during the early years of Ostpolitik. Nothing, in fact, was ever really decided. The Brandt government preferred that the radios abandon Germany for another home but was unwilling to directly challenge the American government by refusing a license renewal. The Nixon administration was not interested in "helping" Bonn by offering to close or move the radios; indeed, President Nixon is reported to have exploded in anger when the Germans unofficially asked American cooperation in the matter.[13] Yet although the German government preferred to avoid a direct confrontation with Washington over a secondary issue like the radios, it was unwilling to resolve the issue once and for all by making clear to the Poles and other East bloc countries that the status of the radios was nonnegotiable. Typical was the comment of Herbert Wehner, then SPD deputy chairman, after listening to Polish complaints about RFE during a Warsaw visit, that he was "not in a position to change anything regarding the existence of this institution."[14] Such expressions of ambivalence fortified the Communist resolve to continue to demand RFE and RL's expulsion, which in turn gave the Brandt government justification for a tentative exploration of alternative arrangements—meaning a different location—for the radios.

In the meantime, the controversy had emerged as something of an issue in internal German politics. The Free Democrats, the SPD's coalition partner, were generally supportive, as the party's two leading personalities, Foreign Minister Walter Scheel and Hans-Dietrich Genscher, at the time interior minister, distanced themselves from the SPD forces pressing for the radios' removal.[15] Naturally enough, leading figures from the opposition Christian Democrats and Christian Social Union were even more aggressive in affirming their support.

When asked about attempts to expel RFE, Manfred Woerner, the shadow defense minister, explained, "If this is détente, we don't want it."[16] Likewise, CSU leader Franz-Josef Strauss scoffed when asked by a Soviet journalist whether the two American stations might prove a disruptive influence during the Olympics. "I'm rather well-informed about the output of other radio stations," Strauss said, "and if we discuss Radio Liberty and Radio Free Europe, we should also discuss the German language programs of Radio Peace and Progress [a Soviet propaganda service], Radio Prague, and others."[17] The anti-Brandt press, especially the journals published by the conservative and anti-Communist Springer group, also took up the radios cause to buttress the argument that détente SPD-style entailed a dangerous shift toward neutralism.

These expressions of support could be helpful, especially when newspaper reports of rumored schemes to evict the radios compelled the government to issue a denial. But officials at RFE were not enthusiastic about the extra attention from the media. From the opening of the Munich headquarters in 1951, RFE—and even more so RL—had maintained a low public profile. Even when under public attack the radios had avoided engaging in debate with German critics, instead relying on diplomatic channels between Washington and Bonn to iron things out. Now, according to Ralph Walter, RFE had "become something of a touchstone for those who are not willing to accept Ostpolitik as an unmixed blessing." Walter feared that "some of those who currently concern themselves with RFE are motivated more by suspicion of Ostpolitik—and, quite clearly, the government which directs it—than they are with the fate of RFE."[18] To be publicly embraced by the opposition meant risking a further alienation of the SPD and a transformation of the SPD's vague wish for RFE's disappearance to a determined effort to rid Germany of this roadblock to détente.

It was not only the German government's attitude toward the radios that had changed. In Germany itself, as in the United States, a hostility toward the institutions established to wage the Cold War and defeat communism marked the culture of the liberal Left. The Young Socialists, or Jusos, the SPD's youth wing, began to openly oppose the radios' presence in Germany. Several chapters adopted resolutions calling for their expulsion as Cold War anachronisms and emblems of Germany's lack of full sovereignty. Both the Jusos and the youth group of the Free

Democrats refused to grant interviews to RFE's Hungarian service, which in 1972 was preparing a series of broadcasts on the innocuous subject of youth participation in presidential election campaigns.[19]

The radios also became a target for West Germany's noisy New Left. In March 1972, eight young SPD Bundestag members sent an open letter to Brandt and Nixon asking that the two radios be removed from German soil. The letter declared that the radios' presence in Germany "is such as to allow doubts to arise about the sovereignty of the Federal Republic of Germany." The eight were members of the Thursday Circle, a group of left-leaning SPDers who concerned themselves with America's global misdeeds—in Greece, Vietnam, and elsewhere—and similar issues considered too controversial for the party's mainstream to bother about. One of the eight, Bjoern Engholm, later rose to the party leadership position.[20] Another, Karl-Heinz Hansen, later wrote a pamphlet called *Radio Free Europe: Child of the Cold War,* which was published by Democratic Action, a leftist organization originally founded to combat the influence of neo-Nazism and later shifted toward a more overtly pro-Communist stance.[21]

While the Thursday Circle occupied the SPD's far fringes, a group of seventy-four Social Democratic members of the Bundestag subsequently endorsed the anti-Radio document, a not-inconsequential number. The statement also generated confusion within the government. Conrad Ahlers, a press spokesman, asserted that the federal government recognized the importance of the radios for the "free information of the people in the East bloc," but then balanced this bit of praise by declaring that the two stations' programming should not hinder Bonn's foreign policy. Several newspapers also quoted Ahlers as saying that the West German and American governments were already holding discussions on the future of the radios, a statement that was probably not accurate and certainly not reassuring to RFE and RL or to their audience, who were constantly being told by the Communist press that the demise of these criminal stations was imminent.[22]

One consequence of RFE's German troubles was a heightened sensitivity over broadcast content. Radio Free Europe's American managers were determined to give the station's German critics no reason to question its journalistic judgment. There were, in any case, unmistakable signs that the Foreign Ministry intended to step up the monitoring of RFE broadcasts on potentially troublesome themes, subjects having less to do with Germany than with Germany's eastern neighbors. In September 1971, the Foreign Ministry asked Ralph Walter to pass along recent scripts from the Polish service, the first time such a generalized request had been made since the Hungarian Revolution. The Foreign Ministry made a number of subsequent requests on such topics as a Brezhnev visit to Germany and relations between Poland and the FRG.[23] Perhaps sensing RFE's vulnerability, the Polish regime escalated its complaints; in March 1970, Warsaw issued a furious objection to RFE's coverage of negotiations between Bonn and Warsaw. It is, in fact, highly unlikely that RFE violated it own guidelines or the rules of basic prudence, given the Germany political environment at the time.[24]

In 1974 Willy Brandt resigned as chancellor after it was discovered that his personal secretary was an East German agent. His successor, Helmut Schmidt, was looked on favorably by official Washington as more pro-NATO and less inclined to a fast-track Ostpolitik. In fact, Schmidt's relations with the United States were marred by frequent controversy. And he was no more favorably disposed toward RFE and RL than was Brandt.

Schmidt was, if anything, more open about his desire for the radios' departure from Germany than Brandt had ever dared to be. While sitting with the chancellor during a campaign train tour in 1976, Kurt Dewitt, RFE's veteran German correspondent, was the startled recipient of a Schmidt diatribe: "You people are causing us a lot of trouble, you know," Dewitt quoted Schmidt as saying. Schmidt went on to suggest that RFE seek a new location, perhaps in Spain or Portugal. The following day, Dewitt had a conversation with a Schmidt aide that was even more troubling. "You must realize that you are a problem," he was told. "The subject is being brought up again and again. And no one can identify himself *in toto* with these enterprises."[25] Schmidt went on to raise the issue during a May 1977 conversation with Zbigniew Brzezinski, who had just taken over as President Jimmy Carter's national security adviser. As Brzezinski described the encounter, Schmidt made a series of aggressive complaints about RFE, saying that "he was tired of [RFE] . . . operating on German soil, that its presence was contrary to détente, and that he would like to get it out of Germany." This provoked an equally blunt response from Brzezinski: Radio Free Europe, he declared, "was an important element of the overall U.S. policy toward the East, including our interest in the security of Germany, and that such matters could not be decided unilaterally or outside the larger security context." In other words, for Germany to raise the question of the radios was to risk opening the broader question of America's security presence in the Federal Republic. According to Brzezinski, Schmidt dropped the issue there and then, and there is no evidence that Schmidt pressed the issue again during his term as chancellor.[26]

While Schmidt's successor, Christian Democratic leader Helmut Kohl, embraced many of the SPD's Ostpolitik initiatives, he made certain that in pursuing détente with the East, West Germany kept its identity firmly anchored in the West. Under the CDU–Free Democrats coalition, the radios' status was secure.

12

Senator Fulbright's Crusade

The most serious threat to the radios was not Ostpolitik, but Senator J. W. Fulbright. Whereas German leaders such as Brandt and Schmidt declined to provoke a confrontation with the American government over the freedom radios' presence in their country, Fulbright attacked the stations head-on. He pursued his campaign with the same zeal that drove his campaign for a U.S. military withdrawal from Vietnam. He was both shrewd and tenacious, and he believed passionately in the rightness of his cause. He also came reasonably close to achieving the total shutdown of RFE and RL.

For those who were involved in projects to advance America's Cold War objectives, the sixties are remembered as a period of intellectual assault on the foundations of the country's postwar foreign policy. Every institution that served the Cold War was scrutinized and cross-examined, from the military to universities that were involved in defense research or strategy studies. Moreover, a new and increasingly influential group of "engaged" scholars were casting doubt on every assumption on which the legitimacy of American policy rested. The revisionists argued that America adopted the containment policy because of ambitions for world domination and insisted that America's hostility to the Soviet Union had driven Stalin to impose the Communist system on the East European satellites. And they identified anticommunism as the source of everything that had gone wrong in America, from racial division to the alienation of youth.

This reexamination spawned a thoroughgoing journalistic investigation into the Cold War's impact on American domestic life, and led, inevitably, to the Central Intelligence Agency, with its far-flung empire of proprietary organizations, foundations, and publications, which had been set up to ensure that the West would be well armed in the war of ideas with communism. Radio Free Europe and Radio Liberty were the largest, most expensive, and most successful of the CIA's intellectual properties; it was thus only a matter of time before the relationship between the radios and the CIA was made public.

In its March 1967 issue, *Ramparts* magazine, a freewheeling forum of New Left journalism, published an article that probed the CIA's role as funding agency for putatively nongovernmental domestic political organizations. The article concentrated on the National Students' Association, for years the recipient of CIA subsidies. Neither the radios nor the Free Europe Committee were mentioned. Yet even before the magazine's official publishing date, journalists who had seen advance copies were asking pointed questions about the source of the radios' funding. Thus in a column on the broad issue of the CIA's domestic projects, Max Frankel of the *New York Times* asked, "How can the citizens be protected against campaigns which solicit financial contributions to Radio Free Europe, an intelligence agency operation represented as a non-profit enterprise."[1] For a few weeks thereafter, the "open secret" of CIA funding became a matter of frequent press comment.

The radios' most vulnerable point was less the fact of having been sustained by the intelligence budget than the revelation that the Crusade for Freedom had engaged in a massive deception of the public. A CBS television documentary on the CIA zeroed in on the fund-raising duplicity when narrator Mike Wallace declared, "If you responded to the many appeals of Radio Free Europe on television, in magazines, even in buses and subways, then you became part of a CIA cover."[2] Putting aside the overblown rhetoric, Wallace raised a legitimate issue. Whereas other CIA-funded entities claimed to derive their funds from corporations or foundations, RFE created a myth of massive public financial support. In a sense, the public had been duped into believing that its contributions were responsible for "keeping hope alive" behind the Iron Curtain, when in fact the overwhelming portion of

RFE's budget was provided, covertly, through federal funds. In the wake of the CIA documentary, CBS announced that it would no longer run commercial announcements for RFE that had for years been placed by the Advertising Council, an organization that sponsored public service spots for noncontroversial causes. Within a day, CBS claimed that the announcement had been in error, and that the RFE commercials would be aired as in previous years. The episode was highly embarrassing to the network's president, Dr. Frank Stanton, who was serving as chairman of the Radio Free Europe Fund, which raised private funds for the station.[3]

This was the first time that the mainstream press had zeroed in on the intelligence community's relationship with RFE and RL. In the past, journalists, who presumably knew the truth, would drop tantalizing suggestions about an unofficial government role when writing about the radio's finances. But the issue of radio funding had been raised more directly on occasion by commentators with sharp ideological profiles or by political gossip columnists. Fulton Lewis Jr. had linked RFE to the CIA more than once in his radio broadcasts, and Drew Pearson, an RFE enthusiast, had dropped hints about RFE's reliance on CIA dollars during the fifties.

In 1964 two investigative writers, David Wise and Thomas B. Ross, devoted most of one chapter to RFE and RL in their anti-CIA study, *The Invisible Government*.[4] Despite its polemical tone, *The Invisible Government* was accorded respectful attention by reviewers. Nevertheless, no newspaper saw fit to pursue what would have been a relatively easy exposé in the story of the agency's instruments of "black propaganda," as Wise and Ross referred to the radios. Indeed, even after the *Ramparts* report, the press did not subject RFE and RL to the intense attention paid to defense research by universities or the CIA's covert action campaigns. Had the press been so inclined, it might well have discredited and ultimately destroyed the radios by raising question after question about CIA influence, fund-raising duplicity, and budgets shielded from public scrutiny.

There is, ironically, evidence that by the late 1960s the radios did not enjoy universal support within the CIA. According to Victor Marchetti, coauthor of *The CIA and the Cult of Intelligence,* many high-ranking agency officials were convinced that the radios had outlived their usefulness and favored phasing them out or placing them under different sponsorship. While those urging the elimination of the CIA's relationship were not necessarily dissatisfied with the radios' broadcast performance, they felt that RFE and RL no longer served the interests of the agency to the same extent as in their early years, when RFE maintained its network of information bureaus, conducted interviews with thousands of refugees, and functioned as a scholarly and informational nerve center on matters concerning East European communism. The radios were expensive; furthermore, some CIA officials believed they were widely infiltrated by Soviet bloc agents. Although those favoring elimination were fortified by the conclusions of several internal studies, the radios survived, Marchetti claims, because they continued to enjoy the support of important CIA veterans, presumably including Richard Helms, the director of Central Intelligence at the time. The radios' position was reinforced by the presence on the Free Europe Committee of such influential figures as Lucius Clay and James Roche, the chairman of General Motors. Finally, Marchetti said, some CIA officials were unwilling to jettison the radios out of fear that if the annual subsidies were ended, that money would not be transferred to other agency projects, but simply eliminated from the budget altogether.[5]

Marchetti was considered a CIA renegade; he wrote his book after quitting the agency with fourteen years of service under his belt, including a stint as executive assistant to the deputy director. Marchetti certainly knew a great deal about the inner workings of American intelligence, and while his credibility was damaged by the perception that his revelations amounted to an unpatriotic act, many scholars of American intelligence regard Marchetti's reporting, if not his interpretations, as generally accurate.

With the debate over America's policy in Vietnam at fever pitch, the story of the CIA's relationship with the radios disappeared from the media rather quickly. Editorial comment was largely favorable to RFE and RL, although a few newspapers urged that a new source of funding be sought. But President Lyndon Johnson, already under siege for his policies in Vietnam, showed no inclination to salvage what were being called the "CIA orphans." Johnson was less impressed by arguments for a vigorous American role in the ideological struggle than previous presidents, and he seemed willing to sacrifice the CIA-financed institutions, including the radios, if for no other reason than to relieve himself of yet another foreign policy headache.

Johnson appointed Undersecretary of State Nicholas Katzenbach to chair a committee to make recommendations about the fate of the CIA assets. The Katzenbach committee—the other members were John Gardner, secretary of Health, Education, and Welfare, and Richard Helms—took only two weeks to issue its findings, which reached the president's desk on March 29. The recommendations were stark: "No federal agency shall provide covert financial assistance or support, direct or indirect, to any of the nation's educational or voluntary organizations." And in a passage that would seem to ring the death knell for the radios, the report declared, "No program currently would justify any exception to this rule."[6]

At the time Radio Liberty derived its entire budget from the government through the CIA. Radio Free Europe received a small percentage of its budget through private contributions; the overwhelming percentage was supplied by the intelligence budget. A literal interpretation of the Katzenbach recommendations would have meant immediate liquidation absent an arrangement for alternative funding sources, an unlikely prospect in the midst of the Vietnam War. Lyndon Johnson is said to have been divided over the radios' disposition; he eventually decided to spare them because of the persuasive powers of Helms as well as a personal appeal from Senator James Eastland, a Mississippi Democrat and old presidential friend. After wavering over his decision, Johnson announced that the radios would be allowed to remain on the air on the grounds that they "were not private and voluntary organizations but rather government proprietaries established by government initiative and functioning under official policy direction."[7]

Thus the radios survived under the same funding arrangement as before. If Johnson feared that his decision would trigger another round of criticism over government secrecy or CIA abuse, the public response soon dispelled his apprehensions. The decision provoked hardly a murmur of criticism from the press or Congress.

There had been some discussion of funding the radios through an overt vehicle, and a committee was established, chaired by Secretary of State Dean Rusk, to explore alternative arrangements for the CIA orphans. Rusk, however, ruled that the radios fell outside his committee's purview for national security reasons. Rusk requested instead that consideration of the radios' future be undertaken by the 303 Committee of the CIA.[8]

For the next three years, the CIA wrestled with the problem of the radios' future without finding a satisfactory solution. Indeed, internal CIA memoranda suggest that the agency anticipated a decision to liquidate the radios. Commenting on the response abroad to a decision to close the two stations out of embarrassment over revelation of their covert funding by the CIA, one agency official wrote, "The reaction to this would be puzzlement, and it would be the one reaction common to interested opinion in both Western and Eastern Europe." He added: "Where the fact has not actually been known, covert support has long been assumed in Europe and would not be considered reprehensible. The oddity for Europeans would be that such activity by government should fall of legalistic-moralistic criticism at all, and that an American administration could be forced by it to disavow a policy pursued for two decades. Far from granting moral credit for the move, most Europeans would see it as reflecting a somewhat quaint approach to international politics." The memo added that Soviet dissidents and intellectuals would regard a shutdown as a "loss to their cause" and would regard the reasons for liquidation as "incomprehensible."[9]

There was, in fact, consideration given to retaining RFE while closing down Radio Liberty. In early 1968 the CIA gave thought to closing down RL on budgetary grounds (RL, unlike RFE, received its funds entirely from the CIA) and because RL's signals were heavily jammed; also, the VOA and BBC provided programming to the Soviet Union, and RL's liquidation "could be considered as a U.S. move to improve relations with the USSR." This alternative was abandoned after the Soviet-led invasion of Czechoslovakia in August 1968.[10]

Little changed for the next three years. Officials of the two stations held a few inconclusive meetings with CIA liaison representatives to explore alternative sponsorship. All agreed that the ideal solution would entail the creation of some form of public-private collaborative effort, whereby a sponsoring organization would receive government funds but set its policies independent of Washington. Some advanced the British Council, which sponsored various cultural projects abroad, as a model; others proposed that the radios affiliate with the Smithsonian Institution. All agreed to avoid placing the radios under direct government supervision, either through the United States Information Agency (USIA) or the State Department. The success of the radios was due to their independence; government control, especially State Department control, would have subjected them to the same political influences that burdened the VOA throughout the Cold War.

Yet despite the recent brush with liquidation, the radios did not approach the question of funding sources with special urgency. The subject of ending the CIA relationship had come up during the period in which the Cold War consensus prevailed. A.A. Berle had proposed formalizing the government's sponsorship during a conversation with Allen Dulles in 1957, advancing the dubious argument that government was a more flexible instrument than private administration might prove to be.[11] But neither the radios nor the CIA had given the matter more than cursory consideration. The CIA funding channel had worked well, and there was little reason to believe it would not work well in the future. Furthermore, a change in sponsorship would have meant public acknowledgment of the CIA tie, a prospect RFE in particular preferred to avoid, since it would mean that the truth about the Crusade for Freedom would emerge.[12]

Even after the revelations about the CIA orphans, the agency remained committed to covert funding for the radios. A memo from an agency official to Richard Helms concluded that there was "no satisfactory alternative" to covert funding. Open funding, the memo declared, would subject the radios to public scrutiny and debate and would require an explanation of their "more politically charged missions." "This would firmly fix the radios as official instruments of the U.S. government, which, in turn would jeopardize their positions in all their host countries and present the target regimes with an easy rationale for discrediting them." The memo went on to recommend that if covert funding was deemed unacceptable, "the only alternative would be termination."[13]

In the altered political environment of the early seventies, however, the maxim "If it ain't broke, don't fix it" was no longer appropriate. The Cold War consensus lay in tatters. Prominent members of Congress were embracing theories about America's global role that a few years earlier had been limited to a few historians of revisionist bent. Thus Mike Mansfield, the respected Senate majority leader, was pressing for the removal of American troops from Europe, an act that would have meant the effective destruction of the NATO alliance. Furthermore, President Richard Nixon, a politician of impeccable anti-Communist credentials, had launched an ambitious policy of détente with the Communist world, centered on a series of summit meetings, trade initiatives, and arms control agreements. While Nixon believed in a tough-minded détente, in which the United States maintained its leadership role within the Atlantic Alliance and continued to engage communism in the ideological struggle, more dovish-minded politicians saw détente as supplying the opportunity to rid American policy of "needless obstacles to mutual understanding" between East and West. At the same time, the CIA was fast becoming the most unpopular institution of government; its actions were blamed for Cold War scandals in every part of the world.

The radios thus were vulnerable. Though still popular with public and press, their existence could easily be placed in jeopardy by a sensational press revelation or congressional investigation.

Or by the hostility of an influential member of Congress, such as Senator J. William Fulbright. For years the Arkansas Democrat had commanded the nation's attention as chairman of the Senate Foreign Relations Committee. Fulbright was best known as an acid-tongued critic of American involvement in Vietnam. Liberals adored Fulbright to the point of forgiving him his unbroken record of opposition to civil rights legislation. When Robert Kennedy sought the presidency in 1968, the Democratic Party's antiwar wing urged that Fulbright be made the vice-presidential candidate. And when George McGovern won the presidential nomination on an anti–Cold War platform in 1972, the Left promoted Fulbright as a future secretary of state.

By the early seventies, Fulbright had moved beyond war critic to embrace much of the revisionist argument about the basic thrust of postwar American foreign policy. While never subscribing to the view that American policy was motivated by economic self-interest, he did accept the thesis that America had been corrupted by its commitment to containing the spread of communism. Fulbright came to regard anticommunism as America's original sin, and he devoted his energies to the removal of Cold War influence from America's conduct of international affairs.

Fulbright laid out his critique in *The Crippled Giant,* a 1972 book that was remarkable for the radicalism of its analysis, given the author's position within the political establishment. Harking back to the postwar origins of U.S.-Soviet hostilities, Fulbright praised Henry Wallace's noninterventionist perspective while charging that President Truman had welcomed Stalin's aggression in Eastern Europe as a convenient rationale for the Cold War. Fulbright was especially concerned with what he perceived as the immature unwillingness of America's Cold Warriors to accept Moscow's domination of its neighbors. He thus declared, "Insofar . . . as we raise false hopes with provocative propaganda, maintain high troop levels, and continue the arms race, we retard the natural process of European reunification, lingering morbidly and uselessly in the graveyard of Cold War relics."[14]

To reassure the Kremlin of our peaceful intentions, Fulbright proposed the withdrawal of American troops from Europe and the liquidation of Radio Free Europe and Radio Liberty.[15] Fulbright was particularly churlish toward the radios: "Purporting to show [East Europeans] that there is a better 'way of life' outside the 'Iron Curtain,'" he wrote, "we foster futile discontent, not for any discernible purpose of policy, but for purposes of ideological mischief. In this way we detract from the broader purposes of our own policy and of world peace, which requires us to live in the greatest attainable harmony with the Communist governments of the world." As chairman of the Foreign Relations Committee, Fulbright carried out a two-year crusade to put these purveyors of "ideological mischief" off the air. Fulbright's single-minded campaign did not succeed, but it was the most serious threat to the radios' existence during the Cold War.[16]

On January 21, 1971, Senator Clifford Case, a New Jersey Republican with a liberal orientation and a record of opposition to the Vietnam War, rose on the floor of Congress to read a statement about the radios. Case began by "revealing" the links between the radios and the CIA—the first time, incredibly, a public official had acknowledged the relationship. Case was a determined opponent of government secrecy, and it was to this aspect of the radios' history that he addressed his most acidulous remarks. He noted that millions of Americans had contributed to the Crusade for Freedom under the impression that their "Truth Dollars" enabled RFE to broadcast its message to those living under Communist tyranny. "Several hundreds of millions of dollars in United States government funds had been expended from secret CIA budgets to pay almost totally for the costs of these two radio stations," he declared. "[At] no time was Congress asked or permitted to carry out its constitutional role of approving the expenditures."[17]

Some State Department officials believed that the man responsible for Case's "revelation" was not the senator, but his aide, John D. Marks, a disgruntled former State Department and CIA official who had left the government and joined Case's staff. Marks was Victor Marchetti's coauthor in writing *The CIA and the Cult of Intelligence,* and he knew the facts about the radios' CIA ties.[18]

Ultimately, whether the impetus came from Case or Marks is irrelevant. If Case had not gone public with the truth about the radios' funding, someone else would have. Case, furthermore, was favorably disposed toward the radios' broadcast mission. He even introduced a bill to remove the radios from the CIA, provide $30 million in federal funds for their operation in fiscal 1972, and place them, temporarily, under the supervision of the State Department while a permanent solution could be arranged.

To win passage, Case needed to secure approval from the Foreign Relations Committee, chaired by the radios' most powerful adversary. To complicate the matter further, several committee members shared the chairman's skepticism toward RFE and RL: Frank Church, an Idaho Democrat who later chaired investigations into CIA abuses and who had once headed a Crusade for Freedom campaign in his home state; Stuart Symington, a Missouri Democrat who had moved in an increasingly dovish direction since serving as secretary of the air force in the Truman administration; and Majority Leader Mike Mansfield, who counted Fulbright as an important ally in his campaign to pull American troops out of Europe.[19]

For Church, Symington, and Mansfield, the fate of RFE and RL was a secondary issue. Not so for Fulbright. Fulbright had grown increasingly bitter about America's political direction and was prone to mutterings about a developing "cult of the personality" around the president and a "breakdown of our democratic system."[20] His distemper seemed to reinforce his resolve to change the course of American policy. When responding to those he respected or who agreed with him on the importance of détente, Fulbright chose his words carefully in justifying his opposition to the radios. To Marshall Shulman, a Soviet expert from Columbia University who went on to serve in the administration of President Jimmy Carter and who supported RFE and RL, Fulbright cited economic factors: America, he wrote Shulman, could no longer afford both the freedom radios and the VOA.[21] On other occasions, he allowed his true sentiments to pour forth. During a committee hearing, Fulbright complained of the large number of East European émigrés on the radios' staff. "They have their biases," he warned, "which is not necessarily and always coincident with the interests of the United States."[22] On the floor of Congress, he described the radios as part of a "big lie" that had corrupted American policy and as a "product of the U-2, Bay of Pigs, and Tonkin Gulf imagination."[23]

Fulbright also conducted a search for evidence of scandal or malfeasance. He wrote Secretary of State William P. Rogers to inquire whether RFE or RL had a connection with Soviet dissident Pyotr Yakir, who had been arrested for, among other things, passing information along to Radio Liberty. He also asked for the transcripts of the broadcasts reporting Yakir's arrest, an unusual request given Fulbright's lack of interest in the content of the radios' broadcasts. Fulbright's staff displayed some confusion on radio operations. J. Allen Hovey, a Free Europe Committee official, seemed bewildered when Robert Dockery, a committee aide, inquired as to why RFE was so preoccupied with the internal political developments of its audience countries, particularly since, Dockery added, broadcasts on internal themes irritated Communist Party leaders. An exasperated Hovey replied that given the option of offending the leadership or the listeners, RFE had decided that an irritated Communist leadership was a price worth paying for the loyalty of its listeners.[24]

In fact, Fulbright's effort to win support for his antiradio drive was a notable failure. Congress, including most Democratic doves, favored retaining RFE and RL under non-CIA administration; more than half the Senate endorsed a statement supporting the radios sponsored by Senators Hubert Humphrey, the former vice president, and Illinois Republican Charles Percy. When the matter of providing one-year funding came before the full Senate in March 1972, only six senators voted no: Fulbright, Mansfield, Symington, and three other Democrats, William Proxmire of Wisconsin, Harold Hughes of Iowa, and Allen Ellender of Louisiana.[25] A similar measure that came before the House in November 1971 passed 271 to 12. Those in opposition included archsegregationist John Rarick of Louisiana, a John Birch Society supporter; John Schmitz of California; and liberal doves such as Don Edwards of California and Bob Kastenmeier of Wisconsin.[26] The nation's newspapers supported the radios with near-unanimity; only *Newsday* of Long Island editorially called for elimination. A similar outpouring of support came from the European press.

Most pro-détente members of the Washington establishment also favored a continuation of the radios' broadcasts. A number of Fulbright's acquaintances joined a citizens' committee to support the radios chaired by George Ball, who as undersecretary of state was one of the earliest critics of the Vietnam War in the Johnson administration.[27] By contrast, Fulbright's support was limited to marginal figures, such as Cyrus Eaton, an eccentric millionaire with pro-Soviet views, and Fred Warner Neal, a professor who was to play a key role in the Committee on East–West Accord, an organization established in the mid-1970s to promote détente.[28] But isolation seems not to have weakened Fulbright's resolve. He was convinced that the world was moving inexorably toward détente, and that the process could be accelerated if the few remaining obstacles could be pushed aside. As he told the American Bankers Association in an otherwise glowing *tour de horizon* on U.S.-Soviet relations, "All that remains of the 'liberation' policy are the mewlings of Radio Free Europe and Radio Liberty, which liberate nobody but greatly annoy the governments of Eastern Europe."[29]

It is unlikely that a familiarity with the content of RFE and RL broadcasts would have persuaded Fulbright to abandon his crusade for liquidation. While the broadcast tone of both instruments had changed since the fifties, their reason for being remained a commitment to undermine Communist regimes. They pursued this objective through uncensored news and reasoned analysis, not polemics. The radios might best be compared to a politically aligned American newspaper, in which there was separation between news and the editorial page, where opinions were expressed, sometimes strongly, and where commentaries were dictated by an overarching philosophy.

The radios seldom blamed communism per se for the social ills that plagued the audience societies. Instead, commentaries tended to focus on specific problems within the context of the limited solutions available under the Communist system. Commentators did not insist that endemic housing shortages could only be dealt with by the free market. Rather, they might propose a reallocation of resources from the military or heavy industry to the needs of consumers, or social democratic type reforms.

The principal challenge remained providing accurate reports on developments that the Communist media ignored, censored, or distorted. Radio Free Europe had launched its broadcasts in 1950 to give Eastern Europe an alternative to a censored media, and twenty years later it continued to fulfill that basic role. Communist media were more informative and less bombastic than in the past, in large measure, no doubt, because of the challenges posed by foreign broadcast services. But censorship—systematic and thorough—remained fundamental to Communist control.

The case of Poland is instructive, since that country enjoyed a reputation for cultural liberalism. Yet according to Jane Leftwich Curry, who analyzed seven hundred pages of documents smuggled out of the censor's office by a censor who defected to the West, the press was more rigidly controlled during the 1970s, under the leadership of Edward Gierek, a man lauded by the West as a reformer, than it was under the dogmatic Gomulka.[30]

Gierek saw the censor as occupying a pivotal position in mobilizing support for the regime's economic strategy. Whatever legitimacy Gierek enjoyed was predicated on the fulfillment of his vow of economic betterment for the country's restive workers. A crucial element of this strategy was what came to be known as the "propaganda of success," which amounted to an endless stream of articles extolling Gierek's policies and ignoring the nation's gathering crises. Central to the censor's mandate was to ensure that no criticism of Gierek's economic strategy reach print. The list of forbidden subjects reached well beyond questions of economic policy, narrowly defined. It included a complete ban on references to pollution, food contamination, agricultural disease, and other health-related topics.

The censors also participated in rewriting Polish history. It was, in fact, instructions to falsify information about the Katyn forest massacre, in which thousands of Polish officers, including his own grandfather, were murdered by Soviet troops during World War II, which prompted the defection of the censor who smuggled the material to the West. In this particular case, censors were compelled to change the date of the massacre from 1940 to 1941 in order to remove any evidence of possible Soviet guilt.

As long as RFE and RL remained on the air, the attempts to airbrush inconvenient facts from the news pages and history books usually ended in futility. Radio Free Europe maintained a battery of analysts who scrutinized historical writings for evidence of chicanery. If a falsification was discovered, broadcasters would make sure that it became public knowledge. More often, RFE and RL provided information that was suppressed rather than distorted. In 1970, for example, RFE's Czechoslovak service broadcast the contents of a special report, prepared dur-

ing the period of relative freedom in 1968, that reached critical conclusions about the political trials of the early fifties. The report's existence was acknowledged by the authorities only after RFE had aired
its contents for several weeks.[31]

Ironically, given Fulbright's frequent citing of President Nixon's
trip to China as proof that the world was moving toward détente and
away from Cold War, it was this very event that gave the radios an
opportunity to provide their audience with an alternative to the slanted
coverage in the official Communist press. Both RFE and RL offered
in-depth coverage of the historic event, much of which was taken
directly from American and West German television stations, while
commentators countered the quasi-official Soviet view that the visit
smacked of "collusion" between Washington and Beijing. Détente, in
fact, provided numerous opportunities for the radios to correct Communist press errors or to simply fill in the gaps left by the censors.
Radio Liberty, for example, told its listeners about the huge amounts
of grain purchased by the Soviet Union from Western countries, a fact
the Soviet media ignored.[32]

jeszcze Polska ....

For Radio Free Europe, the most formidable challenge, and greatest
opportunity, was again to be found in the melodrama of Polish politics. By the mid-sixties, Gomulka had abandoned all pretense of reform, and as the decade ended, his position as party leader became
increasingly tenuous. In 1970, the party announced, to great fanfare, a
series of desperation measures billed as major steps toward economic
reform. Radio Free Europe was unimpressed, and pronounced the
new actions as inadequate. In a prescient commentary in October, a
Polish analyst declared, "There is widespread disbelief in the economic
miracle which the system of incentives was expected to bring.... The
working class, which invariably has to suffer because of the effects of a
badly managed economy, sometimes loses its temper."[33] On December 12, the regime announced sweeping price increases on a wide
range of necessities—food, clothing, and fuel primarily—theoretically
balanced off by a reduction in the price of household goods. Again,
RFE's analysis foresaw trouble ahead: "The political consequences of
these economic measures could well be very serious. The timing of
higher prices on major foodstuffs just before Christmas will seriously
deepen the already strong dissatisfaction. It could also arouse dissatisfaction within the party itself."

_12/70_

amen....

Three days later, Poland's Baltic coast erupted in protests and riot-
ing. Initially, the news was concealed from the outside world. Soon,
however, a refugee living in Sweden picked up a report from Gdansk
radio about spreading disorder. He told a friend in Copenhagen about
the upheaval, and the friend in turn passed the information along to
RFE. The station's monitors picked up a weak signal from Radio
Szczecin and later one from Gdansk. Radio Free Europe immediately
began issuing reports on the situation; it was the first news organization to cover the disorders.

The importance of the RFE reports was reinforced by the news
blackout imposed by the authorities in Warsaw. Aside from those in
the coastal areas, Poles knew little of what was happening in what
would become the bloodiest upheaval in postwar Polish history, with
several hundred deaths, a much greater loss of life than during the
imposition of martial law in 1981. Only on the afternoon of December 16, many hours after RFE had begun coverage, did the regime
allow Radio Warsaw to offer an account of the coastal events, albeit a
slanted version that blamed the troubles on hooligans and adventurers.
Placing the blame for popular unrest on antisocial elements was a shop-
worn Communist tactic. As Jan Nowak noted in the Polish service's
first commentary on the crisis, "The well known propaganda trick of
presenting people who have been led to despair as hooligans, social
scum, provocateurs, and troublemakers can no longer mislead anyone;
it was used in the past too often. If the demonstrating workers committed acts of violence, then their behavior can only be compared to a
man who, led to total despair, breaks everything that falls under his
hand in an outbreak of fury. Responsibility for this kind of outburst
falls on the people and circumstances which led to such a state of
mind." Soon, Radio Free Europe was identified by the official press as
the source of Poland's miseries. *Trybuna Ludu,* the organ of the party's
central committee, accused the "subversive" RFE of having abetted
the internal enemy: "It calls for excesses, and pushes [people] to irresponsible and harmful acts, the costs of which are not to be paid by the
hirelings in Munich, but by all of us, the whole society."

The official line shifted dramatically on December 20, after Edward Gierek was named to succeed Gomulka. The new party chief
and the media now explained the upheavals in language not very different from RFE commentaries. *Trybuna Ludu* blamed the tragedy on
"ill-conceived conceptions of economic policy," while the daily news-

paper *Zycie Warszawy* wrote of a need to "change the mode of government at all levels." The lesson RFE drew was that "the workers, together with the whole community, have won their first great victory. They have shown that their will and their demands must be taken into consideration by the authorities, that there are limits which no one can exceed." Polish communism had been shaken to its roots. And for the next two decades, Radio Free Europe's most important story would be the steady unraveling of the party's control over the economy, culture, and people of the Soviet Union's most important satellite.

Poland was not the only country in which Communist authorities were singling out the radios for special attention. What appears to have been a coordinated antiradios press campaign was launched throughout the Soviet bloc in the early 1970s, inspired, no doubt, by the conviction that détente offered a unique opportunity to discredit the stations. In January 1972, a time when the debate over the fate of the radios was at its height, an influential Soviet editor suggested to a visiting American congressman that if Western radio stations stopped what he described as their anti-Soviet propaganda, the Soviet Union would ease its restrictions on political dissent and Jewish emigration, two key stumbling blocks to improved ties at the time. The "unofficial" sounding was made by Aleksandsr Chakovsky, the editor of *Literaturnaya Gazeta,* during a meeting with Representative James Scheuer, a Bronx Democrat whose district included a high percentages of Jews. Referring to Radio Liberty and the VOA, Chakovsky told Scheuer, "If you change these broadcasts, we will change the way we handle dissidents and those who want to emigrate."[34]

But the propaganda offensive was even less convincing than past campaigns of denunciation. In 1956, the last time the entire Soviet bloc made the radios a target, RFE was vulnerable because of its blunders during the Hungarian Revolution. But in 1971, the charge that RFE was interfering in the internal affairs of regimes that practiced systematic censorship rang hollow. Even party propagandists realized the absurdity of constantly placing the blame for Communist failures on foreign broadcast stations. The Soviet party newspaper *Komsomolskaya Pravda* wrote in 1971 that "it is always better for us to analyze [social problems] than to wait for commentaries by various 'voices' which reach our country one way or another." Added *Magyar Hirlap,* a Hungarian party newspaper, "All in all, it is undeniable that we can learn from the methods of RFE; namely [we must provide] more publicity, still more stimuli for thinking, still more published facts."[35]

On the other hand, some party officials detected a new and sinister role for the radios in their ability to amplify isolated acts of dissent that were beginning to spread from the Soviet Union to Eastern Europe. According to a Polish official: "Even insignificant troubles caused by reactionary forces may [assume] great importance. . . . The danger of each hostile action can no longer be measured by the force and extent of the local group which starts that particular move. It must be multiplied by the power of the facilities for ideological subversion available abroad, as well as by certain elements of our own weakness."[36] Communism could no longer isolate expressions of discontent. International broadcasting ensured that samizdat from Lviv, a riot in Gdansk, or a demonstration in Tbilisi would be quickly relayed throughout the entire Soviet bloc. Due in large measure to the efforts of RFE and RL, there was no such thing as purely local protest.

The context in which the debate over the radios' future took place was dominated by America's pursuit of détente with the Soviet Union. It was not only RFE and RL that found it necessary to make adjustments in light of the policy shifts in Washington. The United States Information Agency and its broadcasting arm, the Voice of America, were embroiled in a series of controversies with the State Department and Congress over what critics called a failure to fall in line behind the new détente orientation. Frank Shakespeare, a high-ranking CBS executive, had been appointed director of the USIA during Nixon's first term. Shakespeare made little secret of his anti-Communist convictions; naturally, he believed that the USIA, as the agency responsible for the promotion of American values around the world, should take the leading role in carrying out the global war of ideas. Unfortunately for Shakespeare, the Senate Foreign Relations Committee, chaired by Fulbright, enjoyed oversight authority over the USIA. Fulbright developed an antipathy toward Shakespeare from the very beginning, and was constantly on the hunt for evidence that Shakespeare was "politicizing" the agency. In one famous incident, a deputy to Shakespeare, Bruce Herschensohn, publicly called the senator's foreign policy views "naïve and stupid." Herschensohn, who later became a well-known figure in conservative circles in California, subsequently resigned, but he did not apologize for his remarks, which were provoked, in part, by Fulbright's attempts to liquidate RFE and RL.[37]

In 1973, shortly after Shakespeare had returned to private life, a report was issued that urged changes in USIA policies designed "to reflect and encourage" East-West détente. The report was prepared by the U.S. Advisory Commission on Information, chaired, ironically, by Frank Stanton, a former chairman of RFE's private fund-raising effort. The report was, in effect, a criticism of Shakespeare's continued insistence on a critical stance toward the Communist world. It urged that the agency overhaul its policies and methods to "convey this new atmosphere of improved relations between the U.S. and two historically hostile powers [the Soviet Union and China] to the rest of the world." Even before his departure, Shakespeare had been pressured by the administration to soften coverage of the two major Communist powers and had ordered changes in VOA coverage of China and the USSR before Nixon's visits to the two countries. Alexander Haig, then the president's national security adviser, had instructed the USIA to continue "eschewing polemics, not seeking quarrels and not attempting to magnify small incidents in your broadcasts to the Soviet Union."[38]

Soon, changes were made, only to generate a new set of controversies. James Keogh, a Nixon speech writer and former *Time* magazine correspondent, replaced Shakespeare and immediately transformed coverage of Communist world affairs. Now, however, agency employees were charging that the new administration was quashing programs that might be deemed offensive to Communist leaderships. The VOA abandoned several frequencies at Soviet request. It eliminated several longstanding political programs in favor of programs featuring popular music. Programming decisions were increasingly influenced by a policy of avoiding material that might irritate the Kremlin. A series of broadcasts on Aleksandr Solzhenitsyn's monumental study of Soviet oppression, *The Gulag Archipelago,* was canceled. A proposed series on young workers in the Soviet Union and Eastern Europe was turned down because, according to a VOA official, "if it had been honest and accurate, it would have been offensive to the governments involved; it would have seemed gratuitous and ideologically polemical." Keogh denied that his policies amounted to censorship, but he defended a policy of avoiding material that might offend Communist regimes. He dismissed broadcasts of the Solzhenitsyn book as "advocacy journalism," and declared, "Détente has changed what we do in USIA.

Our program managers must be sensitive to U.S. policy as enunciated by the President and the Secretary of State. That policy is that we do not interfere in the internal affairs of other countries."[39]

As a reward, the Soviets temporarily suspended the jamming of VOA broadcasts.[40] But what the Voice gained in audibility was counterbalanced by a loss of credibility with the Russian audience. Kirill Chenkin, a Soviet journalist who emigrated to Israel in the early seventies, said that by avoiding broadcasts that might offend the leadership, the VOA had suffered a loss of credibility and audience. "Something that's inoffensive to the government isn't likely to be worth tuning in," he asserted.[41]

Thus while Radio Free Europe and Radio Liberty had been established as the quintessential instruments of anticommunism, their defenders studiously avoided any reference that might link the radios to their Cold War past. A special RFE report, issued for public relations purposes, carried the title "Radio Free Europe in an Era of Negotiation." In testimony before Senator Fulbright's committee, supporters argued that the radios' role was entirely consistent with the objectives of détente. There were, of course, differing versions of détente. Some, like Senator Fulbright, maintained a narrow definition centering on arms agreements and the expansion of trade. Others insisted that détente would be incomplete unless accompanied by greater freedom for the people of the Communist world. Those drawn to the more expansive view usually favored continuation of the radios' broadcasts. Senator Case, for example, justified his legislation on the grounds that "the conditions for peace and understanding do not exist when the closed society limits the information that its people receive." The radios also counted among their admirers those who were skeptical of détente from the outset and believed that RFE and RL remained subversive of the Communist system. Yet no one ever actually defended the radios with the argument that they subverted the Communist system or weakened Soviet domination of its neighbors. Indeed, one is struck by how seldom the word "Communist" was uttered during the hearings before the Foreign Relations Committee.

The radios' most eloquent defenders turned out to be foreign correspondents with experience in the Soviet bloc. Robert S. Elegant, a reporter for the *Los Angeles Times,* wrote that it was unfortunate that the radios were criticized by "men of good will who champion free exchange of ideas and want to end the Cold War." He added:

True liberals should . . . support the stations' aims: free
information and East–West relaxation. Fundamental rapprochement between East and West is impossible as long as
insecure Eastern governments must rule by physical and
psychological repression. Both RFE and RL discuss the
problem of peaceful evolution in Communist societies in
language immediately comprehensible to generations trained
in the intellectual discipline of Marxism. . . . Both stations
are byproducts—not causes—of fundamental tensions.
Despite their human imperfections, both seek to reduce
internal and international tensions by the best means yet
known to man.[42]

The radios also received a glowing endorsement from David
Halberstam, who had become acquainted with RFE broadcasts during a stint as correspondent in Warsaw for the *New York Times*. At the
time of his testimony before the Foreign Relations Committee,
Halberstam was a celebrity on the antiwar Left because of publication
of his best-selling attack on the Vietnam policies of the Kennedy and
Johnson administrations, *The Best and the Brightest*. Halberstam's committee appearance, during which he gave an impassioned defense of
the radios from the position of someone who could speak with authority about their impact on the audience countries, may have helped
dispel lingering doubts about the importance of the radios among
dovish senators such as Frank Church. Halberstam had reason to be
appreciative of RFE's role; in 1965 he had been summarily expelled
by Communist authorities for writing about the economic frustra-
tions of the Polish people. The very night of his expulsion, RFE broadcast the texts of the articles that had provoked the authorities.
   More than any other witness, Halberstam demolished the various
arguments advanced by Fulbright for liquidation. Whereas Fulbright
derided the radios as propaganda tools, Halberstam compared them to
NBC, CBS, or the *Times* when judged on performance and accountability. Whereas Fulbright argued that the radios had little influence or
listenership, Halberstam testified that they enjoyed a high degree of
credibility among the most sophisticated East Europeans. To Fulbright's
denunciations of the radios as Cold War relics, Halberstam retorted,
"To judge [RFE] as part of the Cold War is to find the broadcaster as
guilty as the jammer." To Fulbright's complaint that RFE and RL an-

noyed regime officials, Halberstam observed that, in private, the East European journalists who held their jobs because of their presumed political reliability praised RFE broadcasts for contributing to the process of opening up Communist societies to outside ideas. Halberstam concluded with a tribute to the radios' contribution to the struggle for freedom in the closed societies of the East: Communist authorities "would like to stomp [RFE] out. It is the one thing in their society they can't control in any way. It does heighten the aspirations [of the people]. It does heighten the sophistication and the level of knowledge of their population. It is something that they cannot quite control. Therefore, [the authorities] have to be accountable, too."[43]

Fulbright was no more inclined to accept the testimony of Vietnam critics like Halberstam than State Department officials or the émigrés who appeared before his committee on the radios' behalf. Nor was he deterred by his isolation within Congress. In 1971, Fulbright had commissioned studies of both radios by the research service of the Library of Congress. To his considerable annoyance, the completed drafts amounted to unalloyed endorsements of both RFE and RL. Fulbright thereupon tried to withhold the reports from public release and requested that the drafts be rewritten. On February 17, 1972, the syndicated columnists Rowland Evans and Robert Novak published a column accusing Fulbright of attempting to quash the studies because of their inconvenient conclusions. Speaking on the House floor, Robert Steele, a Connecticut Republican, demanded that the reports be made public.[44]

The studies were thereupon released, but Fulbright lashed back by questioning the integrity of the surveys, noting that James Price, who wrote the RFE study, had worked for a time with the CIA. In fact, both Price and Joseph Whelan, the author of the RL report, had conducted numerous studies into subjects that were related to the U.S.-Soviet rivalry, and neither seemed inclined to question the basic assumptions undergirding America's Cold War involvement.

Fulbright managed to prevent a resolution of the controversy for many months, during which time the radios existed thanks to continuing resolutions providing stopgap, temporary funding. He forestalled the adoption in 1971 of a plan formulated by Cord Meyer of the CIA and several State Department officials, including David Abshire, assistant secretary of state for congressional relations and John Baker, director of East European affairs. Their plan called for the radios to be administered by a presidentially appointed committee, the American Council on Private International Communications. The board would be funded by Congress, but function independent of the federal government on policy matters.[45]

The State Department–CIA plan was introduced as legislation by Senator Case. The Senate, however, was unenthusiastic about appropriating money for an independent agency over which it would have no control. Instead, the Senate adopted Case's original, interim proposal, calling for a one-year appropriation to maintain the radios under State Department jurisdiction.

In the House, there was little opposition to the radios; the chairman of the Foreign Affairs Committee, Thomas "Doc" Morgan, was a strong supporter, as were such key committee members as Clement Zablocki and Dante Fascell. The House adopted a measure that differed significantly from the Senate version, and it took many months of negotiations before the House agreed to accept the Senate measure.

Throughout the debate, Fulbright showed himself a master tactician. Depending on the audience, he might characterize the radios as an impediment to détente, a drain on the budget, or an ineffectual duplication of the VOA. As a final ploy, he raised the absence of financial support from America's NATO allies. If the Europeans think that the radios are so valuable, he mused, why aren't they contributing their fair share.[46]

The question of European participation in RFE-RL funding was contrived and irrelevant. European funding would inevitably raise the prospect of European participation in management and policy-making, an unworkable arrangement given each country's special sensitivities and objectives in relations with the East. But no one was willing to challenge Fulbright. Instead, the radios engaged in an elaborate charade to convince the Senate that every avenue of possible foreign funding had been explored.

In the aftermath of the Hungarian Revolution, RFE had had the foresight to establish what was known as the West European Advisory Committee. The members were drawn from influential European political circles—former officials and diplomats who also served on such bodies as the Council of Europe and the North Atlantic Assembly. To these experienced European politicians, the controversy over CIA-RFE ties reflected a typically American naïveté; the CIA's role, they believed, was neither surprising nor objectionable. They were, however, concerned that the turmoil might destroy the freedom radios. It was therefore arranged that a small delegation of WEAC members visit the United States in hopes of influencing the debate, led by the committee's chairman, Dirk Stikker, a former foreign minister of the Netherlands.

The delegation asked to meet informally with members of Fulbright's committee. Fulbright, however, insisted that Stikker appear before the committee in a public session. At the hearing, Fulbright badgered Stikker about who had paid for the trip (RFE had), whether the Europeans were prepared to share in the radios' costs (Stikker hemmed and hawed), whether he knew of any CIA agents on the RFE staff (Stikker denied it), and carried out a prolonged argument over Stikker's contention that RFE was a representative example of a free press. Stikker became so agitated that radio officials feared he might suffer a heart attack, as Fulbright contested every assertion and fulminated about European unwillingness to help pay for the freedom stations.[47]

In any event, RFE solicited funds from governments, Atlanticist organizations such as the North Atlantic Parliament and the Council of Europe, and private foundations and corporations. No serious money was raised from any European sources, and the issue died a natural death.

In May 1972, President Nixon entered the controversy by appointing a special commission to make recommendations about the radios' future. He named Milton Eisenhower, the former president's brother, as chairman. The other members were John P. Roche, a professor of politics at Brandeis and a former aide to President Johnson; Edmund A. Gullion, dean of the Fletcher School of Law and Diplomacy at Tufts University; Edward W. Barrett, former assistant secretary of state for public affairs and dean of the School of Journalism of Columbia University; and John A. Gronouski, former ambassador to Poland, former postmaster general, and dean of the Lyndon B. Johnson School of Public Affairs at the University of Texas.[48]

Given the political character of its composition, it was preordained that the Eisenhower Commission would support the radios' continued role in American diplomacy. Roche had a reputation as a militant anti-Communist, Gronouski had testified before the Foreign Relations Committee on RFE's behalf, and Barrett had played an important role in setting policy for America's international broadcasting program in the early years of the Cold War, and had served as director of the VOA.

The appointment of the commission and the passage of a bill that funded RFE and RL for fiscal 1973 finally settled the issue of the radios' existence. The principal lingering question was how the radios would be funded and governed, and it was to this question that the commission's report, released in early 1973, addressed itself. First, the report concluded that the radios contributed to détente on the assumption that "peace is more secure in well informed societies than in those that may be more easily manipulated." Second, the commission recommended against soliciting funds from foreign governments on the ground that shared funding would inevitably raise the question of shared management and policy responsibilities.

Finally, there was the central issue of creating an organizational structure to ensure adequate funding, journalistic independence, and accountability to Congress. The commission proposal borrowed heavily on the original State Department plan for an American Council for Private International Communications, which had been proposed, and rejected, in 1971. The commission called for funding to be provided openly by Congress. A new structure, called the Board for International Broadcasting, would serve as a link between the federal government and the radios; the radios, in turn, would continue to be run by their separate corporate boards. The BIB would act to protect the radios from political pressure while at the same time ensuring that broadcasting was "not inconsistent with broad U.S. foreign policy." The double negative formulation, attributed to Milton Eisenhower, was a genius stroke, insofar as it implied a policy that was at once politically responsible while allowing a wide latitude of broadcast discretion.[49]

The recommendations embedded in the commission report won the endorsement of President Nixon, who called the stations "voices of free information" that "serve our national interest and merit the full support of the Congress and the American people." In a passage meant to answer Fulbright's assertion that RFE and RL were incompatible with détente, Nixon declared, "The free flow of information and of ideas among nations is a vital element in normal relations between East and West and contributes to an enduring structure of peace."[50] The report formed the basis for legislation introduced by Senators

Humphrey and Percy. The measure was quickly adopted, 313 to 90, in the House. In the Senate, Fulbright remained defiant to the bitter end. He introduced an amendment that would have prevented the United States from paying more than half the radios' budget after 1975, and when that failed, he tried unsuccessfully to have the radios combined with the operations of the VOA. Having dispensed with the Fulbright proposals, the Senate approved the BIB legislation, 76 to 10. On October 19, 1973, Public Law 93–129, the Board for International Broadcasting Act, was enacted into law.

There was a bizarre footnote to the controversy over the radios' future existence. In the midst of Senate hearings, Fulbright read into the record the texts of letters, signed by Jan Nowak and written on RFE letterhead, which were highly critical of the Arkansas senator. The letters were addressed to the editor of a Polish American newspaper. One letter accused Fulbright of continuing his campaign against the radios out of vengefulness and made reference to Fulbright's "pro-Communist sympathies." The letter also charged that Fulbright "made his first trip after completion of his education to no other place than Moscow."

Fulbright was furious, and the matter was potentially damaging to RFE given the Senate's sensitivities to attacks on its members. It appears, however, that Nowak was at least in part the victim of a dirty-tricks campaign orchestrated from Poland. To begin with, the letters were never published; they were stolen from the editor's desk and passed along to Fulbright. Second, at least some of the letters were apparently written in Poland. Indeed, several months prior to the Senate hearing, excerpts from the purloined letters had been published in *Zycie Warsawy,* a regime paper. At least one letter was an outright forgery as part of a campaign to discredit both RFE and Jan Nowak. No lasting damage was suffered by RFE, although Nowak's reputation was tarnished a bit since he had, in fact, sent letters to various Polish American acquaintances to encourage a campaign against Fulbright's liquidation efforts within the Polish American community. In his memoirs, Nowak asserts that the theft of the letters and the fabrication was part of a secret police campaign to discredit RFE and contribute to the station's demise.[51]

During the 1970s, the State Department began to take a more systematic interest in the content of RFE broadcasts. American diplomats stationed at embassies in Eastern Europe monitored RFE broadcasts and discussed the station's programs with regime officials, local journalists, and members of the democratic opposition. Complaints would routinely be passed along to higher-level officials in Washington, who would then pass along the information to RFE management. The State Department officials with whom RFE dealt directly were usually favorably disposed toward the station's mission and understood that RFE was meant to play a different role than the Voice of America. Nevertheless, some could not understand how a station funded by public money could be given the high degree of autonomy that RFE continued to enjoy; these officials occasionally suggested the institution of prebroadcast script reviews. The issue, however, was never pressed, and the policy of permitting individual broadcasts a high degree of journalistic independence remained in place.

Some suspected that the principal reason for enhanced diplomatic monitoring was a desire to ensure that RFE broadcasts conformed to the objectives and spirit of détente, then at high-water mark. A more likely reason is simply the fact that the State Department was obliged to pay additional attention to RFE and RL after the CIA relationship was broken. Naturally enough, the State Department was concerned principally with broadcasts that might be interpreted as jeopardizing American relations with East European countries with which the United States hoped to forge closer ties.

One such country was Romania. Radio Free Europe was an influential force in Romania, and its broadcasts were withering toward Ceausescu and his clique. The embassy in Bucharest frequently complained of what was called an "overly biased approach" and an "overly personal manner used to criticize members of the Romanian leadership." The problem, from the embassy's point of view, was spelled out in a 1974 memo: "U.S. policy is to 'support Romania's independent posture,' and the embassy has striven to gain the confidence of a wide variety of officials in the Romanian government. This task is not made easier if RFE adopts a carping or ad hominem approach to this leadership, who wonder whether the [American government] 'speaketh with forked tongue.'"[52] Eventually, radio officials directed the Romanian chief editor, Noel Bernard, to tone down the polemics.[53]

The other major problem country was Poland. Polish officials complained incessantly about RFE broadcasts. The State Department generally supported Gierek's policies and was intent on solidifying relations with Poland. Radio Free Europe, however, was unimpressed by Gierek;

the radio regarded his reforms as little more than a public relations offensive designed to convince America and other Western governments to offer economic concessions. From the very beginning, therefore, RFE's view of things clashed with the objectives of official diplomacy.

The American embassy in Warsaw was not inclined to give credence to the regime's complaints about RFE. Occasionally, however, the embassy did weigh in with complaints. One of the most notable occurred in the early seventies, when Gierek paid a much-ballyhooed visit to the United States. The regime press covered the event as a major success for Gierek, who was reported to have won enhanced support from the American government and strengthened relations with the Polish American community. Radio Free Europe coverage was less enthusiastic and gave considerable coverage to the demonstrations and protest statements that greeted Gierek at his various stops. The embassy seemed to take the regime's side, accusing RFE of exaggerating the extent of anti-Gierek manifestations. More broadly, the station was accused of having worked against the national interest, insofar as "some of the broadcasting . . . was at cross purposes with what we . . . sought to achieve." The radio management conducted an investigation of the disputed scripts, and concluded that while a few were in violation of broadcast guidelines, the overwhelming majority of the scripts posed no problem in content or tone.[54]

Eventually, a team of scholars headed by Bill Griffith and Zbigniew Brzezinski conducted a study of the Polish service programming, and gave it a strong endorsement.[55] Griffith suggested in a letter to Secretary of State Henry Kissinger that the State Department was overly critical of RFE. Kissinger, however, contended that some programs during the Gierek visit "fell outside the boundaries of appropriate broadcasting." Nevertheless, he reaffirmed the government's support for the RFE mission: "We will continue to make it clear that we regard the radios as an important element contributing to our foreign policy objectives, no less during a period of détente than heretofore."[56] In fact, some RFE veterans questioned Kissinger's commitment to the independence of the freedom radios. Others came to believe that controls instituted during the détente period seriously jeopardized the radios' mission. The debate over the impact of détente would have serious implications for the radios' future once Ronald Reagan was elected president.

13

Frequency Wars

Perhaps the greatest compliment paid Radio Free Europe and Radio Liberty was the extraordinary steps the Soviet bloc took to prevent their message from reaching the people of Eastern Europe and the Soviet Union. From the moment the two stations went on the air, Communist authorities deployed the most technologically advanced methods to interfere with, or "jam," their signals and, in some cases, render the broadcasts unlistenable. In response, RFE and RL hired a team of radio engineers whose principal mission was to develop strategies to break through the static. The result was a constantly escalating battle of the airwaves.

The first extensive use of jamming came during World War II, when both sides tried to disrupt their adversary's military communications. Germany also jammed the BBC and other foreign services that broadcast to the people under Nazi control. As the Cold War got underway, the Soviets used jamming sporadically. Jamming was begun in earnest after an incident in August 1949, when a woman jumped to her death from the window of the Soviet consulate in New York. Predictably, the Soviet press ignored the story; the VOA, just as predictably, gave it extensive coverage, forcing Moscow to concoct a version that provoked snickers from the Soviet public. After this embarrassing episode, the Kremlin decided to take whatever measures were necessary to prevent Soviet citizens from hearing anything but the officially sanctioned version of events.

By the end of 1951, the Soviets had put in place a small army of jamming devices, more than one thousand in all, and were interfering with the broadcasts of all Western radio services. By 1956 the number of devices may have reached three thousand throughout the Soviet bloc. Although jamming was initially directed at the entire panoply of Western broadcasts, the principal targets over the years were the two American freedom stations. The Soviets stopped jamming the BBC, the VOA, and other Western stations during periods of thaw and détente, but they jammed Radio Liberty broadcasts right up until the dying years of the Cold War. Radio Free Europe was more fortunate. The Polish regime ended jamming in November 1956, after Gomulka assumed power—a time when RFE broadcasts were perceived as helpful to the new leadership. (Poland would reinstate the jamming of RFE in 1971, after the upheavals on the Baltic coast.) In 1963 Hungary ended jamming; Romania followed suit one year later. On the other hand, Czechoslovakia and Bulgaria kept the jamming machines in operation almost to the Cold War's conclusion.[1]

The simplest and most common form of jamming is to set a noise machine in front of a microphone and broadcast loud, shrill sounds on the same frequency as the broadcast one wants to blot out. In the early days, jamming noises were created mechanically and transmitted via recordings. A more effective technique was later developed: white noise, which covered the entire range of an audio spectrum with headache-inducing shrieks and squawks. An alternative was to broadcast loud, boisterous music to drown out the offending signal.

The conflict over jamming was one of the many miniwars fought within the overall context of the Cold War, albeit one waged by scientists and engineers rather than generals. It took on many of the attributes of real war, with the obvious exception of human casualties, of whom there were few, those being the East Europeans who were punished for listening to foreign broadcasts during the Cold War's first few years. The jamming war was an emblematic Cold War contest, since it indirectly involved the competition of ideas. It required tactics and strategy, special projects, intelligence. And like modern warfare in general, the jamming war depended on each side's ability to develop more powerful and sophisticated technology.

The Kremlin entered this struggle with an attitude similar to that which guided its arms buildup. Just as Moscow was determined to match the United States, weapon for weapon, bomb for bomb, no matter how onerous the burden to the creaking Soviet economy, so the Kremlin leadership was willing to devote billions of dollars to minimize the influence of foreign ideas on its population. Some Western analysts estimate that by the 1970s, the Soviets were spending more to jam Western broadcasts than the West spent on its broadcasts to the Soviet Union and Eastern Europe.

In the Soviet Union, jamming stations worked closely with an extensive monitoring network, to which they were linked by a centralized control system. The monitors audited the incoming broadcast signals and reported changes in the frequency patterns. This information enabled the central control system to order adjustments in the jamming stations. Warsaw Pact countries worked in close cooperation to limit the impact of foreign broadcasts. The officials responsible for the administration of jamming met periodically to discuss the most effective allocation of resources. Sometimes jamming was implemented along transnational lines. A jamming station in Ukraine, for example, might be used to intercept a signal directed toward Prague. In some locations, jamming farms were constructed, from which signals could be beamed immediately to deflect programs headed toward the country where the jammers were situated or to a neighboring fraternal state. There was also Western speculation that those countries that had ostensibly suspended jamming sometimes used jamming devices from neighboring countries to do the job for them.

If the Soviet goal was to make life difficult for the radios and their listeners, they can certainly be said to have succeeded. Stanley Leinwoll, an RFE-RL frequency expert who was involved in the airwave wars for nearly four decades, is candid in acknowledging that jamming was highly effective in the large cities. He compares the RFE-RL listener under conditions of jamming to an American baseball fan who is forced to adjust and readjust his AM receiver in order to listen to a game broadcast from a distant city. Reception will fade in and out, static will be a constant irritant, other stations will interfere from time to time. But the dedicated fan will continue his search for the right signal, undaunted by these annoyances. Likewise, RFE-RL depended on the dedication of its listeners in those countries where serious jamming was practiced.

Leinwoll and his colleagues in the radios' engineering section devised various strategies to thwart the jammers, some more useful than others. One technique was used in broadcasts to countries that practiced selective jamming, whereby jamming was limited to news and political programs. In broadcasts to Czechoslovakia, RFE would schedule a series of innocuous, and therefore unjammed, programs—poetry readings, music, and so on—and intersperse the cultural items with news or political commentary. The jammers caught on rather quickly; eventually, the Czechoslovaks returned to a policy of jamming all programming. Another tactic was to switch frequencies during the day in the hope of evading the interference, if only for a while. Here the problem was two-fold: First, the jammers were usually savvy enough to grasp what was going on and redirect the jamming transmitters. Second, the switching back and forth of frequencies was a burden on the listeners, who had to constantly adjust their shortwave receivers throughout the day, even in the middle of programs. A more successful technique was called saturation broadcasting, by which RFE might send its signal through as many as twenty-five frequencies toward a major city like Prague, with the expectation that some programs would reach the audience unhindered.

The result of the frequency wars was something of a stalemate. Communist authorities were never able to completely blot out the freedom radios. Those who wanted to listen found ways to do so, even under the most intense jamming. They took their receivers to the countryside, where jamming was less effective, listened at twilight, or late at night, when atmospheric conditions enhanced reception, and became adept at discovering the one or two frequencies the authorities left unjammed in order to monitor what RFE and RL were saying. Or they simply suffered through the static, adjusting the dial and placing the receiver in different positions in the hope of getting a slightly clearer signal. At the same time, there is no question that jamming made listening a difficult and often unpleasant experience, and reduced the listenership for RFE and RL by discouraging the occasional listener who did not share the political passions of the core audience.

If jamming presented a serious obstacle for Western broadcasters, RFE and RL above all others, the practice represented a humiliating admission of weakness by the Soviets. After decades of state Socialist rule, the Kremlin still feared the power of outside ideas—even straight news reporting that the censors were unable to control. Furthermore, jamming probably violated several international agreements, including the Montreux International Communications Act, the Helsinki Final Act, and the Universal Declaration of Human Rights. The latter spoke of the right to "seek, receive, and impart information and ideas . . . regardless of frontiers." Until the Gorbachev era, however, the Soviets remained unmoved by arguments based on international law. When challenged, they would bluster and fume about acts of ideological hostility and interference in their internal affairs. The Kremlin's position was stated with colorful bluntness in a 1958 United Nations debate by Arkady Sobolev: "Moscow has atomic bombs to reply to aggression and jamming transmitters to take care of subversive broadcasts beamed to the USSR."[2]

Of course, Sobolev and other officials did have access to foreign broadcasts through the daily summaries supplied by the KGB. Those citizens who actually had to contend with jammed broadcasts regarded the practice as an annoyance and further evidence of the illegitimacy of the Communist system. Alexander Solzhenitsyn couldn't repress a sense of outrage when the subject of jamming was raised. As he told a 1973 interviewer,

> What jamming of radio broadcasting means is impossible to explain to those who haven't experienced it themselves, who haven't lived under it for years. It means daily spittle into your ears and eyes, it is an offense and a degradation of man to a robot's level.... It means that grown persons are reduced to infants: swallow what your mother has already chewed for you.... Even the most benevolent broadcasts during the most friendly visits are jammed systematically: there must not be the slightest deviation in the evaluation of events, in the nuances, in the accents—everybody has to be informed about and remember an event one hundred percent the same way.... Moscow and Leningrad have paradoxically become the most uninformed big cities in the world. The inhabitants ask people who come in from the countryside about news. There [in the provinces], because of cost (our population has to pay very dearly for these jamming services) the jamming is weaker.[3]

Aside from the various schemes their engineers developed to thwart the jammers, RFE and RL relied principally on the construction of more and more powerful transmitters to ensure that their message penetrated the Iron Curtain. In the early years, the need for better transmitting equipment was critical. The equipment the two stations inherited in Germany was outdated and far from adequate given the realities of jamming. For Radio Liberty, the situation was desperate. Inferior transmitters plus heavy jamming plus the formidable challenge of reaching the vast regions of the Soviet Union combined to render the RL signal barely audible to its intended audience.

Several problems confronted the radios as they searched for ways to enhance their signals. One problem was technical: the radios required sites that were ideally situated to beam shortwave broadcasts to the East. An ideal transmission site was not necessarily located in close proximity to the target country; for various reasons relating to how shortwave signals are projected, the best location might be far distant from the audience country. The second problem was political. As RFE learned during its search for a country that would play host to its European headquarters, most European democracies were not enthusiastic about permitting the United States to establish an anti-Soviet radio facility on their territory.

The solution to both problems was to be found on the Iberian Peninsula. Spain and Portugal were perfectly situated from a technical point of view, offering shortwave broadcasters a clear signal to the Eastern bloc. The political situation was more complex. Both countries were run by conservative dictators who were firmly anti-Communist and generally pro-West. A nod of assent from the leader was sufficient to guarantee the success of an enterprise, and there was little likelihood that opposition parties or parliaments would interfere with the process. On the other hand, both Spain's Franco and Portugal's Salazar were reviled as Fascists by much of the world; Franco was especially disliked because of his brutality during the Spanish Civil War.

In late 1950 the Free Europe Committee authorized one of its members, H. Gregory Thomas, to negotiate with the Portuguese government for a transmitter site. Thomas was an ideal choice for the assignment. As the owner of a company that distributed Chanel products in North America, Thomas had gained extensive experience in international business. During the war he had worked for the OSS in Portugal, and had made important contacts among leading political figures, including the dictator Antonio de Oliveira Salazar. After the war Salazar had moved Portugal into NATO and wanted very much to win acceptance for his country as a full-fledged member of Western Europe. He agreed to meet with Thomas, approved the basic terms of the proposal, and directed the relevant officials to cooperate with the

American. The negotiations were thus quickly consummated with a minimum of complications.

A site was soon found in a desperately poor village named Gloria, located on the Tagus River. Land for the transmitters was purchased with funds provided by the CIA, but the facility was technically under the ownership of a majority Portuguese corporation. By April, less than four months after Thomas had opened negotiations, the deal was made final. By the end of the following February, four transmitters were operational, a remarkable achievement even by the standards of the early fifties. With the construction of the Gloria transmitters, and the facilities that already existed in Germany, RFE had its technical facilities in place for the duration of the Cold War.[4]

Radio Liberty began investigating additional transmitter sites soon after it went on the air in 1953. A consulting firm hired by Amcomlib recommended a location either in Spain or North Africa. There were a number of potential sites in Spain, including several in the then undeveloped Costa Brava. Although the State Department was apprehensive about dealings with Spain because of Franco's image as the murderer of the Spanish Republic, Howland Sargeant, the new president of RL, traveled there in 1955 to seek an agreement with the government.

Sargeant had an advantage as he approached the negotiation. Several years earlier, he had served as America's delegate to UNESCO. Spain had applied for membership. But because of the country's pariah status, a favorable vote was by no means assured. The United States had supported Franco in the UNESCO vote, and Sargeant had conducted the negotiations that enabled Spain to win admission. Franco himself sent Sargeant a personal note of gratitude for his diplomatic assistance.

Initially, the Spanish bureaucracy was unforthcoming. Sargeant finally requested an audience with Franco, using the note of gratitude as a trump card. Franco received him for more than an hour, after which previously closed doors miraculously swung open. A site in the village of Pals on the Costa Brava was found, and an agreement reached with the government. But it was not until March 1959 that the first Pals transmitter was in operation. Construction on the remaining transmitters continued into the mid-sixties; when all was completed, RL had some of the most powerful shortwave transmitters in the world.[5]

In neither Portugal nor Spain did the radios actually own the land on which the transmitters were located. Thus fluctuations in the political climate were a potential problem, as a new and less sympathetic government might refuse to extend the leases that allowed the radios to operate the transmission facilities. As long as Franco and Salazar were in control, relations with the government went smoothly. In the 1970s, however, political upheavals shook both countries: Franco gave way to a democratic system, and in Portugal a revolutionary military regime, led by left-wing officers, swept the dictatorship from power and gave rise to fears of a Marxist regime in Lisbon.

For the radios, the Portuguese situation seemed the more ominous. Communist elements were spearheading the takeover of large estates and businesses in various parts of the country, including the section around the Gloria transmitters. But even though Communist militants would have been eager to shut down an institution that existed to undermine the Soviet system, no action was taken against RFE. One reason was RFE's status as the largest employer in the region. While the local population may have sympathized with the radicals on certain issues, they did not want to jeopardize the principal source of local prosperity. Eventually, the radicals in Lisbon were removed in a countercoup, democracy was instituted, and RFE reached agreement on a fifteen-year lease.[6]

Spain proved a more difficult challenge. The Costa Brava site, worthless when the original lease was signed, was now valued at many millions. Furthermore, the Soviets were putting pressure on the new, democratic Spanish government, offering inducements, such as diplomatic recognition and trade incentives, if the Pals lease was not extended. Finally, the government feared that the lease might provoke a raucous political debate in Parliament and might even lead to a deterioration of relations with the United States. At one point the radios were told that the lease would not be renewed. The Board for International Broadcasting immediately began making contingency plans, but requests for transmitter sharing arrangements were turned down by both the BBC and Deutsche Welle. Even the VOA was reluctant to lend its transmitters to RL; the Soviets had recently stopped jamming the Voice, and it was felt that an association with Radio Liberty might jeopardize the no-jamming agreement.

In fact, no conclusive agreement was made with the Spanish government. Officials told the BIB that a parliamentary debate over lease extension might prove volatile. At the same time, the government did not want to jeopardize relations with the United States by evicting RL from its territory. The deal, or nondeal, that was struck allowed RL to continue to operate Pals without a formal lease agreement. The Spanish government did not publicize details of this peculiar arrangement, and the BIB had to accept a deal that was considerably short of satisfactory but that ultimately enabled Radio Liberty to continue its broadcasts to the Soviet Union without interruption for the rest of the Cold War.[7]

By the late 1980s, the practice of jamming became increasingly difficult for the Soviets to justify. This was particularly the case after Mikhail Gorbachev initiated his policy of glasnost, or openness. One sign that a change might be in the offing was a declaration in June 1986 by Vladimir Posner, the unofficial Soviet spokesman who became something of a media celebrity in America, that jamming was "counterproductive." In a talk before the conservative American Enterprise Institute, Posner asserted that jamming could be terminated if the United States toned down the "subversive" broadcasts of RFE-RL. According to Posner, jamming actually enhanced public interest in the freedom radios, thus attracting attention "to something that is not all that interesting."[8]

The next indication of a shift in the Kremlin's attitude toward international broadcasts was a declaration by Gorbachev that the reason the USSR jammed the VOA was the lack of a transmitting base near the American mainland that would enable the Soviets to broadcast their views to the American public. Gorbachev followed up this statement with a proposal at his summit meeting with President Reagan at Reykjavik that the two countries swap air time, with the Soviets broadcasting their perspective on events over American radio and the United States broadcasting programs over radio networks in the USSR.[9]

To iron out the details of an agreement, Charles Z. Wick, the director of the United States Information Agency, held an informal negotiating session with Alexander Yakovlev, a key figure in the Gorbachev leadership team. Wick was a close personal friend of the president and had a reputation as a fervid anti-Communist. But Wick was also a man of enthusiasms, and in 1986 his greatest enthusiasm was the reform course promised by Gorbachev. According to the notes taken by the American side at the Wick-Yakovlev meeting, Yakovlev "stated that if the U.S. government in fact did not object to the Soviets using a transmitter on or near U.S. territory, the Soviet Union would respond by ending jamming. It would be a fair deal, Yakovlev said, where each side would present its point of view without insulting the other." At this point, Wick is recorded as saying, "You've got a deal." Yakovlev then replied, "I am only talking about VOA,'" as regards the cessation of jamming.[10]

There were a number of problems with this arrangement, the most important of which was the exclusion of RFE-RL from the settlement. The arrangement appalled officials at the State Department and National Security Council. Wick's efforts at diplomacy drew scorn from columnist William Safire and a sharp rebuke from the conservative Heritage Foundation. Wick soldiered on, however, and actually lined up American radio networks willing to donate air time for Soviet broadcasts before the NSC announced that there would be no deal unless RFE and RL were included.[11]

Radio Liberty had reason to be concerned about the Soviet Union's jamming policies. After the Kremlin stopped jamming the BBC, nineteen additional jammers were directed at RL's signals, and radio officials feared that an agreement to end the jamming of the VOA would bring the entire force of Soviet jamming against RL.[12]

In late November 1988, without warning or fanfare, the Soviet Union stopped jamming foreign radio broadcasts—including those of Radio Liberty. Gene Pell, the president of RFE-RL, recalls being called during the night by the station's engineering chief, George Woodard. "The skies are clear; the jamming has ended," Woodard reported.[13] If asked, Soviet officials would contend that foreign broadcasts held little interest for their people and therefore posed no danger to their political control.[14] Some speculated that the decision was influenced by Gorbachev's scheduled visit to the United States in December, as well as by the Soviet leader's planned human rights conference in 1991. Some even theorized that Gorbachev was motivated by the expectation that Western stations, including RFE and RL, would support his initiatives and side with the reformers in their debates with the Old Guard. Soviet officials later told Pell that the decision to end jamming had been the subject of a lengthy and rancorous debate in the Politburo. Vladimir Kryuchkov, head of the KGB, reportedly said that jamming would be ended "over my dead body." In the end, Gorbachev's arguments against jamming carried the day.[15]

One reflection of glasnost was a new candor in discussing the censorship apparatus, including jamming. In 1989, *Pravda* revealed the existence of a secret communications ministry jamming department, which had recently been disbanded. The department was known by those who worked there as the Krestyaninova Department, after Natalia Krestyaninova, who headed it for a quarter-century. The jamming operation was established in 1939 and eventually commanded a vast network of facilities in every Soviet republic and major city.[16]

To what degree economic factors dictated the decision is not clear. Certainly, the Soviets were spending massive amounts to limit Radio Liberty's impact—between $750 million and $1.2 billion, according to Western estimates, more than twice the amount America spent on the VOA and RFE-RL combined.[17]

The end of jamming gave RFE and, especially, RL a major ratings boost. But the postjamming environment presented new challenges, as did the policies of Mikhail Gorbachev. Now that the playing field was level, the radios would be judged by more exacting standards. And the competition, especially in the Soviet Union, would be much more substantial in light of the new and unprecedented policy of glasnost.

14

Bombs, Spies, Poisoned Umbrellas

Although jamming was the preferred method to thwart the radios, much rougher tactics were also employed. Journalists were blackmailed, threatened, beaten, and murdered—in the most notorious case, by a poisoned umbrella. Their relatives behind the Iron Curtain were persecuted. Spies found their way to key staff positions, where they remained, undetected, for years. And in the most serious attempt to silence Radio Free Europe and Radio Liberty, the radios' Munich headquarters was bombed in an operation masterminded by the legendary terrorist Carlos.

Bombings and assassinations were not, in fact, a Soviet trademark in its dealings with the United States. The Kremlin generally adhered to a gentlemen's agreement whereby both sides avoided violence against their rival's citizens, including intelligence agents. Communist regimes usually followed this informal code in their policies toward the radios. There was, however, something in the nature of the freedom stations that occasionally brought out communism's primitive instincts. Communist authorities did not regard the broadcasters as American nationals, but as treasonous citizens of their own lands, as guilty of betraying the motherland as a defector who volunteered for the CIA. Radio Free Europe broadcasts inflicted lasting wounds on the East European party leadership. Some RFE and RL commentators had been members in good standing of the cultural elite back home. From their Munich studios, they explained why communism could not produce decent homes or shoes that fit. They also related intimate details about the despots who presided over the people's democracies—about court intrigues, betrayals, the malicious treatment of subordinates, about the extravagant life-styles of men who preached a gospel of equality. The more thick-skinned party chieftains shrugged it all off, but others were driven to a frenzy when broadcasts zeroed in on their personal affairs. This was particularly true of those Communists who were the object of personality cults, such as Romania's Nicolae Ceausescu or Bulgaria's Todor Zhivkov, both of whom used violence against their RFE tormentors.

While violence was used sparingly, Communist intelligence worked assiduously to penetrate the staffs of the language sections. Sometimes radio employees were recruited by Communist spymasters through bribery, blackmail, or even an appeal to patriotic sentiments. In some cases, trained agents were sent abroad with the mission of landing a staff position in Munich; once hired, they sometimes provided information on the station's internal workings for years before being brought back home. By the end of the Cold War, practically every language section at RFE and RL had been penetrated; in the most serious known case, a KGB agent worked in the Russian section for some twenty years and was a candidate for the chief editor's post when he was called back to Moscow by his superiors.

In the end, the impact of the threats, the occasional violence, the spies, and the moles was negligible. Even the bombing must be counted a failure, since RFE and RL were able to continue their broadcasts without interruption. While the agents could provide many items of interest to Communist security officials—staff biographies, program schedules, technical data, internal memos, information about the American managers (always of interest to East bloc security)—no agent, so far as is known, succeeded in influencing broadcast content. There is, in fact, evidence that agents were discouraged from meddling in broadcast policy, since that might lead to their unmasking. The spies provided their masters with cabinets full of files, and all manner of interesting gossip. But the radios' message remained unchanged.

Although Soviet bloc regimes eventually adopted a policy of extreme cautiousness in the use of "wet operations"—murder, kidnapping, bombing and the like—their intelligence services were relatively unencumbered by such scruples during the Cold War's early period. Radio

Free Europe was seen as an instrument of ideological subversion during a period in which Communist rule was on shaky ground in some satellite countries, and it was thus considered fair game for sabotage projects. In November 1954, German authorities picked up two strangers who were acting suspiciously near one of the RFE–Free Europe Press balloon sites. The two were armed and finally confessed to working for Czechoslovak security. Their mission, according to a statement given to the police, was to "reconnoiter thoroughly and thereafter to lead across the border from Czechoslovakia a party which would destroy the installation by fire and explosion." The orders for the raid had come down from the Czechoslovak Ministry of the Interior.[1]

Prague was also responsible for another operation: a strange attempt in November 1959 to poison the salt in the RFE canteen. Apparently a Czechoslovak diplomat posted in Vienna, acting on instructions from Prague, conceived a plan to introduce atropine, a derivative of deadly nightshade, into the salt shakers, in a dosage sufficient to induce illness but not to kill. Before this scheme could be implemented, it was revealed by an RFE employee acting as a double agent.[2] In any event, the plot's repercussions were serious, since the press played the issue as a Communist murder scheme. In fact, atropine can be fatal in high doses. Jaroslav Němec, a Czechoslovak espionage agent posted as a consular official in Salzburg, was publicly named as the plot's mastermind, and security officials from Prague moved quickly to hustle Němec out of Austria, where he did not enjoy diplomatic immunity.[3]

Some anti-RFE operations bordered on the absurd. Hungarian intelligence devoted much time and energy to screening all letters written from Hungary to RFE's Munich headquarters. A few of the letters were approved and sent along to Munich; the rest were retained in Budapest. Most were addressed to RFE's music program, *Teenager Party,* and were nonpolitical in tone. But the authorities exploited the letters as a means of intimidating Hungary's youth. If a return address was included, the letter was turned over to counterintelligence, which informed the parents that their son or daughter was corresponding with an American spy agency. In addition, Hungarian intelligence created a network of Radio Free Europe listeners—putatively ordinary Hungarians who wrote letters to the station for disinformation purposes. The object was to persuade RFE to shift its format from political programs to music and entertainment.[4]

The Soviets were less concerned with Radio Liberty's broadcasts, barely audible because of RL's antiquated equipment, than with the scheming of prominent exiles from Ukraine, Belorussia, and other non-Russian republics. Exile leaders, some of whom had intensely loyal followings within the Soviet Union, were dealt with by threats, kidnapping, and occasionally murder. In the most notorious case, a Soviet agent assassinated Stepan Bandera, a Ukrainian nationalist who had led armed resistance to the Soviets during and after World War II. The killing took place in West Germany, and when, several years later, the assassin confessed, Nikita Khrushchev put a stop to political killings because of the diplomatic repercussions.

Throughout its history, the non–Russian sections of Radio Liberty maintained close relations with organizations in the West dedicated to the preservation of national culture and the political independence of their peoples. They made liberal use of national patriots on the air. Thus working in tandem with national patriotic institutions committed to the breakup of the Soviet Union, RL's nationality services became a target of the KGB.

In 1954, a Belorussian staff member, Leonid Karas, was found drowned in a river near Munich under suspicious circumstances. Two months later, another RL staff member was found dead in a clear-cut case of murder.

On November 22, an elderly Munich landlady was cleaning her apartment when she discovered a man's body underneath a couch, lying face down with his hands tied behind his back. She told the police that the dead man was Michael Ismailov, an émigré who sometimes used the kitchen in her apartment. The coroner determined that the man died of strangulation after having been hit over the head by a blunt object. The body of the man known as Ismailov was buried, and the police proceeded with their investigation.

At the same time, Abdulrachmann Fatalibey, the editor of RL's Azeri service, failed to show up for work on several consecutive days. His apartment was searched, to no avail, and the police listed Fatalibey as a suspect in Ismailov's killing. Then a rumor began circulating that the man buried as Ismailov was in fact Fatalibey. The body was exhumed, and the rumor proved accurate: Abo Fatalibey had been murdered, probably by Ismailov, who disappeared and likely returned to the Soviet Union.

Fatalibey had a fascinating political biography. He was born in

Azerbaijan and later moved to Leningrad, where he joined the Communist Party and entered military engineering school. He remained in the military for about ten years. But in 1936 he was expelled from the party, charged with having lied about his social origins—he was not, as he had claimed, of peasant stock. When World War II broke out, Fatalibey was sent to the Finnish front, where he distinguished himself and was awarded the Red Star.

In September 1941, Fatalibey was captured by the Germans and sent to a prisoner of war camp. The Germans were in the process of organizing Soviet nationality battalions comprised of POWs and others who were willing to fight against Stalin. Fatalibey agreed to join the Nazi-sponsored Azerbaijan Legion. He distinguished himself at the front, won a Nazi decoration, and returned to Germany, where he was elected to the Azerbaijan Congress, a Nazi puppet organization.

In 1945, Fatalibey was sent to the Italian front, where he was captured by American forces and sent to a POW camp. Somehow he avoided repatriation to the Soviet Union, where his execution was a near certainty. After settling in Rome, he became a publicist for anti-Soviet and pro-Muslim causes. His pamphleteering drew the attention of Palestinian Arabs, and Fatalibey was invited to Egypt, where he became a military adviser to the Arabs involved in the struggle against Israel. He may have fought in the 1948 conflict, and he claimed to have drawn up battle plans that were never implemented.

Fatalibey said that he established contact with American and British intelligence officials while in Egypt. It is not clear whether the CIA helped secure his position at RL. In any event, when the American Committee for the Liberation from Bolshevism was established, Fatalibey was one of the few Azeri exiles available with journalistic skills.[5]

That a man who had served the Nazis and fought against Israel obtained a position as a chief editor at Radio Liberty suggests that the station did not always adhere to its expressed policy of hiring individuals whose pasts were clean and political sympathies within the mainstream. As we will see, charges that the radios had employed war criminals, extremists, and anti-Semites were to be a source of embarrassment in later years.

The intimidation of Radio Free Europe journalists was carried out by every Communist regime in Eastern Europe. Threatening phone calls were placed, notes slipped under doors. Exiled journalists were followed and told that unless they stopped broadcasting messages of subversion, their aging parents would lose their homes or their cousins would be deported to the provinces. Communist officials maintained dossiers on all exiled journalists; what they couldn't discover from internal sources they learned from the moles and agents who had wormed their way onto the station staff.

One of the most successful agents was Andrzej Chechowitz, who worked in the Polish section from 1965 until 1971, when he suddenly surfaced in Warsaw as an officer of the Ministry of the Interior. Chechowitz was hardly the first RFE staffer to return home; others had done so out of disillusionment with the West, homesickness, or in response to Communist threats against friends or relatives. Usually, the "redefectors" were put on public display as unfortunates who, having succumbed to Western propaganda, had been sickened by the spiritually empty life in the Capitalist world and alienated by the cynicism they encountered at RFE.

With Chechowitz, the script was changed. Instead of a soap opera-like story of human redemption, the Poles boasted of having infiltrated RFE with a trained intelligence officer. The regime's motives in presenting the case as a straightforward spy operation were varied. First, the authorities hoped that revelation of a major penetration would stimulate uncertainty in the RFE staff at a time when the future of the station was in doubt due to Senator Fulbright's campaign for liquidation. Second, the announcement that a spy had gained access to sensitive RFE files was certain to unsettle Poles who may have collaborated with the station. Finally, the Chechowitz affair was a warning to the German government that if it intended to play host to a subversive American organization, it would face the prospect of further embarrassing spy scandals. Thus Chechowitz reinforced the regime's diplomatic offensive to convince Bonn to expel RFE from its Munich headquarters, a campaign that was in full swing in 1971.

In 1965, Chechowitz was hired for the Polish section by Jan Nowak; Chechowitz claims, with probable accuracy, that Nowak was enthusiastic about the opportunity to hire a young exile with potential journalistic skills for his aging staff. Nowak, however, was apparently not overly impressed, for he assigned his new recruit to a low-level position in the evaluation department, where he read Polish newspapers and periodicals and selected items for a program featuring a digest of the Polish press.

Chechowitz portrayed his RFE work as serving intelligence, and not journalistic, purposes. At a Warsaw press conference, Chechowitz claimed that the CIA dominated the station's activities. His account was lurid:

> A job with the Free Europe radio means cooperation with representatives of the U.S. intelligence service. Working [there] opens the most secret doors to the most secret department, the so-called East Europe Analysis and Research Department, where one has access to the most secret matters connected to the intelligence and subversive activity of the Munich center, to its plans towards Poland and other social- ist countries . . . to its financial, personal, and organizational links with the intelligence service, the links with Zionist centers, the norms and methods of action, of acquiring information, etc. Only twenty to thirty percent of the materials gathered at the Free Europe were used as a basis for broadcasts. . . . The gist of them constituted valuable intelligence material.[6]

Chechowitz added that while a Pole was nominally in charge of the evaluation unit where he worked, the real bosses were "Colonels Cook and Brown," referring to Richard Cook, a deputy to Ralph Walter, then the director of RFE, and Jim Brown, the director of research. Neither Cook nor Brown ever worked as an intelligence officer or achieved the rank of colonel in military service. Chechowitz seems to have developed some respect for Brown, a prominent scholar of East European politics. He called Brown the "brains" behind the station and its "wisest" leader.

Chechowitz depicted the Polish section as composed of elderly, spiritually broken exiles who were hired solely to carry out the direc- tives of American intelligence. There was an obvious contradiction here, since Chechowitz described RFE as ineffective while blaming it for the Polish coastal uprising of 1970. He also insinuated a bit of anti- Semitism into his story. He claimed that RFE had hired only a few of those Poles who went into exile after the 1968 anti-Semitic campaign, adding that those Jews who had been hired were treated badly. At the same time, he suggested that the departure of the Jews, many of whom held responsible government positions, had deprived RFE of the bulk of its sources within Poland. In essence, Chechowitz was charging Polish Jews with disloyalty, and suggesting that their expulsion was justified.

One apparent motive for the carefully orchestrated series of press conferences and television interviews was to send an ominous message to those Poles who maintained a relationship with the radio station. Jan Nowak had a wide list of Polish contacts with whom he would meet during their trips abroad. They ranged from party officials to high-ranking members of the Catholic Church hierarchy to scholars, journalists, and political dissidents.

One of Nowak's regular sources was Jan Kott, a respected Warsaw theater critic and member of the intellectual establishment who later broke with communism and moved to the West. Kott had known Nowak in Poland, and though he was loyal to the system, regularly met with Nowak during his visits to Paris. His first visit took place in a Paris burlesque house, where a young Polish woman was the star, or rather the starlet, of the latest show:

> I had seen her in Warsaw a couple of months earlier at a
> student cabaret. Naked and half-naked girls rushed by us,
> hurrying up and down the stairs, through the corridors, and
> along the narrow passageway behind the stage, giving off the
> sweet scent of cheap perfume mixed with sweat and swirling
> clouds of powder.
>
> Slowly and methodically Nowak dusted off the lapels of
> his jacket. He paid not the slightest attention to the girls, as
> though they did not exist, or rather as though they were an
> annoying cloud of powder. . . . I don't know why Nowak
> chose that strange place for our conversations—perhaps for
> conspiratorial reasons, but certainly not for its ambiguous
> charms. He was the most austere of all my friends from the
> old Warsaw days, as he would also be later on.
>
> On each of my subsequent trips abroad I called him
> collect—two or three times—at an agreed-on number from
> public telephone booths, never from the hotels where I was
> staying. Once I even went to see him in Munich. I told him
> in as much detail as I could what was going on in the party.
> Even now I am unable to explain exactly why I did that. No
> doubt I was fascinated by the risk, the element of play, and

the new conspiratorial game, especially in Munich, where
Nowak kept me hidden in the apartment of a priest he
knew and allowed me to go out into the town only in the
evenings.[7]

For RFE editors, regular contact with visitors from the audience
countries were extremely important. Radio Free Europe faced the
challenge of reporting on the political developments of societies from
their isolated headquarters in Munich. The station's credibility depended
not just on its accurate news reporting, but on the authenticity of its
vocabulary and its ability to reflect the popular mood. An editor could
not grasp the attitude of the working class in Gdansk by reading *Trybuna
Ludu* or listening to Radio Warsaw. Thus radio editors sought out every available live source: visitors from the East, Western newsmen, researchers and scholars, whomever might provide some firsthand account
of political and social conditions in Eastern Europe. Sometimes they
paid their informants, especially travelers from the East with little hard
currency to spend, or rewarded them by buying them dinner.

For those Poles who had talked with Jan Nowak or other editors,
the return of Chechowitz must have been something of a jolt. He
claimed to have a lengthy list of "collaborators" and threatened to
"unmask" the most serious offenders. He also expressed astonishment
at the number of "seemingly honest and intelligent people" who had
acted as RFE informants, mentioning a certain newspaperman B, and
adding, "One would really be surprised that this man had anything to
do with [RFE] and was giving them various information."[8]

After a flurry of media appearances, Chechowitz wrote his memoirs, after which he faded into obscurity. In later years, he would occasionally make joint press appearances with another of RFE's Communist
agents, Pavel Minarik. In Czechoslovakia, Minarik had worked for the
underground freedom radio station that operated in Brno for a while
after the Soviet invasion. He left after the Prague Spring was crushed,
and, given his contribution to the antioccupation cause, Minarik was
hired by RFE. Blessed with a first-rate radio voice, Minarik was used
as an announcer and news reader.[9]

Minarik was very helpful to his colleagues; he would chauffeur
them around and help run errands. His library, colleagues recall, was
devoted to books on espionage, although no one seriously held him in
suspicion. Minarik was dismissed by RFE during a budget crisis in the

early seventies. He returned to Prague in 1976, to great fanfare. Authorities claimed that he had been trained by Czechoslovak intelligence from the very beginning, with a planned mission of infiltrating RFE. There were a few press conferences, where he asserted that Alexander Dubček and other Prague Spring leaders were working clandestinely for RFE. Afterward, he dropped from sight.

Unlike other former Communist countries, which kept their Communist-era security files locked away after 1989, the Czech Republic publicized the names of security agents, released thousands of pages of intelligence files, and began prosecutions against those accused of more serious crimes. One of those to face criminal charges was Pavel Minarik.

Minarik was accused of nothing less than conspiracy to blow up the RFE headquarters in Munich. According to his indictment, Minarik had been recruited by the intelligence service in 1967, trained, and given the code name Ulyxes. In April 1970, not long after his employment at the station, Minarik is said to have presented his superior, Jaroslav Lis, with a plan to detonate a bomb of sufficient power to destroy the Munich facility or, at minimum, to put the station temporarily off the air. Lis expressed interest; he asked for a floor plan and other details. In November, Minarik made a second request and offered to carry out the mission himself. He pressed the matter, noting that an action taken before the 1972 summer Olympics, to be held in Munich, would create demoralization within RFE. Lis called the proposal "interesting" but declined to give a go-ahead.

In June 1972, Minarik was at it again. This time he proposed that a bomb be placed in a cart used by cleaning personnel, which could then be placed next to the wall of the master control room and detonated. Lis praised the plan but said nothing could be done during the Olympics. The next month, Minarik had a revised plan. He tried several more times, providing floor plans, a film of the master control area, and various alternative options. Finally, Lis told his eager understudy that his schemes to bomb the Munich facility were too risky given the international situation.

When confronted by Czech authorities after the fall of communism, Minarik first denied planning to destroy the headquarters and also denied a charge that he had proposed to kidnap the grandson of the chief editor of RFE's Czechoslovak section. He finally confessed after being shown the minutes of his meetings with Lis and the reports he had sent his intelligence chiefs. Minarik's defense was that he had never carried out the bombing; the documents, however, suggest that this was only because Czechoslovak intelligence never approved his ideas. He also claimed that his proposals were naïve and unrealistic, given his lack of familiarity with explosive devices.

The case against Minarik was eventually dropped. He is said to have become a private businessman and has prospered in the free market environment of post–Communist Prague.

When Yuri Handler, at the time Radio Liberty's chief Russian editor in its New York bureau, visited Munich in 1986, he was told by several colleagues that Oleg Tumanov was a leading candidate for the Russian section's chief editor position. One week later, Tumanov disappeared, only to turn up back in Moscow, where he revealed that he had been working for the KGB from the moment he began work in Munich in the late 1960s.[10]

Clearly, Tumanov was the most successful Communist bloc spy to have infiltrated the radios, at least of those whose identities have been made public. If his account is accurate—and some dispute many of his assertions—Tumanov enjoyed an impressive espionage career if measured by longevity alone. He was, to be sure, a heavy drinker; a photograph in his memoirs shows Tumanov working away at his typewriter with a bottle of Ballantine's scotch whiskey standing at the ready by his side. But addiction to alcohol afflicted many of the exiles. Tumanov was quiet, unassuming, not given to displays of temperament. Yuri Handler found him one of the steadier hands among the chief editors, a competent man who could be counted on to provide precise answers to difficult questions. Tumanov reinforced his image as even-natured and dependable by avoiding involvement in the rancorous staff disputes that pitted the proponents of Russian nationalism against those with a liberal democratic orientation.

Tumanov claims that he was trained as an agent while a young man in the Soviet Union and given the express mission of landing a job at Radio Liberty. He says that he was allowed to "defect" by jumping ship in North Africa, after which he found his way to Germany and eventually to RL.[11] (Oleg Kalugin, the former chief of Soviet counterespionage, told an RFE-RL security official that Tumanov was in fact recruited after he joined RL; the recruitment, he said, was achieved through a relative of Tumanov.)

According to Tumanov, his KGB superiors regarded an assignment as an important mission. To Soviet officials, RL represented the equivalent of the NTS, the Ukrainian OUN, and other nationalist-oriented organizations that "burned with hatred for everything Soviet." "It would be no exaggeration to say that members of the Soviet Politburo feared 'Liberty' more than any other American weapon," he wrote.[12]

Tumanov's control agent, whom he met regularly in East Berlin, had a detailed knowledge of RL's Russian staffers. He had photographs of the chief staff members and gave explicit instruction on how Tumanov should deal with the various personalities in Munich. Tumanov was told to stay out of internal controversies but to send along reports of the political divisions within the staff. The KGB was also interested in RL's audience research unit, located in Paris. To get a reading on what Russians did and did not like in RL programs, the audience research unit relied on interviews with émigrés and travelers. This required personal contact between the RL staff and Soviet citizens, which to the KGB mindset smacked of espionage. The KGB was convinced that audience research was an espionage setup that sought state secrets from gullible Soviet travelers and worked to convince Soviet citizens to defect to the West.[13]

Tumanov was instructed to make no effort to influence broadcast content. Instead, he spent his time photocopying documents and gathering staff gossip, which he passed along to his KGB superiors. According to Tumanov, KGB headquarters in Moscow had thousands of pages of material that he and other agents had passed along. Tumanov claims, probably with some exaggeration, that numerous agents had infiltrated the Russian section. Clearly, however, Tumanov was not the only KGB spy in the Munich headquarters.

Although Tumanov was generally liked and valued as a competent administrative editor, many of his colleagues considered him their intellectual inferior. "As a journalist, he was a zero," asserts Lev Roitman, a Russian commentator. "He was unable to do intelligent commentaries; he was an alcoholic; yet he continued to move up the editorial ladder because he was a competent manager and a yes man."[14] Yuri Handler spent an evening with Tumanov in Munich and came away shocked by what he described as Tumanov's low cultural level. He was particularly taken aback when his host put on a video of an old Soviet patriotic movie, whose melodramatic and sentimental plot brought

Tumanov to tears. Recalled Handler: "I could not believe that this man, whose cultural tastes were so completely Soviet, had such high authority in our service."[15]

Radio Free Europe and Radio Liberty forbade their employees travel to the Communist world during the Cold War. The countries to which they broadcast considered the stations nests of subversion and espionage and their employees CIA agents. An RFE journalist who visited friends in Poland or Hungary, or attended the funeral of a parent in Bulgaria, faced the real possibility of arrest and a lengthy prison sentence. Or an attempt might be made to compromise them, either by entrapment or through relatives who were subject to police pressure.

Only once was an RFE or RL employee arrested by Communist authorities. His name was Fred Eidlin, and at the time of his arrest he was a former employee of RFE, having left the station more than half a year earlier. Eidlin was an American citizen who was pursuing doctoral studies in East European politics at the University of Toronto during the mid-sixties. He took a year off from his studies to work in RFE's policy office. Eidlin was no hard-edged anti-Communist; he joined RFE only after assuring himself that the station broadcast balanced news and reportage. He wrote background studies on Czechoslovakia, the country of his principal scholarly interest, and devoted his spare time to combing RFE's treasure trove of archival material. Eidlin left in November 1969, with plans to resume his studies and to travel throughout the Communist world. Officials at RFE warned him that travel in Eastern Europe could be dangerous for someone who had worked for the station. But Eidlin reckoned that he faced little danger since it had been some years since a Western scholar had been arrested in the Soviet bloc.[16]

On July 22, 1970, Eidlin crossed the border into Czechoslovakia. Four days later, while taking photographs of Prague from a hill overlooking the city, he was arrested and taken to police headquarters, where two officials from the Ministry of Interior met him. The subsequent interrogation suggested that the case was no minor affair. As Eidlin later described the questioning, "They wanted to know . . . when I had first made contact with the CIA, to whom I was reporting, who was reporting to me, whom I had recruited for emigration and for which espionage agencies these people were working, why I carried personal weapons and so on."

After a week of questioning, the Interior Ministry men turned Eidlin over to counterespionage. Eidlin was kept in solitary confinement in the main Prague police jail, was not allowed to see the American consul, and was told that if didn't come clean, things might go quite badly.

Eidlin faced two basic charges. First, he had worked for RFE and therefore was accused of "aiding and abetting the subversion of the Republic." Second, he was charged with having attempted to recruit as CIA agents two Czechoslovak students whom he had met in Germany. Eidlin had in fact encountered the students in a bar, and had subsequently invited them to lunch, along with several RFE colleagues. One of the colleagues was Pavel Minarik, then working as a Czechoslovak spy. Minarik may well have provided the information that led the authorities to arrest the American.

His two acquaintances testified against Eidlin, no doubt under police pressure. One gave a statement, ludicrous on its face, that described the young scholar as a high-level spy: "In the bar I was sitting next to Eidlin. By chance I brushed against him and felt a long metal object in the breast pocket of his sport coat. Later, when we took off our sport coats, the lapel of his was turned up a bit on the back of the chair and I saw the bakelite handle of his pistol. It was this . . . realization that Eidlin carries personal weapons which convinced me that . . ."

Eidlin was tried five months after his arrest. His court-appointed attorney was of little help, and Eidlin conducted much of the defense himself. Nevertheless, he remained optimistic that the logic of his defense combined with the sheer silliness of the charges (he never carried weapons of any kind) would produce a verdict that, at worst, would mean expulsion. He was therefore stunned when the court found him guilty and handed down a sentence of four years in prison. Eidlin would not serve out his term. On February 24, 1971, he was brought from his cell, placed on a plane, and flown to Amsterdam. He had served seven months in various Czechoslovak jails.

Fred Eidlin was fortunate that he chose to travel in Czechoslovakia rather than Romania. No one nursed a more passionate hatred for RFE than Nicolae Ceausescu, and no Communist leader was as willing as the Romanian dictator to employ violence to neutralize his adversaries in Munich.

Ceausescu ran his country in the manner of a traditional Balkan tyrant rather than along the collective, bureaucratic lines preferred by Brezhnev, Gierek, and Kádár. He was megalomania personified, casually issuing decrees that caused the razing of entire villages, the destruction of historic buildings in Bucharest, or the construction of grotesque, Fascist-style government structures at a time when the regime could not afford street lighting for the capital. Ceausescu considered himself the supreme leader, the supreme city planner, the supreme architect and supreme music critic.

The political commentary of RFE's Romanian section was of a different nature from the other RFE language sections. Under its two most famous editors, Noel Bernard and Vlad Georgescu, the Romanian section carried out a relentless polemical offensive against Ceausescu, his imperious wife Elena, and the court camarilla around them. The tone was biting, personal, and sarcastic. During Bernard's editorship, the Romanian section was not infrequently cited for violations of the station's strictures against vituperation and rhetorical excess. The American management considered Bernard one of the station's most gifted editors, and his commentaries were extremely popular with the Romanian audience. Although Georgescu was less strident, he continued Bernard's anti-Ceausescu policies, to which he brought a unique personal perspective, having been a member of Bucharest's intellectual elite and a leading dissident figure before coming to the West.[17]

The Romanian section's broadcasts were a source of tension between RFE and the State Department. While he ruined Romania's economy and despoiled its culture, Ceausescu gained a reputation as a maverick in foreign affairs. Romania was the only Soviet bloc country to refuse to break diplomatic ties with Israel after the 1967 Six-Day War and Ceausescu had declined to participate in the 1968 invasion of Czechoslovakia, an act of independence that elevated him to a hero's status for many East Europeans, if only briefly. For a while in the 1970s, Ceausescu was treated as Washington's favorite Communist: Romania was granted most-favored nation trade status, President Nixon paid a visit to Bucharest, and the United States said little about the regime's atrocious human rights record. Meanwhile, at Radio Free Europe Ceausescu was treated as Enemy Number One due to the tenacity of the Romanian section editors.

Furthermore, RFE had a huge, and devoted, audience in Romania. Indeed, the Romanian section's listenership was proportionately the highest of any of the RFE or RL services, and quite possibly the highest of any Western service that broadcast to the Soviet bloc. Bernard had assembled a team of professional journalists, including several who were well known in Bucharest before they defected. His staff employed a vocabulary and personalized style that held a great appeal for the Romanian audience. Radio Free Europe also benefited from the primitive level of the Romanian Communist press, which had as its principal mission the celebration of the Ceausescus, their achievements, their diplomatic successes, and the respect they enjoyed in Washington, Paris, and other world capitals. In order to save money, Ceausescu actually cut television broadcasts to two hours daily, and as wits had it, one and a half were devoted to the *conducatore* himself. This made foreign broadcasting even more essential. Finally, Ceausescu contributed to RFE's popularity by agreeing not to resume jamming, presumably to ensure normal trade ties with the United States.

Ceausescu no doubt had occasion to regret the absence of jamming. According to Ion Mihai Pacepa, RFE broadcasts frequently sent the dictator into apoplectic rages. Pacepa was a member of Ceausescu's inner circle of security officials; until his defection to the United States in 1978, he was chief of the DIE, Romania's equivalent to the KGB. Among other things, Pacepa was responsible for carrying out Ceausescu's commands regarding the fate of his foreign enemies, usually dissident exiles. And unlike other East European leaders, Ceausescu had no scruples about ordering beatings, killings, or wet operations in general.

Although Ceausescu was not in the habit of listening to RFE, he kept abreast of what was being said about him through daily transcripts or summaries prepared by his intelligence service. After poring over the broadcast digest, an enraged Ceausescu would often summon Pacepa to his office and demand that action be taken to neutralize those RFE Romanians he regarded as the most obnoxious. A particular hate object was Emil Georgescu, a well-known Bucharest prosecutor until his 1974 defection. Georgescu aired biting commentaries on the Ceausescu personality cult and the abuses of the security apparatus. Finally, Ceausescu had had enough. "Emil Georgescu must be silenced, forever," he announced at an August 1976 meeting of top security officials. "He should have his jaw, teeth, and arms broken, so that he will never be able to speak or write again."

On October 18, Georgescu was seriously injured in an automobile accident, an operation carried out by a team of French drug smugglers hired by the DIE. Fortunately, passing motorists prevented the assailants from delivering the beating that was to put an end to his radio career. Georgescu was back on the air a few months later. The DIE thereupon launched a campaign of psychological terror. Agents sent menacing letters, drafted as if written by exiled Fascists. They sent anonymous letters to top RFE officials accusing Georgescu of enriching himself through shady business dealings. Georgescu was blackmailed and told that his aged mother could receive an exit visa if he would resign from RFE. Having failed at the "soft" approach, the DIE tried more direct methods. In July 1981, Georgescu was stabbed more than twenty-two times after leaving his apartment; again the operation was carried out by French drug smugglers. The two assailants were captured and received relatively light prison sentences. Georgescu died not long afterward.[18]

On another occasion, Ceausescu became enraged after scrutinizing anonymous letters that were sent to RFE by Romanian citizens and intercepted by authorities and RFE infiltrators. The letters were replete with attacks on Ceausescu, Elena, and the rest of his family, and Ceausescu was determined to discover the identity of the authors. He thus ordered that handwriting samples be taken of the entire nation, and compared to the RFE letters. He also ordered what came to be known as the typewriter law. Henceforth, all Romanians were required to get police permission to own a typewriter, and samples of each type face were to be filed with the authorities so that the Securitate could track down those who wrote slanderous letters about the first family.[19]

The DIE maintained a female agent at RFE—she worked for the director of the news department. Her husband also worked for the DIE, providing information on military installations in Munich. It was the woman agent who sent copies of the anonymous letters back to Bucharest. Ceausescu once discussed having her place a plastic explosive device in the director's office; apparently the idea was not followed up. Eventually the woman was discovered, though no criminal charges were filed against her. Ceausescu was also obsessed with placing an agent within the RFE staff, then having him redefect to Bucharest, from where he could make sensational revelations about the station's role as a haven for CIA spies—just as Andrzej Chechowitz had done for the Polish regime. Edward Gierek had boasted to Ceausescu of Chechowitz's exploits, and the Romanian would not be content until he could brag about his own superspy in Munich. Pacepa claims that the DIE did in fact have an agent within the Romanian section, code named Ionescu. Ionescu was offered the rank and pension of a general if he would return and denounce RFE. Ionescu, however, declined after his French lady friend balked at the prospect of living out her days in Bucharest.[20]

One of the most controversial revelations made by Pacepa concerns "Radu"—the code name of a form of radiation that, he claims, was given to political prisoners during their incarceration, with fatal results. Pacepa claims that Ceausescu was enthusiastic about the weapon; he would order, "Give Popescu Radu!" when he wanted an adversary finished off. In fact, both Noel Bernard and Vlad Georgescu died of cancer at relatively young ages—fifty-seven and fifty-one respectively—giving rise to the belief, widespread among Romanian dissidents and exiles, that they had been given lethal doses of radiation by the DIE. Western experts tend to dismiss the theory, although the FBI did conduct an inquiry into the deaths of Bernard, Georgescu, and two other top editors who died of cancer at relatively young ages. Georgescu had served time in a Romanian prison; Bernard had not. Pacepa, who was already in exile when the two chief editors succumbed, finds the idea credible. He tried to dissuade Nestor Ratesh, the Romanian section's Washington correspondent, from accepting the chief editor's position in 1989. Ratesh took the job anyway. But RFE took no chances. Ratesh wore a geiger counter while on the job that year.[21]

The suspicion that Romanian intelligence had succeeded in assassinating RFE editors without leaving a trace of evidence is not as far-fetched as one might think, given the experiences of Bulgarian exiles who ran afoul of Todor Zhivkov. Although the world now knows that Bulgarian intelligence murdered a leading exiled writer by stabbing him with a poisoned umbrella and apparently nearly succeeded in killing off a second exiled journalist through similar means, the fact is that without determined forensic sleuthing, both incidents might have been ascribed to some sort of freakish accident.

The victim in the notorious poisoned umbrella case was Georgi Markov. Before moving to the West in 1976, Markov, a novelist and playwright, had been a member of the Bulgarian cultural elite whose friendship was courted by Zhivkov. After receiving political asylum from Great Britain, Markov landed a job at the BBC and also began submitting scripts on a free-lance basis to RFE.

It was his RFE broadcasts that were to cause the greatest furor back home in Sofia. Markov was the author of a regular Sunday series, *In Absentia: Reports from Bulgaria.* In addition to reflections on Bulgarian literature and culture, the scripts included embarrassing revelations about Zhivkov and other party leaders. In 1977, Markov wrote a series of eleven scripts he entitled *Personal Meetings with Todor Zhivkov.* The program was relentlessly critical of the party chief's hypocrisy and aristocratic life-style.[22]

Like Ceausescu and all other Communist leaders, Zhivkov familiarized himself with the content of RFE broadcasts through daily summaries provided by the State Security Directorate for Struggle Against Ideological Subversion. Although Bulgaria jammed RFE broadcasts, state security left one frequency unjammed to allow the scripts to be transcribed. Each day Zhivkov received transcripts of the previous day's broadcasts; he also received a daily report, "Anti-Bulgarian Propaganda Bulletin," that summarized the Bulgarian-language broadcasts of all Western radio services.[23]

Markov received regular death threats from the time he began working for the BBC and RFE. Markov's stock response was to inform the caller that if he were killed, he would die a martyr, and the accuracy of his claims about the brutality of Bulgarian security would be demonstrated. Shortly before his death, however, Markov's caller warned that he would be killed by a poison no Western scientist could detect and thus denied a hero's stature.

The Markov assassination is one of the better-known Cold War murder stories. On September 7, 1978, he was waiting for a bus on Waterloo Bridge. Suddenly, he felt a pain in his leg; he turned and saw a man retrieving an umbrella that he had just dropped. Markov went to work as usual. But the pain worsened, and Markov checked into a hospital. He went into shock and died three days later, leaving a wife and small daughter.

Medical authorities were baffled by the case. They believed Markov had been poisoned, but could find no trace of a deadly substance in his system. After months of investigation, Scotland Yard concluded that Markov had been killed by a dose of ricin, a highly toxic poison, which had entered his system through a pellet that had been injected by the umbrella.

Markov was not the only intended victim of Bulgarian intelligence. Another exile, Vladimir Kostov, was attacked in a similar fashion while in a metro station in Paris. Kostov was a well-connected Sofia journalist who had recently defected. He had good contacts within the Bulgarian security apparatus; he knew, for example, the details of Zhivkov's scheme to have Bulgaria incorporated as the sixteenth republic of the Soviet Union. He survived the attack. Apparently the pellet failed to disintegrate, and he was subsequently hired by RFE as a broadcaster specializing in Bulgarian foreign policy and security affairs.

With the collapse of East European communism, new possibilities opened up for the solution of Markov's murder. But in March 1991, Bulgarian authorities announced that the Markov files had been destroyed by the chief of intelligence, Gen. Vladimir Todorov. Shortly thereafter, another security official, Vassil Kotsev, the man identified as responsible for organizing the Markov and Kostov operations, died in a mysterious automobile accident. Todorov, meanwhile, fled to Moscow, ostensibly for treatment of a heart ailment, but more likely to avoid questioning about the Markov case by Scotland Yard investigators who were in Bulgaria. Todorov denied personal involvement in Markov's murder, though he did not deny Bulgarian government involvement. However, he emphatically denied that Kostov had been an assassination target and suggested that Kostov had invented the assassination story to enhance his value to RFE. Todorov was eventually found guilty of destroying the Markov files and handed a light prison sentence.

The best available information suggests that Markov was killed by a combination KGB-Bulgarian intelligence operation. According to Oleg Kalugin, Markov's fate was sealed at a meeting in KGB headquarters in early 1978. At the meeting were Yuri Andropov, then chief of the KGB and later Soviet leader, Vladimir Kryuchkov, chief of intelligence, and Kalugin, then head of foreign intelligence. Kryuchkov had received an urgent message from Dimiti Stoyanov, the Bulgarian minister of internal affairs. The message said that Todor Zhivkov wanted Markov removed, permanently, and was requesting KGB assistance.

Kalugin claims that Andropov initially resisted the request; but Kryuchkov remonstrated with his chief: the request had come from Comrade Zhivkov. If the KGB turned the Bulgarians down, it would put Stoyanov in an embarrassing position, since it would appear to Zhivkov that his Interior Minister no longer enjoyed the KGB's respect. Finally, Andropov relented, but he limited Soviet involvement to the technical side; there would be no KGB agents assigned to the actual murder.[24]

The job was then passed along to the KGB's scientists, who already had experience in the development of poisons for political killings. Kalugin claims that an initial attempt on Markov was planned for a trip he made to Munich; the idea was to poison his drink during a party. After this plan aborted, the umbrella scheme was hatched. The KGB purchased several American umbrellas, fitting them with firing mechanisms to shoot small pellets from close range. The scientists selected ricin as the poison. A derivative of castor oil seeds, ricin is said to be seventy times as toxic as cyanide. The KGB took the poison and umbrellas to Sofia, where agents instructed the Bulgarians on their use. One glitch occurred when the Bulgarians decided to run a trial test, with a condemned Bulgarian prisoner as the victim. Surprisingly, he survived. At this point, an alternative plan was suggested. Markov would be killed while vacationing in Sardinia through toxic material that would enter his system by human touch—opening a car door or touching a wall sprinkled with the poison. This plan was dropped when it was realized that the poison might kill Markov's wife or small daughter.

Officially, the Markov case has never been solved. An Italian with Danish citizenship was identified as the murderer but was never brought to trial. And in 1995, the neo-Communists who were then governing Bulgaria issued a White Book on the country's international relations. The White Book blamed the previous liberal government for "the self-denigrating confession of involvement in crimes such as the attempt against the Pope . . . and the concurrent link of the name of Bulgaria to the tragic demise of Georgi Markov without a final and unequivocal explanation of the incident."

At 9:47 on the evening of February 21, 1981, a large explosion caused extensive damage to the Munich headquarters of RFE-RL. The blast occurred on a Saturday night, when few employees were in the building. Nevertheless, four employees were injured, two of whom were initially listed in critical condition. The explosion's cause, it soon became clear, was a bomb placed by one of the station's many enemies. The crime was the work of professionals; the bomb was a sophisticated and fairly large device, holding somewhere between ten and twenty kilos worth of explosive material, affixed to the wall near the offices of the Czechoslovak service. The concussion caused $2 million of damage to the headquarters and blew out windows and rattled homes for miles around.[25]

Among the questions that may have been answered with the end of the Cold War is the identity of the parties responsible for the bombing. The solution to yet another Cold War puzzle was found not in the files of the countries to which RFE and RL broadcast, but in the files of the Stasi, the notorious East German secret police.[26]

Richard Cummings, the chief of security for the radios, was permitted to examine Stasi materials relevant to the bombing after the fall of the Berlin Wall. What he discovered was a story that contained many of the trappings of a spy novel—except for a credible motive.

According to the Stasi documents, the operation was carried out by Carlos, the most famous international terrorist of the late Cold War period. Although best known for his work on behalf of radical Arab and Palestinian causes, Carlos had close links to the intelligence services of the Soviet bloc. In 1979, in fact, Carlos moved his base of operations to Budapest, where he remained for several years with the approval of the Kádár regime.

On October 14, 1980, Carlos chaired a meeting of followers from various European terrorist organizations at which the subject was the RFE-RL assignment. The operation was apparently funded by the Ceausescu regime in Romania. The Carlos group conducted a surveillance study of the station headquarters, with the apparent purpose of determining when the fewest number of employees would be in their offices. A Saturday evening date was decided on in order to minimize the risk of casualties. Among those involved in the planning were Magdalena Kopf, Carlos's lover, known as "Lilly," and Johannes Weinrich, Carlos's most trusted aide, known as "Steve." Weinrich took extensive notes during the meeting, which were later sent by Hungarian intelligence officials to their East German counterparts.

Romanian intelligence supplied the equipment: blocks of explosives, radio transmitters and receivers to detonate the explosives, walkie-talkies, nine pistols—two with silencers—and hand grenades, to be used if West German police took pursuit. In the event, the guns and grenades proved unnecessary. There was little security at the Munich headquarters at the time and the building was poorly illuminated. There were only two security guards; one acted as a parking attendant, the other conducted patrols around the building. The patrols took eighteen minutes, more than enough time to plant the device and make an escape.

The team selected for the operation represented a multinational cross-section of European terrorism. Weinrich led the expedition; the bomb was detonated by Bruno Brequest, a member of a Swiss terrorist group, and the rest of the team included members of the Spanish Basque ETA. After the bombing one car was abandoned a few hundred meters from the radio headquarters; when police checked the automobile several months later, they discovered several grenades inside.

Ceausescu was apparently pleased with the outcome; Carlos was feted by high-ranking security officials in Bucharest, although soon after he was told to leave Hungary and subsequently relocated his operation in Damascus. Meanwhile, Ceausescu's obsession with RFE remained undiminished. In 1984, West Germany expelled five Romanian diplomats for allegedly plotting to bomb the RFE-RL headquarters and to kidnap and possibly assassinate a Romanian exile. All five were reportedly agents of Romanian intelligence and were said by German sources to have been involved in various "criminal acts."[27]

During their early years, RFE and RL drew the bulk of their staff from what was known as the postwar wave of emigration, comprised of those who had fled their native countries to escape Communist rule. The postwar generation came in many ideological varieties, ranging from Social Democrats to the far Right. Some were deeply committed to democracy; some were motivated by religious convictions; some had had their property confiscated.

Radio Free Europe tried to fill its staff with an ideologically diverse collection of journalists representing mainstream parties and excluding ultrarightists and Communists. Nevertheless, some journalists with tainted pasts did gain employment with the station. George Urban, who worked for RFE in the early sixties and was later appointed the station's director, recalls encountering Emil Csonka, the leader of the youth section of the Hungarian Fascist movement, the Arrow Cross, while working in Munich. Csonka was at the time a member in good standing of the Hungarian section.[28]

The problem of staff recruitment was more complex for Radio Liberty, since the various nations that made up the Soviet Union had little experience with democracy or party politics. For the non-Russian nationalities, the fight against communism took the form of a fight for national survival, an emphasis reflected in the programming of the RL nationalities' services. Many Russians regarded Marxism as an alien ideology that was preventing Russia from achieving spiritual greatness.

East European nationalism was sometimes tainted by ethnic chauvinism. Balts hated the Russians, Hungarians had little use for Romanians (and vice versa), Bulgarians disliked the Turks. The management of the radios made the promotion of ethnic harmony a programming priority; RFE in particular encouraged its language sections to broadcast items about the amicable relations between different ethnic and religious groups in the democracies. The management was also attentive to the possibility of expressions of anti-Semitism. Anti-Semitism had been the curse of Eastern Europe, and the disgraceful behavior toward Jews who returned to their homes from the death camps suggests that anti-Semitism persisted even after the truth about the Holocaust was known. Anti-Semitism over the airwaves was never a serious problem at RFE or RL. Indeed, the radios consistently denounced the repression of Jews and Jewish culture in their broadcasts and included Jewish religious programs on their schedule. Anti-Semitism in relations between staff members was another question. Bad blood between Jewish staff members and nationalist oriented staff caused serious divisions within the Russian section during the 1970s, and there were similar, if less rancorous, problems within the Ukrainian section.

There was also the question of the political history of some members of the radios' staff. During the war, collaboration with the Nazis had occurred in a number of East European countries and in many of the non-Russian regions of the Soviet Union. The motives for collaboration varied. In some countries (Romania most notably) there were sizable Fascist movements that, without much prodding from Germany, carried out despicable atrocities against the Jews. But in the non-Russian republics of the Soviet Union, collaboration could be a more complex phenomenon. Some did it for money; some did it because they hated the Jews and enjoyed persecuting them. Others cooperated with Germany because they despised what communism and Russian imperialism had done to their nations.

After the war, some with questionable political pasts managed to slip into the United States. The United States had an official policy against granting visas to exiles with records of collaboration, but given the chaotic wartime circumstances in Nazi-occupied Europe, it was impossible to conduct a thorough investigation of all those who applied for residency in America, and some gained admittance by simply falsifying their biographies. Others were admitted through national security waivers issued by the CIA or State Department because of their cooperation with American intelligence, because they possessed special expertise (German scientists, for example), or for other security-related reasons. According to some accounts, the Office of Policy Coordination under Frank Wisner made widespread use of the anti-Soviet intelligence network organized by Nazi spymaster Reinhard Gehlen. Gehlen's network included a good number of East Europeans, Ukrainians, Balts, and Belorussians, some of whom were given American citizenship as reward for their assistance to the United States.[29]

It is clear, as the case of the ill-fated Abo Fatalibey demonstrates, that some exiles with collaborationist records found their way to the staffs of both RFE and RL. Fatalibey, of course, was not an American citizen, but he had secured employment with a Cold War radio station funded by the American government. And while some collaborators may have gone to some length to conceal their pasts, this was not the case with Fatalibey, who provided the information about his role with Nazi military units and Nazi puppet organizations in a biography he wrote for RL after he was hired.

How many exiles with records similar to Abo Fatalibey's landed positions with Radio Liberty or RFE is unclear. During the 1950s the fact that accused war criminals had gained entrance to the United States elicited little public furor. By the 1970s, when demands were raised for action against Nazi accomplices, many of those who might have worked for RL or RFE had died or retired. It is also possible that the CIA removed the personnel files of tainted radio employees when the decision was made to end the relationship between RFE and RL and the intelligence agency.

During the 1970s, the American government began to take the issue of Nazi war criminals seriously. A special investigative unit was set up in the Justice Department to sift through the records and bring deportation cases against those who gained admission to the United States illegally. Some of the accused voluntarily surrendered their American citizenship and moved abroad; a few were deported to other countries, in a few cases, to the Soviet Union. In the most notorious case, John Demjanjuk, a Ukrainian American living in Cleveland, was accused of being "Ivan the Terrible," a feared death camp guard. Demjanjuk was sent to Israel, where he was put on trial and eventually freed for lack of clearcut evidence. Afterward, he returned to Cleveland; although his citizenship was restored, the Justice Department reopened its case in 1999.

The Demjanjuk case points up the difficulties faced by government prosecutors. The events in dispute had taken place forty years previously, and the witnesses and the defendants were quite old. Often, documentary evidence was provided by the Soviet Union, and was thus regarded with suspicion. The accused were often able to present witnesses whose testimony contradicted the death camp inmates.

While some investigative journalists claimed that RFE and RL had provided jobs to many exiles with questionable pasts, the actual number was quite low. Few radio employees, past or present, were accused of war crimes or collaboration during the period when the most intensive investigations were taking place. And most of those worked as free-lancers rather than as full-time employees.

Although the cases against some free-lancers were relatively strong, no one was ever convicted and stripped of citizenship. Vilis Hazners, a free-lancer with the Latvian service, was accused of having persecuted Jews in Latvia during the war. Radio Liberty suspended him after the Justice Department filed a deportation case against him. But while a number of witnesses testified against Hazners, an immigration judge found in his favor, and he was reinstated by RL.[30] Stanislaw Stankievich, a free-lancer for the Belorussian service and a former employee of the Institute for the Study of the USSR, was also the target of deportation proceedings, having been named as a participant in the massacre of Jews in the town of Borissow. Stankievich died before his case was heard.[31]

Another Belorussian, Anton Adamovich, admitted on national television that he had worked during the war for a newspaper in the Belorussian capital of Minsk that advocated independence from the Soviet Union. Interviewed by Mike Wallace for the television program *60 Minutes,* Adamovich also made statements that could have been interpreted as an admission of having worked as a Nazi propagandist, but according to William Kratch, the director of the RFE-RL office in New York who witnessed the interview, Wallace badgered the elderly émigré and continually prefaced questions with "When you

TRIFA 1979

were a Nazi propagandist . . ." Kratch claims that Adamovich denied on several occasions that he had worked for the Nazis but eventually grew flustered and simply gave up trying to refute the charge. Adamovich did, however, acknowledge that he had worked for U.S. Army intelligence after the war.[32]

No deportation case was brought against Adamovich. But the *60 Minutes* segment earned the radios considerable press criticism and provoked U.S. Representative Barney Frank to issue a demand for Adamovich's dismissal—which the radios rejected. In a sense, Adamovich suffered for his openness; another RL employee, a Ukrainian named Leonid Lyman, declined to appear before the *60 Minutes* camera after one of Mike Wallace's assistants asked if he was known by a certain pseudonym during the war. By refusing to submit to a televised interview, Lyman ensured that his name never came up during the subsequent furor.[33]

For Radio Free Europe, the most serious war criminals' controversy involved a broadcast, not an employee accused of a collaborationist past. On May 1, 1979, RFE's Romanian service aired a forty-five-minute interview with Bishop Valerian Trifa, the head of the Romanian Orthodox Church of America. The interview did not touch on political matters, focusing instead on the fiftieth anniversary of the Romanian missionary church in the United States.

Trifa had for years been the object of charges of membership in the Fascist Iron Guard in Bucharest. He was said to have encouraged Iron Guardists to carry out pogroms against the city's Jewish population. The Trifa case had been given widespread attention by the media, and Trifa himself was already facing denaturalization hearings when the interview took place.

Noel Bernard had decided to include the interview in the coverage of the church anniversary, and had directed Liviu Floda, a Romanian staff journalist in New York, to prepare the story. Floda, who was Jewish and despised Trifa, dragged his heels but finally complied after Bernard insisted that the interview be carried out. There is evidence that several of Bernard's subordinate editors questioned the wisdom of featuring the alleged war criminal on the air. Bernard, however, pressed ahead. He was convinced that coverage of the church anniversary would be incomplete without some comment by the head of the Romanian church in America. He was also motivated by the existence of a splinter exile church that was regarded as controlled by the Communist regime in Bucharest. Bernard felt it would be a mistake for the only voice from America to be that of a puppet church.[34]

News of the Trifa broadcast eventually filtered back to the United States, where it provoked a storm of protest from the press, Jewish organizations, and, most notably, from Representative Elizabeth Holtzman, a New York Democrat who was passionately committed to the campaign against Nazi war criminals.

With the Trifa case, the radios learned that one of the byproducts of the new environment of open congressional funding and public accountability was an intensified political scrutiny of the stations' internal affairs. As a result of this one script, a hearing was conducted, at Holtzman's insistence, by a subcommittee of the House Committee on Foreign Affairs. Fortified by information from disgruntled Romanian section journalists, Holtzman used the opportunity to denounce Bernard's stewardship, and came close to demanding his dismissal.[35]

The controversy also ensnared Paul Henze, who was working as a deputy to Zbigniew Brzezinski in the National Security Council. Henze, whose portfolio included foreign broadcasting, was on hand at a meeting of the Board for International Broadcasting when the Trifa matter came up. Henze dismissed the controversy as "silly," a comment that nettled Walter Roberts, the BIB's executive director, who called the Trifa program "a very serious issue." Henze shot back that the issue "certainly isn't serious from the point of view of the White House." Henze then clashed with BIB member Rita Hauser, Henze insisting that RFE was "not a court of judgment" but a "means of communication," and Hauser insisting that he take back his remarks. The transcript of the meeting was leaked to the press, whether by a board member or staff is not clear, another sign of the new and more open environment.[36]

Trifa left the United States a few years later to avoid deportation. Radio Free Europe and Radio Liberty became more attentive to the political ramifications of their programs, but the end of the Trifa episode did not mean an end to allegations that broadcasts were politically insensitive, chauvinistic, or anti-Semitic.

15

The Reagan Years

Of America's nine Cold War presidents, none was as committed to the mission of the radios as Ronald Reagan. Although principally remembered for his defense buildup and support for anti-Soviet forces in various Third World locales, Reagan also believed that America should conduct a vigorous offensive in the global war of ideas.

Reagan therefore embarked on a program to strengthen the instruments of what had come to be known as "public diplomacy." Reagan himself set the tone by trumpeting the superiority of American democratic capitalism and speaking of communism as an evil and doomed system. He created new projects to carry on the war of ideas, most notably the National Endowment for Democracy, a quasi-governmental entity that provided financial assistance to the democratic opposition in dictatorships of both the Right and the Left. Reagan's tenure also saw the creation of Radio Marti, a surrogate home service for Cuba modeled after Radio Free Europe but administered by the United States Information Agency. And he gave priority to the reinvigoration of the existing weapons of ideological warfare. Thus Reagan unveiled an expensive, and ultimately unfulfilled, program of technical modernization for the Voice of America.

For Radio Free Europe and Radio Liberty, Reaganism first meant more money. The era of budget stringency and staff reductions came to an end with the election of the Great Communicator. In the late seventies, there had been serious talk about moving part of the radios' operation to the United States due to the high cost of doing business in Germany. In 1979, the RFE–RL budget stood at more than $80 million, a major increase from the $45 million six years earlier. And this despite a 26 percent reduction in staff.[1] Under Reagan, little pressure was exerted to relocate the broadcast headquarters. In budget after budget, Reagan raised the appropriations for both the VOA and RFE-RL, even as he hacked away at the spending levels of a long list of domestic programs. The radios were able to overhaul antiquated equipment, hire new staff, add correspondents to cover the war in Afghanistan, and launch a new service, Radio Free Afghanistan, beamed to the mujahedeen and their supporters.

Yet it cannot be said that this new abundance made the headquarters in Englischer Garten an especially happy place during the early 1980s. Reagan's policies were divisive at home and abroad; they were equally divisive within RFE and RL. The men Reagan appointed to overhaul America's international broadcasting stations were bent on recasting the RFE-RL message along more muscular lines. When they hired managers and staff, they sought men who shared their hatred of communism and disdain for détente. They encouraged sharp, hard-hitting commentaries—restrained polemics that would zero in on Communist failure, Communist hypocrisy, and Communist immorality.

Some welcomed the changes, but many did not. The radios were no strangers to controversy, having survived the Hungarian Revolution, the CIA revelations, and Senator Fulbright's machinations. But where previous controversies had revolved around broadcast performance or organizational questions, the Reagan-era disputes were directly related to the stations' political orientation. And as is often the case with ideological controversies, the argument over editorial direction left little room for compromise.

The Reagan upheaval struck Radio Free Europe during a period of relative stability. The station had received widespread praise for its coverage of the Prague Spring and the Polish worker rebellions of 1970 and 1976. Its listenership in Poland, where the trade union Solidarity had just been launched, and Romania, where RFE was revered for its relentless criticism of the Ceausescus, had never been higher. The station's management was in the hands of capable veterans; the director, James F. Brown, a British native who had taken American citizenship, was a respected scholar of East European politics and the man credited with forging RFE's research department into an institution respected throughout the academic and journalistic worlds.

Brown and Ralph Walter, who remained at RFE-RL as executive

vice president, were by instinct and experience cautious in their management policies. While committed to the eventual overthrow of East European communism, they were skeptical of a Soviet bloc collapse in the foreseeable future. This was particularly true of Brown, whose views about the future of Eastern Europe were reflected by his assertion, made in private conversation, that Kádárism was the best possible outcome to which the Hungarian people could aspire.[2] Brown was unimpressed by Westerners, particularly Americans, who insisted that a revivified Free World was capable of rolling back Communist power in Eastern Europe.[3]

Walter had served on the policy staff during the Hungarian Revolution, and Brown had arrived at RFE soon after. For both, the lesson of Hungary was that prudence was almost always the better part of valor. Was it possible that they had learned the lesson of Hungary too well? Some critics believed that, a quarter-century after the event, RFE was overly preoccupied with the events of 1956 to the detriment of its message.

Questions were also raised about RFE's support for reform Communists. During the 1960s, RFE had used its broadcasts to encourage the forces aligned against Novotný in Czechoslovakia, and had also given tentative support to János Kádár in Hungary. The station's leadership reasoned that after the Hungarian Revolution had been crushed, incremental reform inspired from within the party structure represented the most likely route to liberalization and economic change. Radio Free Europe was not alone in its embrace of reform communism; its hopes for gradual, party-led change was shared by the State Department and most scholarly experts on Eastern Europe.

The 1968 Soviet invasion of Czechoslovakia represented a major setback to RFE's expectations for gradual change under reform communism. Jim Brown says that the Warsaw Pact occupation of Prague "knocked the idea that serious reform could come from within the party on its head."[4] In Czechoslovakia, the postreform regime of Gustáv Husák systematically purged the officials associated with Dubček; other potential reformers quickly got the message that conformity was a prerequisite for a successful career. In Bulgaria, Todor Zhivkov employed a mixture of repression and cooptation to stifle the advocates of change, and in Romania, Nicolae Ceausescu ruthlessly purged those who questioned his peculiar brand of neo-Stalinism.

This left Poland and Hungary. In Poland, RFE had greeted the

1970 replacement of Gomulka by Edward Gierek as a hopeful sign, especially in the light of the unsavory character of some of the more prominent alternative leaders. Yet Gierek's reformist rhetoric was not matched by his actions. According to Jim Brown, RFE decided to no longer place its bets on reform communism, "when we began to understand what a charlatan Edward Gierek was." Brown says that RFE effectively wrote Gierek off in 1973, two years into his rule and five years before the American government began to cool on the Polish leader.[5]

The one country in which the notion of reform communism was still treated respectfully was Hungary. Radio Free Europe had excoriated Kádár as one of the great villains of the Hungarian Revolution but shifted its perspective in the mid-1960s, when Kádár made his famous pronouncement that those Hungarians who "are not against us are with us." While Kádár remained a gray, undynamic figure, a reliable supporter of Soviet foreign policy, and cautious in his approach to domestic affairs, he did permit a carefully controlled policy of cultural and economic change. In response, RFE covered the regime's policies with a more approving eye, praising the reforms and attacking those figures who were regarded as impediments to liberalization.

By the mid-1970s, RFE became more deeply involved in internal Hungarian politics. Joseph Szabados, who succeeded István Bede as Hungarian director in 1972, was a proponent of aligning RFE with the positive aspects of Kádárism. "If we praised the positive policies," he reasoned, "the reformers would be encouraged to continue and expand on those policies. . . . We did not criticize the reformers."[6]

Szabados went one step beyond simply promoting the reform agenda in RFE commentaries. He would hold meetings with representatives of the regime at discreet locations in Western Europe, usually Vienna or Rome. The Hungarian delegation included acknowledged leaders of the reform camp, as well as a more controversial figure, Gyorgy Aczel, a Politburo member whose abilities were recognized but whose reform credentials were a matter of dispute.

In discussing the meetings years later, Szabados said it was clear to both sides that each was trying to put across its own agenda: "They tried to manipulate me, and I in turn tried to outmanipulate them." The Hungarian goal was to convince RFE to put its muscle behind some new policy that was running afoul of conservative resistance. The Hungarians would pass along information that was not available in the Hungarian press, enabling the radio to broadcast expert, informed analysis unavailable anywhere else. The Kádárists, for example, urged RFE to support the breakup of large industrial enterprises into smaller entities that could be run as cooperatives. Such a request posed no problem for Szabados, since he favored almost any proposal that contributed to the dismantling of the Stalinist economic structure.

The Kádárists also asked RFE to say some kind words about certain reform favorites, especially those involved in economic policy, and to praise Aczel, the cultural chief. Some observers would not have included Aczel in the reform camp. But Szabados views him as "a convinced Communist who was nevertheless the main instigator of reform from inside the party." Among the antireform figures whom RFE was urged to criticize were Bela Biszku, the chief of party administration, and Sandor Gaspar, the trade union chief.[7]

For obvious reasons, these off-the-record sessions were kept confidential, known only to a handful of officials in the American management. Even in an era dominated by East-West détente, the revelation that an RFE editor was holding face-to-face meetings with Communist officials would have raised serious questions for the station's management. Furthermore, the station's tilt toward Kádárism was not universally popular within the Hungarian service. Eventually, RFE's coverage of Hungarian affairs was to be an important point of contention between the RFE leadership appointed after Reagan's election and holdover editors from the previous administration.

By 1980, many anti-Communists had reached the conclusion that U.S. policy had been enfeebled by a decade of détente—in every dimension, military, diplomatic, and in the realm of public diplomacy. As evidence, they cited the Soviets' attainment of military parity with the United States and the success of pro-Soviet movements in the Third World.

Some suspected that a creeping form of anti-anticommunism had infected the instruments of public diplomacy, including the VOA and the freedom radios. The most thorough exposition of the critics' case was made by James L. Tyson, in a study published by the National Strategy Information Center. Tyson charged that a commitment to détente had weakened the RFE message, to the point where "criticisms of the Communist governments and the Soviet power behind them became rarer, and the political commentary in general became blander." Tyson placed much of the blame on Henry Kissinger; he quoted anonymous RFE editors as complaining that the former Secretary of State had placed restrictions on broadcast content. As evidence of RFE's détenteist mindset, Tyson noted a report by Henry Kamm in the *New York Times* that quoted an editor in the Hungarian section as asserting, "We are not asking the Communists to give up Communism. . . . We would like a beautiful Communism, or as Khrushchev said, a goulash Communism."[8]

Tyson drew much of his material from disgruntled RFE journalists. Radio Free Europe staff members who were dissatisfied with the broadcast tone also met privately with Americans who were believed to have influence with the Reagan administration. Carnes Lord, a member of the Reagan transition team on public diplomacy, had meetings with a number of RFE staff members who complained that some of the language services had fallen under the domination of editors who favored a Euro-Communist perspective or leaned toward the kind of "socialism with a human face" orientation embodied in the policies of the Prague Spring.

The attempt by staff dissidents and their allies within the ethnic lobbies in Washington to use political clout to influence the direction of program policy was an entirely new development. During the days when the Central Intelligence Agency had the ultimate authority over radio policy, staff members seldom took their discontents outside the organization. While ethnic organizations did attempt to influence programming and staffing decisions, the CIA acted as an effective firewall between the political realm and the radios' management. The CIA was also effective at deflecting the attention of members of Congress.

This changed with the creation of the Board for International Broadcasting (BIB) and the decision to fund the radios through open congressional appropriations. Although the BIB was established to prevent political meddling in RFE-RL affairs, the very fact that Congress provided funds for the stations' operation guaranteed a measure of political interference, which was not long in coming, as the Trifa case demonstrated. Furthermore, while the mission of the BIB's professional staff was, in part, to serve as a watchdog, its allegiance was not primarily to the RFE-RL management in Munich, but ostensibly to members of the BIB. In practice, the BIB staff often resisted control by either the radios' management or board members. If they were dissatisfied with the BIB's policies, staff members were known to take their concerns to the press, Congress, or ethnic organizations.

The RFE-RL staff learned quickly that leaking sensitive internal information seldom elicited serious retribution. Diverse complaints found their way to American sources; editors were accused of harboring anti-American attitudes, programs were said to be overly sympathetic to communism, broadcasts were alleged to contain anti-Semitic overtones, commentaries were reported to have insulted ethnic minorities. Usually the information was leaked through covert channels, but not always. German labor law granted extraordinary protections to workers, to the point where outright dismissal became a near impossibility. Although there was a clause in the union contract meant to discourage employees from publicly criticizing the radios, German courts tended to rule in the worker's favor, even in cases in which the employee had published critical articles in publications hostile to RFE-RL.

The evidence suggests that the fears about RFE and RL having abandoned an anti-Communist stance were exaggerated, if not unfounded. The debate over the future of American Cold War policy did reveal a growing acceptance of Communist expansionism in the Third World and willingness to accept the status quo in relations with the Soviets on the part of America's elite institutions. Some Reaganites, however, were inclined to interpret conditions at RFE-RL in the light of the ongoing American debate, leading them to mistake a caution bred of hard experience for the attitudes of anti-anticommunism that they encountered in the domestic debate.

There were, nevertheless, important differences over RFE's broadcast strategy that divided Reagan's supporters from the holdover managers. A high proportion of RFE's managers and editors had spent most of their lives in Western Europe, and their political perspectives had been shaped by the European environment. They were unenthusiastic about the Reaganites' aggressive anticommunism, and some were no doubt disdainful of Reagan himself. Their economic views tended toward the social democratic, and they were unimpressed by the new president's free enterprise crusade. Where American neoconservatives regarded Eurocommunism as an essentially irrelevant phenomenon, Jim Brown encouraged his broadcasters to feature items about the rift in the global Communist movement caused by the ferment in the Italian and Spanish parties.[9]

It is also possible that RFE contributed to its image as bland and unwilling to challenge the existing state of affairs by its public relations strategy during the Fulbright crisis. In interviews with journalists, radio officials went out of their way to emphasize the noncontroversial nature of their programming and to reassure America that the RFE mission was compatible with détente. In attempting to persuade skeptical Americans that the station presented no obstacle to improved East–West ties, indeed, in seldom using the word Communist in describing the radio's objectives, RFE was sowing the seeds of future troubles when the political winds shifted in Washington.

In the aftermath of the 1980 election, the Reagan campaign established a series of transition teams to prepare recommendations on policy and appointments. One team was devoted to public diplomacy and international broadcasting. During the presidential campaign, Reagan had promised that he would "communicate with the world" about the superiority of the American system in its duel with communism. Overseas broadcasting was seen as the most cost effective method of carrying out this mission. At the urging of two National Security Council aides, Soviet scholar Richard Pipes and Carnes Lord, who was responsible for public diplomacy, along with national security adviser Richard V. Allen, a decision was made to assign prime responsibility for this campaign to the BIB and the radios. Emphasis was placed on strengthening RL's broadcasts to the peoples of Soviet Central Asia, an area that the administration saw as a zone of vulnerability for the Kremlin.[10]

From the administration's perspective, the key appointment was chairman of the BIB. Since its establishment in the mid-seventies, the BIB had led a problematic existence. Its first chairman, David Abshire, had served in the State Department and understood the workings of international radio. But Abshire, a Republican appointee, resigned with the election of Jimmy Carter, and Carter's choice to succeed him, John Gronouski, proved a disappointment. Gronouski qualified for the position on the basis of having served as ambassador to Poland and because of his leadership role in the Polish American community. Unfortunately, he is best remembered as BIB chairman for proposing that spokesmen from the Soviet bloc be given free air time to present the Communist side of the argument. The idea, needless to say, was rejected almost immediately.[11]

Aside from weak leadership, the BIB suffered from a lack of authority. Under the original legislation, which brought the radios under the congressional appropriations process, the stations were to be governed by two entities: the BIB, which determined budget priorities and functioned as a liaison between the radios and official Washington, and an entity created from the merger of the old RFE and RL corporate boards, which retained responsibility for broadcast policy. In 1982 this state of dual authority was ended when Congress adopted legislation, sponsored by Senator Claiborne Pell, a Democrat of Rhode Island, that had the effect of abolishing the corporate board and invested the BIB with full powers of administration and oversight. With the Pell amendment in place, the new chairman was assured of considerable power over the future course of RFE-RL.[12]

Initially, the chairmanship was offered to William F. Buckley Jr., the conservative columnist and editor of *National Review* magazine.[13] After Buckley turned down the proposition, the position was offered to Frank Shakespeare, who had chaired the public diplomacy transition team. Shakespeare had spent his life in the broadcasting industry and was at one time considered a leading candidate to become president of CBS. A conservative and ardent anti-Communist, Shakespeare was among a small group of media people who prepared Richard Nixon for his television appearances during the 1968 presidential campaign. Joe McGinniss portrayed Shakespeare as a hard-Right, anti-Communist zealot in his account of the campaign, *The Selling of the President 1968*. Of all Nixon's campaign associates, Shakespeare came across as the most committed to the roll-back of Soviet power and the least likely to favor détente with the Kremlin.[14]

A devout Catholic—he would later be named ambassador to the Vatican—Shakespeare was a great admirer of Pope John Paul II; his other idol was Alexander Solzhenitsyn. He was a close friend of another New York Irish Catholic Republican, William F. Casey, who was about to begin his tenure as director of Central Intelligence. Like Casey, Shakespeare demanded wide latitude in policy making and personnel appointments. Once the administration accepted these conditions, he assembled a board of men who were respected both for their intellectual accomplishments and their ability to wield political power.[15] Democratic members all came from the Scoop Jackson wing of the party: Ben J. Wattenberg, an author and columnist affiliated with the American Enterprise Institute; Michael Novak, a noted writer on religion, ethnicity, and economic themes, who was also an AEI fellow; Lane Kirkland, the strongly anti-Communist president of the AFL-CIO; and James Michener, the author. According to William F. Buckley, the White House initially vetoed the choice of Kirkland because of his sharp criticism of Reagan and his policies. The nomination was approved after Buckley, at Shakespeare's behest, interceded with administration officials.[16] Aside from Shakespeare, the most prominent Republican appointee was Malcolm S. (Steve) Forbes Jr.

Despite its bipartisan character, the board was united in sharing Reagan's anti-Soviet passions. Wattenberg was a champion of the American system and unabashed in his contempt for those who contended that American capitalism and Soviet communism were equally flawed. Novak was prominent among a small group of writers who identified capitalism as not only more efficient than other arrangements but also as virtuous. As chief officer of American labor, Kirkland presided over an ambitious project to provide through covert channels various forms of material support for Poland's Solidarity. Clearly, these were men who did not accept the global status quo as immutable. Nor would they go weak-kneed at the first sign of criticism. For Shakespeare, the board's willingness to stand up to public attack was essential, since he had plans for changes that, he suspected, would roil the waters both within RFE-RL and in Washington.

Once the board was in place, Shakespeare moved to overhaul the radios' leadership. He removed the president, Glenn Ferguson, and Ralph Walter, vice president, programs and policy, who functioned as the chief day-to-day administrator. Ferguson, a Democrat, was dismissed because Shakespeare wanted a chief officer who shared his ideological perspective and activist goals. As for Walter, who had kept a nonpartisan profile during his many years in Munich, his dismissal was due to Shakespeare's conviction that a man who had been in a position of high authority for so many years would be likely to resist the changes that the new board intended to institute.[17]

To replace Ferguson, the BIB appointed James R. Buckley. The brother of William F. Buckley, Jim Buckley had won election to the Senate in 1970, running on the Conservative Party ticket in New York. Buckley had won praise for his integrity during his term in the Senate and had been helpful to the radios during the Fulbright liquidation attempt. Shortly after Buckley's appointment, Jim Brown resigned as director of RFE. Brown's departure was triggered by the appointment, over his vehement objections, of a man he considered unqualified as director of the Czechoslovak section. Brown's resignation, however, was inevitable, given his differences with the Reaganites over broadcast strategy. In press interviews, Brown cited "political differences with the way the Reagan administration is now directing the radio" as well as the increasing pressure by émigré organizations to gain influence over internal RFE affairs.[18]

As new RFE director, Shakespeare selected George Urban, a native of Hungary who had emigrated to Great Britain after World War II and had established a reputation as a leading anti-Communist intellectual. Urban came to his position after years of experience in international broadcasting, having worked for the BBC during the fifties and served as a researcher and program developer for RFE during the 1960s. Urban had come up with the idea for one of RFE's more interesting projects, the Radio University of the Air, which featured interviews with leading European intellectuals, including prominent former Communists such as Arthur Koestler and Ignazio Silone.

Urban shared the Reaganites' apprehensions over the direction of RFE programming. He was convinced that the station was overly enamored of Eurocommunism; he also believed that many RFE editors had come to accept the view that "there was not much to choose from between the 'shortcomings' of Communism and those of American capitalism."[19] Radio Free Europe, he believed, was "suffering from the effects of détente and a loss of purpose and direction." "There was," he asserted, "growing doubt within senior management whether the conflict with the Soviet system could be won and whether winning it unconditionally was desirable. A thirty-year organizational fatigue was taking its toll. Bureaucrats were replacing men of political commitment; mediocrity and a willingness not to rock the boat were increasingly reckoned as virtues and passports to promotion."[20]

His detractors accused Urban of measuring conditions in Munich by the standards of the political debate raging in Washington.[21] The tenor of that debate can be gauged by the reaction to an interview with President Reagan conducted by James Buckley and broadcast to the Soviet and East European audience over RFE-RL. Although Reagan delivered some pro forma comments about America's commitment to peace and international harmony, the thrust of his remarks was hard-hitting anticommunism featuring a vocabulary not employed by American leaders in many years. He asserted that the United States intends by its example to "demonstrate that Communism is not the wave of the future" and to "show the captive nations that resisting totalitarianism is possible." He added, "What the people of Eastern Europe choose to do to achieve their freedom, of course, is their own decision." The response of the American press was to ask Buckley whether the president's comments violated the radios' guidelines, with the implicit suggestion that Buckley should perhaps have applied the censor's blue pencil to Reagan's remarks.[22]

Given the sweeping nature of Urban's indictment, one might expect major changes under his leadership. In fact, broadcast content changed relatively little during his three-year tenure. Nor were there massive shifts in staff. The one exception was the Hungarian service. Unlike previous managers, Urban understood Hungarian and listened constantly to RFE's Hungarian programs. He was not impressed by the pro-Kádár orientation of the broadcasts and bombarded Joseph Szabados with memos demanding that broadcasts stop praising reform communism, that broadcasts concentrate on Kádár's failings instead of his achievements, and insisting that certain staff members be prevented from writing on sensitive themes, or urging that they be fired. Soon Szabados resigned; as replacement, Urban hired Laszlo Ribanszky, a veteran BBC broadcaster and a political moderate.[23]

Urban's attempts to change the direction of Hungarian programming quickly ran into opposition from the State Department. When he informed Jack Matlock, at the time an adviser to President Reagan on Soviet affairs, that he had removed Szabados because he was dissatisfied with the Hungarian section's unwillingness to criticize the presence of Soviet troops on Hungarian territory, he was surprised to learn that Matlock agreed with Szabados's restraint on the troop question. According to Urban's account, Matlock indicated that the American government was satisfied with political conditions under Kádár, and expressed the view that as long as the Hungarian leader remained silent on the troop presence, the United States should do the same. Urban's broadcast strategy was also criticized by the U.S. ambassador to Hungary, a Hungarian American named Nicholas Salgo, who remonstrated with Urban over the radio's sharp criticism of Kádár and of its dim view of the country's elections, which RFE treated as a sham.[24]

Another of Urban's goals was to bring to an end the practice of hiring former members of East European Communist parties. "I was especially determined not to allow the libertarian ideas we stood for to be mocked by people who had made names for themselves as propagandists for the regime and were known to our audience as such," he explained in his memoirs. "Nothing could have done greater damage to our credibility than allowing former propagators of Marxism-Leninism to be heard on our airwaves enlarging on the virtues of the market economy, liberal parliamentary democracy, and individual freedom."[25] But the issue was not quite so black and white. Each service had on-air broadcasters who had had party connections back in the home country, either as members or as journalists who, while technically not party members, were given official approval to work in the media. Some were talented commentators whose broadcasts were highly popular with the RFE audience. Emil Georgescu, for example, had been a prosecutor in Bucharest; at RFE, his broadcasts so infuriated Ceausescu that he ordered his secret police to carry out several assassination attempts. Similarly, Vladimir Kostov, a Bulgarian journalist who defected to the West and was hired by RFE, was a target of a "poisoned umbrella" assassination attempt like the one that killed Georgi Markov.

Within the Czechoslovak service, however, the addition of a number of "official" journalists who had emigrated after the 1968 Soviet invasion was a source of internal strife. The newcomers—Sláva Volný, Karel Jezdinský, Milan Schultz, and others—were first-rate radio commentators and were given responsibility for important programs on internal Czechoslovak politics. While Volný had been a party member and had made some blatantly propagandistic broadcasts during the 1950s, he had distinguished himself during the Dubček era. Jezdinský had been a mainstay of a clandestine freedom broadcasting operation that remained in operation for some time after the Soviet invasion. The RFE broadcasts of Volný and the other newcomers were thoroughly hated by the Prague regime; Prague radio attacked its former colleagues mercilessly as renegades who had sold themselves for the American dollar. But veterans of the RFE Czechoslovak service resented the prominent role the "68ers" were given and complained to émigré groups and sympathetic politicians that "Communists" had come to dominate the station.[26]

Urban's policy shifts met with predictable resistance from inside RFE. Many in the Hungarian section resented his treatment of Szabados, his demands for change in the broadcast tone, and his appointment of staff members whose views were more compatible with the views of the Reagan administration. Géza Ekecs, a leading editor under both Szabados and Ribanszky, derided Urban for his "Boy Scout anti-Communism" and was especially critical of Urban's strictures on political language. Urban, for example, instructed editors to refer to trade unionists and parliamentarians from Communist countries as "so-called trade unionists" and "so-called parliamentarians" to reinforce the bogus nature of Communist institutions. Ekecs and other critics asserted that Urban's language guidelines—generally ignored in practice, RFE veterans contend—betrayed a lack of understanding of the RFE audience, which, they asserted, fully grasped the false character of Communist unions, parliaments, and constitutions but would have regarded such blatant reminders by RFE as unnecessary and silly. Barry Griffiths, an editor in the news division, claimed that the staff was bored by Urban's lectures on the history of the anti-Communist struggle, much of which, Griffiths claimed, involved American debates—whether Alger Hiss was guilty, for example—of little relevance to RFE listeners.[27]

Urban was also accused of trying to impose a form of ideological censorship on RFE broadcasts. Exhibit A of Urban's detractors was the Reagan joke incident. On August 11, 1984, Reagan was preparing for a radio address. Thinking the microphone was turned off, the president quipped that he had "just signed legislation which outlaws Russia forever. We will begin bombing in five minutes." In fact, Reagan's words were recorded and reported by all major American media.

The Reagan joke occurred on a Saturday. On Monday, James Edwards, the chief of the radios' news division, proposed that the incident be reported as a normal news item. Urban, however, refused to approve the inclusion of the joke in RFE broadcasts. In his memoirs, Urban claimed that he was concerned that the Kremlin "would misinterpret the joke and take it to be an American threat to Soviet security" and feared that the Soviet public might not know how to interpret the joke and "conclude that nuclear war was imminent."

Edwards and others regarded this explanation as nonsense. They noted that other international broadcast services had reported the joke and concluded that Urban's real motivation was to quash a news item that placed President Reagan in a less-than-favorable light. Going further, they accused Urban of pressuring broadcasters to slant news about Reagan by accentuating his achievements and minimizing his missteps.[28] If their assessment was true, it was in a certain sense irrelevant, since most RFE exile journalists tended to be strongly pro-Reagan, and took no pleasure in reporting news that placed the United States in an embarrassing light.

There were also grumblings about Urban's policy of circulating memos that he personally drafted suggesting the political line on certain subjects. For example, Urban wrote the following regarding the U.S. debate over the CIA's role in mining Nicaraguan harbors: "While taking no position on how the mining was done and by whom it was done (we institutionally abstain from all comment on intelligence operations), we stress that the net result of the expansion of Soviet influence in the world has always been the suppression of freedom, the collapse of civil society, and the institution of the police state. Nations that take preemptive actions to slow down, stop, or reverse the violent expansion of Soviet-sponsored power act defensively in the legitimate interests of the freedom and welfare of their own people."[29] Many broadcasters, perhaps baffled by the complexities of the Central America debate in Washington, no doubt found Urban's arguments helpful in providing a framework for coverage. Urban never insisted that his memos be incorporated into the broadcasting schedule, and the principle of the editorial freedom of the individual language desks was respected during Urban's tenure.

For RFE, the major story of the 1980s was the ferment in Poland, beginning with the rise of Solidarity and followed by the imposition of martial law, the Cold War between the Communist authorities and the Polish people, and, finally, the election of 1989, an event that signaled the effective end of Polish communism.

After nearly a quarter-century as editor of the Polish section, Jan Nowak retired in 1975. His departure came under not entirely happy circumstances. He doubted the American commitment to the freedom radios following round after round of budget cuts and staff reductions. His credibility had suffered a bit due to the public disclosure of his private criticisms of Senator Fulbright. Members of his staff chafed under his autocratic leadership style. He also had to endure false—and outrageous—accusations, emanating from East German sources, that he had collaborated with the Nazis during World War II and that he or a member of his family had served as a *treuhandler,* or manager of confiscated Jewish property in German-occupied Poland.

Nowak was succeeded by his deputy, Zygmunt Michalowski.

Michalowski maintained Nowak's policies of supporting the liberal democratic wing of the dissident movement, of differentiating between the various factions and personalities within the party, and of cooperating closely with the Catholic Church. Michalowski, however, soon realized that the balance of power had shifted due to the rise of the dissident opposition, the corrupt nature of the Gierek regime, and the tenuous state of the Polish economy. Even before Solidarity, the regime could not afford to ignore demands to maintain price controls for consumer goods, and to cede a degree of cultural autonomy and religious freedom. Two developments further weakened the regime: the beginnings of samizdat publications and the installation of Karol Wojtyla as Pope John Paul II. Radio Free Europe devoted hour after hour to the underground essays and manifestoes of the democratic opposition, a practice that enabled the authors to reach millions of listeners instead of a few hundred. The radio received documents from an ideologically diverse collection of opposition groups and faced the challenge of deciding which to broadcast and which to discard. The general rule was to favor those groups that best reflected Western democratic values as opposed to those of a nationalist or populist stripe. Michalowski preferred the material issued by the KOR, the leading democratic group formed after a series of strikes in 1976 to provide assistance to persecuted workers. Michalowski found the KOR documents factual and interesting and favored the group because its members were often in the thick of the most significant controversy of the day. By contrast, he usually ignored the samizdat of the KPN, a nationalist organization that Michalowski criticized as sloganistic and replete with exaggerated claims of the KPN's importance.[30]

As for the pope, the general rule was to give his every action extensive and favorable coverage. As Michalowski observed, "In my view, RFE was obliged to cover the entire scope of his work, his every movement, every word, all the echoes in the Western press, and to expose all the tricks employed by the Communists to censor him."[31] Radio Free Europe hired a Polish correspondent for assignment to the Vatican, from where he provided daily reports on the latest papal developments. It also gave minute-by-minute coverage of the pope's first visit to Poland in 1979. Even though it was prevented from assigning correspondents to cover the pageantry on the scene, RFE kept its listeners informed by the simple trick of reporting the event as it happened from American and West German television. Radio Free Europe devoted a full thirteen of its nineteen on-air hours to the pope's visit; Western reporters quoted Poles who claimed to listen to RFE's coverage eight hours each day. Meanwhile, official Polish television limited its coverage to two-minute segments on the evening news and edited out the pope's calls for religious freedom while stressing his politically safe comments about peace, cooperation, and the Catholic Church's traditional stance against divorce, abortion, and materialism.[32]

SOLIDARNOŚĆ

Radio Free Europe responded to the emergence of Solidarity with a combination of enthusiastic support and caution. Michalowski, who was editor-in-chief from Solidarity's founding in the summer of 1980 through the early stages of martial law, was determined that RFE would not be accused of destabilizing an already precarious situation: "We supported the democratic opposition by spreading information about their program and commenting favorably when the situation warranted. But we were careful not to increase the existing tensions. On the contrary, on numerous occasions we urged restraint on both sides, pointing to unforeseeable and potentially dangerous developments if the situation became uncontrollable. Sometimes we referred to the possible drastic response of the Soviets."[33] To Marek Latynski, a chief deputy to Michalowski and later director of the service, the early Solidarity period is memorable for the enthusiasm it generated within the journalistic staff: "There was a great deal of euphoria within RFE over Solidarity. We thought that with Solidarity there was a force to which we could give our utmost support, as opposed to supporting one party faction or leader against another party faction or leader. We now had a truly national force, a force which represented the aspirations of the Polish nation."[34]

Like Michalowski, Latynski kept his enthusiasm under restraint. If anything, RFE underplayed the more sensational episodes in the pre–martial law period. Thus the station devoted little coverage to a Solidarity congress' declaration of solidarity with the oppressed workers throughout the Communist world, a measure adopted over Lech Walesa's objections and widely regarded as unnecessarily provocative. Nor did RFE ever accept the notion that power actually resided with the people in the streets, as some Solidarity leaders claimed. A few weeks before martial law, Latynski broadcast a commentary that dismissed the notion that Poland could rid itself of Communist rule as a dangerous illusion. Michalowski went even further. He reminded his

SELF-LIMITING REVOL'N

listeners that Solidarity's gains had come through "self-control . . . political judgment . . . awareness of the possibilities and limits imposed by geo-politics." He cautioned against "frustration, impatience, bitterness, a feeling of being wronged, even when fully justified." He was conciliatory toward the party group then in power, and he reminded Poles "in which part of Europe Poland lies and what duties that entails." "Anti-Sovietism," Michalowski declared, "is not the essence of the political attitude of Poles who want to put their house in order. Both the party and the nation must take into account the stand of the Soviet Union."[35]

In its coverage of martial law, the Polish service was not subject to the same strict script controls that Ralph Walter had imposed during the 1968 Soviet invasion of Czechoslovakia, although items that involved commentary or analysis were given prebroadcast vetting. Michalowski kept Jim Brown and his deputy, Robert Hutchings, informed of the general tenor of the broadcasts, and there were daily conferences over broadcast strategy. But with few exceptions, scripts were not read in advance. If anything, RFE was more cautious in its news coverage than were Western newspapers and press services. The station refused to report accounts of massacres or alleged atrocities unless they could be verified, and refused to broadcast information about casualties unless there were corroborating reports from several responsible Western media. Almost always, RFE's judgment was vindicated, as the rumors of mass killings, assassinations, and burial sites never proved accurate.[36]

Michalowski retired in 1982; his successor, Zdzislaw Najder, was one of the most fascinating, and controversial, figures in the station's history. Najder was a highly regarded scholar of the life and work of Joseph Conrad, the Polish-born author whose works on politics, terrorism, espionage, and colonialism presaged the crucial struggles of the Cold War. Najder had a number of acquaintances within the RFE management, including Jan Nowak and Jim Brown. When martial law was declared, Najder happened to be in Britain, where he was teaching at a university. Given his pro-Solidarity sentiments, Najder decided that it would be foolish to return to arrest or political marginalization. On Nowak's strong recommendation, Najder was hired as Polish service director; he was the first section director in the station's history to have come directly to his position from Eastern Europe.[37]

Initially, his appointment seemed a brilliant stroke. In the spring of 1983, the regime tried him in absentia and handed down a sentence of death on charges of having collaborated with American intelligence services. Najder was the third exile Pole to be handed a death sentence during martial law; the other two were the ambassadors to the United States and Japan, an indication of how seriously the regime regarded Najder's having accepted the RFE post. Najder himself called his new job "the most important position for a politically active Pole."[38] But Najder's tenure at RFE proved a stormy affair. Intellectually brilliant, he was an indifferent administrator and even poorer as a manager of personnel. The staff was soon divided into pro-Najder and anti-Najder factions. The critics circulated petitions and engaged in acts of defiance; at one point Najder and certain members of his staff would not communicate unless in the presence of witnesses.

Najder also sharpened the service's broadcast tone. He had a wide network of contacts among the opposition within and outside Poland and used his contacts to acquire inside information for broadcast commentaries. Some assert that Najder went a step further and used his position at RFE to influence the internal debate within Solidarity; some even speculate that Najder himself was the author of manifestoes that were smuggled into Poland and issued as expressing the views of a Solidarity faction.[39] Furthermore, Najder did not appreciate the distinction between news and opinion. He tried to suppress pessimistic news about Solidarity, deepening the rifts within the staff and incurring the displeasure of the Americans.[40]

Najder's attitude toward the Catholic Church was also a subject of contention. Unlike his predecessors, Najder did not regard the church as immune to criticism. When he believed the church was adopting an overaccommodating stance toward General Jaruzelski, he would broadcast indirect but, for the politically sophisticated listener, obvious attacks on the church hierarchy. One method of getting his message across was to broadcast a commentary praising the militancy of the Nicaraguan Catholic leadership in standing up to the Sandinistas at a time when the Polish church was advocating compromise with the regime. Within Solidarity, Najder's commentaries on the church and politics had a certain resonance, since Archbishop Jozef Glemp, the Polish primate, was regarded as too willing to cut deals with Jaruzelski. Others, however, argued that despite Glemp's mediocrity, the church's authority should remain inviolate except in truly exceptional circumstances. According to Marek Latynski, a critic of Najder, a high official of the Polish church eventually complained to the American management about Najder's broadcasts.[41]

If the Catholic Church was disturbed by RFE's broadcasts, the Jaruzelski regime was apoplectic. The view of the martial law regime, as put forward by its spokesman, Jerzy Urban, in a 1984 interview with the *Wall Street Journal,* was that support for Solidarity was dwindling and would diminish even further if the Solidarity underground lost its access to Western radios. As Urban put it, "If you would close your Radio Free Europe, the underground would completely cease to exist."[42] While the regime admitted that foreign broadcasts enjoyed more credibility than did Communist media, they ascribed this state of affairs to the "mistakes" committed during Gierek's time, when official propaganda portrayed Poland as an idyllic place where conditions were constantly getting better and better. But the official press did not burnish its reputation by printing ludicrous charges that RFE maintained a secret blacklist of Communists who were to be imprisoned or liquidated in the event of a successful uprising.[43]

Some RFE programs used hard-hitting language to attack the party leadership. For example, one program ended with a quote from Albert Camus's novel *The Plague* that a persecuted nation must constantly struggle in order not to be brought to its knees. In January 1985, an RFE broadcast caused a minor sensation when it included a segment taken from a satirical journal published by Polish émigrés. The item was a parody of a speech by Adolf Hitler in which the fuhrer's boasts came across as quite similar to the declarations of the Jaruzelski regime during martial law. It drew a self-righteous protest from Polish officials. The State Department thereupon issued a public apology; a State Department spokesman declared, "The U.S. government disassociates itself from that broadcast and regrets any implication of similarity between Nazi Germany and present day Poland and particularly between Adolf Hitler and General Jaruzelski."[44]

Despite the occasional polemics, most of the RFE coverage during the martial law period amounted to a measured critique of Communist policies. Najder created a program entitled *The Poland that Could Be,* in which he speculated on the future of Polish society after communism. Radio Free Europe also concentrated on the woeful condition of the Polish economy. Leszek Gawlikowski, the editor of the economics program, explained why it would be impossible for Poland to emulate the model of authoritarian economic change set by Chile, an important subject given Jaruzelski's well-known fascination with Gen. Augusto Pinochet, the Chilean strongman who instituted economic reforms while keeping his country under dictatorial grip. Nor did the regime press automatically respond to RFE criticism with shrill polemics or diplomatic demarches. When Gawlikowski broadcast a series of programs detailing the economic burden of arms spending, the leading party newspaper, *Trybuna Ludu,* published a lengthy article of rebuttal.[45]

Due to mounting criticism of his leadership style and the deepening divisions within the staff, Najder was forced out in 1987. After communism was overthrown, he returned to his native land, where he played an important role in party politics for a few years. But controversy was to dog him even in the post-Communist era. Files buried away in the party archives indicated that in the 1950s Najder cooperated with the secret police and was paid for his services. His code name was "Zapalniczka," or Lighter. The information was, ironically, made public by Najder's old nemesis, Jerzy Urban.[46]

For Radio Liberty, the 1980s were a time of unprecedented opportunity. The Soviet populace may not have been in a state of rebellion, but the evidence of ferment and discontent was obvious. Although the regime had effectively crushed the organized dissident movement, samizdat publications continued to flow to the West. They covered a wide range of subjects, from political rights to religious freedom to the rights of the non-Russian peoples and assertions of Russian nationalism. There were even samizdat materials advocating what today might be called identity politics—women, the handicapped, minority groups.

Emigration from the Soviet Union continued at high levels throughout the 1970s. While few exit visas were issued after the West boycotted the 1980 Moscow Olympics in response to the invasion of Afghanistan, there remained a large pool of candidates for journalistic positions in Radio Liberty's Russian section. By the early 1980s, RL had assembled a staff that included some of the best-known names in Russian cultural life, experts in music, literature, sports, science, economics, history, as well as writers and musicians.

With its talented commentators and intensive coverage of Soviet political developments, Radio Liberty gained new stature among Soviet listeners. It was on Radio Liberty that Russians heard the forbidden writings of Solzhenitsyn, broadcast day after day, in their entirety.

Radio Liberty broadcast hours of samizdat programming, as well as discussions of the fate of Russian culture and the future of Russia in a post-Communist world. Despite heavy jamming, RL was the station of choice for dissidents and independent minded officials; many report taking to the countryside on a weekend simply to find a spot where RL broadcasts could be heard free of the incessant static encountered in the cities. Indeed, RL was judged the most important foreign broadcast service in an informal, underground, listener analysis compiled by two Russian dissidents, Viktor Nekipelov and Felix Serebrov in 1980. The report praised RL for "the variety and scope of its programming and, above all, for its understanding of our problems." Listeners were said to regard RL as "our national home station."[47]

Many dissidents developed a proprietary interest in the content of RL broadcasts. In typically Russian fashion, they did not hesitate to voice objections when they disagreed with station policies. In 1977, fresh from his release from the gulag, Vladimir Bukovsky derided RL's policy guidelines, which he compared to the instructions for censorship imposed by Soviet authorities.[48] Solzhenitsyn also weighed in, accusing RL in 1982 of self-censorship, and writing in *National Review* that RL broadcasts "have degenerated to such an extent that, if they continue the way they are going, it would be better to do away with them altogether."

The addition of literally dozens of new hires created rifts within the RL staff. On one side were members of the older generation, ethnically Russian, advocates of an "authentically Russian" programming orientation, devoted to Solzhenitsyn, fervently anti-Communist but inclined toward skepticism about Western democracy. On the other side were the new arrivals, often Jewish, suspicious of Russian nationalism, critics of Solzhenitsyn, and strong advocates of democratic change in the Soviet Union. Within the RL staff, in other words, the age-old struggle between the Slavophiles and Westernizers was being played out.

The internal bickering soon led to charges of anti-Semitism. Newly hired Jewish staff members accused colleagues from earlier waves of emigration of Great Russian chauvinism; the Jews, in turn, were charged with a failure to appreciate the Russian character. In one notable mid-seventies incident, Victoria Semenova, a producer-announcer, wrote a memo charging that many RL programs did not have "a Russian spirit . . . the Great Russian culture . . . and by spirit I mean one based on *it was in*

Christianity and Orthodoxy." Jewish staff members regarded Semenova's memo as anti-Semitic, and she was reprimanded by American officials. But some believed that management was weak and indecisive in dealing with anti-Semitism within the staff. At a meeting addressed by the Soviet dissident Leonid Plyusch, a staff member allegedly asserted that Jews were the source of all Russia's problems. This prompted a complaint by Rachel Fedoseyev, a Jewish broadcaster who concentrated on the Soviet human rights movement. Both she and the staff member were reprimanded, a Solomonic decision that satisfied no one. In a subsequent reorganization of the service, several Jewish staff members lost high editorial positions; one chief editor, Vladimir Matusevitch, was encouraged to transfer to London because of the staff turmoil; Matusevitch had demanded that the BIB conduct an investigation of internal staff affairs.[49]

There is evidence that the divisions between Russians and Russian Jews were inflamed by the KGB, working through staff members who had been recruited by Soviet intelligence. In his memoirs, Oleg Kalugin claims that Oleg Tumanov, the Soviet agent who worked his way into a key editor's position, contributed to the acrimony by spreading rumors and disinformation. Tumanov, Kalugin writes, wrote anti-Semitic letters that led to open clashes within the Russian section staff during the mid-1970s.[50] Presumably, Kalugin was referring to two anonymous letters that mysteriously appeared on the RL bulletin board during the mid-1970s. One listed the names of certain Russian staff members with the label "Jew" attached, accused Jews who served the Soviet regime of having "drowned the country with innocent blood," and asserted that the Russian section "cannot be called Russian if it is in the hands of Jews." The second letter singled out by name the more prominent Jewish members of the newly hired staff for various forms of abuse and called them agents of the secret police and Russophobes. Both letters were signed "The Russian Nationalists."

Eventually, the internal struggle within Radio Liberty became a matter of public concern. In January 1981, James Critchlow, a member of the BIB staff, drafted an internal memorandum that cited what were described as widespread violations of RL guidelines by Russian broadcasters. In his most serious charge, Critchlow claimed that Russian broadcasts included "expressions of Russian nationalistic and xenophobic views" that encouraged "attitudes of aggression towards other peoples." Critchlow also said that programs dealing with historical themes "regularly discredit democracy and disseminate authoritarian ideas." While Critchlow was overly sweeping in his generalizations, the evidence he cited, in the form of direct quotes from a number of broadcasts, amounted to a serious indictment of the station's leadership. Critchlow quoted from broadcasts that gave a pessimistic view of democracy, criticized Poland, attacked the Uniate Catholic Church of Ukraine, and portrayed the Russian Orthodox Church as the only true faith. The report was leaked to the press—Critchlow himself denied responsibility for the leak—and caused some embarrassing headlines in the American press.[51]

Radio Liberty had been without a strong director since the retirement of Howland Sargeant in the mid-1970s. In 1982, Frank Shakespeare offered the directorship to George Bailey, an American writer who had spent practically his entire life in Europe. Bailey had an interesting background. During World War II, he had served as an American liaison officer with the Red Army—a colleague was William Sloane Coffin Jr., better known as a radical clergyman during and after the Vietnam War. After the war, Bailey served with the occupation forces in Germany, where he witnessed the forced repatriation of Soviet citizens to certain death or imprisonment in the Soviet Union. Bailey developed a healthy dislike for the Soviet system as a result of these experiences; at the same time, he gained a profound respect for Russian history and culture. After leaving the military, Bailey worked as East European correspondent for the *Reporter* magazine and later served as an aide to the West German publishing magnate Axel Springer.[52]

Bailey's appointment was a source of controversy from the beginning. To his hard-edged anticommunism was added a reputation as an admirer of the nationalist wing of the Russian emigration. There was something patently unfair in the whispered charges that Bailey sympathized with an authoritarian brand of nationalism, and it was especially unfair to label him an anti-Semite; among other things, his wife was Jewish. Bailey was the author of a laudatory book about Andrey Sakharov, the leading figure of democratic dissent in the Soviet Union, and while at RL he named former dissidents to important editorial positions. But Bailey did not limit his relationship to members of the Sakharov wing of Soviet dissent. He was friendly with Vladimir Maksimov, the editor of *Kontinent,* an émigré journal of nationalist inspiration—a publication Springer helped finance—and included among his contacts members of the NTS, the semisecret Russian nationalist organization whose views were regarded as strongly authoritarian.

Bailey thus began his tenure under inauspicious circumstances. Outside the radios, he was regarded as yet another ultra-anti-Communist hired to transform RFE-RL into a propaganda instrument. In Russian exile circles, he was seen as an ally of anti-Western authoritarians. Bailey added to his problems through his lack of interest in administrative affairs. Behind his gruff exterior, he was relatively easygoing, too much so, some say, given the difficult challenges in running a staff of temperamental exiles.[53] And while Bailey never attempted to foist a political agenda on RL, he firmly believed that the exposition of the ideas of Russian nationalism deserved a prominent place on the broadcasting schedule. Along with the samizdat programs and the news about democratic dissidents, RL's Russian broadcasts included contributions by Maksimov and his co-thinkers from *Kontinent*.

It did not take long for questions about the changes Bailey was implementing to appear in the press. In 1983, two respected political writers, Josef Joffe and Dmitri K. Simes, accused RL of having broadcast items that suggested that democracy was corrupt and decadent and not appropriate for Russia. The principal piece of evidence was a speech delivered by Solzhenitsyn in Taiwan, broadcast by RL in full.[54] Soon afterward, the debate over RL broadcast content reached Congress. Senator Charles Percy, ordinarily a supporter of the radios who was instrumental in putting together the plan that brought the stations under open government sponsorship, criticized a Ukrainian program as possibly anti-Semitic. Although the BIB had initiated an internal investigation into the broadcast, Percy prematurely went public because, he said, he did not believe that the oversight agency was taking the matter seriously enough.

The Percy statement drew an angry response from the BIB. "It would be difficult to exaggerate how offensive we find these reckless charges," Frank Shakespeare declared. Ben Wattenberg, the BIB vice chairman, actually read the disputed script to his eighty-five-year-old father, a Jew who had been born in Ukraine near a village discussed in the program; the elder Wattenberg concluded that the script was not offensive or anti-Semitic.[55]

In this case, as in most other RL programming controversies, matters of historical interpretation were involved. Nationalism, chauvinism, and anti-Semitism were ingrained in the history of Eastern Europe; it would have been impossible to limit programs on historical themes to a discussion of figures who had championed the ideals of Western democracy. To broadcast the anti-Semitic utterances of a turn-of-the-century official did not necessarily signify an anti-Jewish broadcast; it all depended on the historical context and the explanatory comments of the broadcaster. In the case cited by Percy, the broadcast revolved around the memoirs of Mykola Kovalevsky, a minister of agriculture in Ukraine during the early 1900s. A passage describes a pogrom that took place in the village of Proskurov. It noted that often after acts of terror carried out by the Bolshevik Cheka in which Jews played a prominent role, "the population generalized the circumstances and identified Bolshevism with Judaism, which was a huge mistake."

As the above example suggests, not every charge of anti-Semitism was necessarily justified. Upon careful scrutiny, some charges seem unfair and others ambiguous. To cite another example, the *New Republic* accused RL of having broadcast a section from the notorious anti-Jewish tract, *Protocols of the Elders of Zion*. In fact, the commentator had noted that the Protocols were a "vile anti-Semitic forgery."[56] Nevertheless, headlines reading "Anti-Semitism at Liberty" began appearing in newspapers throughout the United States. Shakespeare, Urban, and Bailey interpreted the bad press as a reflection of liberal media bias. They may have had a point. The radio leaders were unabashed anti-Communists and Reagan supporters. While the press had reported previous charges of questionable broadcast policy—after the Critchlow report, for example—it had never before attempted to place the blame on a particular editor or administrator. There was no evidence that violations of broadcast guidelines were more numerous under the Reaganites than during previous administrations. Thus to conclude, as George Urban does in his memoirs, that a liberal media were actively seeking out evidence to discredit the Reagan administration's appointees at RFE-RL was not irrational.

There is, on the other hand, evidence that Russian nationalists were given too much air time freedom during Bailey's directorship. Like Polish nationalism or Ukrainian nationalism, Russian nationalism represented a powerful idea to people seeking an alternative to communism. The Russian idea was a subject of serious debate among the giants of the dissident opposition, including Solzhenitsyn and Sakharov. To insist, as some did, that Russian nationalism had no place on RL broadcasts was in effect to demand that the station censor not simply one broadcast, but an idea of central importance to many Russian listeners.

But like other nationalisms, Russian nationalism has its dark corners. If anything, the Russian nationalist variant is more inclined to chauvinist excess than other varieties. Radio Liberty included staff members who favored a revival of the monarchy, were skeptical about the benefits of democracy, were convinced that Russian culture was superior to the cultures of the small nations in the empire, and who probably believed that Jews could never qualify as authentic Russians.

Furthermore, the management can also be blamed for failing to take strong steps to deal with the problems after they had become an issue of public comment. After accusations of anti-Semitic programming appeared in the press, George Bailey issued a directive requiring that he personally review any script that dealt with Jewish subjects. The order was rescinded after a few days, but the confusion about effective broadcast control lingered on.[57] Having spent his adult life in Europe, Bailey was unfamiliar with the ways of Washington and never fully grasped the potential damage of allegations of national chauvinism and anti-Semitism.

Nor did Bailey or his colleagues in the American management fully comprehend the role that staff members were playing in the dissemination of unfavorable publicity. Indeed, staff members became increasingly brazen in making their discontent public. Where previously information had been leaked to the press or friendly intermediaries surreptitiously, now some staff took their complaints directly and openly to the public. Vadim Belotserkovsky, a Russian staffer, attacked RL in the course of an anti-Solzhenitsyn screed published in the *Nation,* a leading left-wing magazine.[58] After the article appeared, RL officials asked Belotserkovsky to promise to refrain from further public protests. When he refused, he was fired on the grounds that he had violated a clause of the labor contract prohibiting "journalistic activities . . . that adversely affect the legitimate interests of RFE-RL." Belotserkovsky, however, had the final laugh: the German labor court ordered his reinstatement; meanwhile, RL's critics added violations of an employee's rights of free speech to its bill of indictment.[59]

Because Belotserkovsky's article was tendentious and was published in a journal notorious for its hostility to American Cold War policy, its impact was marginal. The same, however, could not be said of a critical assessment written by Ludmilla Alexeyeva. Alexeyeva was a heroine of the dissident movement, having served as a founding member of the Moscow Helsinki Watch Committee. After emigrating to the United States in 1977, she continued to work for change in the Soviet Union and made regular commentaries on human rights for Radio Liberty. In 1986, she wrote a scathing report on the Russian language services of both RL and the VOA. Once again, Solzhenitsyn was singled out for criticism; RL was accused of tolerating broadcasts that featured expressions of extreme Russian nationalism and a hostility to pluralism and democracy. The report was published by the respected human rights organization, Helsinki Watch, guaranteeing that it would be taken seriously by policy makers in Washington. As a freelancer, Alexeyeva did not enjoy the normal protections of American labor law; nevertheless, RL took no action against her, and she continued to work for the organization she had publicly attacked.[60]

Eventually, Washington became directly involved in the controversy. In mid-1984, a Democratic staff member of the Senate Foreign Relations Committee, Geryld B. Christianson, was dispatched to Munich on a study mission. Christianson visited Munich for three days, after which he issued a report whose conclusions were less than earth-shaking. He found no evidence of anti-Semitic broadcasts, though he concluded that Solzhenitsyn's Taiwan speech and some of Maksimov's broadcasts were anti-Western in character. In addition, while he discovered no "pattern of widespread policy violation," he asserted that the "potential" for abuse had increased due to the lack of control exercised by Bailey and other editors.[61]

A more thorough study was conducted by the General Accounting Office in 1985. Its conclusions mirrored Christianson's. The report, which dealt with both RFE and RL, noted eighteen policy violations in the first half of 1984, not a large number given the thousands upon thousands of broadcasts over the Radios. The violations included a reference to the Soviet foreign minister as a bandit, the comparison of former Soviet officials to war criminals, the use of an anatomical obscenity to describe a Polish official, the description of an unidentified American actress as harboring "warm feelings" for the Soviet Union (the broadcaster probably had Jane Fonda in mind). Again like the Christianson report, the GAO assessment seemed more concerned with the process than with actual violations, and recommended that additional controls over broadcast content be added.[62]

The measured conclusions of the GAO and Christianson reports were in sharp contrast to the polemics of Rep. Lawrence Smith, a Florida Democrat. Following a brief visit to Munich, Smith accused Shakespeare of politicizing the radios, and charged that RFE-RL tolerated extremist, anti-Semitic, and antidemocratic programs. And he accused Urban and Bailey of having moved the radios in the direction of a "less subtle, uniform anti-Communist line."[63]

The antipathy that some members of Congress felt toward the BIB leadership lingered even after Shakespeare, Buckley, Urban, and Bailey had left the radios. Thus when the BIB drafted a new mission statement, the House International Operations subcommittee subjected the document to a line-by-line critique. Ironically, the new statement had been mandated by Congress as one means of preventing violations of policy guidelines. And the drafting committee was comprised of men of impeccable credentials: Michael Novak, James Michener, and Clare Burgener, a former congressman from California. Nevertheless, the subcommittee chairman, Florida Democrat Dan Mica (who would serve as BIB chairman after leaving Congress in the 1990s), questioned a statement calling the family "the most basic of all institutions" and fretted that the formulation might invite a debate over birth control or abortion. Lawrence Smith found some sections too strident—"more of the . . . stuff that got us into trouble in the past." He singled out statements referring to "state-controlled media whose methods are often unscrupulous," "false theories of moral equivalence as between free and unfree nations," and "ideologically distorted definitions of reality."[64]

The Shakespeare team had moved on by the fall of 1986. Shakespeare was appointed American ambassador, first to Portugal and later to the Vatican. Buckley was named to the federal judiciary. Urban and Bailey left to write books about the Cold War. In Urban's case, departure was clouded by a controversy over an op-ed essay in which he volunteered his advice to President Reagan on his upcoming summit with Mikhail Gorbachev. James Buckley thought it inappropriate for an RFE-RL official to be publicly dispensing wisdom to the president and told Urban so. For his part, Urban accused Buckley of being overly attentive to Washington's political winds.[65] Malcolm S. Forbes Jr. was named BIB chairman; after considering a long list of candidates that included members of Congress and high-ranking diplomats, the BIB selected E. Eugene Pell, a former television correspondent for

NBC and at the time director of the VOA, as president of RFE-RL. Forbes and Pell were Republican conservatives with strong anti-Communist convictions. They were, however, more attuned to the mores of Washington than the previous leadership. They made an effort to smooth the ruffled feathers of congressional critics such as Claiborne Pell and Larry Smith and took measures to prevent further scandals over script content. Pell ended the relationship with Maksimov and other *Kontinent* editors and imposed stricter controls over the content of Russian broadcasts.[66] When a Polish free-lancer described New York mayor Ed Koch and San Francisco mayor Dianne Feinstein as homosexuals in a broadcast, he was summarily fired, the two editors who had allowed the script to go on the air were reprimanded, and an apology and retraction were made.[67]

Any assessment of the legacy of the Shakespeare era must balance the obvious negatives—internal turmoil and a consistently bad press—against the realities of broadcast content and audience reaction. Never before or since were RFE-RL broadcasts subjected to such intense scrutiny by journalists, government agencies, and constituency organizations. These various investigations did uncover shortcomings in Radio Liberty programs. But the nature of the problem was not shrill or propagandistic scripts but broadcasts that treated often arcane historical themes in a tendentious or chauvinistic way. Expressions of Russian nationalism had plagued RL before George Bailey was appointed director, and while he can be faulted for giving nationalists too much freedom at the microphone, media accounts of RL as a mouthpiece for anti-Semitism and czarism were exaggerated and, in some cases, motivated by ideological hostility to the Reaganites' bare-knuckle anticommunism. Nor is there evidence that RFE-RL's audience was alienated by the policies of the Reagan era. The radios' own polls indicated high listenership throughout Eastern Europe and an increasing audience in Russia. As in the past, the radios' listeners tuned in primarily for news and analytical reports; the historical items that created such furors in the United States enjoyed limited audiences in the Soviet Union.

In any event, by 1986 the question facing the radios was no longer whether their broadcasts were sufficiently tough on communism, but whether they were prepared to meet the unprecedented challenge of the Gorbachev leadership, with its policies of glasnost and perestroika, its seeming youth and vigor, and its unpredictability. With Gorbachev in power, there would be no time to argue over historical interpretation; events were moving at a dizzying pace, with new initiatives an almost daily occurrence. Clearly, RFE and RL would have to undergo rapid change if they were to remain on the cutting-edge of the revolutionary developments in the Communist world.

16

Victory

At the time of his ascension to power, Mikhail Gorbachev was regarded in the West as a formidable adversary—a leader who was committed to economic modernization, an aggressive diplomacy, and military parity with the United States. Despite his dissatisfaction with the Soviet system's inefficiencies, there was nothing in Gorbachev's biography that suggested anything less than total belief in communism. Nor was there any reason to believe that Gorbachev would tolerate a non-Communist path in any of the East European satellites or a retreat from the USSR's involvement in Afghanistan, Africa, Central America, or other Third World outposts. That his policies would lead to freedom in Eastern Europe, the collapse of communism throughout the world, and the breakup of the Soviet Union never occurred to Western experts, who predicted that the superpower rivalry might well intensify if Gorbachev's reforms paid dividends.

One man who believed that Gorbachev posed a greater threat to the Socialist system than to capitalism was Vladimir Matusevitch. Since joining Radio Liberty in the early 1970s, Matusevitch had been among the Russian section's star commentators. Brusque and outspoken, he was not universally popular among his colleagues. He had engaged in some heated arguments with leading members of the Russian nationalist faction during the 1970s and spent much of the 1980s as RL correspondent in London, well away from the hothouse atmosphere in the Munich headquarters.

At about the same time that Gorbachev was elected party leader, Matusevitch began a new program—a review of Soviet television. In the past, television reviews had been impossible since RL correspondents had no access to Soviet stations. The introduction of the satellite dish, however, enabled Matusevitch to receive Moscow stations in the comfort of his London home. "One of the most unforgettable moments of my life was when I was first able to watch Moscow One [a leading Soviet channel] in my living room," he recalled years later. "I felt like an American cowboy in Montana must have felt the first time he heard the voice of Tito Gobbi."[1]

Television reviews were new not only for RL; they were new to the Soviet Union. Matusevitch had been a film reviewer in the Soviet Union; his specialty was the Scandinavian cinema. In his commentaries on Soviet television, he soon found that he was mainly reviewing Gorbachev: "I followed Gorbachev's path as leader through television. Even under conditions of harsh censorship, television gave me an insight into Gorbachev's character which I could never have gotten from books or newspapers. . . . I vividly remember a moment two or three months after he came to power. There was a meeting in a provincial city, and Gorbachev abruptly broke off the ritual of the five-minute standing ovation for the leader. These Communist rituals may have seemed ridiculous to outsiders, but they were very important to the system. And I realized right then that this guy could destroy everything."[2] Matusevitch was also impressed by the decision, apparently initiated by Gorbachev, to film him in full front view, which allowed Soviets to see the large birthmark on his forehead, instead of in profile, which concealed the discoloration.

The first big story of the Gorbachev era was the Chernobyl nuclear disaster, a major embarrassment for the new leader and a near catastrophe for his country. On April 26, 1986, one of the four reactors at the Chernobyl complex in Ukraine exploded, killing thirty-one people and sending clouds of radiation throughout Eastern Europe. The disaster was seen as the first important test of glasnost, the policy, recently announced by Gorbachev, of candor and honesty in discussing the Soviet Union's shortcomings. The official response to Chernobyl was not impressive. Indeed, the Soviet press gave every indication of trying to cover up the accident just as it had ignored or lied about previous disasters, natural as well as manmade.

Here, then, was the ideal story for Radio Free Europe and Radio Liberty. All the elements were present: Soviet incompetence, censorship, the lack of sovereignty of the East European countries, whose press, following the Soviet lead, downplayed the incident. Chernobyl also stoked the fires of anti-Russian sentiments among the Soviet Union's non-Russian peoples, especially in Ukraine and the Baltic republics, whose people lay in the direct path of the fallout. The radios understood the ramifications of Chernobyl and devoted hour after hour to the story. Broadcasts gave instructions on the decontamination of food and clothing and the protection of children. The radios interviewed Western nuclear experts, energy officials, and anti-nuclear activists. They explained the accident's implications for neighboring countries, and they covered its internal political repercussions, such as the resistance of army reservists from Estonia, who had been called to help decontaminate the area around the Chernobyl reactor.

This would be one of RFE-RL's finest hours. All indications suggest that listenership rose dramatically throughout the early stages of the crisis. The Communist media fumed and complained about what Poland's regime spokesman, Jerzy Urban, called RFE's "unjustified, unfounded, but deliberate actions intended to scare [the] population." But there is no evidence that the radios practiced irresponsible journalism. As was usually the case in times of crisis, the radios were more cautious than the mainstream Western press; they did not, for example, broadcast the wildly exaggerated claims of two thousand deaths in the Chernobyl area that had been reported by the UPI and had run in many newspapers.[3]

In the midst of the crisis, the Kremlin trotted out Oleg Tumanov for a press conference. Tumanov had recently returned to Moscow after serving as a KGB agent inside the Russian service; before the Western press, he charged that the CIA called the shots at Radio Liberty. Western correspondents were unimpressed. The whole affair led some to conclude that Mikhail Gorbachev's glasnost was little different from Leonid Brezhnev's censorship.

There is evidence that the Chernobyl calamity fortified Gorbachev in his resolve to reduce censorship, promote openness, and bring the Soviet Union into the modern era where the rapid transmission of accurate information was critical to economic success. Although he initially dithered on the issue of jamming foreign broadcast services, Gorbachev unleashed a measure of internal press freedom unprecedented in Soviet history. Finally, in late 1988, Gorbachev summoned up the will to end jamming not simply on the VOA and BBC but on all foreign stations, including Radio Liberty.

Gorbachev may have concluded that allowing the Russian people to hear a station that enjoyed greater credibility than the Soviet media was well worth the risk. Gorbachev was already celebrated in the West as a reformer, a man of peace, and the most dynamic leader of the decade, if not the entire postwar period. At home, however, his policies were meeting growing resistance, first and foremost from traditionalists within the Communist Party. Nor was Gorbachev especially popular in the non-Russian republics, where national consciousness, long suppressed by force, was rising to the surface. And in some East European countries, party leaders reacted with dismay as the new Soviet leader dropped broad hints that the Kremlin would no longer intervene to prevent the overthrow of the people's democracies. Under these circumstances, Gorbachev may have calculated that the Western broadcast media, including Radio Liberty, would be more likely to support his course than the Soviet media itself, at the time divided between those who embraced glasnost and those who were serving as defenders of orthodoxy.

If the end of jamming represented a great opportunity for RL, it also posed a serious challenge. The Soviet press was in transition from totalitarian conditions to relative freedom. It was experimenting with Western techniques and openly reporting controversies and scandals that would have been ignored in the past. Radio Liberty also had a psychological adjustment to make. For if the Soviet media were weighed down by the vestiges of a totalitarian mindset, Radio Liberty was burdened by the notion that it was something less than normal news radio, an attitude that had been inculcated by years of serving as the target of Soviet propaganda.

To lead RL's Russian service at this critical juncture, the station's management brought Vladimir Matusevitch back from London and appointed him service director. Matusevitch quickly made a number of programming changes. He eliminated programs on political prisoners as well as readings of banned literature, reasoning that under Gorbachev few political prisoners remained in the gulag and even fewer writings were proscribed. In their place, he launched several new cultural programs through which he hoped to convey a special perspective about the political changes underway in Russia. Matusevitch also paid attention to the station's production techniques. Because of jamming, announcers had gotten into the habit of pronouncing each word slowly, clearly, and loudly; with jamming abolished, RL adopted a normal radio voice. The changes seem to have worked. Although RL had been the station of choice for the political opposition, its ratings consistently lagged behind the VOA due to the jamming. With an unjammed, level playing field, RL's ratings soared, as did its influence.

The station also scored some hard news coups. One of the most sensational was an interview with Boris Yeltsin, at the time a pariah to the political establishment, in which he accused the KGB of having threatened to kill him with a low-frequency transmitter that could stop his heart.[4] The station also covered an investigation by two independent-minded prosecutors into allegations that Yegor Ligachev, the leading defender of party orthodoxy and a critic of Gorbachev, had accepted a bribe from the party chief of Uzbekistan. When the investigators ran into trouble in getting their story covered by the Soviet press, they turned to RL, which gave in-depth coverage to the charges.[5]

The appointment of Matusevitch was among a number of personnel moves made by the management team that succeeded Frank Shakespeare and James Buckley. Although Steve Forbes was in basic agreement with Shakespeare's view that the radios were in need of an overhaul, the new BIB chairman was considerably more low-key than his predecessor. Forbes commanded bipartisan respect in Washington, and he proved effective at persuading the key congressional committees to increase the radios' budget and provide the supplemental appropriations that seemed an annual necessity given the American dollar's weakness against the German mark.

Gene Pell, the new president, paid much of his attention to improving the technical quality of the stations' broadcasts. He secured new equipment and hired William Marsh, a veteran of international broadcast news, as executive vice president for programming with the assignment of improving the radio professionalism of the staff. Pell was determined to avoid the kind of negative publicity that had bedeviled Radio Liberty during the previous administration. He thus eliminated a consultant arrangement with George Bailey, severed the Russian service's relations with the *Kontinent* writers, and imposed a system of prebroadcast controls on the Russian service broadcasts.[6]

Throughout its history Radio Liberty had treated the non-Russian-language services as the station's stepchildren. Whereas Russian broadcasts were on air nearly all day, the nationality services broadcast an

hour or so of original programs, which were repeated once or twice each day. Whereas the Russian service commanded a staff of some ninety journalists and support people, the nationality services made do with seven or eight editors and broadcasters, or in the case of the Ukrainian service perhaps fifteen to twenty. When the station's managers set out their annual priorities, the number one item was likely to be buttressing the Russian-language broadcasts; the nationality services were invariably a secondary priority.

There were practical reasons for the stress on Russian broadcasts. Russians were by far the largest language group in the Soviet Union, and Russian was the lingua franca of government, business, and, in most parts of the country, education. Furthermore, the educated elites of the non-Russian republics tended to speak Russian, which meant that even in republics such as Uzbekistan, Georgia, and Turkmenistan, RL's Russian-language broadcasts had far higher ratings than RL's broadcasts in the language of the republic.

On the surface, the question of whether to give more emphasis to the nationality broadcasts was a simple one. If Radio Liberty were to maintain broadcasts to Ukrainians, Armenians, and Tatars, then the station should offer a high quality product. This required adding more and better-qualified staff, overhauling the programming, and broadcasting more hours each day. Unfortunately, decisions regarding the nationality services could not be made on the basis of broadcast quality alone. To assign the non-Russian broadcasts a higher priority in the overall RL mission was at heart a political decision, which involved the State Department and National Security Council as well as Radio Liberty. The United States was both officially and unofficially opposed to the breakup of the Soviet Union. That Radio Liberty maintained a network of non-Russian broadcasts could in itself be interpreted as a contradiction of official policy; certainly the Soviet Union considered it so. Nor were Kremlin officials mollified by RL's stricture against broadcasts that endorsed a republic's secession from the union. Mark Pomar, who served as an editor in the Russian service and later worked as executive director of the BIB, observed that to nationalist minded Ukrainians, Uzbeks, and Georgians, the nationality services signified that if the United States was not willing to champion the Soviet Union's splintering, it was prepared to offer a gesture of sympathy to their aspirations to independence. "Even if few listened to the Tatar service," Pomar said, "its existence indicated to Tatar intellectuals that America recognized their cause." For the non-Russian republics, and especially for the smaller ones, Radio Liberty was, in Pomar's opinion, "the standard bearer of an alternative way of existence."[7]

The editors and commentators for the nationality services were primarily drawn from among the partisans of national independence, and they proved intrepid and guileful in getting the basic message across. If the guidelines forbade calls for national independence, this did not prevent the broadcasters from emphasizing the pre-Soviet cultural heritage, the historic struggles against foreign aggressors, the plight of national patriots who had been packed off to the gulag, and the tragic fate of those who had been persecuted for their "national deviation" policies under Lenin and Stalin.

During the 1970s, when Zbigniew Brzezinski was national security adviser and Paul Henze a Brzezinski deputy, the NSC reached a decision to strengthen RL's broadcasts to the peoples of Soviet central Asia. Brzezinski and others saw the Moslem republics as the Soviet Union's weak link. They were economically backward, their religion was suppressed, and their people were treated with condescension by the Russian leadership in Moscow. To add further insult, the Soviets were waging a merciless war against Afghanistan, a Moslem country whose people shared an ethnic heritage with several of the Soviet central Asian groups. The Carter administration, however, balked at Henze's proposal to build new transmitters on the grounds that there was no hospitable location for construction and that new facilities would take years to build.[8]

Reagan administration officials were also interested in beefing up the central Asian broadcasts. In 1985, Congress authorized the BIB to establish a new entity, Radio Free Afghanistan, which broadcast to the peoples of Afghanistan in their native languages. The service broadcast limited hours each day and was shut down after the Soviets withdrew from the conflict.[9]

Yet despite the support of officials within the government, little headway was made until 1988, when Radio Liberty named S. Enders Wimbush as its new director. Wimbush was a central Asia specialist who had worked for the RAND Corporation and had served as director of an institute on central Asia at Oxford University. Wimbush was more than an academic expert on the region; he was among a small group of scholars—Paul Henze, Alexander Bennigsen, and Helene Carrere D'Encausse were others—who saw the restiveness of the non-

Russians as the Soviet Union's Achilles heel. Wimbush thus assumed his responsibilities at RL determined to use the non-Russian broadcasts as a weapon toward the breakup of the union:

> My thinking was quite simple. The Soviet Union was a multinational empire. Multinational empires don't survive. The Soviet Union was an evil empire, one of the most pernicious experiments in human history. And its very existence was contrary to the interests of the United States. My view was very different from those who believed that dissent or economic failure would bring the Soviet Union down. I always believed that the nationality problem was the Soviet Union's most serious weakness. And I believed that it was in the American interest to prevent the Soviet Union from feeling that it had complete control over its border regions. Because if the Soviet leaders felt their country's borders were secure, they were more likely to become aggressive internationally.[10]

Wimbush and his cothinkers were known among Kremlinologists as "disintegrationists." Their perspective on the USSR's future represented a distinctly minority view. According to the mainstream position, Moscow had done an adequate job in giving each group a stake in the union's preservation; while nationalism posed a challenge to the Kremlin, there was no reason to see it as a threat to the Soviet Union's existence.

Although there was some talent in the nationality services when he took over, Wimbush found the overall quality insufficient to carry forward his ambitious goals. Programs showed little imagination, broadcasters lacked basic skills, the intellectual level was uneven, and scripts were tainted by émigré thinking, with too much air time devoted to arguments over long-ago controversies that meant little to the audience. Wimbush therefore undertook to transform the programs and staff of the nationality services, with a special focus on the central Asian services. During his five years at RL, Wimbush hired new chief editors for practically all the services, added staff, and increased the number of broadcast hours.

Soon, RL's audience began to grow in the non-Russian republics, partly due to changes adopted by the station, and in part due to a rise in national consciousness among the non-Russian peoples. As totalitarian controls were relaxed, the republics became assertive in demanding first more autonomy, and then, eventually, freedom from the union. In republic after republic, powerful movements for national independence formed, either as coalitions of the national front variety, or as political parties with a nationalist orientation. In most cases, Radio Liberty served as the media of choice for the partisans of independence; indeed, in some cases, RL, or in the case of the Baltic states, RFE, effectively functioned as an instrument of the independence forces. Radio Liberty interviewed leading independence politicians, reported on their speeches and manifestoes, and gave extensive coverage to demonstrations and other proindependence manifestations. The station made excellent use of its contacts during periods of crisis, such as the disturbances between Armenians and Azeris over control of Nagorno-Karabakh and the massacre of demonstrators in Tbilisi, Georgia, by the Soviet army. Although radio policy demanded balanced, accurate, and nonprovocative reporting of violent clashes, the heavy reliance on sources from within the republics guaranteed a particular tilt to the broadcasts.

In its coverage of the accelerating pace of Soviet events, RL was given a considerable assist by glasnost. For the first time in its history, RL could interview government critics directly over the telephone without fear that association with the instrument of imperialist propaganda would earn the interviewee a term in the gulag. Radio Liberty hired stringers in each of the republics to cover local political developments. The station also began to experiment with live broadcasts, something that had never been attempted before.

Radio Liberty's nationality services faced a particularly tricky challenge. They were small and their staff, which ranged widely in talent and political sophistication, was overworked. Only recently had they been asked to enter the world of regular radio journalism. Moreover, where the anti-Communist revolutions in Eastern Europe were, with the exception of Romania, nonviolent affairs, the republics experienced wave after wave of riots, upheavals, interethnic clashes, and violent confrontations pitting local nationalists against the Soviet military. Nor were nationalist leaders necessarily of the caliber of a Walesa or Havel. Some resembled Zhviad Gamsakhurdia, the mercurial leader of the Georgia opposition who, once in power, proved just as autocratic as any Soviet viceroy.

BROADC

294

In the i
control br
both th
edge
st

Azer

Soon enough, one of the nationality
its journalistic abilities under crisis condit
a source of bitter controversy within Ra

In early 1989, the Red Army was d
of Azerbaijan, an oil-rich, predominant
involved in a violent dispute with neig
on the source of information, the strife w
attempt to win control of Nagorno-F
enclave in Azerbaijan, or by anti-Arm
Baku and other Azeri cities. Wherever the responsibility lay, the fact
that it was Azerbaijan that Moscow selected as the target of a full-scale
military operation.

Wimbush had recently hired a new editor for the Azeri service,
Mirza Michaeli. Wimbush felt he had real talent in Michaeli, who had
previously served as chief editor of the VOA's Azeri service, and he
used the Azeri broadcasts as a testing ground for new journalistic techniques, such as the use of free lance stringers and live broadcasts. When
Baku was invaded, Wimbush was vacationing with Gene Pell in the
United States. Several days after the clashes began, he received a telephone call from Bill Marsh, who informed Wimbush that the Soviet
foreign ministry had issued a complaint through diplomatic channels
about the content of the Azeri broadcasts.

The questionable broadcasts occurred during the invasion's first
two days, after which Radio Liberty took measures to monitor the
content of Azeri programming. Surprisingly, the Soviet press took little
notice of the broadcasts, and the American press, with the exception of
a single article in the *Los Angeles Times,* ignored the controversy. Unlike
in Hungary in 1956, the Azeri crisis did not do lasting damage to the
credibility of the radios.

But the potential for serious embarrassment was clearly present.
Radio Liberty stringers in Baku provided what amounted to live battleground reporting, complete with the rumbling of tanks, machine-gun
fire, and the cries of the terrified civilians. There were interviews with
respected Azeri cultural and political figures, who denounced the
Russians as invaders and occasionally as Fascists or worse and urged
the Azeri people to stand firm in the face of foreign occupation. Although RL editors did not suggest that outside aid might be forthcoming, they openly sympathized with the Azeri people and
encouraged their resistance.

vasion's aftermath, various measures were instituted to
oadcast content, including prebroadcast review of scripts of
e Azeri and Armenian services. But while Wimbush acknowl-
d that the Baku events should have been covered with more re-
aint, he was loath to apologize for the Azeri service's handling of the
affair. Indeed, Wimbush took pride in the Azeri performance and argued that the coverage may ultimately have served American interests
insofar as Radio Liberty had made a "strong statement against naked
aggression." He later declared, "Had I been there I would probably
have stopped the live broadcasts and been more careful about what
went out over the air. I'm glad I wasn't there, because I'm glad that the
station was able to get its message across. While those broadcasts might
not have been good as policy, they were good politically. Those two
days of broadcasts probably earned the United States more good will
in Azerbaijan than anything else we ever did. The Azeri ambassador
told me an entire generation of Azeri intellectuals was in America's
debt because of those broadcasts. I'm glad we did them."[11]

This was very much a minority view at Radio Liberty. Mark Pomar,
a member of the BIB staff at the time, called the broadcasts "uncon-
firmed, exaggerated, hysterical hyperbole." He also criticized Wimbush's
policy of stirring up discontent among the Soviet nationalities as an
irresponsible strategy and a serious breach of RL's broadcast code.[12] An
investigation by the inspector general's office concluded some broadcasts were "inflammatory, highly emotional, lacked objectivity, and supported a specific national liberation organization."[13] Others were
disturbed that Wimbush actually proposed that the Azeri service be
rewarded at a time when others thought its performance merited dis-
missals and stricter control. Yet Bill Marsh, a respected manager known
for a generally cautious approach to broadcast content, says in retrospect that some of the criticism was unwarranted. To Marsh, the issue
came down to a problem of handling vivid, highly emotional, life-
and-death events. "An American radio station might win an award for
a similar series," he claims.[14]

Ironically, at the very time that the events in Baku were coming to
a boil, Wimbush was addressing a meeting of the BIB in Washington.
In a triumphalist mood, Wimbush declared that RL was functioning
like a "well-oiled machine." That phrase would return to haunt him in
the wake of the Azeri controversy. The whole incident, including
Wimbush's lack of repentance, was to destroy his relationship with

Gene Pell and Steve Forbes. Wimbush stayed at his post for several more years, after which he returned to nonpolitical work in the United States. He did, however, have the satisfaction of witnessing the vindication of the disintegrationist interpretation. When the Soviet Union collapsed, it was the national consciousness of the Estonians, Azeris, Tajiks, and other non-Russian peoples that led the way.

The vanguard of opposition to Soviet rule was not to be found in central Asia but in the Baltic republics of Estonia, Latvia, and Lithuania. The Baltic states had enjoyed intermittent independence during their long histories, most recently during the interwar period. They were incorporated into the Soviet Union during World War II in what amounted to an act of military conquest. The Balts detested Soviet rule, which they identified as Russian imperialism enforced by local Communist quislings. They were alarmed by policies of Russification, by which Moscow sought to suppress the Baltic languages and cultures, and, to the degree possible, replace the Baltic peoples, many of whom were deported to the gulag, by Russian immigrants. Given the Baltics' tiny populations, Russification signified eventual cultural extermination.

In light of the Baltic peoples' strong sense of national consciousness and hatred of communism, it is surprising that the radios made no broadcasts in the their languages until 1975. When the Free Europe Committee was established in 1949, it included representatives from the various Baltic exile organizations. The exiles lobbied for the inclusion of the Baltic languages in the new Radio Free Europe, yet for practical and technical reasons RFE's management had mixed feelings about adding Baltic services to the five original East European–language divisions. Some questioned whether the Baltic peoples would survive what was perceived as a Soviet campaign of cultural genocide. Even into the 1950s, Stalin continued to carry out massive deportations in the Baltic republics, with the educated classes a special target. The ferocity of the campaign caused C.D. Jackson to speculate that within five years the Baltic peoples would either be removed from their native lands or killed off.

Nevertheless in 1951 RFE, apparently with the approval of the State Department, was moving ahead with plans for services in Estonian, Latvian, and Lithuanian, and had actually begun the process of hiring a broadcast staff for the Baltic sections. Then the State Department changed its mind. Radio Free Europe, it pointed out, had been established because the Voice of America, as an official instrument of the American government, could not broadcast hard-hitting propaganda to Communist countries with which the United States maintained diplomatic relations. But this restriction, the State Department claimed, did not apply to the Baltics, whose incorporation by the Soviet Union had never been recognized by the United States. Thus it was decided that the VOA would function as the sole American propaganda instrument in the Baltic languages. As A.A. Berle, one of the more active Free Europe Committee board members, noted at the time, "I stated off-the-record that unless the State Department was prepared to support a liberation of the Baltic states, I was opposed to broadcasting or starting movements which could only end in the slaughter of the people. For this reason I was opposed to the [FEC's] getting involved in it until a firm policy was made. . . . At the board meeting today [November 28, 1951] we took up the matter and decided to play 'out.'"[15]

The Baltic organizations continued to press for inclusion in RFE, and in 1953 the State Department removed its objections, having concluded that it made no sense to forbid RFE broadcasts to the Baltic peoples when the rest of the Soviet Union and Eastern Europe were already the targets of broadcasts by RFE and RL. By this time, however, RFE's leadership had cooled to the idea of broadcasts to the Baltics. Bob Lang, the director of RFE, argued that the station did not need the added burden of three new broadcast services at a time when it was just beginning to achieve a measure of success in its programs to Eastern Europe. He also expressed the view, widely shared within the organization, that broadcasts to the Baltics did not merit the added cost and technical complications given the small number of potential listeners involved. In subsequent years, similar objections were invariably voiced whenever Baltic representatives placed their case before RFE.[16]

The advocates of Baltic freedom did not give up. They acquired airtime over Radio Madrid and even broadcast programs over the station operated by the NTS, the only condition being that the broadcasts not take on an anti-Russian tone. But the exile leadership balked when suggestions were advanced to ask Radio Liberty to expand its programming to include Baltic broadcasts. Radio Liberty was established to speak to the peoples of the Soviet Union, and it was a cornerstone of the Baltic ideology that the three small countries were not legally part of the union. For Radio Liberty to sponsor broadcasts to the Baltic republics might be interpreted as an acknowledgment of Baltic incorporation.[17]

By the mid-seventies, however, Baltic organizational leaders were prepared to put aside their objections. The State Department was persuaded to approve the addition of the Baltic services, and Radio Liberty agreed to add the three republics to its target audience. And in the end, the Balts got what they wanted. Under the Reagan Administration, a decision was made to move the Baltic services to RFE as a gesture of continuing American support for the cause of Baltic independence.

Until the late 1980s, Baltic programming consisted of the usual mixture of émigré voices, cultural news, and reports about political dissent. Although many Baltic broadcasters harbored strong anti-Russian sentiments, they were under strict instructions to avoid ethnic slurs, and in identifying the adversaries of Baltic independence, RFE broadcasts concentrated on a combination of Russian imperialism, communism as an idea, and the functionaries of the local Communist parties. They did not, as one editor put it, distinguish between bad Russian Communists and good Lithuanian Communists.[18] Once Gorbachev launched his reform program, however, events began to move swiftly, and RFE was compelled to make adjustments in its political strategy and programming approach.

One immediate problem was the coverage of Gorbachev. Was he a reformer, as many in the West claimed, or simply another Russocentric Communist bent on economic modernization? The Lithuanian service decided initially on a cautious approach. "We were sensitive to the Western proclivity to treat each successive Soviet leader, from Malenkov to Andropov, as a reformer," explained Kestutis Girnius, the Lithuanian section chief. "Given that history, we were skeptical about Gorbachev for some time."[19]

For Toomas Ilves, the chief editor of the Estonian service during the crucial years of the independence struggle, the broadcast mission was to accelerate the freedom process by whatever means prudence allowed. Ilves was an Estonian American who combined a fierce commitment to the Estonian cause with a shrewd instinct for American politics. He pushed the limits of the permissible right to the edge but was careful to avoid rash acts that would embarrass Radio Free Europe and set back the cause generally. Thus when in 1988 the old-line leader of the Estonian Communist Party was replaced by a Gorbachevian man of Euro-Communist sympathies, Ilves was unimpressed. "I felt that my job was to show that this Gorbachev idea of Communism with a human face was still Communism."[20]

Like Enders Wimbush, Ilves believed that RFE should be a participant in the struggle for the dissolution of the Soviet Union. Fortified by a sense of historic mission, he and his small staff worked twelve hour days—longer in times of crisis—to inform the Estonian people about the fast-moving developments in their own country and in the greater world. But Ilves adhered to the established guidelines. When in 1991 President Bush betrayed a lack of sympathy toward Baltic demands for independence—an attitude that infuriated most Balts—RFE avoided editorial comment and instead kept its listeners informed through reports on what the world press was saying about the American policy.[21] A similar, if more nuanced, approach was adopted by the Lithuanian service. In reporting on the Western reaction to Baltic events, Kestutis Girnius stressed the distinctions among a newspaper editorial, the declaration of a member of Congress, and an official State Department position. He also endeavored to explain the realpolitik behind the official statements—why, for example, America might not want to support Baltic independence, given its stake in Gorbachev's survival. "We tried to explain why Denmark could openly support independence, but why Germany might be less enthusiastic," he said. "We didn't dampen hope. But we tried to give a realistic picture of the outside world's thinking."[22]

The extremes to which Ilves would go for a good story are exemplified by an incident involving an appearance by Arnold Ruutel, an Estonian party leader, at a conference in Paris sponsored by the journal *Entendu*. In its reports on the event, the Estonian party press claimed that Ruutel had placed himself squarely within the independence camp. Ilves, however, had assigned a correspondent to cover the conference, and the reporter said that far from endorsing independence, Ruutel asserted that Estonians supported the union and Gorbachev, and that claims to the contrary were Western fabrications. When the RFE report was aired, Estonian party propagandists labeled it yet another falsehood meant to damage Estonia and communism. In the past, RFE would have simply ignored the name calling. In the new, open environment, however, Ilves thought it important to demonstrate conclusively that the party had lied. He therefore asked *Entendu* for a transcript of the proceedings. The journal's response was that a transcript could be provided—for eight thousand dollars. Ilves thereupon persuaded the RFE management to provide the money, purchased the transcript, and proved that his correspondent's coverage had been accurate.

In January 1991, events came to a boil. Units of the Soviet military lay siege to government offices and television stations in both Tallinn, the capital of Estonia, and Vilnius, the principal city of Lithuania. Radio Free Europe had anticipated that things might spin out of control; early in the month, Robert Gillette, the RFE director, issued a memorandum directing the Baltic services to exercise caution in quoting sources who threatened armed resistance in the case of Soviet attack. When the assault did come, RFE services kept their lines open to the embattled countries, and were able to provide detailed and accurate coverage of the conflict.[23]

The Baltic events posed a tricky problem for the State Department. The invasion occurred just days before the United States and its allies launched the Desert Storm offensive against Iraq. American diplomats were desperate to prevent any weakening of Gorbachev's position because of the potential impact on the anti-Iraq coalition and thus regarded Baltic calls for secession with dismay. They understood that the nationality services of RFE and RL were contributing to Gorbachev's problems by their encouragement of the forces of union dissolution, yet the State Department was hesitant to intervene in the radios' affairs for fear of negative domestic political repercussions. As Paul Goble, who worked both for the State Department and RFE-RL, observed, "The thinking at State was to avoid the tar pit of involvement in the radios' affairs because of the reaction it might cause in Congress and in the ethnic communities in America."[24] Indeed, advocates of Baltic independence had already criticized the Voice of America, claiming the Voice was downplaying demands for independence and supporting Gorbachev in his efforts to hold the union together.[25] In the end, the Desert Storm coalition remained firm and the Baltics got their freedom. The one clear loser was Mikahil Gorbachev, whose reforms backfired in ways he never anticipated.

For Radio Free Europe, 1989 represented the culmination of nearly forty years of service in the cause of East European liberty. To say that it was a year of astonishing developments is an understatement. No one, and certainly not RFE, believed that by the end of the year, communism would no longer survive as a governing system in its target countries.

It was, of course, apparent that the system was facing serious challenges as the fateful year began. This was especially true in Poland, where talks between Solidarity, which until recently seemed a spent force, and the Jaruzelski regime produced an agreement calling for partially free elections. For the Communists, this represented a remarkable concession. It was an article of anti-Communist faith that communism could never compete effectively under democratic conditions, and Communists historically had given every indication of agreeing with that assessment. When the deal calling for elections was announced, the reaction in the West was restrained. Some speculated that Poles might opt for Jaruzelski and stability; others expressed doubts that the party would permit honest balloting; still others wondered whether Gorbachev would in the end tolerate a Polish government dominated by Solidarity.

Marek Latynski, RFE's chief Polish editor, took the attitude that the elections constituted a remarkable opportunity—both for Poland and for the radio. He proceeded on the assumption that the balloting would not be rigged and that the Communists faced the prospect of a devastating setback. Elections had already been conducted in Lithuania, and the result was a complete rout for the party. Latynski therefore believed that the Polish election might revolve around the single issue of whether a candidate was or was not a Communist.[26]

The elections were conducted on a nonparty basis; candidates ran without affiliations, a policy insisted on by the Communists. Radio Free Europe therefore saw its job as making sure that the Polish people knew which candidates were representing the party and which were not. During the campaign, RFE attempted to interview as many non-Communist candidates as was possible by telephone. As polling drew near, RFE announcers read out the names of the nonparty candidates for each election district, dull radio for sure, but quite possibly helpful to the opposition. The radio also summarized the most important articles in *Gazeta Wyborcza,* the leading opposition newspaper, which was unable to print enough copies to reach its potential audience.[27]

Radio Free Europe's coverage was thus nonpolemical, but hardly nonpartisan. Its pro-Solidarity tilt was likely not welcomed by the

State Department, which privately fretted that a Solidarity landslide would erode Gorbachev's precarious standing in Moscow. Some high American officials, in fact, were known to be favorably disposed toward Jaruzelski. John C. Whitehead, assistant secretary of state for Europe, had at one point demanded to review RFE scripts after getting an earful of complaints from Jaruzelski. The BIB declined to provide the scripts, and the issue was smoothed over by lower-level officials.[28] Yet despite its high interest in the Polish elections, the State Department did not intervene in RFE's coverage, and after Solidarity scored a smashing victory at the polls, RFE moved quickly to establish bureaus and assign correspondents to cover news from inside the country.

Events in Czechoslovakia were moving at a much slower pace than in Poland, or so it seemed. At the year's beginning, Vaclav Havel, the dissident playwright and unofficial leader of the opposition movement, was given yet another prison sentence for incitement; among the evidence brought against Havel were interviews he gave RFE.[29] This act provoked the predictable protests from the outside world, but the regime seemed not to care about what others thought of its internal policies.

But beneath the surface, elements within the party were increasingly dissatisfied with the leadership's course. They were unhappy with their country's pariah reputation, embarrassed by the mediocrities who dominated the government, and convinced that the forces that were threatening party control in other countries posed a threat to the system in Czechoslovakia as well. And where in the past Moscow had backed up the dogmatists who held the reins of party control, now, under Gorbachev, elements who favored a measure of liberalization believed they had a patron in the Kremlin.

In the fall of 1989 came the incident of the Jakeš tape. Miloš Jakeš had only recently been elevated to succeed Gustáv Husák as party leader. Jakeš was an uninspiring time-server who was committed to the status quo. Earlier in the year, he had addressed a conference of local party activists. The speech was an embarrassment to the leadership, in every respect. It was candid about the party's woeful standing among the people. It was also ungrammatical, rambling, incoherent. Thus speaking about responsibility for past errors, Jakeš declared, "Comrades . . . yes . . . this person [it isn't clear to whom he was referring] made some mistakes. . . . Every one of us makes mistakes[,] . . . but always . . . who's this government. . . . When I ask, it's a Communist government. . . . Communist it was, it is, it always will be." Jakeš also said, regarding his regime's isolation, "Sometimes I feel like the last post in a fence."[30]

Within a few weeks, a tape of the speech made its way to Radio Free Europe. Irena Lasota, an activist on behalf of East European democracy, was given the tape by Jan Ruml, a dissident who later became a government official in the post–Communist period; she then passed it along to the radio.[31] The original source of the leak, though, came from within the party, from those who hoped to undermine Jakeš and others in the leadership. This goal was certainly achieved. The Jakeš tape was the talk of Prague, as people passed around cassettes recorded from RFE broadcasts and mimicked the semiliterate words of their country's leader.

Even more important than the Jakeš tape was RFE's intense coverage of the massive movement of East Germans to Czechoslovakia and Hungary, and from there to West Germany. The significance of East German events in accelerating the pace of Communist disintegration throughout the rest of Europe cannot be overemphasized. The German Democratic Republic was notorious for the strict control of its citizens; it was also the most economically successful Communist state. Moreover, it had always been assumed that however much experimentation and liberal change Moscow might permit in the other people's democracies, its tolerance for change in East Germany was limited. Yet here was East German communism coming apart at the seams, and a passive Soviet Union unwilling to utter a word of support for the party leadership. Events in East Germany at once lifted the fear of Soviet intervention from the people of Czechoslovakia, Bulgaria, and Romania, while sending the message to the dispirited party leaderships that they could no longer depend on the Soviet Union as the ultimate guarantor of their survival.

Romania was the last of the Communist dominoes to fall. The Romanian revolution was to be the most violent in East Europe, and it also gave the appearance of the most spontaneous, there being no dissident opposition to speak of in the country. In fact, elements within the party had been conspiring against Ceausescu for some years, and these oppositional elements often used RFE as the mouthpiece for their views. In 1988, Silviu Brucan, a Marxist theoretician and something of a dissident, gave an interview to RFE in which he declared

that Romania had become intellectually dead, that Ceausescu was sti-
fling the party, and that the country was heading toward "neocolonial
status."[32] Then, in February 1989, RFE received a copy of the "Letter
of the Six," a manifesto drafted by Brucan and signed by six prominent
party members that raised objections to Ceausescu's course. The authors specified that RFE was not to broadcast the contents until a
more traditional news agency broke the story. In March, after the BBC
ran excerpts from the letter, RFE broadcast the entire text, along with
commentaries from leading editors.[33]

By December, Romania was the only East European country in
which the old system—and the old leadership—survived. On December 17, both RFE and the BBC announced that a disturbance had
broken out in the Transylvanian city of Timisoara. In fact, security
forces had fired on civilians, and an undetermined number had been
killed. Within a few days, RFE was broadcasting eyewitness accounts
from travelers who had witnessed the massacre. The radio also received
a tape that included the sounds of shots and the screams of the terrified townspeople.

Clearly, something important was underway. But covering Romanian developments posed a greater challenge than RFE had confronted
in Poland or Czechoslovakia. There were few Western reporters in
Romania and correspondents were generally restricted to Bucharest.
Romania was awash in rumors—there were wild stories of thousands
massacred by the Securitate, of Arab terrorists forming a palace guard
for Ceausescu, of conspiracies among Ceausescu's allies and his adversaries. Thus while RFE quickly went on a twenty-four-hour broadcast
schedule to Romania, there was often a dearth of new, reliable information to tell the listeners.

One objective of RFE coverage was to encourage the Romanian
military to at minimum remain neutral in the struggle. Romanian
army men were reminded that to retain its credibility as a national
institution, the military should either remain neutral or side with the
people. In response, RFE received calls from parents who requested
that RFE broadcast its military scripts over the frequency to which
their sons, who were serving in tank brigades, had access. Munich also
received calls from Securitate agents who understood which way events
were headed and wanted to be of some assistance to the revolutionary
cause. These agents provided the addresses of safe houses, the location
of secret airfields that might be used by Ceausescu, and information

about Bucharest's vast tunnel network. Radio Free Europe did not broadcast the information about the safe houses for fear the addresses might be inaccurate, but it provided the details about the airfields and tunnels. These broadcasts reached important listeners. At one point, the radio received a telephone call from the Romanian general staff, asking that information about tunnel locations be rebroadcast; the original broadcast had apparently been garbled in transmission.[34]

Unlike in Poland, where Solidarity served as a government-in-waiting, or Czechoslovakia or Hungary, where nonparty figures were prepared to govern, Romania had no significant dissidents outside the party who enjoyed popular credibility. The dissident movement had been thoroughly infiltrated by the Securitate; it was generally believed that many "dissidents" who were allowed to go to the West were working as regime agents. With no Havels, Walesas, or even Yeltsins to align with, RFE gave guarded support to various figures within the party as the only realistic alternatives to Ceausescu. Ion Iliescu, one of those given favorable treatment on RFE, did in fact succeed to the country's leadership after Ceausescu's execution. Afterward, RFE had reason to question whether it had followed a wise course in promoting the cause of so-called party dissidents. For while many Romanians gave RFE credit for its role in bringing Ceausescu down, the station was also blamed for having built up Iliescu, an unpopular leader.[35]

With the demise of Ceausescu, communism came to an inglorious end in central and Eastern Europe. In the Soviet Union, the system lingered on until August 1991, when the failed coup against Mikhail Gorbachev brought about the demise of communism and catapulted Boris Yeltsin back into the political spotlight. Yeltsin had little interest in the survival of the union; his personal ambition was to rule Russia. He thus quickly agreed to the dissolution of the Soviet Union, and at year's end, the huge, terrifying Socialist empire founded by Lenin and consolidated under Stalin ceased to exist.

That Yeltsin remained a formidable Russian political figure is due in some part to Radio Liberty, which devoted considerable coverage to his pronouncements during his years in the wilderness. There is some irony here, since most leading Russian editors at RL preferred Gorbachev, the steady reformer, to Yeltsin, with his bouts of instability and his tendencies toward demagogy. But despite its support for glasnost and perestroika, RL probably damaged Gorbachev's prospects by simply providing honest coverage of Soviet developments, which were dominated by economic decline, political unrest, industrial strikes, coup rumors, and anti-Russian manifestations throughout the non-Russian republics.

Although many in the Soviet hierarchy remained cool to RL, no one could afford to ignore the station given its growing audience and enhanced political influence. Vladimir Kryuchkov, the KGB chief who had argued strenuously against the lifting of jamming and, in 1990, accused the CIA of trying to destroy the Soviet Union through RL broadcasts, gave several interviews to RL reporters, as did other leading members of the national security apparatus. The prevailing attitude seemed to be, as one official put it, that it made no sense to refuse an interview to a station to which one regularly listened.[36]

Radio Liberty was also the subject of revisionist treatment by the Soviet press. In 1990, Leonid Shinkarev, a correspondent for Izvestia, wrote a laudatory commentary after visiting RL's Munich headquarters: "In the empty years of our isolation from the world (and in spite of being labeled cosmopolitans, traitors, and so on), it was [RL] which brought us the voices of Sakharov and Solzhenitsyn, which day-after-day informed us about the human rights movement, which read us underground samizdat documents. What we talk about today, they talked about twenty and thirty years ago."[37] Shinkarev described a station that approached its coverage of Soviet politics with the utmost seriousness, that supported perestroika almost to a man but also was marked by a wide diversity of opinion, ranging from monarchist to liberal democratic. He was particularly struck by the station's ability to give intelligent coverage to Soviet affairs despite its decades of physical isolation from its audience. He noted with awe that Lev Predtechevsky, RL's military affairs correspondent, had access to Western military journals and official reports that would be restricted as top secret documents in the Soviet Union.

Radio Liberty progressed from filling the gaps in glasnost—the station was cited by Soviet officials for its superior coverage of the catastrophic 1988 earthquake in Armenia, an event that confounded a Soviet press conditioned by years of censorship to ignore natural disasters—to functioning as a normal radio station, with correspondents in all the major cities. When the August 1991 coup took place, the years of careful preparation paid off. Radio Liberty had over 100 stringers in the Soviet Union; the Russian section was thus able to assign reporters to cover every aspect of the crisis. Two reporters focused entirely on Boris Yeltsin and remained at Yeltsin's side in the Russian White House throughout the critical days. Radio Liberty gave Yeltsin crucial access to the Russian people, especially those outside the major cities. It was over RL that Yeltsin made his call for a general strike on the coup's first day. Radio Liberty also covered the coup plotters, providing interviews with such hard-liners as Viktor Alksnis, the "Black Colonel," and Alfred Rubiks, a leader of the Latvian party.

On the coup's second night, Mikhail Sokolov, who was there in the White House with Yeltsin, told his listeners, as he watched tanks advance on the building, "Farewell, I'm afraid this is my last report." But the telephone line was kept open, and a short time later Sokolov came back on the air to report that the tanks had turned back and the imminent danger was past. That same night, a CNN reporter filmed a crowd manning a barricade outside the parliament building. Many were huddled around fires listening to portable radios; when the reporter asked to what station they were listening, they replied, "Svoboda"—Liberty.[38]

The RL staff labored round the clock during the coup week and was never cited for a serious error or the use of inflammatory language, an impressive testimony to the station's professionalism. Indeed, RL chose to ignore a report of Gorbachev's death that the BBC and other stations broadcast and later retracted.

In the coup's aftermath, RL received testimonials from both Mikhail Gorbachev and Boris Yeltsin. Gorbachev had relied on RL and other foreign broadcast stations during the critical days of August; Yeltsin, of course, had relied on RL to maintain contact with the Russian people. Meanwhile a revolution had swept away both communism, one of the most repressive political systems invented by man, and the Soviet Union, an empire that had endured for decades by force of arms but split apart almost without resort to violence. To Paul Goble, Radio Liberty's greatest achievement was in discouraging the use of force during the final, convulsive years of the empire. "I think we helped make the revolution, and I think we helped make it peaceful," he recalled several years later. "If it hadn't been for Radio Liberty, I'm sure there would have been more killing. Whatever we can be taxed for, the fact remains that there are a lot of people who are not dead because of this radio station."[39]

Epilogue

The end of the Cold War brought a brief period of recognition and acclaim to Radio Free Europe and Radio Liberty. On returning to their native lands, the exiled editors and commentators were hailed as comrades-in-arms of the freedom struggle. Jan Nowak received a tumultuous welcome when he arrived in Warsaw in 1989. Kyrill Panoff, chief editor of the Bulgarian section, was asked by the leader of the democratic opposition, Zhelyu Zhelev, to address a huge Sofia May Day crowd in 1990, something Panoff recalls as one of the most thrilling experiences of his life. Mircea Carp, an editor in the Romanian section, was given a standing ovation when he was summoned forth during a cultural program in a Bucharest theater. Dagmara Vallens, a fixture of Latvian broadcasts from the very beginning, was speaking to her brother while riding on a bus in Latvia when the passenger directly in front turned and declared, "I know your voice."[1] And practically every RFE-RL personality claims to have been recognized by taxi drivers who refused to accept payment from a hero of the revolution.

The euphoria was short-lived. Eastern Europe was impoverished and politically unstable. Whereas Radio Free Europe and Radio Liberty had been praised for their steadfast opposition to communism, they were now blamed for supporting—or seeming to support—political parties that proved unable to put things in order. There was also the question of the radios' reason for existence. Should they be retained as instruments that taught the rudiments of democracy and free markets to societies with little experience of either? Or as an insurance policy against the return of communism or the rise of extreme nationalist movements? Or simply as a model of a free press in countries where the media, even after communism, remained highly partisan? In 1993, the new Clinton administration decided the issue by eliminating much of the operation, placing what remained of the radios under the oversight of the United States Information Agency and moving the headquarters from Munich to Prague after Czech president Vaclav Havel offered the radios a rent-free headquarters in the city's central district. Broadcasts to Hungary were eliminated altogether, and broadcast hours to Poland and the Czech Republic were reduced considerably, while the Polish and Czech sections looked for private sponsors to replace American government funding. But RFE retained its other services, including Slovak, now operating as a completely separate entity, and even added a South Slav service, which broadcast to the new nations of the former Yugoslavia, while Radio Liberty retained its entire roster of language services. In 1998, Congress approved a measure that placed two new surrogate services, Radio Free Iran and Radio Free Iraq, under the administration of RFE-RL, a testament to the American political leadership's confidence that the model established by the radios could be utilized for the promotion of democracy in other parts of the world.

Many of the old exiles left the radios after the move to Prague in 1995. Some returned to their native countries to take up positions in the press or to work as representatives of Western corporations interested in gaining a foothold in the emerging post-Communist market. For those who remained in the West, the going could be rough. In RFE's early years, exiled editors worked for a few thousand dollars a year with few benefits and modest housing. By the 1990s, salaries often reached the range of fifty to sixty thousand dollars, more than most journalists in the United States or Germany were making, for that matter, and compensation was even higher for chief editors and managers. The radios leased apartments for staff in the nicer parts of Munich, and provided generous benefits and home leave for American citizens. An exiled journalist who left the radios discovered that there were few jobs for writers with limited proficiency in English or German; many made do with poorly paid jobs in the ethnic press or as American correspondents for the media in post-Communist Eastern Europe.

For some radio veterans, the end of the Cold War brought vindication for a life's work. This was certainly true for Jan Nowak, who had emerged, after a few years' retirement, as director of the Polish–American Congress and a consultant to the National Security Council. In 1996, Nowak received the Medal of Freedom, the highest civilian honor in the United States. Even in his mid-eighties, he kept busy lobbying for the expansion of NATO to include Poland and other countries of east and central Europe. Cord Meyer, who was present at the creation of the radios, was still writing a syndicated column. George Kennan, the "father" of Radio Free Europe, also lived to see the collapse of the Communist system, although he was not inclined to take credit for his role in the system's demise.

Vladimir Matusevitch remained as director of Russian broadcasting for a few years, and then moved to Washington, where he served as a commentator for RL. Matusevitch was fired under somewhat murky circumstances. Matusevitch thereupon sued the station. Matusevitch was no stranger to law courts. During his stint in London, he was sued for accusing another Russian exile journalist of advocating a "racialist recipe"; the journalist had written in the *London Telegraph* that the BBC hired its Russian staff almost exclusively from "Russian speaking national minorities," a phrase some interpreted as anti-Semitic. Matusevitch lost, and the court awarded the plaintiff more than $400,000. By this time Matusevitch had left England, and he never had to pay the judgment.[2]

Tributes poured in from the radios' loyal listeners. Some recalled the dangers of listening to foreign broadcasts during the Cold War's early days. Grigory Yavlinsky, a reformer and presidential candidate in Russia, recalled that his father and grandfather had been regular listeners to RL. "Because it was forbidden to listen to Radio Liberty, they used to tell me to warn them if someone was coming up the stairs of our apartment building. When I was a little older, they asked me not to say anything to my friends in school about what they did every evening."[3] Andrei Codrescu, a Romanian émigré who attained some notoriety as a humorist on National Public Radio, recalled listening to RFE in his youth, "with the shades drawn, the lights off." He added, "If I walked down any darkened street at that hour, I would have seen the lowered shades and the furtive dark in which glowed the soft dial of the radio."[4]

Poland must figure prominently in any assessment of the radios' Cold War legacy. Throughout the Communist era, Poland remained in a state of constant potential rebellion. The Catholic Church was never brought under regime control; neither, for that matter, was the peasantry, which alone among the people's democracies successfully resisted collectivization. Radio Free Europe was regarded by most Poles as the most powerful voice of the opposition; its influence over the course of Polish politics was incalculable. Because the service was led by patriotic Poles, who loved their country more than they detested communism, RFE was never accused of egging people on to suicidal gestures. And because the Polish editors hated communism, they ignored the American diplomats who urged support for the leader of the day, whether it be a "national Communist" such as Gomulka, a "pragmatic reformer" such as Gierek, or a "national patriot" such as Jaruzelski.

For Lech Walesa, a listener at a young age, Radio Free Europe broadcasts were partly responsible for his commitment to the political opposition. Walesa became acquainted with RFE at age thirteen, during the Hungarian Revolution. "You had to listen very intensely because of the jamming," he recalled many years later. "But as a result you remembered it all the more. I think my whole career went the way it did because we lived those days so intensely."[5] In another, almost lyrical tribute, Walesa declared, "Presenting works that were 'on the red censorship list,' it was our ministry of culture. Exposing absurd economic policies, it was our ministry of economics. Reacting to events promptly and pertinently, but above all truthfully, it was our ministry of information."[6] Walesa's sentiments have been repeated, though seldom with his eloquence, by many others. Which raises the question: Why were the radios so highly valued by the democratic opposition of Eastern Europe? What accounts for the credibility of what the Communist leadership and many in the West regarded as instruments of American propaganda? The United States, after all, showed little enthusiasm for international broadcasting before World War II, and even during the war its propaganda broadcasts were regarded as inferior to those of the BBC.

Part of the answer lies in the nature of communism. In its very essence, communism relied on a series of lies and myths—about capitalism, about the nature of democracy, about religion, about the achievements of the Soviet Union, about Lenin, Stalin, and their lesser acolytes. To compensate for the weakness of their argument, Communists sought absolute control over the means of communication. The state or the party owned the media, foreign newspapers were banned, and foreign broadcasts jammed. The subjects of Communist regimes understood that they were living under a system constructed on a foundation of lies. They were eager for a free press and truthful commentary, and in the absence of indigenous alternatives, they cared not at all whether the sponsor was the American government, the CIA, or a committee of concerned American citizens. And they respected RFE and RL for their having promoted change, not suicidal gestures or violent revolution.

If Communist repression created what amounted to a captive audience, the fact that the radios were free from direct American government control made an enormous contribution to their success. Operating under the covert and relatively relaxed oversight of the CIA ensured that the radios could avoid the meddling of congressional critics, be they rightwingers on the lookout for ideological softness or liberals who feared that criticism of the Soviet Union might impede the progress of détente. Whereas the Voice of America operated under the perpetual threat of congressional harassment and frequently changed its program composition and ideological tone because of shifts in the political environment, RFE and RL maintained a relatively consistent voice, especially in the years following the Hungarian Revolution.

The radios maintained relative independence due to the talents and judgment of their staff. Had their staff been dominated by mediocrities, the radios would have lost the loyalty of their audience. Had the radios been captured by zealots, they would have lost the support of the American government. The radios understood that their audience preferred accurate news and restrained commentary to blatant propaganda. The radios did, of course, retain a clear point of view. Eventually, they evolved into something akin to National Public Radio (NPR), a radio network devoted to public affairs and culture, but with a clear anti-Communist perspective.

The comparison with NPR can be extended to the area of staffing. Just as certain NPR correspondents have become important journalistic voices in the United States, so RFE and RL built an audience through the abilities of staff reporters and analysts. Certain language services hired commentators with established reputations as writers and critics back home. This was especially true of the Russian broadcasting service, which boasted the cream of the Russian intellectual diaspora among its contributors. The very fact that these noted writers and critics had forsaken their native country for an American-sponsored forum was itself a powerful rebuke to the Soviet system. More to the point, their participation enabled Radio Liberty to present broadcasts that were intellectually and journalistically superior to Soviet media offerings.

The radios owe a measure of their popularity to their role as a counter to Soviet and Russian imperialism. This was especially true of Radio Liberty. No single issue was as central to the collapse of communism as the desire for independence of the non-Russian peoples of the Soviet Union. Without directly inciting the non-Russian nationalities, RL supported their cause by serving as the voice of the cultural opposition. Radio Liberty broadcast prohibited literature, banned music, plays that could never be openly produced, it interviewed exiled writers and reported on the fate of those persecuted for participation in the independence cause. It helped sustain the movements for national sovereignty even though American policy, official and unofficial, opposed the breakup of the Soviet Union.

Finally, the radios were instrumental in thwarting communism's attempt to isolate and atomize its subjects. Especially in its early years, communism succeeded in demoralizing the people of Eastern Europe by convincing them of the futility of united opposition. Marcin Krol, a prominent historian and essayist, has written of RFE's impact on Poland during the Cold War's early years: "Several conditions defined the situation of the individual under totalitarian rule in Eastern Europe. Persecution and terror were among them; so was an endless amount of lies. What is perhaps less known—and has not yet been properly described—is how lonely everyone felt and how cut off from the greater tradition of Western learning and thought. . . . Even the most innocent meetings were thought by the regime to be dangerous. . . . Family life flourished under these restraints, but one cannot live a full life only among the members of one's family. Listening to Radio Free Europe created for a vast number of Poles the perhaps artificial but nevertheless essential sense that one was living in larger company."[7] Some commentators cultivated a radio style through which they seemed to speak directly and personally to each listener. They projected the message that others understood their plight—not simply the commentator but millions in the Free World as well. The radios paid particular attention to the acts of protest and rebellion, and by instantaneously relaying accounts of dissent, promoted the idea that events in Krakow carried important implications for listeners in Kiev, Brno, and Sofia. Through RFE-RL and the other foreign broadcast entities, the Communists were never able to gain a media monopoly, and were thus deprived of the most potent tools of totalitarian control.

It is unfortunate that most histories of the Cold War deal with RFE and RL as footnotes, or as CIA-manipulated propaganda instruments. For in fact the radios proved one of the most successful institutions of America's Cold War effort, and made an important contribution to the peaceful nature of communism's demise. Their success can be measured by the gratitude expressed by millions of listeners, for whom the radios often served as a voice of hope and sanity in an often hopeless and insane world. Or by the fury their broadcasts generated among the Communist party elites—who listened in spite of their anger in order to find out what was really going on in the world. In the war of ideas between communism and democracy—and this, after all, was the central conflict of the Cold War—the freedom radios proved to be one of democracy's most powerful weapons.

Appendix:
Policy Guidances

From their inception in the early 1950s until the late 1970s, Radio Free Europe and Radio Liberty established broadcast policy through the issuance of regular directives, or guidances. In most cases, the guidances were drafted by members of the American management and circulated to the editors of the various language services. On occasion, the guidances were written by RFE or RL administrators and then sent for approval to the Central Intelligence Agency or the State Department before being implemented as official policy. In a very few cases, broad policy documents were written by the State Department itself.

Several different types of guidances were issued by the two stations. Radio Free Europe issued daily guidances, which suggested points that broadcasters might highlight in commenting on the major news items of the day. Broad thematic guidances on subjects like Hungarian agriculture or the Sino-Soviet split included lengthy background analysis and recommendations as to how broadcasters should cover the particular issue. Finally, "country papers"—lengthy guidelines for RFE's strategy toward its target countries—were issued after consultation with the CIA and State Department.

Radio Free Europe issued hundreds of guidances during the 1950s. As RFE and RL evolved into normal international broadcasting networks, they made less frequent use of guidances and relied more on the professional judgment of the language service editors. By the late 1970s the use of policy guidances had been almost entirely discontinued.

This was the first guidance issued by Radio Free Europe. Written in 1950, it spells out the station's mission and objectives at its inception. The language reflects the political environment of the early Cold War; indeed, by the standards of the time, this was a moderate document.

REVISED

(September 21, 1950)

POLICY GUIDANCE MEMORANDUM NO. 1

Objective of Radio Free Europe.

The objective of Radio Free Europe is to prevent, or at least to hinder, the spiritual, economic and military integration of the nations of Eastern Europe into the Soviet bloc. To this end we seek to hold or to capture, insofar as possible, the allegiance of the peoples in the nations to which our programs are beamed, and to undermine Soviet and native Communist influence in that area by every means available to propaganda.

Character of Audience.

To develop a line of approach calculated to attain our objective it is necessary first of all to consider the composition of our audience. In each of the prisoner states, in varying proportions, it will fall largely into the following occupational categories:

1. Peasants.
2. Industrial workers
3. Intelligentsia
4. Military
5. Church
6. Functionaries
7. Business

For each of these categories specific topics and lines of approach should be developed with a minimum of delay, having due regard for such differentiating factors as sex and age. However, this memorandum is limited to the discussion of certain topics and lines of approach calculated to interest and influence our audience as a whole. To assist in the selection of these, the following assumptions have been made in regard to the proponderant majority of our listeners:

1. That there is an almost universal and burning desire to be freed from foreign domination,

2. that, with the exception of those who profit directly from it in terms of power or privilege, there is a general detestation of the police state in all its aspects,

3. that life in a police state has enormously stimulated the longing for a measure of personal freedom, and in particular for freedom of worship,

4. that there is a widespread divergence of opinion as to the most suitable form of political, social, and economic organization to be instituted once national independence has again been achieved,

5. that the spirit of nationalism has lost none of its vitality,

6. that the attachment of the peasant to his land is as passionate as ever; and that there is a welling desire for land reform wherever feudal tenure has persisted,

7. that there is a general desire for economic betterment,

8. that life goes on in these countries and that the attitude of certain members of the population towards the regime may be conditioned by the way it has affected their personal situation,

9. that there is a certain amount of disappointment among the peoples of the target area in regard to the past policies of the Western world towards the enslaved countries of Eastern Europe,

10. that there is a strong desire to preserve the ties with Western culture and to prevent integration into the Soviet system.

Topics and Lines of Approach

The foregoing assumptions suggest certain topics and lines of approach with which it is now proposed to deal.

Liberation

For the peoples of the prisoner states everything else hinges upon the question of liberation. This is for them the vital preoccupation. Accordingly, liberation must be the predominant theme in any effective long-range program of propaganda.

This confronts Radio Free Europe with a dilemma. It is absolutely essential to keep the hope of liberation alive. Yet we should recognize that for the peoples of Eastern Europe another world war appears to offer the only chance of realizing this hope. If, accepting this thesis, we state quite frankly that in our view there can be no lasting peace until Eastern Europe has been freed from the domination of the Soviet Union, we play into the hands of the Kremlin, who with their "peace" campaign are exploiting in every corner of the globe the almost universal fear and detestation of war. If, on the other hand, we do less than this, we run the risk of weaking the morale of our friends behind the Iron Curtain, who will surely be told, and may actually believe, that we have abandoned them.

Under these circumstances, what should be our line? The following suggestions, by no means all-inclusive, are put forward in a tentative vein. We should:

1. Make it clear on every appropriate occasion that the United States had not forgotten the pledge of national independence contained in the Yalta declaration and so flagrantly violated by the Soviet Union—that we expect to see this pledge eventually redeemed.

2. Make the point that because of the attitude of the Soviet Union, the world situation is at present in flux and that the time and manner of liberation will of necessity depend upon the way in which the conflict between the free world and the Soviet despotism may develop—a question which is still not yet clear.

3. Emphasize the growing awareness in the western world of the Soviet objective of world domination.

4. Recount the stages of increasing resistance to Soviet pressure, culminating in the action of the United Nations in Korea.

5. Tell of the overwhelming strength of the free world in terms of raw materials and industrial potential.

6. Tell of the increasing military strength of the free world and notably of the United States—making much of the readiness with which our industrial potential, designed for the purposes of peace, can be converted if need be from civilian to military production.

7. Develop the thesis that the first step in bringing about a retreat of Soviet power must be to arrest its further advance and that we are presently engaged in taking this step.

8. Draw attention to the forces of disintegration at work within a despotism, and their tendency to grow by leaps and bounds once the period of easy conquests has come to an end.

9. Express the hope, possibly with tongue in cheek, that when finally confronted with preponderant strength in being, the masters of the Kremlin may accept the ever open invitation to abandon their

mad dream of world domination and join with other nations of the world community in laying the foundations for expanding prosperity in a world at peace.

10. Define what we mean by peace, i.e., peace through freedom, the only peace that under any circumstances we would accept.

11. On every possible occasion make it clear that the existing world tension is not based upon a struggle for power between the United States and the Soviet Union, as it is so often represented, but that it is a recrudescence of the ancient struggle between freedom and tyranny, that in this struggle there can be no neutrals, that in this struggle we consider all of Eastern Europe, whether at present under Russian domination or not, by its whole history and tradition inevitably on our side.

After Liberation, What?

Our friends in the prisoner states are profoundly interested to learn what we see in prospect for them once liberation has been achieved. The answer to the question, "After liberation, what?" is to be found in certain fixed principles of American policy. We believe that once the prisoner states have been liberated they should be free to form governments of their own choosing without interference by any outside influence, including our own. We believe that in this manner they will be able to adopt whatever form of political, social, and economic organization is best suited to their needs. We stand ready to be of assistance to them in overcoming their initial economic difficulties.

Whenever there have been social advances, as for instance, in the opening of educational opportunities to a wider group, our disposition would be to see that the gains made were held as a prelude to further progress. It should be pointed out, however, that in a climate of freedom, teachers would once again be permitted to seek the truth and impart it to their pupils, who would no longer have to play the part of the propagandists for an alien philosophy or the mouthpieces for a steady stream of Soviet lies.

We hold the view that the nations of Eastern Europe form an essential and an integral part of any viable European economy. In general, we favor the maintenance of a high degree of national cultural autonomy within the framework of a European federation. We look upon such a federation as the best means to provide for the prosperity and the security of the European continent.

Under the stress of war we accepted the notion that the Balkan

States with the exception of Greece should fall within the Russian sphere of influence under certain very definite conditions. These conditions, agreed to by the Soviet Union, have not been met by them in practice. Accordingly, the whole question of spheres of influence can fairly be re-examined. Without prejudging this issue, we strongly inclined at present to the organization of peace through the instrumentality and under the supervision of the United Nations without conceding to any nation that degree of authority over its neighbors which the Soviet Union has read into the conception of spheres of influence. We believe that the prisoner states must be freed of Russian domination. This means for us as a minimum the withdrawal of the Soviet Army and its Secret Police, free elections effectively supervised, and the repeal of all measures illegally adopted. In general it means that frontiers imposed by the Soviets should promptly be brought under review and wherever possible finally determined by friendly negotiation between parties originally involved.

The American Example

Our friends in the prisoner countries are subjected to a constant barrage of misrepresentation about the United States. No opportunity should be lost to set this matter right.

A rising standard of living, an ever-widening horizon of opportunity, the dignity and worth of the individual, personal freedom and national independence in a world at peace are ideals responsive to the deepest longings of our people. We seek these things for others no less than for ourselves. Our thoughts are directed to the ever-present American vision of a brighter future. By way of demonstrating the truth of these assertions, we have but to present in broad outlines our national behavior in the domestic and in the foreign field.

In the domestic field we can point to the enormous advances in the sphere of social legislation. A developing industrialism, together with the spread of popular education, has brought to masses of people a larger share of the good things of life than ever before, and this movement continues in the United States because we believe that in the world of today it is essentially just and right. We have thus placed ourselves securely on the side of progress. There has been recurrent criticism of the so-called "welfare state," but very little criticism of the obligation of the government to interest itself increasingly in the general welfare of the citizen with the result that a growing sense of well-being and of security has been brought to the average man and woman. In the process our economy has <u>not</u> been disrupted, and our actual and potential productivity has reached previously undreamed of heights. It can safely be asserted that no other system devised by man has demonstrated such flexibility in the face of changing conditions as the American system, or such outstanding success in meeting them. Our propaganda should take full advantage of these facts.

In the foreign field we can underscore the efforts we have made to improve the standard of living in other countries and to advance the cause of world peace. The first of these was of course our major participation in U.N.R.R.A., an act of generosity never fully appreciated and already largely forgotten. Then came the Marshall Plan, which would have brought material help to many of the countries behind the Iron Curtain had it not been for the intransigence of the Soviet Union. Beyond this we stand committed to the widest possible extension of multilateral trade as a condition essential to world prosperity. And we have made a modest beginning in the implementation of that "bold new program" for the development of backward areas known as Point Four.

In the interests of peace with justice we have given wholehearted support to the United Nations, which we joined in good faith in the hope that it would be able to maintain international peace and security. Because this hope has for the moment been dimmed by the conduct of the Soviet Union, we have felt obliged to take measures both within and without the Charter which we deemed necessary to maintain security, if it did not maintain the peace, of the free world. We have scrupulously observed our international commitments to the utmost of our ability. We need not hesitate to spread these facts on the record.

Russian Objectives

Our friends in the prisoner countries have had experience enough of their own to have a pretty clear view of the objectives of the Soviet Union. It would not be surprising if they wondered at times whether our view was equally clear—whether we had at last taken the measure of the menace and whether we were prepared emotionally to meet it at whatever cost.

We should state without hesitation that the Soviet Union, in our view, is today an imperialist power seeking world domination as its undisguised objective. It has made a prisoner of many states and now threatens the free world. Promising the millennium, it enlists the support of the toilers in many lands, postponing the disclosure of the emptiness of its promises until it is so well entrenched in power that the disillusioned have no longer any choice but to obey. It is this Bolshevik imperialism, using Communism as a weapon, which is the real enemy. And it is Bolshevik imperialism that should be the principal target of our attack. This is tyranny—naked and aggressive—with all the strength and with all the weakness of tyranny. We should point out that the strength of tyranny is notoriously transient, while its weaknesses, as history reveals, leads to its inevitable doom. We should play on the growing objection of the satellites to the Soviet Union's disregard for their rights, prestige and interests. Many useful variations can be developed on this theme.

Semantics

Wherever the voice of the Soviet reaches, the meaning of words is twisted out of all recognition. It is important on this account to devote some effort to clarification. The corruption of the idiom by the propagandists of the Kremlin should be debunked. The "peace-loving people's democracy" must be shown up for what it is—a totalitarian despotism bent upon conquest by subversion, or if need be by force. Communism as a weapon of subversion must be exposed. Its appeal lies in the fact that since the early days of the Russian revolution it has carried overtones of a release from oppression. On this account it has proved a useful slogan about which to rally the unwary. But however useful as a slogan, we should recognize and bring others to recognize that in no country, including the Soviet Union, has the visionary and unworkable system of Communism been tried as a form of economic organization. Wherever the power of the Kremlin extends, the form of organization is that of a tyrannical oligarchy enforcing its will on a mass of reluctant serfs by the adroit and unscrupulous use of the secret police. Misrepresented as a liberating movement, Bolshevik imperialism is in fact reaction incarnate. It is Red Fascism, and should be so designated. Other striking examples will no doubt suggest themselves.

Useful topics briefly noted.

American Democracy

Recognizing our shortcomings, we make no claim to perfection. We do claim, however, that we strive to attain it, and that under our system injustices gradually yield to correction and the lot of the average citizen improves from year to year.

Fear

Native Communists in the prisoner states live in constant fear of liquidation from above or vengeance from below. We should recurrently play upon this fear. At the same time we should draw a distinction between those Communists who have behaved in a traitorous manner and who have shared in the responsibility for the sufferings of their fellow citizens, and those Communists who have merely passively accepted the party line as a means of self-preservation. To the latter we should offer the hope that the error of their ways may be forgiven.

Nationalism

We should do everything in our power to fan the flames of nationalism as distinct from chauvinism. Nationalism of the twentieth century contemplates the maintenance of the greatest possible degree of economic, political and cultural autonomy having due regard for the necessity of regional groupings and of world organization. This twentieth century nationalism may prove in the end to be one of the most effective forces working against the ambitions of the Kremlin.

Oppressors Versus Victims

We should make the point as frequently as possible that we never cease to distinguish between oppressors and their victims; that we have the most profound sympathy for the peoples of the prisoner states, including the Russian people; that our quarrel is exclusively with the tyrannical governments which oppress them.

Frank Altschul.

The guidance on the coverage of anti-Semitism was included in RFE's first policy manual, issued in 1951. East European anti-Semitism was a major issue at the time, since many of the defendants of the purge trials that swept the Communist parties of the region were well-known Jewish party officials. Both RFE and RL regularly condemned anti-Semitism in their broadcasts and frequently linked the persecution of Jews to Communist ideology and tactics.

Anti-Semitism

1. Anti-semitism in the Soviet orbit has two aspects. The minor aspect, which is virulent in Hungary and to some extent in Romania, where a relatively large number of Jews still live, is a carry-over from an earlier time, now reinforced by the presence of an appreciable number of Jewish communists in high governmental and party posts. With regard to the status of the Jews of these two countries, RFE's position is as follows:

   a. For Hungary, a special guidance has been written, recommending that Christian speakers warn against making scapegoats of the Jews, and pointing out that Jewish Hungarians suffer equally with other Hungarians under the Rakosi regime; that suffering should unite men and not divide them; and that Rakosi the Communist, not Rakosi the Jew, is the nation's oppressor—the oppressor of Jews and Christians alike.

   b. For Romania the situation is somewhat different. There are said to be 350,000 Jews in the country. By arrangement between Tel Aviv and Bucarest, Jews have been allowed, for about a year past, to leave Romania for Israel (at the reported rate of 2,000 a month). Our Romanian station should <u>not</u> discuss the subject of anti-semitism in order to avoid doing anything which might cause the regime to cancel the arrangement whereby Jews are allowed to leave the country.

2. The major aspect of Soviet anti-semitism is of a new kind for which the Stalinists have found the name of "anti-cosmopolitan-

ism." This is the Soviet-Russian counterpart of Hitlerian anti-semitism. That is to say, it is not a mere sentiment in the population, it is a conscious governmental policy. The German doctrine was founded on the notion of race and "blood"; the Soviet doctrine is founded on the notion of race and history. The Jew is deemed inapt for Sovietism because he is historically a citizen of the world—specifically of the bourgeois world. He is therefore intellectually incapable of loyalty to a doctrine that is marked by two great negatives—for Sovietism is not merely atheistic, it is also not humanistic. Its core is not man—not even man without God; its core is the State, incarnate in a dictator. The Jew is deemed to be innately incapable of worship of the State.

3. Supplementing this fundamental doctrine, three considerations have impelled the Kremlin to intensify its anti-semitism:

a. The awareness of every people behind the Iron Curtain that they are being governed by agents of the Kremlin and exploited in the interest of Soviet imperialism, and the resultant threat of "Titoism," have impelled the Kremlin to try to resolve a contradiction in its rule: it has sought, at one and the same time, to replace "national communists" by more reliable agents, and to pose as the defender of the national aspirations of each of the peoples we address.

The clearest example of how anti-semitism is used to further this purpose is to be seen in Czechoslovakia. In that country the regime began by placing Jewish Communists in "unpopular" functions, particularly the police. Beginning a year ago, when the regime started to crack, Moscow chose its scapegoats among its Jewish agents, both on the highest levels (Slansky) and on lower levels (Frejka, R. Margolius et al). The Czechoslovak purge has been notably a purge of Jews; and an important objective of the purge has been to give emotional satisfaction to people for whom a Jew is a proper scapegoat.

b. Secondly, since the concentration of Soviet fire against the USA (with a considerable diminution of attacks against our allies) the Soviet rulers have bethought themselves that European Jews are people who have relatives and friends in the United States, and that to attack a Jew is to attack a "natural" ally of America. Jewish Communists, therefore, have become "unreliable" communists.

c. Finally, affairs in the Middle East encourage anti-semitism in the Soviet orbit. The Arab nations are anti-Israel; the Jews are pro-Israel. The Arab nations are anti-West; Israelis are pro-West. The West is "capitalist;" or at least anti-communist. Ergo. . .

4. This situation, which is clear enough in Czechoslovakia, is not one of which RFE can take advantage in Romania at this time, for the reason cited in par. 1 (b) above. It may be exploited in Hungary (chiefly) and in Poland, not in broadcasts to the nation at large but in scripts addressed directly to the Jewish members of the regime. We are already pointing out to members of the several regimes that their careers are, of necessity, short; their triumph can only be brief, in the nature of things. They are like the King-priest of Nemi (see Fraser, The Golden Bough, vol. I, ch. 1) who must prowl day and night, weapon in hand, because he who became king by murdering his predecessor is doomed to be succeeded by one who will murder him. To the Jewish official we say that his insecurity is greater than that of his Christian colleague because the Politburo, exactly like the Nazis, refuses to believe what everybody else know to be true—that a Jew can be a loyal citizen of his political nation.

5. We take appropriate occasion to make clear that RFE is anti-racist on principle: that as Poles, Czechs, Slovaks, Hungarians, Romanians, Bulgarians, Albanians, we know that so-called race theories are scientific absurdities and we believe in the brotherhood of man under the fatherhood of God.

The 1957 country paper for Hungary is interesting for several reasons. To begin with, the paper was drafted by the State Department and imposed on RFE and the Voice of America as a broad guideline for coverage. This was the first country guidance issued after the 1956 Hungarian Revolution, and its language and tone reflect the American government's determination to bring the policies of its foreign broadcasting stations in line with the government's policy toward Eastern Europe. The paper is also important for its instruction that RFE should regard itself more as a European station rather than an American station.

SECRET [stamped on original document]
Approved by Committee on Radio
Broadcasting Policy, 20 August 1957

RFE BROADCASTING POLICY
TOWARD HUNGARY

I. Objectives:

In the interest of assuring maximum possible impact and effectiveness of the total U.S. broadcasting effort directed to the USSR and to the Soviet-dominated countries of eastern Europe, the methods and aims of both official and unofficial American radio stations broadcasting to the area have been thoroughly reviewed in the light of current U.S. policy objectives. In accordance with instructions of the Committee on Radio Broadcasting Policy, upon whose request this review has been undertaken, individual papers have been prepared for each of the target countries on each of the broadcasting operations concerned, outlining the role each should play in the furtherance of both general and specific American objectives in the area, and recommending such changes or modifications of present operating practices as may seem desirable to this end.

The following paper concerns only Radio Free Europe broadcasts to Hungary. It establishes practices and policies to be followed by Ra-

dio Free Europe in its broadcasts to Hungary with a view to assuring
close conformity of the activities and aims of the station with current
policy objectives of the U.S. with respect to Hungary and to achieving
maximum effectiveness in this regard by defining RFE as a "gray"
station a constructive and essential role, clearly distinct from that of the
official Voice of America.

II. Policy Considerations:

A. Background of U.S. Policies:

The fundamental objectives of U.S. policy are to preserve the security of the U.S. and the vitality of its fundamental values and institutions, and to promote the general
welfare of its people.

The greatest threat to these objectives at present is the
Soviet Union, with its determination to destroy all rival power.

There is no foreseeable prospect of significantly reduc-
ing Soviet military strength, which is the core of Communist
power, except by mutually acceptable agreements with the
Soviets or by large-scale military action. The initiation of
such military action is not an acceptable course for the U.S.

Accordingly, it is U.S. policy, approved June 3, 1957, to
seek (a) to affect the conduct and policies of the Communist
regimes, especially of the Soviet Union, in ways that further
U.S. interests; and (b) to foster tendencies that lead them to
abandon expansionist policies. This offers the best hope of
bringing about at least a prolonged period of armed truce,
and ultimately a peaceful and orderly world. . . .

In the exploitation of Soviet bloc vulnerabilities, it is
national policy, approved June 3, 1957, that the U.S. should
seek to:

a. Promote evolutionary changes in Soviet policy and conduct in ways that further U.S. and Free World security;

b. Weaken the ties which link the Soviet Union and Communist China and their Satellites;

c. Encourage bureaucratic and popular pressures inside the bloc for greater emphasis by the regimes on their internal problems; the effort should be to pose the necessity of devoting attention and resources to solve them or facing increased disaffection if they are ignored;

d. Undermine the faith of the Communist ruling classes in their own system and ideology.

B. U.S. Policy Toward Hungary:

In the foregoing context, U.S. policy toward Hungary plays an important but a definitely subsidiary role. All actions with regard to Hungary must be considered with regard to their effect on the overall situation, particularly with reference to U.S. efforts to affect the conduct and policies of the Soviet Union.

Among long-term U.S. objectives are the complete independence of Hungary from Soviet domination and the establishment in Hungary of a representative government resting upon the consent of the people.

Recognizing the unlikelihood of attainment of this goal through internal revolutionary means, our short-term aim is to foster an evolutionary development resulting in the weakening of Soviet controls and the progressive attainment of natural independence. In doing this, we must seek to maintain the morale and the hopes of the Hungarian people, while indicating that their basic problems can only be solved in the long-term by pacific means and that patience and enduring quiet effort will be required on their part.

An initial U.S. objective is to encourage, as a first step toward eventual full national independence and freedom, the establishment of a "national Communist" regime which, though it may continue to be in close political and military alliance with the USSR will be able to exercise to a much greater degree than in the past independent authority and control in the direction of its own affairs, primarily confined in the first stage to its internal affairs. However, "national Communism" and other tendencies and developments which may tend to weaken Soviet controls but which in themselves retain a basically authoritarian character do not offer solutions consonant with the ultimate aspirations of U.S. policy toward Hungary. Though they may be judiciously exploited in the interest of the immediate objective of promoting greater Hungarian independence from Moscow, exploitation should never be in the manner or to a degree detrimental in the long-run to the genuinely democratic and Western tendencies and developments which exist within Hungary.

The immediate goal of U.S. policy toward Hungary is to attempt to maintain the deep-seated psychological animus towards the USSR and Soviet communism which expressed itself in the October revolt, and to help preserve such of the gains achieved in the course of that revolt as may be feasible. These gains include greater freedom for the peasant, and a trend away from forcible collective farming. While they may be more emotional and temporary than concrete and permanent, these gains are nonetheless important as a step toward our immediate goal of bringing about a loosening of the ties between Hungary and the USSR. In carrying out this policy, it should be underlined that it is neither feasible nor desirable for us to run the risk of either local or general hostilities. . . .

III. The Role for Radio Free Europe:

The general nature and content of broadcasts to Hungary will be adapted to the characteristics of Radio Free Europe as (1) a voice of the people of free Western nations dedicated to the interests of the people of East Europe, and (2) an instrument, unattributable to the U.S. Government, for the furthering of U.S. policy objectives.

A. U.S. policy will control the overall policy position on RFE.

1. While its broadcasts must adhere to U.S. policy in general and avoid positions which would produce a net result injurious to U.S. policy, RFE will, at the same time, maintain flexibility and objectivity. With respect to the internal and external affairs of the U.S. which merit treatment in news to Hungary, RFE will report objectively, giving fair coverage to legitimate points of view which are not necessarily in accord with the public position of the U.S. Government.

2. Unannounced U.S. foreign policy will from time to time be conveyed to RFE. As an instrument for furthering unannounced policy, RFE will be governed strictly by the policy guidance furnished to it through appropriate channels. This guidance will relate to specific events and conditions and may, in some instances, appear to be in conflict with announced policy. (In most instances, guidance on unannounced U.S. policy will relate to objectives which can be undertaken by RFE as an unattributable radio, but which would be inadvisable or inappropriate positions to be taken by an official organ or spokesman of the U.S. Government.)

3. RFE will seek by all practicable means to broaden and improve its news coverage of world affairs and its cross reporting of events in the Sino-Soviet orbit. In its coverage of world news RFE will strike an appropriate balance between the need to avoid the appearance of an American propaganda instrument, and the interest in U.S. affairs which follows normally from recognition by the Hungarian audience that the United States is the keystone of the free world. In seeking this balance RFE will be guided by (a) impartial and objective selection of news based on its news value to Hungarians, and the reporting and commenting on such news from a viewpoint consistent with its representation of the people of the free world as distinguished

from its covert representation of U.S. policy, and (b) recognition that the principal role of official radios broadcasting to Hungary is to reflect the American point of view and to cover "Americana"; RFE broadcasts in this area should generally be in the European context as seen through European eyes. In its cross reporting of events in the Sino-Soviet orbit, RFE will place emphasis on coverage and comment relating to events and developments which serve to illustrate inconsistencies in the application of Communist methods, conflicts in interpretation of Communist doctrines among the orbit countries, and will treat extensively the gains in other satellite areas in the direction of liberalization and lessening of Soviet control.

4. RFE will avoid a tendentiously negative approach in its broadcasts to Hungary and, when possible, inject constructive criticism into its commentaries. The general tone of its broadcasts will be pro-Western, as distinguished from anti-Communist. Attacks on communist institutions will be characterized to the greatest possible extent by positive suggestions and commentaries which will illustrate for Hungarians possible means for overcoming the evils and defects of such institutions. (RFE will use "black book" technique for exposure of actions by Communist individuals and harsh conditions and excesses, provided the highest degree of care is exercised in the pre-broadcast development and authentication of the facts.)

5. RFE discussions of communist institutions and regime practices will be based on the presumption, rendered irrefutable by the October 1956 revolution, that Hungarians are almost unanimous in their hatred of the communist system and their will to resist Soviet domination. On this basic presumption, discussion and commentary will never suggest to Hungarians that the West has forgotten the lesson of the revolution; it will recognize that Hungarians have no need for purely negative discussions in refutation of communist ideology or condemnation of Soviet practices; but it will not neglect the small but influential group

of intellectuals and convinced Government officials who continue to represent a target for discussions of Marxist/Leninist ideologies.

This same basic presumption dictates the need for a positive practical approach to Hungarian audiences which will implicitly recognize the Hungarian national will to be free of Soviet domination, which will be sympathetic to the enormous difficulties in the way of liberation from the Soviets, but which will illustrate for the Hungarians the world-wide sympathy which their efforts to gain freedom from Soviet domination have won for them. Emphasis will be placed on reporting to Hungarians on the damaging effect which their revolution has had on the world communist movement.

6. Although the U.S. Government and its official media maintain a position of non-interference in the internal affairs of other nations, it is permissible and desirable that RFE, within the limitations indicated in this paper, concern itself with the internal affairs to those matters which have a material bearing on subservience to the USSR, regime practices, legislation and control, and similar factors, the discussion of which will serve to promote policy objectives of the U.S. vis a vis Hungary. RFE will be sensitive to the will of the Hungarian populace and avoid involvement in affairs which Hungarians in general regard as peculiarly the concern of themselves.

7. In its discussion of Hungarian internal political affairs, RFE will not present itself specifically as the voice of the internal opposition to the regime, but it will seek to adapt its programs, insofar as consistent with the policies expressed in this paper, to points of view sympathetic to the Hungarian audience or to specific segments thereof. In making reference to the Kadar regime, RFE will not refer to it as a "government," and will make clear to Hungarians that the West regards the Kadar regime as nothing more

than a puppet which masks the Soviet occupation and responds primarily to the manipulations of the Kremlin.

8. In its discussion of international affairs and political systems RFE will attempt to convey to Hungarians the impression that the West wants for Hungarians a form of government of their own free choice, a government freely chosen and representative of the Hungarian people. While democratic rather than authoritarian forms should be made to seem more attractive, RFE will in no way suggest that the West seeks to impose any particular form of government on Hungary. RFE will not indulge in direct endorsements of the advantages of the various forms of freely chosen governments. RFE will combat the Soviet propaganda line which seeks to picture Western governments as adhering rigidly to the late 19th century pattern of capitalism by pointing to the progressive reforms enjoyed in free nations.

9. RFE will take steps toward a strengthening of its posture as a reflector of the free world to Hungarians. It will increase emphasis on European ideas, events and prospects for the future, both to lay foundations for future association of East European countries in the European Community, and to demonstrate the practices and achievements of free world peoples by the example of European nations whose traditions, resources and physical situations are nearest to those of the audience. This will be accomplished over a period of time by:

> Development of appropriate relationships with "European" organizations, whose expressed interest and practical cooperation will balance the previous identification of RFE with the U.S. alone among the Free World peoples.

> Greater use of European materials, points of view and speakers.

Emphasis on European integration and cooperation movements and trends, with frequent and explicit discussion of the potential role of Hungary in a free community. This discussion would exclude any direct or implied suggestion that Hungary join any western military alliance.

Discontinuation of identification of broadcasts to Hungary as the "Voice of Free Hungary," and the substitution of "This is the Hungarian Service of Radio Free Europe," or some similar designation, to be agreed upon which will foster the "European" concept of RFE while at the same time maintaining the identification of the broadcasts as specifically for and in the service of Hungarians. The approach that RFE represents the views of Hungarian political opposition, or any suggestion that it is an outlet for Hungarian emigre political opinion is to be abandoned.

10. Although RFE will not serve as an organ for the political views as such of the Hungarian emigration, under established policy controls it will make liberal use of outstanding recent Hungarian refugees for both programming and broadcasting purposes, and it will give coverage to those organizations and activities of the new emigration which will serve to convince Hungarians that the free world has not forgotten their heroic revolution and the aspirations of the Hungarian people.

B. In the implementation of the immediate goals of U.S. policy toward Hungary, RFE's programming will be directed toward:

1. Maintaining Hungarian belief in the continuing moral support and understanding of the peoples of the West for Hungarian people in their struggle. Emphasis will be placed on the theme that in the West, Hungary, because of its tradi-

tions and culture, is thought of as a logical and natural member of the community of western European nations.

2. Encouraging regime leaders and functionaries, especially potentially defectionist elements within the regime, to reckon with the eventual freedom of Hungary from Soviet domination, to question the security of their own future, and to think of courses of action independent of Moscow.

3. Encouraging but urging restraint upon the forces of Hungarian nationalism and patriotism, the desire for national independence and the hatred of foreign domination.

4. Satisfying the Hungarian hunger for western intellectual and cultural contacts.

5. Making clear that free men sympathize with those who are resisting regime measures of repression of intellectual and cultural expression.

6. Assuring that Hungarians are accurately and currently informed on events in the free world, in Hungary and within the Sino-Soviet orbit.

7. Negating tendencies toward belief in Hungary that RFE is a spokesman for a rightist West which, by blanket condemnation of all things communistic, appears to condemn some present institutions in Hungary which were established under communist rule and badly administered, but which the majority of Hungarians regard in principle as beneficial; such as land reform, including church estates, nationalization of basic industry, and the broadening of various social benefits to all social classes of the nation.

8. Encouraging thinking of solutions for internal Hungarian political and economic problems in the light of free Europe analogies. In this connection the examples of Finland and Austria may provide useful analogies.

9. Encouraging any developments assisting an evolutionary change in Hungarian political, economic and social life toward more liberal forms.

10. Encouraging Hungarians to measure the degree of basic human rights granted to them in terms of their religious beliefs and the doctrine of dignity and freedom of men...

This guidance on the coverage of Lenin was issued by Radio Liberty in 1970. It reflects the spirit of détente, which set the tone for U.S.-Soviet relations at the time. In many respects, this is a remarkably sympathetic document that presents the founder of Soviet communism in a generally favorable light.

Radio Liberty   October 30, 1970
Program Policy Division

BROADCAST GUIDANCE
RL'S TREATMENT OF LENIN

Assumptions

Of all the top revolutionary leaders, Lenin is the only one to retain real respect and authority among a considerable segment of RL's audience. This is partly the result of propaganda, partly due to the fact that Lenin died at a very convenient time (during NEP, before collectivization, etc.); and, that by contrast with the years of Stalin's rule, he is associated with both the best and most heroic aspects of Bolshevik rule. It is, however, mainly among the lower and the middle strata of population that the cult of Lenin is still deeply rooted. The intellectuals, to a very large extent, have become more critical and usually do not accept the cliches of official propaganda. Youth, especially youth of school age, are submitted to the strongest indoctrination, but saturation breeds indifference and Lenin's image is often relegated to the limbo of a remote and irrelevant past.

An unforeseen by-product of what <u>Komsomolskaya Pravda</u> called the "pomposity and bombast" surrounding the Lenin centenary has been the growing awareness—acute among intellectuals—that the Lenin presented to them by the party is a propaganda creation designed not to celebrate Lenin the man but to serve current party goals. It is probable that Lenin the human being—a man with a sense of privacy and personal modesty, simple in his wants, and an opponent of ceremony—would have been shocked to find himself sanctified, and appalled at the way his successors have wrapped themselves in the mantle of his name to justify pseudo-Leninist policies. Yet he would probably also have acknowledged ruefully that for the sake of an ideal he bequeathed to Soviet society the elements that made possible such distortion—the single party, the bureaucracy the secret police, and the ban on organized opposition that form the basis of the present leadership's power.

It should be assumed, on the other hand, that most party members have a very high esteem for Lenin and that the best of them consider a "return to Leninist norms" as the best remedy against the abuses of Stalinism. Among all elements of the population there persists in general a strong positive attitude toward Lenin and the democratic ideal with which he is identified. Even among more sophisticated individuals who do not accept the "Lenin myth" the positive aspects of his thought are useful in arguing for desired reforms within the system.

In the national republics, Lenin's particular role towards specific national groups may have left an impact that is still remembered by the present generations. Thus, it is possible, for instance, that in Armenia, Azerbayjan, and Georgia, Lenin is still resented as the leader who liquidated national independence, while in the Tatar and Bashkir republics, Lenin's image may have the more positive overtone of a statesman who prompted national autonomy. On the whole, it appears that with time particular national grievances or sympathies in connection with Lenin are gradually being replaced by general concern with more current issues. Those arguing for an extension of national rights are known to rely on Lenin's statements and approach to nationalities' policies as opposed to Stalin's. But many listeners may not be fully aware of the controversy between Lenin and Stalin on this question.

Objectives

1. To show our audience that the officially propagated Lenin legend has little relation to the man and his work. To "demythologize" Lenin by presenting an objective historical perspective, paying him due respect when warranted by historical truth and criticizing his stand or views when they deserve it. To disprove the concept of Leninism as a clear-cut infallible guide to all problems at all times, demonstrating the inconsistency within his own thought and the lack of continuity between Lenin's thought and the sys-

tem he created as well as between Lenin on the one hand, and on
the other, Stalin and subsequent regimes.

2. To assist listeners to think critically about both the positive and
negative aspects of Lenin and Leninist doctrine and where and
how the democratic ideals they associate with Lenin failed to be
realized in Soviet life. To encourage them to counterpose Soviet
realities today to the more positive ideals of Leninism and to explore in what ways these ideals could be realized.

Treatment

RL's approach to all topics dealing with Lenin is very cautious.
Extreme care is taken to avoid any emotional and propagandistic tone.
All emphasis is laid on <u>historical</u> facts. We point out that there were, in
fact, three different aspects in Lenin:

    a. the Lenin before 1917 whose activities were aimed at con-
        vincing and converting potential supporters. A Lenin of gran-
        diose promises for the future; a Lenin insisting on democratic
        principles and human rights;

    b. the Lenin of the Revolution—the heroic and cruel utopian
        who hoped to achieve world revolution and establish a so-
        cialist society by decrees;

    c. the post-revolutionary Lenin who had to drop myths and
        face pragmatic reality. A Lenin who had to abandon or revise
        some of his theoretical principles in order to keep and
        strengthen the grip of power.

We show that it is this many-sided aspect of Lenin which is ignored by official hagiography. Also, it is on the basis of Lenin's contradictions that it is possible for progressive dissenters to quote from Lenin
to justify their causes, just as it is equally easy for the conservatives to
quote the same source in order to denounce any departures from
whatever happens to be the orthodox line of the day.

RL gives a true picture of Lenin the man—contemporary memoirs of people personally associated with Lenin as well as works by
present-day authorities should be used in preference to station-origi-

nated comment. Particular care is taken to avoid any derogatory terminology, which can only alienate listeners and affect adversely the station's credibility. Facts should speak for themselves. It is not the task of RL to denounce Lenin, but to analyze his life and work in the light of objective, historical criteria. RL juxtaposes the different aspects of Lenin's personality and notes that attempts to bring out those views and statements of Lenin which might further progressive reforms in the Soviet system if seriously implemented and which expose the lack of a genuine ideological basis in current Soviet practices.

Lenin revised Marx. This theme, when well-documented, could serve as an excellent platform for the next step: if Lenin found the time ripe to revise Marx, is it not time to revise Lenin in the light of the realities of the second half of the twentieth century?

In treating the whole theme of Lenin and "Leninism" we do not hide the fact that many of the most objectionable practices of Stalinism were rooted in Lenin's teachings and actions—e.g., the concept of terror against political prisoners, the introduction of invectives into political polemics, systematic destruction of traditional and universal moral standards, etc., ruthless persecution of religion, disregard of and cavalier attitude to the heritage of the national past and its treasures.

We also point out that Lenin is practically the only Bolshevik leader whom the present party leadership can describe as a true Communist, Marxist, etc. Indeed, most of the others who were close associates of Lenin—Trotsky, Bukharin, etc.—were repressed by Stalin. We emphasize Lenin's close association and respect for many of those who were, or still are, un-persons.

All shows dealing with Lenin and "Leninism" should be oriented towards present-day issues. We are not primarily interested in history per se and our efforts at demythologizing the Lenin cult are aimed at promoting "glasnost" and at a better understanding of the present situation. We keep in mind the general tedium surrounding Lenin as a topic in the wake of the CPSU's hollow overemphasis during the centennial. RL programming avoids polemics with Soviet statements and carping at specific assertions in Soviet media, and concentrates on initiating its own discussion of Lenin in connection with topics and themes where a real understanding of Lenin or his positions would substantially illuminate present situations and alternatives.

Notes

1. "It Will Be Seen Who Is Right"

1. The quotes from Jackson, Peroutka, and Tigrid came from transcripts of May 1, 1951, broadcasts located in the Radio Free Europe corporate archives in Washington, D.C. Transcript of C.D. Jackson's press conference are also in RFE corporate archives.

2. Childs and Whitton, *Propaganda by Short Wave*, 4–5.

3. Ibid., 12–18, 35–37.

4. Ibid., 44–48.

5. Browne, *International Broadcasting*, 96–100; Tyson, *U.S. International Broadcasting*, 5–12.

6. Mickelson, *America's Other Voice*, 14–16; Miscamble, *George F. Kennan, 1947–1950*, 203–5; James McCargar, interview with author.

7. DeWitt C. Poole to Joseph Grew, February, 16, 1949. Noting Kennan's intention to retire from government service, Poole writes, "Since George was the original father of our enterprise we shall certainly lose something from his departure from government."

8. From *Foreign Relations of the United States, Russia, 1919,* Department of State, publication 987, 42–43.

9. Dulles address to Bond Club of New York, May 6, 1948.

10. Thomas, *Very Best Men,* 60–62.

11. Simpson, *Blowback,* 8–9, 100–101, 171–72.

12. Altschul memorandum, July 17, 1950.

13. "Fight False Propaganda With Truth," text of Truman speech, *New York Times,* April 19, 1950.

14. Thomas, *Very Best Men,* 29–30.

15. May, *American Cold War Strategy,* 29, 35, 74.

16. Isaacson and Thomas, *Wise Men,* 282.

17. Holt, *Radio Free Europe,* 233.

18. From introductory remarks at press conference announcing formation of FEC, June 1, 1949; Mickelson, *America's Other Voice,* 19–22; Henze, interview; McCargar, interview.

19. Poole to Grew, June 10, 1949; Henze, interview; McCargar, interview.

20. Browne, *International Broadcasting,* 132–35; Tyson, *U.S. International Broadcasting,* 12–14.

21. Text of Altschul speech, 1951.

22. Jackson memorandum, n.d.; also see *Time* magazine, January 29, 1950, 19.

23. *New York Times*, October 22, 1953, 17.

24. Quoted in Collins, *Free Europe Committee,* 86.

25. Jackson to H.D. Paine Jr., January 22, 1951.

26. Kovrig, *Myth of Liberation,* 102–3.

27. Joseph Grew, "National Committee for a Free Europe," *American Foreign Service Journal*, September 1949.

28. Herbert Gross memorandum, April 14, 1950.

29. DeWitt C. Poole to John C. Hughes, June 9, 1950.

30. Memorandum on meeting of RFE planning committee, July 8, 1950.

31. Memorandum, November 16, 1950.

32. Mickelson, *America's Other Voice,* 24–30.

33. Undated RFE press release.

34. Numerous internal memoranda show DeWitt Poole and Frank Altschul expressing exasperation over the lack of government guidance on policy matters.

2. Crusade for Freedom

1. The description of the Freedom Bell dedication is taken from *The Story of the World Freedom Bell,* published by the Crusade for Freedom, n.d.

2. Mickelson, *America's Other Voice,* 51–54.

3. Ibid., 51–58.

4. Collins, *Free Europe Committee,* 291.

5. Ibid., 285–86.

6. Comptroller General of the United States, *U.S. Government Monies Provided to Radio Free Europe and Radio Liberty,* 101.

7. Meyer, *Facing Reality,* 115–16.

8. Ibid., 116–17.

9. Altschul memorandum, November 1, 1950.

10. Altschul memorandum of conversation, July 17, 1950.

11. Altschul memorandum, May 28, 1950.

12. William Griffith, interview with author; Henze, interview; Jan Nowak, interview with author.

13. Meyer, *Facing Reality,* 118.

14. Nowak, interview.

15. Altschul memorandum, November 6, 1950.

16. Lang memorandum, October 15, 1974.

17. Henze, interview; Nowak, interview.

18. David Binder, "Embattled Radio Free Europe Defends Role," *New York Times,* March 15, 1971.

19. John Foster Leich, "Great Expectations: The National Councils in Exile: 1950–1960," *Polish Review* 35, no. 3/4 (1990).

20. John Foster Leich, interview with author; J. Russell Poole, interview with author; Stanley Leinwoll, interview with author; Henze, interview; Nowak, interview.

21. Archibald S. Alexander to C.D. Jackson, July 25, 1960.

22. The controversy over Polish broadcasts is discussed in chapter 7.

23. Smith memorandum, May 16, 1962; Poole, interview.

24. Nathan memorandum, November 15, 1960.

25. Ibid.

26. Internal RFE memorandum, June 15, 1960.

3. The Mills of God Grind Slowly

1. See Lewis, *Polish Volcano,* 25–36; Karpinski, *Count-Down,* 30–35.

2. Michie, *Voices Through the Iron Curtain,* 164–66; Holt, *Radio Free Europe,* 140–42.

3. Radio Free Europe press release, n.d.

4. Karpinski, *Count-Down,* 102–3.

5. Frank Altschul memorandum, November 1, 1950.

6. Mickelson, *America's Other Voice,* 26–30. Henze, interview; McCargar, interview; Ralph Walter, interview with author.

7. Frank Altschul memorandum, November 1, 1950; W. Griffith, interview; Nowak, interview; Henze, interview; McCargar, interview; Walter, interview.

8. John Foster Leich, "Great Expectations: The National Councils in Exile, 1950–1960," *Polish Review* 35, no. 3/4 (1990).

9. Undated Crusade for Freedom press release.

10. Nowak, interview.

11. W. Griffith, interview; Henze, interview; Nowak, interview.

12. Mickelson, *America's Other Voice,* 23–24; Henze, interview.

13. *New York Times,* July 9, 1950.

14. Altschul memorandum, October 10, 1950.

15. W. Griffith, interview; Henze, interview; Nowak, interview; Walter, interview.

16. Radio Free Europe Policy Manual.

17. Ibid.

18. Ibid.

19. Special Guidance No. 5 on the Czechoslovak Trials, November 22, 1952.

20. William Rafael memorandum, March 21, 1952.

21. Internal memorandum, May 13, 1951.

22. Galantiere memorandum, June 30, 1952.

23. Galantiere memorandum, October 4, 1951.

24. Internal RFE report, September 1953.

25. S. Brucan, "Slave Drivers Preaching Liberty," *Scinteia,* February 24, 1951, quoted in Alfred Weld memorandum, May 17, 1951.

26. Holt, *Radio Free Europe,* 70–72; Michie, *Voices Through the Iron Curtain,* 52–58; Henze, interview; W. Griffith, interview; Walter, interview.

27. Undated Crusade for Freedom press release.

28. Kenneth Campbell, "Radio Free Europe Adopts Red Tactic," *New York Times,* May 23, 1951.

29. Internal RFE memorandum, September 21, 1951.

30. Michie, *Voices Through the Iron Curtain,* 71–79; RFE teletype message, September 13, 1951.

31. Michie, *Voices Through the Iron Curtain,* 71–79.

32. Ibid.

33. Quoted in Collins, *Free Europe Committee,* 197.

34. Joanna M. Wandycz, "Radio Free Europe: A Key Player in the Downfall of Communism in Poland" (master's thesis, Univ. of Indiana, 1995).

35. Henze, interview.

36. Radio Free Europe Policy Manual; Lovestone attended early meetings of the NCFE's radio committee, where he made recommendations on personnel matters, information gathering, and labor coverage; General Minutes of Radio Committee meeting, March 23, 1950. RFE Archives.

37. William Rafael memorandum, September 21, 1950.

38. Paul Henze memorandum, August 6, 1953.

39. Deák, interview.

40. Spencer Phenix memorandum, June 18, 1953.

41. Berle et al., *Navigating the Rapids,* 628.

42. Peroutka memorandum, June 17, 1953.

43. Policy guidance, June 20, 1953.

44. Gerald Steibel, interview with author; W. Griffith, interview; Henze, interview.

45. Peroutka memorandum, June 17, 1953.

46. Policy guidance, July 21, 1953.

47. Policy guidance, July 11, 1953.

48. Internal memorandum, August 1953.

49. Information from translations of Hungarian service scripts in RFE archives.

50. Berle et al., *Navigating the Rapids,* 631.

4. "We Tore a Big Hole in the Iron Curtain"

1. Mickelson, *America's Other Voice,* 56–57.

2. Collins, *Free Europe Committee,* 201.

3. Abbott Washburn, interview with author; Mickelson, *America's Other Voice,* 56.

4. Michie, *Voices Through the Iron Curtain,* 137.

5. Frederick Sondern, "Balloons Across the Iron Curtain," *Reader's Digest,* January 1953, 61; Michie, *Voices Through the Iron Curtain,* 136–41.

6. *News from Behind the Iron Curtain* (RFE newsletter), July 1953, 23; Michie, *Voices Through the Iron Curtain,* 140.

7. "Operation Veto," internal RFE document; *News from Behind the Iron Curtain,* July 1954, 34, and August 1955, 38–39; Michie, *Voices Through the Iron Curtain,* 144–54.

8. "An Estimate of the Effectiveness of FEP Balloon Operations," internal report, August 1, 1955.

9. Michie, *Voices Through the Iron Curtain,* 160–63.

10. Ibid., 157–58.

11. *News from Behind the Iron Curtain,* December 1954, 38–45.

12. "Estimate of the Effectiveness of FEP Balloon Operations," August 1, 1955.

13. Collins, *Free Europe Committee,* 225–28.

14. Alton Kastner, interview with author.

15. Lang correspondence to FEC executive committee, March 1, 1955.

16. "Estimate of the Effectiveness of FEP Balloon Operations," August 1, 1955.

17. Ibid.

5. Right-Wingers and Revanchists

1. Mickelson, *America's Other Voice,* 24–26; Henze, interview.

2. Karpinski, interview.

3. Passages from Prague Radio appeared in an RFE report on the reaction to broadcasts of the Voice of Free Czechoslovakia, issued in October 1953.

4. W. Griffith, interview; Henze, interview.

5. Reyman, interview.

6. C.D. Jackson memorandum, June 21, 1951; Walter, interview; W. Griffith, interview; Henze, interview.

7. Henze, interview; Walter, interview.

8. Summary of minutes of meeting on RFE policy held in Munich, October 7, 1951.

9. Nowak, interview; Henze, interview; Walter, interview.

10. W. Griffith to Galantiere, June 25, 1951.

11. Galantiere memorandum, November 10, 1952.

12. Memorandum, Galantiere to Whitney Shepardson, March 12, 1956.

13. *Rheinischer Merkur,* October 17, 1952, translation in RFE archives.

14. Minutes of RFE leadership meeting, August 30, 1952.

15. Galantiere memorandum to Robert Lang, November 10, 1952.

16. Robert Lang memorandum to FEC board, November 25, 1951.

17. Langendorf memorandum, September 20, 1954.

18. Minutes of RFE leadership meeting, January 6, 1955.

19. "Attacks on RFE by Slovak and Sudeten Groups," internal report, January 30, 1958.

20. W. Griffith to Jackson, December 26, 1951.

21. Hickenlooper to Sarnoff, December 20, 1951; Jackson to Sarnoff, January 9, 1952.

22. *New York Herald Tribune,* February 15, 1954.

23. Galantiere memorandum, March 16, 1954.

24. "Summary of Available Personality Information," internal RFE memorandum on Peroutka, November 16, 1954.

25. Samuel Walker memorandum, February 8, 1954; Reyman, interview.

26. Thomas Myers memorandum, June 25, 1955.

27. W. Griffith, interview; Henze, interview; Nowak, interview; Walter, interview.

28. Galantiere memorandum, May 13, 1955.

29. Henze, interview; Walter, interview.

30. "Kersten Committee in Munich," foreign service dispatch, n.d., in RFE archives.

31. Barnouw, *Image Empire* 2:134.

32. This and subsequent Lewis quotes from transcripts of radio scripts in RFE archives.

33. "Mr. Lewis and Radio Free Europe," *National Review,* March 29, 1958.

6. Revolution in Hungary and Crisis at Radio Free Europe

1. See Thomas, *Very Best Men,* 142–52

2. See, for example, Brands, *Devil We Knew,* 184; Walker, *Cold War,* 109.

3. Walter, interview.

4. For government handling of the secret speech, see Cline, *CIA Under Reagan, Bush, and Casey,* 185–87.

5. Holt, *Radio Free Europe,* 65; Michie, *Voices Through the Iron Curtain,* 171–73.

6. Meyer, *Facing Reality,* 123.

7. Holt, *Radio Free Europe,* 175.

8. Ibid.

9. Ibid., 177–78.

10. Information on Hungarian language scripts in RFE internal memoranda, June 1956.

11. Nowak, interview; Henze, interview; Walter, interview.

12. "Hungarian Refugee Opinion," January 1957, based on a sample of refugees in displaced persons camps in the United States conducted by RFE; opinion survey among Hungarian refugees in Austria, conducted November 22–26 by Institut fuer Markt und Meinungsforschung.

13. W. Griffith, interview.

14. Paul Henze memorandum, June 7, 1955.

15. Ibid.

16. Confidential report issued in September 1956, probably by the State Department.

17. W. Griffith memorandum, September 26, 1956

18. Holt, *Radio Free Europe,* 181–85; Meyer, *Facing Reality,* 126–30; Henze, interview; Nowak, interview; Walter, interview.

19. Holt, *Radio Free Europe,* 181–85; Henze, interview; Nowak, interview; Walter, interview.

20. Interview with Gyula Borbandi; W. Griffith, interview; Henze, interview; Walter, interview.

21. Bain, *Reluctant Satellites,* 197–208. For other critical accounts of RFE during the revolution, see Lomax, *Hungary, 1956,* 128–29; Barber, *Seven Days of Freedom,* 128–30; and Michener, *Bridge at Andau,* 248–52.

22. W. J. Convery Egan memorandum, November 4, 1956.

23. Correspondence from Egan to Willis Crittenberger, November 27, 1956.

24. Michie, *Voices Through the Iron Curtain,* 255–56; W. Griffith, interview.

25. Condon memorandum, November 20, 1956.

26. Egan memorandum, December 28, 1956.

27. Quoted in Michie, *Voices Through the Iron Curtain,* 251.

28. Quoted in Condon memorandum, January 16, 1957.

29. Egan memorandum, January 28, 1957.

30. Official report of Special Mission to Europe on U.S. Policy Toward the Satellite Nations, Foreign Affairs Committee, United States House of Representatives, report issued May 16, 1957.

31. "Report of the Special Committee on the Problem of Hungary," June 20, 1957, 21–22.

32. Internal RFE report, issued December 7, 1956.

33. The Griffith report was issued December 5, 1956.

34. W. Griffith, interview.

35. Quoted from scripts in RFE archives.

36. Borbandi, interview.

37. Michie, *Voices Through the Iron Curtain,* 225.

38. Ibid.

39. Condon memorandum, December 1, 1956; Condon memorandum, December 13, 1956.

40. Egan memorandum, November 4, 1956.

41. Condon memorandum, December 1, 1956.

42. Howard A. Tyner, "In Hungary, Memories of the Pain," *Chicago Tribune,* November 4, 1981.

43. W. Griffith, interview.

44. Central Intelligence Agency memorandum, "Radio Free Europe," November 20, 1956.

45. Eisenhower quoted by Griffith in 1986 interview by Laszlo Ribanszky, chief editor of RFE Hungarian language service.

46. Walter, interview.

7. Peaceful Coexistence

1. Stuart Hannon memorandum, December 10, 1956.

2. Walter, interview; Mrs. Richard Condon, interview with author.

3. Lewis Galantiere memorandum, January 29, 1959; Henze, interview; Walter, interview.

4. Mucio Delgado memorandum, June 24, 1957; Borbandi, interview; Géza Ekecs, interview with author; Walter, interview.

5. Nowak, *Polska z Oddali,* 31–50.

6. Walter, interview.

7. I had access to country papers for Czechoslovakia, Hungary, and Poland for 1957; Walter, interview.

8. 1957 Czechoslovakia Country Paper.

9. Ibid.

10. Jan Nowak memorandum, February 26, 1958; Nowak, interview; Walter, interview.

11. W. Griffith memorandum, January 21, 1957.

12. RFE program guidance, January 18, 1957.

13. Quoted in memorandum of Joseph L. Ranft on RFE coverage of Polish elections, January 25, 1958.

14. Stuart Hannon memorandum, March 7, 1958.

15. John Dunning memorandum, May 8, 1958.

16. Interview with Yale Richmond.

17. Nowak, interview.

18. Griffith memorandum, December 28, 1958.

19. Nowak, *Polska z Oddali,* 77–83.

20. George V. Allen memorandum to President Eisenhower, August 19, 1959.

21. Ibid.

22. Jackson to Ann C. Whitman, secretary to President Eisenhower, September 4, 1959.

23. A description of the dinner meeting is contained in an undated C.D. Jackson memorandum.

24. Nixon, *My Six Crises*, 284–85.

25. Nowak, *Polska z Oddali*, 83–86.

26. Details of the meeting in memorandum from Archibald Alexander, president of the Free Europe Committee, October 22, 1959.

27. Nowak memorandum, October 30, 1959.

28. Mickelson, *America's Other Voice*, 113–16.

29. Ibid.

30. Ibid., 115–17.

31. Henze, interview; McCargar, interview.

32. Mickelson, *America's Other Voice*, 120; Reyman, interview; Walter, interview; Nowak, interview.

33. Zbigniew Brzezinski and William E. Griffith, "Peaceful Engagement in Eastern Europe," *Foreign Affairs*, July 1961, 642–54.

34. Jan Nowak, "Political Broadcasting to the Communist World," internal memorandum, January, 1961.

35. Ibid.

36. Nowak, *Polska z Oddali*, 224–47.

37. Richard Rowson, interview with author; Nowak, interview.

8. "The Iron Curtain Was Not Soundproof"

1. For discussion of rock music's impact on Communist Eastern Europe, see Ryback, *Rock Around the Bloc*.

2. Michie, *Voices Through the Iron Curtain*, 59.

3. Ibid., 56–57.

4. Ibid., 58.

5. Discussion of Ekecs's disc jockey program taken from interviews with Géza Ekecs and Charles Andras.

6. The attacks on the program were published in an RFE publication, *Teenager Party: The RFE Program Which Has Captured the Hungarian Youth*, 1968.

7. The letters to Ekecs were compiled in an RFE publication, *Bridge Building: Listeners' Response to the Broadcasts of the Hungarian Broadcasting Department*, 1965.

9. August 21, 1968

1. Ralph Walter memorandum, January 5, 1968.

2. Excerpt from letter to Professor Jiří Horák, dated February 29, 1968.

3. Walter, interview; Reyman, interview.

4. Walter, interview.

5. Czechoslovakia Country Paper, internal RFE report, 1965.

6. Karel Jezdinský, interview with author.

7. Walter, interview.

8. Reyman, interview.

9. Walter memorandum, July 19, 1968.

10. Walter memorandum, July 20, 1968.

11. Reyman, interview; Walter, interview.

12. Information from Czechoslovak service scripts in RFE archives.

13. Passages from Husák's inaugural speech to the party central committee delivered April 17, 1969, contained in RFE report, "Radio Free Europe and the New Czechoslovak Regime," 1969.

14. Ibid.

10. From Liberation to Liberty

1. Critchlow, *Radio Hole-in-the-Head,* 4.

2. Mickelson, *America's Other Voice,* 59–60.

3. Ibid., 60.

4. Ibid.

5. Ibid.

6. Ibid., 60–62.

7. "Negotiations for an Effective Partnership," internal report of the American Committee for Liberation from Bolshevism, June 1956.

8. Ibid.

9. Ibid.

10. Ibid.

11. Ibid.

12. Ibid.; Jon Lodeesen, personal note, Lodeesen Papers.

13. Ibid.

14. Ibid.

15. Robert F. Kelley memorandum, December 15, 1953.

16. "Negotiations for an Effective Partnership."

17. Ibid.

18. Critchlow, *Radio Hole-in-the-Head,* 11.

19. See chapter 13.

20. Critchlow, *Radio Hole-in-the-Head,* 5, 20.

21. Ibid., 80–82.

22. Mickelson, *America's Other Voice,* 70–72.

23. Ibid., 71–72.

24. "Negotiations for an Effective Partnership."

25. Quoted in Mickelson, *America's Other Voice,* 69.

26. Ibid., 105.

27. "Negotiations for an Effective Partnership."

28. Francis Ronalds, interview with author.

29. Sargeant memorandum to Amcomlib, February 10, 1958.

30. Kelley memorandum, September 19, 1960.

31. Critchlow, *Radio Hole-in-the-Head,* 22–23.

32. Ibid., 84–86; Ronalds, interview.

33. Critchlow, *Radio Hole-in-the-Head*, 15–17; Ronalds, interview.

34. Mickelson, *America's Other Voice,* 109; Ronalds, interview.

35. Mickelson, *America's Other Voice,* 110.

36. Critchlow, *Radio Hole-in-the-Head,* 73–75.

37. Ibid., 101–2.
38. Lodeesen memorandum, December 30, 1969.
39. Lodeesen memorandum, September 15, 1970.
40. Lodeesen memorandum, June 9, 1970.
41. Van der Rhoer memorandum, August 5, 1971.
42. Jon Lodeesen, personal note, in Lodeesen Collection.
43. Ronalds, interview.
44. Mario Corti, interview with author.
45. Vladimir Matusevitch, interview with author.
46. Radio Liberty Policy Manual, 1976.
47. Ibid.
48. Ibid.
49. Solzhenitsyn statement appeared in *New York Times,* April 9, 1972, and is here quoted from *The Right to Know: Report of the President's Study Commission on International Broadcasting,* 1973.

11. The Perils of Ostpolitik

1. Ernst Langendorf memorandum, February 24, 1967.
2. Interview took place October 16, 1969; translation in RFE archives.
3. Karpinski, *Countdown,* 111.
4. Henryk Birecki, letter to *Washington Star,* September 28, 1971.
5. Walter memorandum, March 25, 1970.
6. Ash, *In Europe's Name,* 287.
7. William Marsh, interview with author.
8. Walter memorandum, April 21, 1970.
9. Jan Nowak memorandum, June 9, 1970.
10. Thomas C. Bodin memorandum, September 7, 1970.
11. Enno von Loewenstern, "Is the Red Pencil Riding *Deutsche Welle,"* *Die Zeit,* March 25, 1975.
12. Walter memorandum, May 21, 1970.
13. David Abshire, interview with author; Thomas Barthelemey, interview with author; Walter, interview; Iain Macdonald memorandum, July 28, 1970.
14. Internal memorandum, September 1970.
15. Walter memorandum, March 15, 1971.
16. Radio Free Europe press release, May 24, 1972.
17. Ibid.
18. Walter memorandum, September 7, 1970.
19. Joseph Szabados memorandum, December 22, 1972.
20. Radio Free Europe news report, March 20, 1972.
21. Langendorf memorandum, August 21, 1972.
22. Joe Alex Morris, *International Herald Tribune,* March 24, 1972; Reuter dispatch, March 23, 1972.
23. Walter memorandum, September 13, 1971.
24. Langendorf memorandum, March 25, 1970.
25. James Edwards memorandum, September 29, 1976.
26. Brzezinski, *Power and Principle,* 293; Zbigniew Brzezinski, interview with author.

12. Senator Fulbright's Crusade

1. The Frankel column appeared February 18, 1967 and is quoted here from an internal RFE memorandum on press reaction to the CIA revelations, April, 1967.

2. Quoted from internal RFE memorandum on press reaction to CIA revelations, April, 1967.

3. "C.B.S., In Shift, Denies Its Report of Ending Radio Free Europe Ads," *New York Times,* March 15, 1967.

4. Wise and Ross, *Invisible Government,* 313–27.

5. Marchetti and Marks, *CIA and the Cult of Intelligence,* 167–70; Victor Marchetti, interview with author.

6. Mickelson, *America's Other Voice,* 125.

7. Ibid., 125–26.

8. "Free Europe, Inc. and Radio Liberty Committee, Inc.," internal CIA memorandum, November 13, 1968.

9. "Reactions to Closing of Radio Free Europe and Radio Liberty," internal CIA memorandum, Abbot Smith to Richard Helms, October 26, 1967.

10. "Funding of Radio Free Europe and Radio Liberty," internal CIA memorandum, L.K. White to Richard Helms, November 15, 1968.

11. Berle et al., *Navigating the Rapids,* 677.

12. John Richardson, interview with author.

13. "Free Europe, Inc. and Radio Liberty Committee, Inc.," op. cit.

14. Fulbright, *Crippled Giant,* 20–21, 34.

15. Ibid., 35–36.

16. Ibid., 37–38.

17. Press release from office of Senator Clifford Case, January 23, 1971; "Case Bill Strips Secrecy from Radio Free Europe," *Washington Post,* January 24, 1971.

18. Mickelson, *America's Other Voice,* 129; Leonard Marks, interview with author.

19. Mansfield announced his opposition to the radios in the course of a report which advocated withdrawing American troops from Europe. The report was submitted to the Foreign Relations Committee, July 23, 1973.

20. Fulbright, "The Senate Surrenders," *Progressive,* January, 1973.

21. Fulbright to Shulman, February 24, 1972.

22. Hearings before the Committee on Foreign Relations, United States Senate, on Radio Free Europe and Radio Liberty, 93d Cong., 1st sess., June 12, 1973, 72.

23. *Congressional Record,* February 17, 1972, S2055–S2057.

24. J. Allen Hovey memorandum, January 22, 1972.

25. Internal RFE memorandum, March 1972.

26. *Congressional Record—House of Representatives,* November 19, 1971, H11332.

27. Fulbright to George Ball, March 8, 1972.

28. Eaton to Fulbright, November 22, 1971; Neal to Fulbright, April 12, 1972.

29. Address to American Bankers Association, July 11, 1973.

30. See Curry, *Black Book of Polish Censorship.*

31. Examples taken from "Radio Free Europe Preliminary Annual Report," for fiscal 1972.

32. Ibid.

33. Material of RFE treatment of the 1970 Polish events is taken from "RFE and the Polish December," published by RFE in 1972.

34. Theodore Shabad, "Soviet Liberalizing Hinted If West Acts," *New York Times,* January 14, 1972.

35. Observations of Communist officials compiled in "Radio Free Europe Preliminary Annual Report" for fiscal year 1972.

36. Ibid.

37. Spencer Rich, "Fulbright Blasts Shakespeare, Scott," *Washington Post,* April 10, 1972.

38. Dusko Doder, "Report Urges USIA to Reflect Detente," *Washington Post,* March 5, 1973; David Binder, "USIA Is Set for Major Changes if Study Group Has Its Way," *New York Times,* January 28, 1975.

39. "Muted Voice of America," *Time,* December 16, 1974.

40. Marilyn Berger, "Soviets Halt Jamming of VOA Broadcasts," *Washington Post,* September 13, 1973.

41. Kirill Chenkin, "Voice of America: Mellow But No One Listens," *Los Angeles Times,* March 12, 1974.

42. Robert S. Elegant, "Communists Get Doses of Information," *Los Angeles Times,* March 22, 1971.

43. Halberstam testimony from proceedings of Senate Foreign Relations Committee hearings on Radio Free Europe and Radio Liberty, 93d Cong., 1st sess., June 23, 1973, 136–41.

44. Rowland Evans and Robert Novak, "Fulbright the Jammer," *Washington Post,* February 17, 1972.

45. Mickelson, *America's Other Voice,* 132.

46. Ibid., 143–47.

47. Ibid., 141–42.

48. Ibid., 150–51.

49. *The Right to Know: Report of the President's Study Commission on International Radio Broadcasting,* 1973.

50. "Nixon to Ask Aid for Radio Free Europe," *New York Times,* May 8, 1973.

51. Nowak, *Polska z Oddali,* 326, 332; Mickelson, *America's Other Voice,* 155–56.

52. Comments by American embassy officials in Bucharest were summed up in a memorandum by Ralph Walter, November 18, 1974.

53. Walter, interview.

54. Warsaw embassy criticism summarized in Ralph Walter memorandum, February 7, 1975

55. "The Polish Broadcasts of Radio Free Europe," April 23, 1975.

56. Henry A. Kissinger to William H. Griffith, May 30, 1975.

13. Frequency Wars

1. Stanley Leinwoll, "Jamming—Past, Present, and Future," *World Radio and Television Handbook,* 1980; Leinwoll, interview.

2. Leinwoll, "Jamming."

3. Quoted in "Radio Liberty: Role and Underlying Idea," Radio Liberty Committee, 1972.

4. Mickelson, *America's Other Voice,* 43–50.

5. Ibid., 75–84.

6. Ibid., 171–75.

7. Ibid., 175.

8. Myron Struck, "Posner Criticizes Soviet Jamming of U.S.-funded Radio," *Washington Times,* June 4, 1986.

9. Gary Thatcher, "US Weighs Swapping Radio Broadcast Rights With Soviet Union," *Christian Science Monitor,* October 30, 1986.

10. William Safire, "'You've Got a Deal,'" *New York Times,* November 10, 1986.

11. George Archibald, "USIA Denies Wick Made Airtime Deal with Soviets," *Washington Times,* November 21, 1986; George Archibald, "Heritage Chides Wick for Airtime Swap Deal," *Washington Times,* November 19, 1986; Charles Fenyvesi, "Radio Moscow on Your AM Dial," *U.S. News and World Report,* November 17, 1986.

12. David Binder, "Soviet 'Voice' Jammers Shift to 'Liberty,'" *New York Times,* June 2, 1987.

13. E. Eugene Pell, interview with author.

14. David B. Ottaway, "After 35 Years, Soviets Stop Jamming of U.S. Broadcasts," *Washington Post,* December 1, 1988; "Moscow Stops Jamming American, Other Radio Stations," *Baltimore Sun,* December 1, 1988.

15. Pell, interview.

16. "Pravda Reveals Secret Radio Jamming Department," UPI, March 15, 1989.

17. Leinwoll, interview.

14. Bombs, Spies, Poisoned Umbrellas

1. Michie, *Voices Through the Iron Curtain,* 284–85.

2. Ibid., 285.

3. Bittman, *Deception Game,* 11–12.

4. Ibid., 148–49.

5. The Fatalibey case is described in an unpublished paper by Richard Cummings, former director of security for RFE-RL.

6. RFE internal memorandum, summary of Polish media coverage of Chechowitz press conference, March 11, 1971.

7. Kott, *Still Alive,* 208–9.

8. Ibid.

9. Information on the Minarik case is taken from a memorandum by Richard Cummings and interviews with Karel Jezdinský, a colleague in the Czechoslovak service, and Samko Bellus, service director during Minarik's tenure with RFE.

10. Yuri Handler, interview with author.

11. Tumanov, *Tumanov,* 33–47 and passim.

12. Ibid., 67.

13. Ibid., 83–86.

14. Lev Roitman, interview with author.

15. Handler, interview.

16. Information on the Eidlin case is taken from an account written by Fred Eidlin.

17. Mircea Carp, interview with author; Liviu Floda, interview with author; Robert Hutchings, interview with author; Walter, interview.

18. Pacepa, *Red Horizons,* 162–64.

19. Pacepa, *Red Horizons,* 223–24

20. Richard Cummings, interview with author; Pacepa, *Red Horizons,* 306–8.

21. Ion Mihai Pacepa, interview with author; Nestor Ratesh, interview with author; Carp, interview.

22. See Markov, *Truth That Killed,* Markov's memoirs of his life in the Sofia elite. It includes a number of stories about Zhivkov that were used as the basis for RFE scripts.

23. The most thorough account of the Markov case is contained in an unpublished article by Richard Cummings.

24. Kalugin, *First Directorate,* 178–86.

25. Mickelson, *America's Other Voice,* 5–10.

26. Cummings, interview; unpublished Cummings account based on material from Stasi files.

27. "Bonn Ousts Five Romanians Tied to Radio Free Europe Plot," *Los Angeles Times,* November 10, 1984.

28. Urban, *Radio Free Europe and the Pursuit of Democracy,* 138.

29. See Simpson, *Blowback;* also Loftus, *Belarus Secret.* Though tendentiously argued, both contain useful background on the employment of suspected Nazis by American intelligence.

30. William Kratch, interview; Board of Immigration Appeals decision in Hazners case, July 15, 1981.

31. Transcript, "60 Minutes," May 16, 1982; Jan Zaprudnik, interview with author.

32. Transcript, "60 Minutes"; Kratch, interview.

33. Kratch, interview.

34. Floda, interview; Carp, interview.

35. See transcript of hearing before the Subcommittee on International Operations of the Committee on Foreign Affairs, House of Representatives, February 21, 1980, "Allegations Concerning the Romanian Service of Radio Free Europe."

36. Mike Feinsilber, "Radio Free Europe Broadcast Attacked," *Houston Chronicle,* December 12, 1979.

15. The Reagan Years

1. Gilbert A. Lewthwaite, "U.S. May Cut Radio Staffs in Europe," *Baltimore Sun,* October 26, 1979.

2. Reyman, interview.

3. James F. Brown, interview with author.

4. Ibid.

5. Ibid.

6. Joseph Szabados, interview with author.

7. Ibid.

8. Tyson, *U.S. International Broadcasting,* 64.

9. Brown.

10. John M. Goshko, "Stepped-Up Radio Propaganda Campaign Planned Against Soviets," *Washington Post,* March 12, 1981.

11. Urban, *Radio Free Europe and the Pursuit of Democracy,* 38.

12. Mickelson, *America's Other Voice,* 189–92.

13. Frank Shakespeare, interview with author.

14. McGinniss, *Selling of the President,* 57–58.

15. Shakespeare, interview.

16. William F. Buckley, "Remembering Lane Kirkland," *New York Post,* August 23, 1999.

17. Shakespeare, interview.

18. "Radio Free Europe Chief Quitting," *Christian Science Monitor,* June 14, 1983; Brown, interview.

19. Urban, *Radio Free Europe and the Pursuit of Democracy,* 38.

20. Ibid., 76.

21. Hutchings, interview; Brown, interview.

22. John M. Goshko, "Reagan Lashes Communism," *Washington Post,* June 15, 1985.

23. Urban, *Radio Free Europe and the Pursuit of Democracy,* 116.

24. Ibid., 116–18.

25. Ibid., 98–99.

26. Reyman, interview; Jezdinský, interview; Bellus, interview; Walter, interview.

27. Ekecs, interview; Borbandi, interview; B. Griffiths, interview.

28. Urban, *Radio Free Europe and the Pursuit of Democracy,* 95–96; B. Griffiths, interview.

29. Richard Whittle, "Some RFE Employees See Politics Behind Fine-Tuning of Broadcasts," *Dallas Morning News,* September 9, 1984.

30. Author's correspondence with Zygmunt Michalowski.

31. Ibid.

32. Michael Dobbs, "Pope's Words Pierce East's Blackout," *Washington Post,* June 7, 1979. For coverage of the pope's 1979 visit to the United States, see Michael Getler, "Poland Tunes in on Pope," *Washington Post,* October 4, 1979; Michalowski, correspondence.

33. Michalowski, correspondence.

34. Marek Latynski, interview with author.

35. Excerpts from Latynski and Michalowski scripts in RFE archives.

36. Brown, interview; Hutchings, interview; Latynski, interview; Michalowski, interview.

37. Nowak, interview; Brown, interview.

38. Harry Trimborn, "Poland Regime Hits at Radio Free Europe Official," *Los Angeles Times,* June 10, 1983; "Absent Polish Writer Given Death Sentence," *New York City Tribune,* April 26, 1983.

39. Irena Lasota, interview with author; Cummings, interview; Latynski, interview.

40. Leszek Gawlikowski, interview with author.

41. Gawlikowski, interview; Latynski, interview; Nowak, interview.

42. Quoted in Arnold Beichman, "A Clear 'Hatchet-Job' on Radio Free Europe by U.S. Propagandists," *New York City Tribune,* January 14, 1985.

43. *Radio Free Europe: An Instrument of Propaganda Aggression,* a polemic published by the Polish regime in 1983; Michael Dobbs, "Poles' Radio Dial Is Battleground of Fierce East-West Struggle," *Washington Post,* May 27, 1982; John Tagliabue, "Poland Censures Old Annoyer: Radio Free Europe," *New York Times,* May 7, 1982.

44. Bernard Gwertzman, "U.S. Tells Poles It Regrets Broadcast," *New York Times,* January 17, 1985.

45. Gawlikowski, interview.

46. Urban, *Radio Free Europe and the Pursuit of Democracy,* 124.

47. "Rating Radios," *Time,* European edition, April 21, 1980.

48. RFE internal summary of Bukovsky press conference in Paris, February 10, 1977.

49. "Feud of Old-Timers, Newcomers," *International Herald Tribune,* September 11, 1977.

50. Kalugin, *First Directorate,* 194–96.

51. Quoted from Critchlow memorandum, January 29, 1981.

52. George Bailey, interview with author.

53. Mark Pomar, interview with author.

54. Josef Joffe and Dmitri K. Simes, "Static at Radio Liberty: Is Propaganda a Turn-Off?," *Newsday,* October 3, 1983.

55. "Percy Rebuked by BIB Officials," *Washington Times,* May 14, 1984.

56. "Taking Radio Liberties," *New Republic,* February 4, 1985; response by James L. Buckley appeared in *New Republic,* February 19, 1985.

57. Bailey, interview.

58. Vadim Belotserkovsky, "Undoing the West in the Soviet Union," *Nation,* March 16, 1985.

59. Katrina vanden Heuvel, "No Free Speech at Radio Liberty," *Nation,* December 7, 1985.

60. Ludmilla Alexeyeva, *U.S. Broadcasting to the Soviet Union.*

61. Geryld B. Christianson, "New Management at Radio Free Europe/Radio Liberty and the Pell Amendment," staff report for the Senate Committee on Foreign Relations, mid-1984.

62. "Improved Oversight Can Reduce Broadcast Violations at Radio Free Europe/Radio Liberty," General Accounting Office, June 24, 1985.

63. "Florida Congressman Says Changes at RFE and RL Have Caused Some 'Inflammatory Statements' to Air," *Broadcasting,* March 18, 1985.

64. "RFE/RL Guidelines Run into House Subcommittee Buzzsaw," *Broadcasting,* June 23, 1986.

65. George Urban, "Mr. President: Some Suggestions," *Washington Times,* November 13, 1985; Urban, *Radio Free Europe and the Pursuit of Democracy,* 155–56.

66. Pell, interview.

67. Harrison Rainie, "Calls Ed Gay, Is Axed," *New York Daily News,* September 15, 1986.

16. Victory

1. Matusevitch, interview.

2. Ibid.

3. Richard Whittle, "Spreading News of the Disaster," *Dallas Morning News,* May 2, 1986; Michael T. Kaufman, "Poland Assails West, but not Moscow, on Reactor," *New York Times,* May 8, 1986; "Pell Praises RFE-RL Coverage of Chernobyl Crisis," RFE-RL news wire, June 9, 1986.

4. "Yeltsin Accuses the KGB," *Baltimore Sun,* October 21, 1989.

5. Scott Shane, "To Soviets, Probe is a Spy Thriller," *Miami Herald,* October 2, 1989.

6. Pell, interview.

7. Pomar, interview.

8. David Binder, "U.S., Wary of Islamic Upheaval, to Increase Broadcasts to Moslems," *New York Times,* December 17, 1979.

9. Lionel Barber, "Afghan Rebels Financed for Propaganda War," *Washington Post,* August 19, 1985.

10. S. Enders Wimbush, interview with author.

11. Wimbush, interview.

12. Pomar, interview.

13. "Review of Programming Lapses in Radio Liberty's Azerbaijani Service," report issued by Office of Inspector General, Board for International Broadcasting, July 13, 1990.

14. Marsh, interview.

15. Berle et al., *Navigating the Rapids,* 597.

16. Mucio F. Delgado memorandum, June 28, 1956; "The Case for Baltic Broadcasts," internal RFE memorandum, August 4, 1961.

17. Uldis Grava, interview with author.

18. Kestutis Girnius, interview with author.

19. Ibid.

20. Toomas Ilves, interview with author.

21. Ibid.

22. Girnius, interview.

23. Ilves, interview.

24. Paul Goble, interview with author.

25. Robert Pear, "Voice of America Drawing New Critics," *New York Times,* October 1, 1989.

26. Latynski, interview.

27. Robert Gillette, interview with author; Latynski, interview.

28. Pell, interview; Pomar, interview.

29. Jackson Diehl, "Dissident Havel Convicted in Prague," *Washington, Post,* February 22, 1989.

30. Edward Lucas, "Fractured Grammar of Communist Boss Prompts Ridicule, *Toronto Star,* October 23, 1989.

31. Lasota, interview.

32. Ratesh, *Romania,* 99–100.

33. Ibid., 11.

34. Gillette, interview.
35. Carp, interview.
36. Scott Shane, "Radio Liberty's Broadcasts to Troubled Soviet Republics Plug Holes in Glasnost," *Baltimore Sun,* November 24, 1989; David Remnick, "Soviets May Have to 'Accept Bloodshed,' KGB Chief Warns," *International Herald Tribune,* December 24, 1990; Wimbush, interview; Matusevitch, interview.
37. Leonid Shinkarev, "Over the Borders," *Izvestia,* March 31, 1990.
38. *Shortwaves,* August–September 1991.
39. Goble, interview.

Epilogue

1. Pell, Nowak, Kyrill Panoff, Carp, and Dagmara Vallens, interviews with author.
2. Bruce D. Brown, "British Libel Law Put to Local Test," *Legal Times,* September 16, 1996.
3. Grigory Yavlinsky, "Whither Russia?" in "Establishing Democracy: Political Reform and Press Freedom in Russia and Eastern Europe," proceedings of a conference sponsored by RFE-RL, September 19, 1996.
4. Codrescu, *Hole in the Flag,* 162.
5. Quoted in the "People" section of the *Minneapolis Star Tribune,* September 24, 1996.
6. Walesa letter to Radio Free Europe, quoted in RFE-RL annual report, 1993, 5.
7. Marcin Krol, "Listening Through the Jamming," *American Scholar* 67 (summer 1992): 431.

Bibliography

The early chapters of this book draw heavily on correspondence and memoranda written by officials of Radio Free Europe. Most of this material is located in RFE's corporate archives, which were located in the RFE-RL office in Washington, D.C., and scheduled for relocation to the Hoover Institution at Stanford University in 2000. The collection of papers left by Frank Altschul to the Herbert H. Lehman Collection at Columbia University was another source for the early RFE period. For the chapter on the early years of Radio Liberty, I have drawn on papers from the Jon Lodeesen and Robert Kelley collections at the special collections division of the Georgetown University library. I have also made some use of correspondence provided by the Fulbright collection at the University of Arkansas library for the chapter "Senator Fulbright's Crusade."

Books

Abshire, David M. *International Broadcasting: A New Dimension in Western Diplomacy.* Beverly Hills, Calif.: Sage Publications, 1976.

Alexeyeva, Ludmilla. *U.S. Broadcasting to the Soviet Union.* New York: U.S. Helsinki Watch Committee, 1986.

Ash, Timothy Garton. *In Europe's Name: Germany and the Divided Continent.* New York: Random House, 1993.

————— *The Polish Revolution: Solidarity.* New York, Charles Scribner's, 1984

Bain, Leslie B. *The Reluctant Satellites: An Eyewitness Report on East Europe and the Hungarian Revolution.* New York: Macmillan, 1960.

Barber, Noel. *Seven Days of Freedom: The Hungarian Uprising 1956.* Newton Abbot, U.K.: Readers' Union, 1975.

Barnouw, Erik. *The Image Empire: A History of Broadcasting in the United States.* 3 vols. New York: Oxford Univ. Press, 1966–70.

Berle, Adolf A., Beatrice Bishop Berle, Travis Beal Jacobs, and Max Ascoli. *Navigating the Rapids: 1918–1971.* New York: Harcourt Brace Jovanovich, 1973.

Bethell, Nicholas. *Gomulka: His Poland, His Communism*. New York: Holt, Rinehart and Winston, 1969.

Bittman, Ladislav. *The Deception Game: Czechoslovak Intelligence in Soviet Political Warfare*. Syracuse, N.Y.: Syracuse Univ. Research Corporation, 1972.

Blazynski, George. *Flashpoint Poland*. New York: Pergamon, 1979.

Brands, H.W. *The Devil We Knew: Americans and the Cold War*. New York: Oxford Univ. Press, 1993.

Browne, Donald R. *International Radio Broadcasting: The Limits of the Limitless Medium*. New York: Praeger, 1982.

Brzezinski, Zbigniew. *Power and Principle: Memoirs of the National Security Adviser, 1977–1981*. New York: Farrar, Straus, Giroux, 1983.

Campbell, John C. *American Policy Toward Communist Eastern Europe: The Choices Ahead*. Minneapolis: Univ. of Minnesota Press, 1965.

Chalidze, Valery. *To Defend These Rights: Human Rights and the Soviet Union*. Translated by Guy Daniels. London: Collins and Harvill, 1975.

Childs, H.L., and J.B. Whitton, eds. *Propaganda by Shortwave*. Princeton, N.J.: Princeton Univ. Press, 1942.

Cline, Dr. Ray S. *The CIA Under Reagan, Bush, and Casey: The Evolution of the Agency from Roosevelt to Reagan*. Washington D.C.: Acropolis Books, 1981.

Codrescu, Andrei. *The Hole in the Flag: A Romanian Exile's Story of Return and Revolution*. New York: William Morrow, 1991.

Collins, Larry D. "The Free Europe Committee: American Weapons in the Cold War." Ph. D. diss. Carlton University, 1973.

Comptroller General of the United States. *U.S. Government Monies Provided to Radio Free Europe and Radio Liberty*. Report to the Committee on Foreign Relations, United States Senate. Washington, D.C., 1972.

Coleman, Peter. *The Liberal Conspiracy: The Congress of Cultural Freedom and the Struggle for the Mind of Postwar Europe*. New York: Free Press, 1989.

Critchlow, James. *Radio Hole in the Head / Radio Liberty: An Insider's Story of Cold War Broadcasting*. Washington, D.C.: American Univ. Press, 1995.

Curry, Jane Leftwich, ed. and trans. *The Black Book of Polish Censorship*. New York: Random House, 1984.

Davison, W. Phillips. *International Political Communication*. New York: Praeger, 1965.

Ebon, Martin. *The Soviet Propaganda Machine*. New York: McGraw-Hill, 1987.

Free Europe Committee. *The Story of the World Freedom Bell*. Minneapolis: Free Europe Committee, 1951.

Fulbright, J. William. *The Crippled Giant: American Foreign Policy and Its Domestic Consequences.* New York: Random House, 1972.

Green, Fitzhugh. *American Propaganda Abroad: From Benjamin Franklin to Ronald Reagan.* New York: Hippocrene Books, 1988.

Hale, Julian. *Radio Power: Propaganda and International Broadcasting.* London: Paul Elek, 1975.

Hersh, Burton. *The Old Boys: The American Elite and the Origins of the CIA.* New York: Scribner's, 1992.

Holt, Robert T. *Radio Free Europe.* Minneapolis: Univ. of Minnesota Press, 1958.

Isaacson, Walter and Evan Thomas. *The Wise Men: Six Friends and the World They Made.* New York: Simon and Schuster, 1986.

Kalugin, Oleg, with Fen Montaigne. *The First Directorate: My 32 Years in Intelligence and Espionage Against the West.* New York: St. Martin's, 1994.

Karpinski, Jakub. *Countdown: The Polish Upheavals of 1956, 1968, 1970, 1976, 1980 . . . .* New York: Karz-Cohl, 1982.

Kostov, Vladimir. *The Bulgarian Umbrella.* New York: St. Martin's, 1988.

Kott, Jan. *Still Alive: An Autobiographical Essay.* New Haven, Conn.: Yale Univ. Press, 1994.

Kovrig, Bennett. *The Myth of Liberation: East-Central Europe in U.S. Diplomacy and Politics Since 1944.* Baltimore: Johns Hopkins Univ. Press, 1973.

Lenczowski, John. *Soviet Perceptions of U.S. Foreign Policy.* Ithaca, N.Y.: Cornell Univ. Press, 1982.

Lendvai, Paul. *Anti-Semitism Without Jews: Communist Eastern Europe.* Garden City, N.Y.: Doubleday, 1971.

————. *The Bureaucracy of Truth: How Communist Governments Manage the News.* Boulder, Colo.: Westview, 1981.

Lewis, Flora. *The Polish Volcano: A Case History of Hope.* London: Secker and Warburg, 1959.

Lisann, Maury. *Broadcasting to the Soviet Union: International Politics and Radio.* New York: Praeger, 1975.

Loftus, John. *The Belarus Secret.* New York: Knopf, 1982.

Lomax, Bill. *Hungary 1956.* New York: St. Martin's, 1976.

Marchetti, Victor, and John D. Marks. *The CIA and the Cult of Intelligence.* New York: Dell, 1974.

Markov, Georgi. *The Truth that Killed.* London: Weidenfeld and Nicolson, 1983.

Marples, David R. *The Social Impact of the Chernobyl Disaster.* New York: St. Martin's, 1988.

Martin, L. John. *International Propaganda: Its Legal and Diplomatic Control.* Minneapolis: Univ. of Minnesota Press, 1958.

May, Ernest R., ed. *American Cold War Strategy: Interpreting NSC 68.* New York: St. Martin's, 1993.

McGinniss, Joe. *The Selling of the President, 1968.* New York: Trident, 1969.

Meyer, Cord. *Facing Reality: From World Federalism to the CIA.* New York: Harper and Row, 1980.

Michener, James A. *The Bridge at Andau.* New York: Random House, 1957.

Michie, Allan A. *Voices Through the Iron Curtain: The Radio Free Europe Story.* New York: Dodd, Mead, 1963.

Mickelson, Sig. *America's Other Voice: The Story of Radio Free Europe and Radio Liberty.* New York: Praeger, 1983.

Miscamble, Wilson D. *George F. Kennan and the Making of American Foreign Policy, 1947–1950.* Princeton, N.J.: Princeton Univ. Press, 1992.

Nelson, Michael. *War of the Black Heavens: The Battles of Western Broadcasting in the Cold War.* Syracuse, N.Y.: Syracuse Univ. Press, 1997.

Nixon, Richard M. *Six Crises.* Garden City, N.Y.: Doubleday, 1962.

Nowak, Jan. *Courier from Warsaw.* Detroit: Wayne State Univ. Press, 1982.

———. *Polska z Odali: Wojna w Eterze—Wspomniena: Tom II.* London: Odnowa, 1988.

Pacepa, Ion. *Red Horizons: Chronicles of a Communist Spy Chief.* Washington, D.C.: Regnery Gateway, 1987.

Plyushch, Leonid. *History's Carnival: A Dissident's Autobiography.* New York: Harcourt Brace Jovanovich, 1977.

Prados, John. *Presidents' Secret Wars: CIA and Pentagon Covert Operations from World War II Through the Persian Gulf.* Chicago: Ivan R. Dee, 1996.

President's Study Commission on International Broadcasting. *The Right to Know: President's Study Commission on International Broadcasting.* Washington, D.C., 1973.

Ranelagh, John. *The Agency: The Rise and Decline of the CIA.* New York: Simon and Schuster, 1986.

Ratesh, Nestor. *Romania: The Entangled Revolution.* New York: Praeger, 1991.

Rosenberg, Tina. *The Haunted Land: Facing Europe's Ghosts After Communism.* Vintage Books, 1995.

Ryback, Timothy W. *Rock Around the Bloc: A History of Rock Music in Eastern Europe and the Soviet Union.* New York: Oxford Univ. Press, 1990.

Schopflin, George. *Censorship and Political Communication in Eastern Europe.* New York: St. Martin's, 1983.

Schweizer, Peter. *Victory: The Reagan Administration's Secret Strategy that Hastened the Collapse of the Soviet Union.* New York: Atlantic Monthly Press, 1994.

Shane, Scott. *Dismantling Utopia: How Information Ended the Soviet Union.* Chicago: Ivan R. Dee, 1994.

Shanor, Donald R. *Behind the Lines: The War Against Soviet Censorship.* New York: St. Martin's, 1985.

Short, K.R.M., ed. *Western Broadcasting over the Iron Curtain.* London: Croom Helm, 1986.

Simpson, Christopher. *Blowback: America's Recruitment of Nazis and Its Effects on the Cold War.* New York: Weidenfeld and Nicolson, 1988.

Skvorecky, Josef. *The Republic of Whores.* Hopewell, N.J.: Ecco Press, 1993.

Snyder, Alvin A. *Warriors of Disinformation: American Propaganda, Soviet Lies and the Winning of the Cold War; An Insider's Account.* New York: Arcade, 1995.

Sorenson, Thomas C. *The Word War: The Story of American Propaganda.* New York: Harper and Row, 1968.

Sosin, Gene. *Sparks of Liberty: An Insider's Account of Radio Liberty.* University Park: Pennsylvania State Univ. Press, 1999.

Staar, Richard F., ed. *Public Diplomacy: USA Versus USSR.* Stanford, Calif.: Hoover Institution Press, 1986.

Syrup, Konrad. *Spring in October: The Polish Revolution of 1956.* London: Weidenfeld and Nicolson, 1957.

Thomas, Evan. *The Very Best Men: The Early Years of the CIA.* New York: Simon and Schuster, 1995.

Tumanov, Oleg. *Tumanov: Confessions of a KGB Agent.* Chicago: edition q inc, 1993.

Tyson, James L. *U.S. International Broadcasting and National Security.* New York: Ramapo Press, 1983.

Urban, George. *Radio Free Europe and the Struggle for Democracy: My War Within the Cold War.* New Haven, Conn.: Yale Univ. Press, 1997.

———, ed. *Scaling the Wall: Talking to Eastern Europe; The Best of Radio Free Europe.* Detroit: Wayne State Univ. Press, 1963.

Walker, Martin. *The Cold War: A History.* New York: Henry Holt, 1993.

Whitton, John Boardman. *Propaganda and the Cold War.* Washington, D.C.: Public Affairs Press, 1963.

Wise, David, and Thomas R. Ross. *The Invisible Government.* New York: Random House, 1964.

Woods, Randall Bennett. *Fulbright: A Biography.* Cambridge: Cambridge Univ. Press, 1995.

Interviews and Correspondence

The author either interviewed or, in a very few cases, corresponded with the following individuals:

David Abshire

Charles Andras

Gabriel Andreescu

George Bailey

Thomas Barthelemy

Samko Belluš

Giovanni Bensi

Gyula Borbándi

James Brown

Zbigniew Brzezinski

James Buckley

William A. Buell

Keith Bush

Robert S. Byrnes

Mircea Carp

Mrs. Richard Condon

Mario Corti

Richard Cummings

Ambassador Richard T. Davies

Ambassador John R. Davis

István Deák

John Dunning

Fred Eidlin

Géza Ekecs

Rolf Ekmanis

Rachel Fedoseyev

Liviu Floda

Malcolm S. Forbes Jr.

Leszek Gawlikowski

Robert Gillette

Kestutis Girnius

Paul Goble

Ukdis Grava

Barry Griffiths

William Griffith

Yuri Handler

Paul Henze

Robert Hutchings

Toomas Ilves

Karel Jezdinský

A. Ross Johnson

Jacek Kalabinski

Jakub Karpinski

Al Kastner

Tom Keri

William Korey

William Kratch

Irena Lasota

Marek Latynski

Stanley Leinwoll

Carnes Lord

Victor Marchetti

John Marks

Leonard Marks

William Marsh

John Mathews

Jack Matlock

Vladimir Matusevich

James McCargar

Zygmunt Michalowski

Sig Mickelson

Jan Nowak

Ion Mihai Pacepa

Martin Palous

Kyrill Panoff

Pavel Pecháček

E. Eugene Pell

Mark Pomar

Russell Poole

Bruce Porter

Lída Rakušanová

Nestor Ratesh

Walter Raymond

Karl Reyman

John Richardson

Yale Richmond

Lev Roitman

Francis Ronalds

Richard Rowson

Evgeny Rubin

Joseph Ruszar

Frank Shakespeare

Gerald Steibel

Joseph Szabados

Pavel Tigrid

Roman Traycey

Dagmara Vallens

Rossen Vassilev

Gerd Von Deming

Ralph Walter

Abbot Washburn

Boleslaw Wierzbianski

S. Enders Wimbush

Jan Zaprudnik

Index

errors 159 – Kerensky was NOT a Menshevic –
160 – Turkestani ≠ a language ....
— no ref to Vlad Kusin being "dirty"